New Netherland
Connections

This book was the winner of the

JAMESTOWN PRIZE FOR 2013

and the

ANNUAL HENDRICKS AWARD OF THE
NEW NETHERLAND INSTITUTE FOR 2013

New Netherland Connections

Intimate Networks and Atlantic Ties in Seventeenth-Century America

◆ ◆ ◆

SUSANAH SHAW ROMNEY

Published for the Omohundro Institute of
Early American History and Culture, Williamsburg, Virginia,
by the University of North Carolina Press, Chapel Hill

The Omohundro Institute of Early American History and Culture is
sponsored jointly by the College of William and Mary and the Colonial
Williamsburg Foundation. On November 15, 1996, the Institute adopted the
present name in honor of a bequest from Malvern H. Omohundro, Jr.

Ship and passengers with flags of Amsterdam. Woodcut. From Pieter
Corneliszoon Plockhoy, *Kort en klaer ontwerp, dienende tot een onderling
Accoort....* (Amsterdam, 1662), aiiir. This item is reproduced by
permission of The Huntington Library, San Marino, Calif.

Library of Congress Cataloging-in-Publication Data
Romney, Susanah Shaw.
New Netherland connections : intimate networks and Atlantic ties in
seventeenth-century America / Susanah Shaw Romney.—1st edition.
pages cm
Includes bibliographical references and index.
ISBN 978-1-4696-1425-0 (hardback)
ISBN 978-1-4696-3348-0 (pbk.: alk. paper)
ISBN 978-1-4696-1426-7 (ebook)
1. New Netherland—History. 2. Social networks—New Netherland. 3. New
Netherland—Ethnic relations. 4. Women—New Netherland. 5. Indians of North
America—New Netherland. 6. African Americans—New Netherland. 7. Dutch—New
York (State)—History—17th century. 8. New York (State)—History—Colonial period,
ca. 1600–1775. 9. Amsterdam (Netherlands)—Emigration and immigration—History—
17th century. I. Omohundro Institute of Early American History & Culture. II. Title.
F122.1.R65 2014   974.7′1—dc23   2013042706

The paper in this book meets the guidelines for permanence
and durability of the Committee on Production Guidelines for
Book Longevity of the Council on Library Resources.

The University of North Carolina Press has been a member
of the Green Press Initiative since 2003.

To Charles, with all my love

Acknowledgments

 This book has come to life with the support of so many people that thanking everyone is a daunting task. But it is easy to know where to begin. Professor Mary Beth Norton has been an unfailing supporter of this project since its earliest days as a paper in her graduate seminar on women's history at Cornell University. I cannot imagine a better intellectual guide, reader, or mentor than she has been: Thank you, MBN. Professors Rachel Weil and Daniel Usner also provided feedback and support at the first stages, and I am truly grateful for their help and guidance. To all my Cornell friends and professors who sustained me as the dissertation took shape, my sincere thanks.

The extensive research this project required entailed many debts. Crucial financial and travel support came from the Andrew W. Mellon Foundation, Cornell University, the Gilder Lehrman Foundation at the New-York Historical Society, the Huntington Library, the Larry J. Hackman Research Residency Program at the New York State Archives, the Monticello College Foundation at the Newberry Library, and the University of Houston. Work at the municipal archives of Amsterdam (now the Stadsarchief Amsterdam) would not have been possible without the support of a Foreign Language and Area Studies grant. Oliver Rink very kindly provided advice and notes about his work in the same records. Professor Pieter Emmer at Leiden University proved a patient adviser while I was in residence there. In New York, Charles Gehring and Janny Venema at the New Netherland Institute were unfailingly generous and helpful, and I appreciate their gracious introduction to Albany and the Dutch records there. The staff at the New York State Archives and Ken Cobb at the New York City Municipal Archives both helped me access key documents.

Getting all that research into shape required input from numerous readers. Thanks for comments on all or part of the manuscript from Jeannine

DeLombard, Michael McGandy, Laura Mitchell, Joshua Piker, Ann Marie Plane, Daniel Richter, Susan Sleeper-Smith, Terri Snyder, and the anonymous readers. Their insights helped make the manuscript better by lighting my way through many a dark patch.

Participants at several scholarly seminars also aided the project. The Newberry Library Fellows' Seminar participants in 2002 gave me essential feedback while I was in Chicago; thanks especially to James Grossman for encouraging me to focus on networks. The crew at the 2003 Atlantic World "summer camp," also known as the "International Seminar on the History of the Atlantic World, 1500–1825" at Harvard, furthered my journey down that path; I am particularly grateful for the remarks of Bernard Bailyn, Emma Hart, and David Voorhees. Finally, the Huntington Library–USC Early Modern Studies Institute American Origins Seminar in 2007 provided a boost just when I needed it most; thanks to all the participants, especially Carole Shammas and Peter Mancall.

Just as the manuscript was coming to fruition, I was lucky enough to find myself among a wonderfully supportive intellectual and social group. I would like to thank the whole gang from my year at the Huntington Library as a Fletcher Jones Foundation Fellow in 2010–2011: Emily Berquist, David Blight, Erika Boeckeler, Jeannine DeLombard, Robin Derby, Mary Fuller, Margaret Garber, Jennifer Greenhill, Steven Hackel, Dan Horowitz, Helen Horowitz, Ted McCormick, Mary Helen McMurran, Bruce Moran, Marcy Norton, Tara Nummedal, Daniel Richter, Seth Rockman, Marni Sandweiss, Ken Warren, and Sean Wilentz. Without the encouragement of the "hit send" celebrations, progress through publication would have been much less fun.

Yet the Huntington Library has been my academic sanctuary for much longer than a single fellowship year. I would like to thank Roy Ritchie for his friendliness and generosity since my first trip to the Huntington as a graduate student. He has made it possible for me to have an intellectual home through thick and thin. I am not certain if this project could have come to completion without the Huntington, and I owe so much of my experience there to Roy.

The book as it is now is not the manuscript that I originally drafted from my desk in the reading room at the Huntington, however. It has improved immeasurably as a result of the insightful work of the people at the Omohundro Institute of Early American History and Culture. Fredrika Teute gave the manuscript a chance despite its many flaws, and I am indebted to her incisive suggestions and kind words. Nadine Zimmerli read these chapters more times than she could possibly care to count, and I appreciate her unflagging ability to salvage analysis from a morass of prose. Kaylan Stevenson, as copyeditor, deserves an award for her fortitude. I feel so fortunate to have been able to work with everyone at the Institute; I cannot imagine a better experience.

I also want to thank the many friends who have helped me see the project through, especially Carla Bittel, Cheryl Koos, and Shireen Rahnema. My deepest appreciation also goes out to the entire bunch from the Ranch: Jennifer Frost, John Herron, Josh Piker, and Francesca Sawaya, plus the inimitable threesome Lachlan, Naima, and Ryce. Our times together enabled me to keep going, despite the ups and downs over the years.

My family has occasionally wondered what has taken me so long, and I thank them for their patience. To my parents, Joe and Mary Ann, and my sister, Karen, here it is, at long last! Enjoy.

Finally, I have to thank Charles Romney, for everything. Without Charles, nothing would be possible.

Contents

Illustrations

Abbreviations and Short Titles

CMNA ◆ Court Minutes of New Amsterdam, "Original Dutch Records, 1654–65," New York City Municipal Archives

Council Minutes, I ◆ Kenneth Scott and Kenn Stryker-Rodda, eds., *Council Minutes, 1638–1649,* trans. Arnold J. F. van Laer, New York Historical Manuscripts: Dutch (Baltimore, Md., 1974).

Council Minutes, II ◆ Charles T. Gehring, ed. and trans., *Council Minutes, 1655–1656,* New Netherland Documents Series, VI (Syracuse, N.Y., 1995).

DRCHNY ◆ E. B. O'Callaghan, ed., *Documents Relative to the Colonial History of the State of New-York; Procured in Holland, England, and France,* 15 vols. (Albany, N.Y., 1853–1887).

Fort Orange Records, I ◆ Charles T. Gehring and Janny Venema, eds. and trans., *Fort Orange Records, 1654–1679,* New Netherland Documents Series (Syracuse, N.Y., 2009).

Fort Orange Records, II ◆ Charles T. Gehring, ed. and trans., *Fort Orange Records, 1656–1678,* New Netherland Documents Series (Syracuse, N.Y., 2000).

GAR ◆ Gemeente Archief Rotterdam

Loockermans Correspondence ◆ Govert Loockermans Correspondence, 1647–1700, Stuyvesant-Rutherford Papers, New-York Historical Society

NNDS ◆ New Netherland Documents Series

NYCM ◆ New York Colonial Manuscripts

NYCMA ◆ New York City Municipal Archives

NYHMD ✦ New York Historical Manuscripts: Dutch

NYHS ✦ New-York Historical Society

NYPL ✦ New York Public Library

NYSA ✦ New York State Archives, Albany, N.Y.

NYSL ✦ New York State Library, Albany, N.Y.

Provincial Secretary, I ✦ Kenneth Scott and Kenn Stryker-Rodda, eds., *Register of the Provincial Secretary, 1638–1642,* trans. Arnold J. F. van Laer, New York Historical Manuscripts: Dutch (Baltimore, Md., 1974).

Provincial Secretary, II ✦ Kenneth Scott and Kenn Stryker-Rodda, eds., *Register of the Provincial Secretary, 1642–1647,* trans. Van Laer, New York Historical Manuscripts: Dutch (Baltimore, Md., 1974).

Provincial Secretary, III ✦ Kenneth Scott and Kenn Stryker-Rodda, eds., *Register of the Provincial Secretary, 1648–1660,* trans. Van Laer, New York Historical Manuscripts: Dutch (Baltimore, Md., 1974).

RNA ✦ Berthold Fernow, ed., *The Records of New Amsterdam: From 1653 to 1674 Anno Domini,* vols. I–V (New York, 1897).

SA ✦ Stadsarchief Amsterdam

VOC ✦ Dutch East India Company (the *Vereenigde Oostindische Compagnie*)

WIC ✦ West India Company

WMQ ✦ *William and Mary Quarterly*

Editorial Note

Over the years, translators have struggled with how to render the terms New Netherlanders used for Native Americans. Nineteenth-century translators gave the most common term, "wilden," as "savages," since both words share a connection with wildness and are not reserved geographically for the people of the Americas. Indeed, "savage" is the only word that can help readers make sense of phrases like "alwaer zy eenighe meest wilde menschen ... hebben ghevonden, doch niet al te wildt," that is, "where they found some mostly savage people, ... but not entirely savage," as Gerrit de Veer wrote about Willem Barents's encounter with the Sami people of Arctic Eurasia in his 1598 travel narrative *Waerachtighe beschryvinghe van drie seylagien, ter werelt noyt soo vreemt ghehoort,* since reprinted in 1917 as *Reizen van Willem Barents, Jacob van Heemskerck, Jan Cornelisz Rijp en anderen naar het Noorden (1594–1597)* (36). Most present-day translators prefer to give the word "wilden" as "Indians," because "savages" in today's English carries heavy negative connotations that the original writers might not have intended. Translators of French documents similarly struggle with the word "sauvage." I worry, however, that using the word "Indians" could be misleading. The Dutch did have the more neutral cognate "Indianen," but they employed it less commonly for the residents of the Americas than "wilden." Also, some writers, such as David Pietersz de Vries, spent time in both America and Asia, and readers should be aware when they chose different terms to name these two very different groups of people. For example, in De Vries's 1655 narrative, *Korte historiael, ende journaels aenteyckeninge, van verscheyden voyagiens in de vier deelen des wereldts-ronde,* he referred to the residents of India as "Indianen" but usually called Native Americans "wilden" (126).

To avoid the risk of whitewashing racial terms from the past, I have chosen not to translate "wilden." The singular masculine, "wilt," and the singular feminine, "wildin," also appear in this text. I reserve the term "Indians" to stand only for "Indianen." When I have been forced to rely on translated sources, the word "Indians" appears more frequently.

Readers will also find that seventeenth-century Dutch naming practices differ considerably from our own. Spellings of given names varied widely, and diminutives and nicknames were common. Most people used first names and patronymics, not surnames. For this reason, husbands and wives do not always appear to have the same "last" name; their fathers' names were different. Patronymics were commonly designated on paper with abbreviations, with no standard spelling predominating, even within a single document. A woman whose father was named Jan, for instance, might appear in the records as Anna Jans, Jansz, Janse, Jansen, or Jansdochter. However, many upper-status people also had surnames that they used on occasion or consistently. Since a person's status could change over their lives, some people were designated by a surname only later in life. Also, a man who became a surgeon or minister, for example, might take or change his surname to reflect his Latin education. Women were sometimes known by their husbands' surnames and sometimes not. Furthermore, the Netherlands' many immigrants brought their own naming practices with them, meaning that lower-status immigrants or the children of immigrants could be known by surnames rather than patronymics, and regional practices in the Netherlands varied. In general, I have tried to use the form that I saw appearing most often or prominently for a particular person, and, for well-known individuals, I have tried to use the received form, but readers should be aware of the many variations possible for a single person.

Translations from Dutch-language books and manuscripts are my own unless otherwise noted. Passages in quotations marked by parentheses and a caret represent marginal or superscript additions in the original manuscripts. I have silently expanded the many abbreviations found in seventeenth-century sources. I have also used published translations when circumstances required.

Prologue

 In 1657, Johannes Vermeer reinterpreted the common Dutch visual image of the girl with a suitor in his *Officer and a Laughing Girl*. He placed a young woman, bathed in the pure light of an open window, at a table with a man, who appears largely in dark silhouette. A map of Holland and West Friesland hangs on the wall behind them. Cradling a glass of wine in her right hand, she smiles plainly at him, holding her left hand out and open. Perhaps Vermeer intended her gesture to suggest merely a welcoming of the man's advances, although the eagerness of her gaze and the forward tilt of her body as she leans toward him lend a greater sense of urgency to her actions (Figure 1).[1]

With the other elements of the painting, Vermeer indicates that the young woman's entreaty has to do with the burgeoning Dutch commercial empire. Painting at the midpoint of the Golden Age, just after the Peace of Westphalia had finally secured Dutch independence from Spain in 1648, Vermeer

1. Johannes Vermeer's depiction of the young woman's status is somewhat ambiguous. The form of the woman's *hooftdoek,* or kerchief, fits with the "Tied Cap" usually paired with the simple skirt and apron attire associated with women below burgher status in Dutch paintings from 1600 to 1650; see Dana L. Chapman, "Dutch Costume in Paintings by Dutch Artists: A Study of Women's Clothing and Art from 1600 to 1650" (Ph.D. diss., Ohio State University, 1986), 128–142. But, such caps were not reserved solely for representations of servants. For an example of this simple headwear worn with a more elaborate bodice, see Gabriel Metsu's *The Intruder,* Andrew W. Mellon Collection, National Gallery of Art, Washington, D.C. Compare the outfit worn by the woman in Metsu's painting to the simpler attire of the servant portrayed in Vermeer's *The Milkmaid* (Rijksmuseum, Amsterdam). The dress worn in *Officer and Laughing Girl* appears in other Vermeer paintings and "can be defined as daily wear." In 1681, concerns about overly fine clothing among servant women resulted in a sumptuary law obliging them to wear a jacket and apron instead of a gown; see Marieke de Winkel, "The Interpretation of Dress in Vermeer's Paintings," in Ivan Gaskell and Michiel Jonker, eds., *Vermeer Studies,* Center for Advanced Study in the Visual Arts, Studies in the History of Art, LV, Symposium Papers, XXXIII (New Haven, Conn., 1998), 328–330 (quotation, 329). Overall, Vermeer leaves open the question whether the young woman is a servant or of burgher status.

FIGURE 1 ◆ *Officer and Laughing Girl.* By Johannes Vermeer. Circa 1657.
Oil on canvas (lined), 19⅞ × 18⅛ in. (50.5 × 46 cm). Henry Clay Frick Bequest.
© The Frick Collection, New York

lived in a Holland already flourishing economically as a result of overseas expansion and new trade with Asia, Africa, and the Americas. The girl's suitor is not just a local burgher; his clothing clearly identifies him as an officer. Not only did officers like him protect cities and towns at home, they also played important roles in the creation of empire. They sailed aboard the ships of the VOC and the WIC, participated in the Anglo-Dutch wars in the battle for Atlantic trade, and manned posts in Dutch colonies around the globe.

Although Vermeer left much about the shadowy officer a matter of mystery, he included an overt reference to the expanding Dutch empire, specifically the growing Dutch trade along the east coast of North America, through one element of the man's outfit: his unmissable, impressive hat. The hat dominates the center of the left half of the painting, its dark shape dramatically emphasized against the light from the window behind it. Made from beaver skins harvested by Mohawk and Munsee people of the mid-Atlantic coast, shipped through the Dutch colonial port of New Amsterdam on Manhattan, sold in the fur market of Amsterdam, felted in Russia, and steamed into the perfect shape in France or England, hats like these commanded high prices in seventeenth-century Europe. Vermeer does not show the officer's face; to the viewer, he is just one of the many officers crowding the streets and towns of Holland during this period. But if the viewer fails to get a good look at him, it is impossible to overlook the product of the Dutch colonial effort in North America that he wears on his head.[2]

The nod to empire signified by the officer and his hat is furthered by the open window, leading to the world outside. Vermeer's inclusion of the map emphasizes commercial growth and movement even more. Maps frequently occur in his paintings, and he rendered this one with special clarity, orienting the western coast of Holland at the top and depicting the seaboard provinces in a vibrant blue. Based on a map by Willem Jansz Blaeu from 1621, it charts the interweaving of coastline and sea that made up the Netherlands. More than fifty boats and ships dot the waters of the North Sea, the inlet of the Zuider Zee, and the waterways at the mouths of the southern

2. On transforming North American beaver skins into hats for sale during the seventeenth and eighteenth centuries, see Ann M. Carlos and Frank D. Lewis, *Commerce by a Frozen Sea: Native Americans and the European Fur Trade* (Philadelphia, 2010), 15–35. For an investigation of the beaver-skin hat and its relationship to the Dutch empire, see Timothy Brook, *Vermeer's Hat: The Seventeenth Century and the Dawn of the Global World* (New York, 2008). Brimmed hats such as these were considered particularly appropriate for men's equestrian wear; see Marieke de Winkel, *Fashion and Fancy: Dress and Meaning in Rembrandt's Paintings* (Amsterdam, 2006), 104. On the man's sash as an indication of officer status, see John Michael Montias, *Vermeer and His Milieu: A Web of Social History* (Princeton, N.J., 1989), 134.

rivers. By casting the border in the same neutral color as the ocean, Vermeer gives the impression of a Netherlands bounded and penetrated by water, and the boats illustrate that, for the Dutch, oceans, seas, and rivers enabled the movement of people and goods to and from faraway lands.

Between the officer, the hat, the window, and the map, the figure of the young girl is nearly encircled by symbols of the increasingly global Dutch commercial empire. This context makes her gesture as she leans toward the officer a gesture not just to a suitor but also to the wider world of overseas expansion. Her open hand and leaning body reverse the idea of a suitor reaching out to a passive young woman; instead, she seems to reach out to him. In bright contrast to the man's dark silhouette, her white linen kerchief frames her fully lit features, emphasizing her expression and her glance. The direction and hopeful eagerness of her gaze point to the intimacy of her appeal. Though viewers cannot see who he is, cannot see him as an individual, she looks squarely into the face of the man within the officer's clothes, under the imperial hat.

Her boldness could make this painting a restrained example of a bordello scene. Perhaps the figures depict, not a suitor and a burgher girl, but, rather, a customer and a prostitute. The modesty of the young woman's dress and the quiet setting of a seeming burgher room, however, indicate that Vermeer did not intend, at least, to make an overt reference to prostitution. Whether he hoped to portray a woman who sought a relationship with an officer as a short-term liaison during which she could obtain some of his foreign riches with her body or one who desired to create formal ties of marriage with a well-employed man matters less than the association he establishes between the intimate and the imperial. In either case, Vermeer makes clear that the relationship between the two would have both personal and commercial aspects. If she is reaching out to a man, she is also reaching out to the world of imperial trade. Her interaction with empire comes through a person, and the intimate gestures between a girl and her potential lover signal the intimate connections that constituted the Dutch empire.[3]

3. Nanette Salomon argues that the proper context for understanding this work is the bordello scene, popular in Dutch genre painting in the first half of the seventeenth century, and that, together with Vermeer's *The Procuress* (Gemäldegalerie Alte Meister, Staatliche Kunstsammlungen Dresden), this painting depicts "mercenary love"; see Salomon, "From Sexuality to Civility: Vermeer's Women," in Gaskell and Jonker, eds., *Vermeer Studies,* 314–315 (quotation, 314). The connections with that body of work cannot be denied. The combination of a smiling woman, wine, and a soldier place the painting squarely in that tradition. But other elements of the painting, such as the absence of other figures, the lack of an explicit commercial presence (such as coins), no physical contact between the man and the woman,

Seventeenth-century Dutch expansion along the Atlantic coast of North America cannot be fully understood without bearing in mind the correlations between intimacy and empire captured in Vermeer's painting. Dutch society relied on families and relationships between women and men to structure economic and political life. Thus, the Dutch Atlantic empire developed in a setting in which intimate ties melded with economics and politics. When seen in this social and cultural milieu, Vermeer's painting reveals in a dramatic, visual way a truth about how people constructed, interacted with, understood, and resisted long-distance trade and colonization. Intimacies did essential social, political, and economic work to sustain the empire.

Dutch society in the early modern period rested firmly on the *huysgezin,* or household. The gendered relationship between husband and wife provided the basis for the home. The master (*huysman* or *huysvader*) and mistress (*huysvrouw* or *huysmoeder*) had the duty to lead and correct the household's children and servants. The huysgezin formed an economic unit, and members of the household pooled resources and engaged in market-based production and consumption together. The household also defined the political bonds between individuals and society. Citizenship depended on residence within a particular city or town, making Dutch citizenship urban, not national; therefore, only residents could apply for the *burgerrecht,* or the ability to do business and be politically active within a town. Having a huysgezin of his own helped make a man an accepted resident in a municipality. Ideally, people's place in Dutch society flowed from a particular set of domestic relationships embodied in the household.[4]

---

the relative chasteness of her dress, and the presence of the map weigh against such an unambiguous reading of the painting. Vermeer might have been playing with the mixed perception of the homes where sailors and soldiers often lived, places where prostitution and marriage occasionally coexisted.

4. In present-day Dutch, the term "gezin" survives as a way of referring to the nuclear family, irrespective of dwelling. In seventeenth-century usage, "huysgezin" did not mean the nuclear family per se but rather the collection of family, kin, and servants who made up a single residential dwelling; see M. de Vries et al., *Woordenboek der Nederlandsche taal* (The Hague, 1882–), s.v. "huisgezin." On the importance of the increasing market orientation of households to the gradual growth in consumption that formed the "industrious revolution" characteristic of Golden Age Holland, see Jan de Vries, "Between Purchasing Power and the World of Goods: Understanding the Household Economy in Early Modern Europe," in John Brewer and Roy Porter, eds., *Consumption and the World of Goods* (New York, 1993), 85–132, esp. 107–113; Jan de Vries, *The Industrious Revolution: Consumer Behavior and the Household Economy, 1650 to the Present* (New York, 2008). For a short exploration of burgher status in comparison with modern Dutch citizenship, see Maarten Prak, "Burghers into Citizens: Urban and National Citizenship in the Netherlands during the Revolutionary Era (c. 1800)," *Theory and Society,* XXVI (1997), 403–420.

The social, economic, and political life of towns arose out of the associations that developed among households. As a federal republic of provinces, the most basic political unit in Dutch society was the *stad,* the city or town. Towns dominated the politics of the Netherlands, giving Dutch government a profoundly local character as kin and politics tightly intertwined. Civic government provided the basis for stability and economic growth through civil laws, civic charity, and city-supported merchant companies. The most important members of Dutch government arguably consisted of the urban merchant elites—the burghers—whose commitment to town life was embodied by their huysgezin. The diffusion of power among these numerous heads of households ensured that gendered notions of family and community remained at the center of Dutch politics and society. Together, these elite, locally grounded, patriarchal merchant families intermarried to form influential networks that sustained the diffuse politics of the Netherlands. As a result, many family lineages and kin groups shared political power and sovereignty for generations.[5]

Commercial enterprises, too, even those reaching offshore, rested on the networks of kin and community that grew out of the household and town. Indeed, the Dutch rise to economic primacy in the late sixteenth and early seventeenth centuries stemmed, in part, from innovative ways of organizing commerce that drew on the resources of entire networks of investors. Rather than relying on the support of a few major merchants, as had been the practice in Antwerp and elsewhere, the Dutch divided ownership of ships into much smaller shares. Investment and risk could thus be spread widely among merchant, middling, and artisanal families. Trading voyages to European ports and fishing voyages to the North Sea were financed by groups of families within particular coastal towns; consequently, shareholders in fishing voyages could include "herring dealers, bakers, block makers, coopers, ropemakers, ship's carpenters, shoemakers, fishing captains, fishermen, sailmakers, crimps, and others" of small means. The burgher leaders of those towns, in turn, used their political leverage to encourage policies in the States General that would support their ships' profitability. In the sixteenth century, Dutch "herring towns," for instance, successfully pushed for better protection against pirates. Regional trading and fishing ships were not only sponsored by communities, they were also staffed from within those communities. The labor pool that worked these ships largely came from

5. Julia Adams, *The Familial State: Ruling Families and Merchant Capitalism in Early Modern Europe* (Ithaca, N.Y., 2005), 34.

the same locality as their employer and often shared social or familial ties. Hiring frequently took place within the master's home. Thus, commercial activity, particularly shipborne commerce, depended on a complex skein of relationships located within Dutch towns and kinship groups.[6]

As Dutch ships began to sail ever farther at the opening of the seventeenth century, the VOC and the WIC, the two major Dutch mercantile companies, continued to interweave intimate connections with the corporate life of politics and economy. Each of these companies consisted of "chambers" based in towns throughout the Netherlands. Vermeer's Delft hosted chambers of both companies, funneling investment and merchandise through local offices and warehouses. Although charters gave the VOC and WIC trade monopolies over vast expanses, both companies remained intrinsically local organizations, and merchant ships sailed with relative independence from the various urban ports of Holland and the other provinces. Following the patterns developed in regional shipping during the sixteenth century, both companies sold small shares to a wide swath of burghers and local institutions, encompassing many kin and social networks. As a result, they secured access to capital that merchants in rival countries like France, Spain, and England could only dream of. What is more, relatively quickly, families laid claim to specific offices and leadership positions of the VOC and WIC. Burgher families turned both companies into patrimonial estates, carving out pieces that acted almost like inheritable property to be distributed within the kin group. Ties of patronage caused the companies to develop a "network structure" of organization that proved both strong and durable while it

6. A. P. van Vliet, *Vissers en kapers: De zeevisserij vanuit het Maasmondgebied en de Duinkerker kapers (ca. 1580–1648)*, Hollandse historische reeks, XX (The Hague, 1994), 35 ("herring dealers"); Jonathan I. Israel, *Dutch Primacy in World Trade, 1585–1740* (Oxford, 1989), 21–22. See also James D. Tracy, "Herring Wars: The Habsburg Netherlands and the Struggle for Control of the North Sea, ca. 1520–1560," *Sixteenth Century Journal*, XXIV (1993), 249–272; Karel Davids, "Maritime Labour in the Netherlands, 1570–1870," *Research in Maritime History*, XIII (1997), 63–64; Paul C. van Royen, "Mariners and Markets in the Age of Sail: The Case of the Netherlands," *Research in Maritime History*, VII (1994), 51. Whaling ships, however, recruited skilled Basque harpooners, rather than local workers; see J. Lucassen, "Zeevarenden," in L. M. Akveld, S. Hart, and W. J. van Hoboken, eds., *Maritieme geschiedenis der Nederlanden*, II, *Zeventiende eeuw, van 1585 tot ca. 1680* (Bussum, Netherlands, 1977), 132–133. The familial and community nature of maritime hiring was not unique to the seventeenth-century Dutch. According to Michael J. Jarvis, the staffing of Bermuda sloops in the late seventeenth- and eighteenth-century British Atlantic was also "mostly a community or family affair"; see Jarvis, "Maritime Masters and Seafaring Slaves in Bermuda, 1680–1783," *WMQ*, 3d Ser., LIX (2002), 603. For a brief discussion of the changes in ownership practices of herring busses, see Jan de Vries and Ad van der Woude, *The First Modern Economy: Success, Failure, and Perseverance of the Dutch Economy, 1500–1815* (Cambridge, 1997), 243–254.

prevented them from becoming wholly unified, top-directed entities. Even the long-distance trading companies that brought exotic new goods like beaver hats into Dutch homes integrated the personal, familial, and local with the political and economic realms.[7]

It is within this context that the blending of intimacy and empire in Vermeer's *Officer and a Laughing Girl* is so revealing. His painting introduces another level to the connections between overseas expansion and the personal ties that defined town and family life. He implies that individuals far below the status of company investors also related to empire and that they did so through the medium of the immediate, bodily, and gendered relationships they formed with others. An officer and a girl of uncertain virtue might have had little to do with the urban regents who ran the wic and voc, but the painting hints that as one traveled down the building blocks of Dutch society—from the upper echelons of politics and the major trading companies, through the level of the community, into the intimate spaces of the home—empire remained a dominant yet personal presence.

Understanding what that presence meant to people requires looking in detail at the traces they left of their personal and economic lives. Focusing primarily on the ships sailing between Amsterdam and the greater Hudson River region makes it possible to uncover the way individuals experienced the construction of empire. Hollanders rich and poor, immigrants and workers from other parts of Europe, Native American residents of the mid-Atlantic coast, and African women and men forced to build and inhabit the colony all had to find ways of coping with the advent of Dutch transatlantic commerce. Facing a social, economic, and political system that rested on the immediate ties of the household and wider networks of kin, all of these people turned to their own intimate relationships and social connections. As they did so, they alternately created, negotiated, and resisted an intimate empire.

---

7. The original license of the VOC allowed all inhabitants of the Dutch provinces to purchase shares "regardless of the amount of money they were able to put into it," meaning that investments varied from fifty to thirty-six thousand guilders. Shares could also be subdivided into smaller amounts and resold, ensuring that a wide range of Netherlanders managed to own a piece of one of the two companies. For a brief English-language overview of the structure of the VOC, which was largely copied by the WIC, see Ella Gepken-Jager, "Verenigde Oost-Indische Compagnie (VOC): The Dutch East India Company," in Gepken-Jager, Gerard van Solinge, and Levinus Timmerman, eds., *VOC 1602–2002: 400 Years of Company Law* (Deventer, Netherlands, 2005), 43–81 ("regardless," 60). See also Julia Adams, "Principals and Agents, Colonialists and Company Men: The Decay of Colonial Control in the Dutch East Indies," *American Sociological Review*, LXI (1996), 12–28.

Introduction

In February 1657, the year Johannes Vermeer captured the Dutch empire on canvas, the small Dutch colony on the mid-Atlantic coast of North America found cause to rejoice. New Netherland, as the colony later renamed New York was then known, was doing surprisingly well. Moved by "the continuation of healthy, fruitful, and peaceable times," Governor Peter Stuyvesant and the colony council called for a day of thanksgiving. To worship "with greater unity," they forbade ordinary work and games on the first Wednesday in March and ordered everyone to gather in "thanks and prayer." The little colony had much to celebrate. Despite an "unexpected massacre by the Barbarians" two years before, peace again prevailed, and even the "lands and plantations" that had been abandoned and "thereafter neither plowed nor sowed" produced a harvest rich "beyond expectations, even to the wonder of every one" who saw it. Colonial authorities lauded God for the remarkable growth of settlement and trade, expressing their gratitude for the "exceptional increase and flourishing of the population and traffic" of the colony. They counted it a special sign of God's grace that he protected the settlers from illness and allowed them to thrive. "Although other places and nations better and worthier than we, even our friends, and religious companions in our Fatherland" suffered from "heavy, and pestilential fevers," the Manhattan port town of New Amsterdam and the other settlements scattered along Long Island and the Hudson River enjoyed "continued health." With such good news on every hand, the council enjoined the settlers to give honor to "his Holy Word" by praising God together.[1]

---

1. Order, Feb. 6, 1657, NYCM, VIII, 458–460, NYSA. Although Stuyvesant's formal title was director general, documents from the time also referred to him as governor, and the two terms will be used interchangeably throughout.

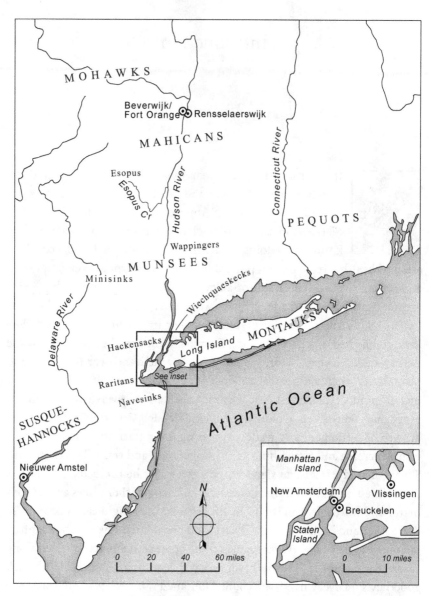

FIGURE 2 ◆ The Mid-Atlantic coast of North America, circa 1660.
Map by James De Grand

At the time of the celebration, Dutch involvement with the mid-Atlantic coast already reached back almost fifty years to Henry Hudson's 1609 Dutch-sponsored voyage to the river that today bears his name. Annual trading ventures in the 1610s gave rise to permanent settlements in the 1620s, which had expanded by 1657 to include villages throughout the Hudson Valley, Manhattan, Long Island, and along the Delaware River. Although Governor Stuyvesant and the council could not have known it when they called the colonists together, Dutch administration there had already entered its final decade. In August 1664, the expanding English empire would successfully challenge the struggling WIC, the Dutch joint-stock company that had governed the colony since the settlers' arrival, for control of the greater Hudson Valley.

Although the Dutch colony's years were numbered, authorities were justified in thinking that prospects looked good. Dutch settlements had increased rapidly in the 1650s, and WIC soldiers had recently succeeded in ousting Swedish-sponsored traders from the Delaware River valley. The colony would continue to grow, reaching a population of somewhere between seven and eight thousand (including some five hundred Africans) by the time of the handover to the English. Although the colony generated only a fraction of the trade produced by the more profitable Dutch outposts in the Indonesian archipelago and elsewhere, private settlers seemed to be doing well, with a rising number of ships arriving annually, connecting them to the wider Atlantic economy. A bountiful agricultural system, sustained by a patchwork of fields worked by Native American villagers, free and enslaved Africans, and settler family farmers, provided sufficient food for all the area's residents. Together, they established a viable regional economy organized around the shared currencies of beaver skins and wampum beads. Trade with indigenous villagers flourished, and particularly strong ties linked the upriver settlement of Fort Orange, at present-day Albany, with nearby Mohawk beaver-skin traders. Though the WIC struggled to cash in on the colony, an increasing stream of migrants came to the greater Hudson Valley, drawn by the profitable trade in beaver skins and the possibility of rich farmland. New Netherland's settlers in 1657 even managed to live in peace with the growing number of English colonists nearby. Though the expanding English colonies proved worrisome in some ways, they also provided more commercial opportunities. No wonder colonial officials wanted to celebrate.[2]

2. For the population of the colony, see Jaap Jacobs, *Een zegenrijk gewest: Nieuw-Nederland in de zeventiende eeuw* (Amsterdam, 1999), 103. See also the English translation, Jacobs, *New Netherland: A Dutch Colony in Seventeenth-Century America* (Leiden, 2005), 93. For an explana-

The small colony that looked so successful in 1657 had not always seemed so promising. The early years witnessed instability engendered by administrators who struck observers as politically inept, tyrannical, or both. Yet the arrival in 1647 of Governor Stuyvesant, who held his post until the end of the Dutch era in 1664, largely ended the first complaint, if not always the second, and, a decade into his rule, he had created a sense of stability. He governed a series of dispersed settlements that had begun patchily, with Fort Orange, a permanent trading post, leading the way in 1614. Family settlement on Manhattan took root in 1623, followed by the creation of a private agricultural patroonship (Rensselaerswijk) and a town (Beverwijk) upriver adjoining the fort. Gradually, settlements along the Hudson and across Long Island supplemented these two key strongholds. In 1655, the takeover of New Sweden made permanent a decades-long, shaky claim to the Delaware Bay. By the time of the call for thanksgiving, the fragility of the first days had faded.[3]

Dutch prosperity in the area depended on a diverse economy and population. The beaver-skin trade, a thriving exchange of pelts hunted by Mohawks, Munsees, and others for goods hawked by Europeans, served as a pillar of the economy within the colony and throughout the entire region during the whole of the Dutch period. Yet, the mid-Atlantic coast also supported profitable agriculture, and the production of corn and food crops by Africans, Europeans, and Native Americans played a fundamental role in the area's economy. New arrivals in the 1650s hoped to export grain and other crops, and wishful settlers made occasional attempts to produce tobacco for European markets. The Manhattan port of New Amsterdam acted as an important stopping place for ships bound to Holland from the Caribbean, and, over time, New Netherland merchants reaped increasing profits from the coastal trade with their English neighbors.

By 1657, the colony had developed considerable political stability as well. Although the Amsterdam chamber of the WIC oversaw colonial authori-

---

tion of why the WIC struggled to make a profit in the more competitive Atlantic trade environment, particularly because its structure so closely followed the VOC system, which was designed for Asian trade, see Jan de Vries and Ad van der Woude, *The First Modern Economy: Success, Failure, and Perseverance of the Dutch Economy, 1500–1815* (Cambridge, 1997), 401.

3. For characterizations of New Netherland's governance as incompetent, see Alan Taylor, *American Colonies* (New York, 2001), 225. For a critique of such characterizations, especially during Peter Stuyvesant's tenure as governor, see Jaap Jacobs, "Incompetente autocraten? Bestuurlijke verhoudingen in de zeventiende-eeuwse Nederlandse Atlantische wereld," *De zeventiende eeuw*, XXI (2005), 64–78.

ties' decisions and employed the governor and other key administrators, the company also allowed significant political authority to devolve to the colony itself. New Amsterdam developed a municipal government in the mid-1650s that provided a city council and a court for the town's residents. Fort Orange and Beverwijk similarly created a municipal council and an orphan's court, two key Dutch civic institutions. Even the governor, also known as the director general or director, and members of the colony's ruling council did not stand somehow apart from the burgher settler population. Though they acted as the local face of the WIC and represented some of the wealthiest and best-connected men in the colony, they were also settlers themselves, with similar interests in beaver-skin trading, agriculture, and commerce as their neighbors. Not everyone was happy with WIC rule, and residents complained repeatedly about the concentration of power in a few hands. Nonetheless, though the colony remained the property of a for-profit, publicly traded company with an appointed ruler, day-to-day governance accorded with many Dutch norms that focused on the interests of the burgher class, just like in the Netherlands.[4]

The residents of the Hudson Valley represented a mixed bunch. Among the European immigrants, Hollanders lived alongside French-speaking migrants from the Low Countries, the children of Scandinavians who had found work in Amsterdam, and a substantial number of German and English folk, along with many others. Together, all of these settlers followed a wide range of religions. Though the official Dutch Reformed Church practiced a form of Calvinism not dissimilar to that of the neighboring New England churches, there were also Lutherans, Quakers, Jews, and others who faced occasional harassment from Governor Stuyvesant but enjoyed unofficial toleration from the WIC.[5]

4. For the political development of New Netherland, see Jacobs, *New Netherland*. On civil institutions in Beverwijk, see Janny Venema, *Kinderen van weelde en armoede: Armoede en liefdadigheid in Beverwijck/Albany (c. 1650–c. 1700)* (Hilversum, Netherlands, 1993); Venema, *Beverwijck: A Dutch Village on the American Frontier, 1652–1664* (Albany, N.Y., 2003); Martha Dickinson Shattuck, "A Civil Society: Court and Community in Beverwijck, New Netherland, 1652–1664" (Ph.D. diss., Boston University, 1993).

5. David Steven Cohen, "How Dutch Were the Dutch of New Netherland?" *New York History*, LXII (1981), 43–60; Oliver A. Rink, "The People of New Netherland: Notes on Non-English Immigration to New York in the Seventeenth Century," *New York History*, LXII (1981), 5–42; A. G. Roeber, "The Origin of Whatever Is Not English among Us: The Dutch-Speaking and the German-Speaking Peoples of Colonial British America," in Bernard Bailyn and Philip D. Morgan, eds., *Strangers within the Realm: Cultural Margins of the First British Empire* (Chapel Hill, N.C., 1991); Evan Haefeli, *New Netherland and the Dutch Origins of American Religious Liberty* (Philadelphia, 2012).

Widespread settlements meant the number of Native American groups who took part, to a greater or lesser extent, in New Netherland's colonial economy remained similarly diverse. Among the Haudenosaunee, or Iroquois, the powerful Mohawks lived close to Fort Orange and provided access to trade routes reaching the Oneida and Seneca. Mahicans on the east side of the Hudson resided just a short way from Rensselaerswijk. Lenapes and Susquehannocks interacted with the trading forts along the Delaware River; Munsee-speaking villagers visited settlers by canoe or foot up and down the Hudson River; and Shinnecocks, Montauks, and other Algonquians shared Long Island with Dutch and English neighbors.[6]

African residents likewise came from a wide array of ethnic backgrounds. Kongolese and other West Africans had lived in the Hudson Valley since the 1620s, many owned by the WIC. By the 1650s, however, these early arrivals were being outnumbered by new importations of slaves from places as diverse as present-day Ghana and Brazil. Increasingly owned by private individuals, these newcomers reflected New Netherland's growing engagement with the Atlantic economy and African trade.[7]

This motley crew of Hudson Valley inhabitants had faced plenty of upheaval by 1657, and they would face still more before 1664. Fighting between indigenous and colonial residents flared up repeatedly during the Dutch colonial period, and even interludes of so-called peace saw occasional violent, if not fatal, episodes. Battles with the Raritans, a downriver Munsee-speaking group, took place as early as the first half of the 1630s. A major, murderous conflict with a number of Munsee villages, known as Kieft's War, erupted in 1640, punctuated by several massacres by WIC forces that disgusted many settlers. Sporadic yet nonetheless gruesome attacks against residents of Marechkawick, Tappan, Wiechquaeskeck, and elsewhere continued until mid-1643. A brief but bloody dispute in 1655 known as the Peach War pitted Hackensack and Wiechquaeskeck combatants against WIC soldiers. Between 1659 and 1664, the theater of war moved to the mid-river area, where the Dutch fought two brutal campaigns, known as the Esopus Wars. Ultimately, the Dutch succeeded in isolating the Munsee-speaking

6. T. J. Brasser, "Mahican," in William C. Sturtevant, ed., *Handbook of North American Indians*, XV, *Northeast*, ed. Bruce G. Trigger (Washington, D.C., 1978), 198–212; Robert S. Grumet, *The Munsee Indians: A History* (Norman, Okla., 2009); Daniel K. Richter, *The Ordeal of the Longhouse: The Peoples of the Iroquois League in the Era of European Colonization* (Chapel Hill, N.C., 1992).

7. Joyce D. Goodfriend, "Burghers and Blacks: The Evolution of a Slave Society at New Amsterdam," *New York History*, LIX (1978), 133–136.

Esopus villagers from their neighbors, with devastating consequences. Each one of these events brought the threat of insecurity, if not violence itself, into every home throughout the greater Hudson Valley.[8]

As deadly and destabilizing as repeated wars with Native peoples were, the greatest threat to the Dutch presence in the area came from their most formidable colonial rival, the English. The First Anglo-Dutch War of 1652–1654 caused considerable unease in the colony, and rumors of an impending English attack, or a combined English-Indian attack, depending on the speaker, surfaced regularly in the 1650s and 1660s. Indeed, the Second Anglo-Dutch War would claim New Netherland as one of its earliest victims. In 1657, however, these threats still seemed distant enough for celebration to feel warranted.

Dutch leaders' optimism in the mid-1650s, the heart of the Netherlands' Golden Age, should not be surprising. During this period, the United Provinces successfully fought for and established their republic's independence from Spanish rule, and the ships sailing from the Netherlands' many ports extended Dutch influence to the far reaches of the globe. With the profits of the new trade that resulted, Amsterdam and other towns throughout the provinces blossomed, attracting migrants from not only the immediate countryside but throughout Europe. The riches from the VOC, headquartered at Batavia on the island of Java, inspired the formation of trading companies to advance Dutch economic interests in other parts of the world, including Africa and the Americas. Within New Netherland itself, towns and trading posts took root on isolated islands and far up river valleys, bringing Native peoples across the middle of the eastern part of the continent into contact with a growing global web. People in the seventeenth-century Hudson Valley region lived in a world that was expanding in all directions.[9]

8. For a survey of wars against the Munsee in New Netherland, see Paul Otto, *The Dutch-Munsee Encounter in America: The Struggle for Sovereignty in the Hudson Valley* (New York, 2006). On the villages targeted during Kieft's War, see Grumet, *Munsee Indians*, 58–59. On Dutch reactions to the massacres, see Donna Merwick, *The Shame and the Sorrow: Dutch-Amerindian Encounters in New Netherland* (Philadelphia, 2006), 133–179.

9. On transatlantic connections, see Oliver A. Rink, *Holland on the Hudson: An Economic and Social History of Dutch New York* (Ithaca, N.Y., 1986); Wim Klooster, "Communities of Port Jews and their Contacts in the Dutch Atlantic World," *Jewish History*, XX (2006), 129–145. On Dutch trade connections throughout the Atlantic, see Johannes Postma and Victor Enthoven, eds., *Riches from Atlantic Commerce: Dutch Transatlantic Trade and Shipping, 1585–1817* (Leiden, 2003). On connections to North American colonies outside the Dutch empire, see Cynthia J. van Zandt, *Brothers among Nations: The Pursuit of Intercultural Alliances in Early America, 1580–1660* (New York, 2008); Claudia Schnurmann, *Atlantische Welten: Engländer und Niederländer im amerikanisch-atlantischen Raum, 1648–1713* (Cologne, 1998). For individual experiences

Just as systems of familial and social relationships supported the society and economy of the seventeenth-century Netherlands, similar webs of connections underlay the colony and the developing empire of which it was a part. Yet the diversity of the people brought together by Dutch transatlantic expansion meant that these networks would follow more than just Dutch patterns. Interpersonal relationships that today seem almost stifling in their intimacy and ubiquity continued to shape most aspects of life in all the cultures—Native American, African, and European—brought together, willingly and unwillingly, by Dutch colonization. Family, kin, clan, and village provided the tools people relied on to function socially and economically.

At the same time, the new circumstances of colonial life challenged these face-to-face relationships and stretched social networks for everyone. As they met people from faraway places, formed new ties across cultural divides, and often endured journeys spanning wide stretches of time and space, the settlers, slaves, and Native Americans of New Netherland lived in a world of ever-increasing distances. Trading voyages and settlements brought together European travelers and enslaved Africans from ports throughout the far-flung Atlantic world. Once they arrived, these settlers and slaves found themselves removed from the circles of kin, faith, exchange, and community that had defined their lives in the Old World. Dutch settlers and sojourners not infrequently had family living as far afield as today's Indonesia. When young Hendrick de Graaf lost his mother, for instance, he found himself marooned in New Amsterdam in the hands of a stepfather who "drinks himself drunk everyday" while his elder brother was "in the East Indies."[10]

Yet, such isolation pales in comparison to that experienced by Africans forced to endure separation from all they had known and to reorient themselves in a hostile and alien colonial geography. Isabel Kisana van Angola had to remake kin and community from scratch following her involuntary migration from her homeland. As Africans and settlers alike continued to make repeated moves within the colony and among the ports of the Atlantic, mobility across vast distances remained a constant feature throughout

---

within the "widespread network" of Dutch commercial activities in Asia, see Vibeke Roeper and Roelof van Gelder, *In dienst van de compagnie: Leven bij de VOC in honderd getuigenissen (1602–1799)* (Amsterdam, 2002), 15.

10. Orphan's Court Records, June 19, 1659, Orphan Masters' Records, Records of New Amsterdam, NYCMA (microfilm, NYSL). This record book has been translated and published, but errors and omissions make the translation unreliable for academic purposes. For the translation, see Berthold Fernow, ed. and trans., *The Minutes of the Orphanmasters of New Amsterdam, 1655 to 1663* (New York, 1902).

many New Netherlanders' lives, posing the threat of multiple upheavals and disconnections.

The arrival of European and African newcomers, and the new diseases, economies, and violence that accompanied them, also confronted Native American communities with the challenges of distance. Quashawam, a Montauk sunksquaw, for example, had to negotiate the shifting political currents of Dutch and English settlement on Long Island in the 1660s at the very moment that a smallpox epidemic dealt the kin and clan ties that mediated power among her people a shocking blow. Montauk residents coping with the destruction of their families and kin groups, Staten Island Munsees responding to the devastation and upheaval of warfare, and even Susquehannock traders reorienting their travel and trade connections eastward all faced disruptions to personal and family ties just as they needed those ties more than ever to help them overcome new and difficult circumstances.[11]

Yet, distances of all kinds proved passable. Extensive transatlantic commerce joined Manhattan to Amsterdam, Africa, Brazil, and ports throughout the Dutch Atlantic and beyond. The overland beaver-skin trade and the regional commodities trade thrived despite topographical and cultural difficulties, becoming essential and fundamental aspects of New Netherland's economy. The disparate peoples of the mid-Atlantic even became so closely tied to one another economically that they shared a common currency and created a frontier exchange economy. Janneken Jans van Leeuwarden, for instance, crossed the Atlantic on her own multiple times. But she did so as a part of her family's growing stake in travel and trade among Brazil, New Netherland, and Amsterdam, and she paid some of her debts in wampum beads manufactured by Algonquian women. Exchanges, like Janneken's, that reached across the ocean, throughout the settlements, to Native American communities depended on debt and credit transactions, showing that this widely dispersed, polyglot set of people did manage to reach across social divisions and establish circuits of trust. The diverse peoples of New Netherland clearly did not exist in isolation or anomie but formed durable connections regardless of the distances that defined their lives.[12]

11. For more on Quashawam, see Chapter 5.

12. On the beaver-skin trade, see Allen W. Trelease, *Indian Affairs in Colonial New York: The Seventeenth Century* (Ithaca, N.Y., 1960); Rink, *Holland on the Hudson*. On frontier exchange economies, see Daniel H. Usner, Jr., *Indians, Settlers, and Slaves in a Frontier Exchange Economy: The Lower Mississippi Valley before 1783* (Chapel Hill, N.C., 1992). All of New Netherland before 1664, not just one particular area, meets the now-classic definition of a "frontier" as a zone of intercultural interaction among previously separate groups. See Howard Lamar and Leonard Thompson, *The Frontier in History: North America and Southern Africa Compared*

The way that the residents of the seventeenth-century greater Hudson Valley wove together their personal relationships to form wider linkages reveals the existence of what I call "intimate networks." These intimate networks consisted of a web of ties that developed from people's immediate, affective, and personal associations and spanned vast geographic and cultural distances. Combining the deep analysis of particular relationships with the investigation of long-distance social webs, a study of intimate networks demonstrates the ways in which people built and negotiated early modern empires. The framework of intimate networks allows for equal emphasis on both the quality and the quantity of people's social ties. By integrating the study of imperial intimacies with the study of imperial networks, this book suggests a new model for the exploration of immediate relationships in early modern empires.[13]

The intimate networks people constructed, rather than actions taken by formal structures or metropolitan authorities, constituted empire. Dutch colonization was thus diffuse, grounded in the petty financial motives and schemes of individual men and women who pursued their own agendas—whether it be to find a marriage partner, make a few guilders in the fur trade, pay off some debts back home, eke out a new status outside slavery, or

---

(New Haven, Conn., 1981), 7. The word "frontier," however, remains somewhat contested. James H. Merrell gives it only backhanded approval by calling it less biased than "backcountry"; see Merrell, "Second Thoughts on Colonial Historians and American Indians," *WMQ*, 3d Ser., LXIX (2012), 451–512. The two most common academic alternatives, "backcountry" and "borderland," poorly match the geography of contact in the Dutch colony. In this period, there was no "front country" equivalent to the tidewater plantation areas of the eighteenth-century Carolinas, colonies for which "backcountry" is frequently used, and the interwoven patchwork of villages in the greater Hudson Valley defies attempts to imagine the area as drawn up of borders or borderlands. On "borderlands," see Jeremy Adelman and Stephen Aron, "From Borderlands to Borders: Empires, Nation-States, and the Peoples in Between in North American History," *American Historical Review*, CIV (1999), 814–841. Only "frontier" combines the geographic and cultural elements of contact so succinctly by indicating cross-cultural contact within a specific region. However, seventeenth-century Dutch speakers used the word "frontier" very rarely, and, when they did, they used it to indicate a military outpost. For instance, regarding fighting in 1655, the council mentioned the burdens borne by the town of New Amsterdam as "frontier en hooftplaets," that is, "frontier and capital" (Petition and Ordinance, Jan. 22–24, 1657, NYCM, VIII, 427–434, NYSA). Thus, describing New Netherland as a frontier follows from contemporary historiography, not early modern pratice. To avoid slippage between the word's older meaning and contemporary academic uses, I employ the word rarely. Nonetheless, this region provides a model of interactions that could help explain patterns in other frontiers in the colonial period.

13. For the networks created by seventeenth-century English travelers, see Alison Games, *The Web of Empire: English Cosmopolitans in an Age of Expansion, 1560–1660* (Oxford, 2008). A robust literature on the British Empire reveals how economic networks functioned on the

keep European trade abuse and expansion at bay. People drew on their personal relationships and sometimes even formed new ones to benefit from, or simply survive, developing overseas connections. As they did this, they built the early modern empire from the bottom up. From an Atlantic perspective, empire consisted of individuals in Amsterdam and beyond who invoked personal relationships to function economically and create new trading opportunities.

Nor did these networks only form transatlantic connections. Intimate networks also constituted empire within the colony itself, structuring imperial links to indigenous communities throughout the region. Both Europeans and Native Americans who engaged in the beaver-skin trade and the essential trade in consumables initiated face-to-face relationships with their neighbors to further their own economic, personal, or communal goals. Cross-cultural interactions in New Netherland were not confined to a small group of go-betweens nor monopolized by state or imperial representatives. Instead, the interface between the Dutch empire and Native America consisted of a highly effective, widespread set of interpersonal and economic networks. The nature of these networks shaped not only the economy but also the course of politics and warfare. Everything about this empire, from its connections reaching into the continent of North America to its transatlantic ties, depended on interpersonal interactions.

Gender roles and relationships between men and women strengthened these intimate networks by coding them as essential personal and familial bonds. These relationships, in turn, laid the groundwork for local, regional, and transatlantic economy, society, and politics. In particular, the specific modes of economic engagement employed by women and men with personal ties to one another helped to maintain New Netherland's critical beaver-skin economy, both across the region and across the ocean. Whether

---

global scale, but their intimate nature and their function at the level of the neighborhood, household, and family rarely receive mention. See David Hancock, "Commerce and Conversation in the Eighteenth-Century Atlantic: The Invention of Madeira Wine," *Journal of Interdisciplinary History*, XXIX (1998), 197; Hancock, *Citizens of the World: London Merchants and the Integration of the British Atlantic Community, 1735–1785* (Cambridge, 1995); Rosalind J. Beiler, *Immigrant and Entrepreneur: The Atlantic World of Caspar Wistar, 1650–1750* (University Park, Pa., 2008); J. Forbes Munro, *Maritime Enterprise and Empire: Sir William Mackinnon and His Business Network, 1823–93* (Suffolk, U.K., 2003); Tony Ballantyne, "Race and the Webs of Empire: Aryanism from India to the Pacific," *Journal of Colonialism and Colonial History*, II (2001); Ballantyne, *Orientalism and Race: Aryanism in the British Empire* (Basingstoke, U.K., 2002); David Lambert and Alan Lester, eds., *Colonial Lives across the British Empire: Imperial Careering in the Long Nineteenth Century* (Cambridge, 2006).

women stayed in the villages of their birth, traversed the ocean, or crossed the cultural divide, they did crucial work building the social and economic connections that sustained Dutch commerce to the mid-Atlantic coast. In short, this early modern European empire would not have functioned without the direct contributions of women. By structuring women's intimate and economic lives, the institution of marriage was as important in the creation of empire as the rule of law or the development of financial instruments of credit and exchange.

Whether negotiating racial difference, building community, or navigating an oceanic crossing, the people of the mid-Atlantic coast initiated and relied on interlinked, immediate relationships that together formed their intimate networks. As people put these relationships to use for personal and economic goals, they wove them into overlapping, branching, and closely connected webs that reached throughout and beyond the Hudson Valley. Rather than cause these ties to rupture, distance and mobility actually allowed people to overcome the dislocation brought about by their expanding world. Together, distance and mobility facilitated the formation of new ties that, alongside old ties, made possible the construction of functional long-distance networks. Thus, people engendered, accommodated, and resisted the new transoceanic economy by drawing on personal relationships.[14]

Often, the function of intimate networks was not benign. Exclusion from and differences among the relationships that constituted these networks meant that they also undergirded colonial inequalities. Personal ties served to locate people and families within developing social hierarchies. Nonetheless, the dynamic nature of those webs left them flexible, and people drew on

14. The multiplicity of geographically dispersed relationships in the Dutch case points out why empire generally can be better imagined in terms of networks than core-periphery models. For the argument that we should conceive "of empire as a set of networks through which knowledge and ideas were exchanged, trust was negotiated, goods were traded, and people travelled," see Natasha Glaisyer, "Networking: Trade and Exchange in the Eighteenth-Century British Empire," *Historical Journal*, XLVII (2004), 451–476 (quotation, 451). Miles Ogborn argues that understanding globalization, of which the building of empires was an important part, requires developing our "ideas of networks or webs of global connection that are built in various ways to link people, places, ideas, and objects together in dynamic configurations"; see Ogborn, *Global Lives: Britain and the World, 1550–1800* (New York, 2008), 5. For a comparison of networks and core-periphery models, see ibid., 4–6. Also see Alan Lester, *Imperial Networks: Creating Identities in Nineteenth-Century South Africa and Britain* (London, 2001), 5; Thomas R. Metcalf, *Imperial Connections: India in the Indian Ocean Arena, 1860–1920* (Berkeley, Calif., 2007), 6–7. Networks can also help us understand empires as processes, not structures; see Eric Hinderaker, *Elusive Empires: Constructing Colonialism in the Ohio Valley, 1673–1800* (Cambridge, 1999), esp. xi.

their immediate relationships in myriad ways to respond to the challenges of race in a colonial setting. Intimate ties within groups enabled cooperation in the face of oppression and provided the basis for survival, especially for Africans and their children in the colony. Native American and white villagers alike relied on intimate networks to both define the differences between their communities and bridge cultural divides. Intimate networks thus provided the framework for the particularities of New Netherland's complex and diverse society.

New Netherland was not the only area of imperial activity where intimacies proved essential to the colonial project. Interdisciplinary scholarly research has shown that the most personal ties between people fundamentally shaped many empires and colonies. Allegiances within colonial regimes often rested on emotions engendered through sexual and domestic relationships. Race-based hierarchies and exclusions, so central to imperialisms, became real through intimate interactions. By regulating people's associations and bodies, laws put intimacies into the service of imperial states, determining, for instance, which family ties could be formalized through marriage and which could not. Deeply personal emotional ties created colonial hierarchies and imperial governance across the globe.[15]

Imperial authorities in different places imposed and proscribed distinct kinds of personal and intimate connections in attempt to create the kinds of colonies they wanted. In New Mexico, the Spanish tried to culturally dominate the Pueblo through everyday relationships within a shared space. On the Pacific coast, Russian men forcibly entered the intimate spaces of Alutiiq families, holding Native women and children hostage while forcing men to hunt for otter pelts, a practice that gave rise to a mixed-race generation that enabled Russian trade in America. In New France, consensual relationships between French traders and Algonquian women fostered and sustained the fur trade at the heart of the colonial economy. A growing literature estab-

15. For an introduction to the literature on empire and intimacy, see Sylvia Van Kirk, "*Many Tender Ties*": *Women in Fur-Trade Society in Western Canada, 1670–1870* (Winnipeg, Canada, 1980); Durba Ghosh, *Sex and the Family in Colonial India: The Making of Empire* (Cambridge, 2006). See also the articles in "Empires and Intimacies: Lessons from (Post) Colonial Studies: A Round Table," *Journal of American History*, LXXXVIII (2001), 829–897; Sudipta Sen, "Colonial Aversions and Domestic Desires: Blood, Race, Sex, and the Decline of Intimacy in Early British India," *South Asia*, XXIV (2001), 25–45; Ann Laura Stoler, "Intimidations of Empire: Predicaments of the Tactile and Unseen," in Stoler, ed., *Haunted by Empire: Geographies of Intimacy in North American History* (Durham, N.C., 2006), 2; Antoinette Burton, "From Child Bride to 'Hindoo Lady': Rukhmabai and the Debate on Sexual Respectability in Imperial Britain," *American Historical Review*, CIII (1998), 1119–1146.

lishes that personal and immediate relationships proved central to ordering life in colonies in North America and beyond.[16]

Although this literature shows that imperial powers employed intimate relationships to shape colonies around the world, it has not yet fully explored how individuals used these same relationships to address the challenges of colonization and distance. Instead, many scholars continue to focus primarily on colonizers' desires to regulate sexual intimacies within colonial locales. Studies of nineteenth-century regimes concentrate on state intervention into the intimate realm as an attempt to establish imperial control over colonized bodies. This emphasis on the bureaucratic imperial state seems an uneasy fit with the early modern period, when colonial regimes remained in their infancy and imperial governments could be quite weak. Janneken Jans, Quashawam, Isabel Kisana, and countless others navigated their challenging times by relying on a wide range of intimate relationships that they shaped for their own ends. Indigenous people within the orbit of colonial power, forced migrants and slaves, and voluntary colonial settlers alike sought to forge particular kinds of societies in the face of overseas expansion by fusing relationships into functional networks.[17]

The distances and problems that these networks enabled people to conquer were hardly unique to New Netherland. Residents of seventeenth-century colonial areas across North America and beyond endured similar separations. Indeed, New Netherland is interesting, not because its distances were atypical, but rather because they were shared. Shortly after arriving in New Netherland in 1641, for example, Geertge Nanningsdochter found

16. Ann Stoler, "Sexual Affronts and Racial Frontiers: European Identities and the Cultural Politics of Exclusion in Colonial Southeast Asia," *Comparative Studies in Society and History*, XXXIV (1992), 517; Damon Salesa, "Samoa's Half-Castes and Some Frontiers of Comparison," in Stoler, ed., *Haunted by Empire*, 71–93. See also Jennifer M. Spear, *Race, Sex, and Social Order in Early New Orleans* (Baltimore, 2009); Nan A. Rothschild, *Colonial Encounters in a Native American Landscape: The Spanish and Dutch in North America* (Washington, D.C., 2003), 3, 23; Gwenn A. Miller, "'The Perfect Mistress of Russian Economy': Sighting the Intimate on a Colonial Alaskan Terrain, 1784–1821," in Stoler, ed., *Haunted by Empire*, 297–322; Susan Sleeper-Smith, *Indian Women and French Men: Rethinking Cultural Encounter in the Western Great Lakes* (Amherst, Mass., 2001); Jean Gelman Taylor, *The Social World of Batavia: European and Eurasian in Dutch Asia* (Madison, Wis., 1983); Sleeper-Smith, "'An Unpleasant Transaction on this Frontier': Challenging Female Autonomy and Authority at Michilimackinac," *Journal of the Early Republic*, XXV (2005), 417–443.

17. Jennifer M. Spear, "'They Need Wives': Métissage and the Regulation of Sexuality in French Louisiana, 1699–1730," in Martha Hodes, ed., *Sex, Love, Race: Crossing Boundaries in North American History* (New York, 1999), 35–59; Spear, "Colonial Intimacies: Legislating Sex in French Louisiana," *WMQ*, 3d Ser., LX (2003), 75–98; Richard Phillips, "Heterogeneous Imperialism and the Regulation of Sexuality in British West Africa," *Journal of the History of Sex-*

herself widowed for a second time, once more a woman without a *huysge-zin,* or household, facing a second long voyage across the Atlantic. But her difficult circumstances seem of a piece with those of women up and down the Atlantic coast in the early years of the seventeenth century. She not only survived her frequent uprootings, she repeatedly formed new intimate relationships and eventually thrived. New Netherland lives like hers raise important questions and suggest patterns to consider elsewhere.[18]

The importance of the contact between Native Americans and settlers, the presence of African slaves, the role of family migration, and the connection to the Atlantic economy also render New Netherland similar to other colonies. Perhaps New Netherland's diverse and dispersed small settlements make the impact of distance more obvious, but distance, isolation, and loss defined the experience of many early American peoples forced to cope with the advent of early modern colonization. When seventeenth-century Africans, Native Americans, and Europeans gazed out across the many gulfs that defined their lives in the greater Hudson Valley, they engaged in a common experience. The tools they used to survive and succeed were likely shared as well.

What makes New Netherland special are the rich, underused sources that offer the potential to investigate people's strategic responses to those challenges. Court and colony records provide particularly detailed access to the lives of not only Europeans like Geertge but also Africans, Munsees, and Mohawks. Notary records not extant in the English legal system reveal the familial and economic tactics of people up and down the social scale, in Amsterdam Old and New.

The relationships cultivated by people as diverse as Geertge Nanningsdochter, Janneken Jans van Leeuwarden, Quashawam, and Isabel Kisana van Angola formed the basis for the stability that New Amsterdammers gathered to celebrate in 1657. Despite the profound changes wrought by distance in people's lives, relationships organized around proximity and interdependence thrived among the Hudson Valley's residents. Immigrants and travelers from Holland and elsewhere established families on American soil, enabling not only Geertge Nanningsdochter and Janneken Jans but even

---

uality, XIV (2005), 291–315; Frederick Cooper and Ann Laura Stoler, eds., *Tensions of Empire: Colonial Cultures in a Bourgeois World* (Berkeley, Calif., 1997). Scholars, including Stoler, have called for greater attention to a variety of intimate relationships, but nonsexual intimacies have garnered less research. For a call to widen the range of relationships studied, see Miller, "'The Perfect Mistress of Russian Economy,'" in Stoler, ed., *Haunted by Empire,* 297–322.

18. For Geertge Nanningsdochter, see Chapter 2.

African women like Isabel Kisana to create the key institution of the huys-gezin, which undergirded the household economy and civic order extolled by colonial authorities. The creation of these new family units incorporated women into kinship networks, thus laying the groundwork for the development of a burgher society in North America. Interdependent and personal relationships even reached across the seas and encouraged the "traffic" in transatlantic trade goods so evident by the time of the celebration. Annetgen Arents Hontoms, for example, the wife of an important skipper and early fur trader to the colony, created and relied on a growing web of personal connections to other maritime couples to support the sale of New Nether-land products in Amsterdam from the 1630s through the 1650s. Networks like hers help explain why settlers in 1657 thought New Netherland's economy was booming even when the WIC struggled to make a profit.[19]

The intimate ties that grew from marriage also flourished among Africans, even though forced migration severed them from their natal ties of kin, clan, and village. Marriage and parenthood joined Isabel Kisana and other African women and men together to form productive households on Manhattan that fit within Dutch ideas of social and civic order. Family and kinship, both fictive and real, allowed Africans to create economic alliances and social protections essential to building stable lives in the colony. Among the families called to honor the day of thanksgiving were Africans, slave and free, who had resisted their threatened social extinction by joining together and recreating intimacy.

Interactions at the mid-Atlantic coast's many cross-cultural meeting points, too, depended on face-to-face encounters. People like Quashawam and her colonial neighbors fashioned trading relationships and sometimes friendships that reached across cultural divides. Mohawks and Mahicans regularly visited settlements around Fort Orange. Settlers and Native peoples upriver got to know one another by name and visited the intimate spaces of one another's homes and communities. Downriver, Manhattan's settlers and slaves frequently interacted with Munsee speakers from villages along the Hudson and on Long Island as they traded in daily necessities. The extension of credit and the formation of enduring trading partnerships show that trust, created through the development of immediate ties, allowed these connections to do economic work essential to the colony's prosperity.

Clusters of close, personal relationships like these intertwined and overlapped to form broader associations. Webs of intimate marital and family

19. On Annetgen Arents Hontoms, see Chapter 1.

ties forged kinship networks that kept money and goods in motion in the service of the small-scale Atlantic economy. Kin and clan networks among Dutch settlers intersected with those among Native peoples, similarly organizing the intercultural exchange systems that created and supported the colony. These networks produced goods and moved goods to the colony's towns, whether those goods came from Amsterdam or from the fields or streams of the Hudson Valley itself. Ties between each huysgezin that settlers formed likewise generated networks, in this case networks of neighborhood and community. The personal and familial relationships that developed among some households while others were excluded produced social hierarchies and lines of power within colonial society. Comparable yet distinct networks of family and clan shaped the lines of political power and authority among Munsees. Yet, even as networks of intimate relationships provided the structure for cultural connections, they also fragmented colonial society. In a period before racial restrictions were fully codified in law, disconnections between personal and familial networks kept Native Americans, forced African migrants, and settlers clearly divided.

If intimate networks formed the backbone of empire, then the actions of all who participated in these networks have to be understood as playing a crucial role in creating the early Atlantic world. Delving into the relationships and families of people like Geertge Nanningsdochter, Isabel Kisana van Angola, Quashawam, Annetgen Arents Hontoms, and Janneken Jans van Leeuwarden has a very important function. Their personal and social webs made possible transatlantic and intercultural trade, structured society and politics throughout the region, established colonial hierarchies, and gave people's lives shape and meaning. Looking at how they built and sustained their most intimate relationships, then, illuminates the gradual construction of the Dutch empire in North America. Only a thorough immersion in people's intimate networks can fully reveal how early modern empire, reaching across the ocean from Amsterdam, took shape in the greater Hudson Valley.

CHAPTER ONE

◆ ◆ ◆

"Goods, Wares, and Merchandise"
Amsterdam's Intimate Atlantic

 In 1619, an Amsterdam woman carefully packed a sea chest. Marritgen Wouters folded shirts and stockings, smoothed down pillows, and counted out coins into a sack. Her husband, Skipper Hendrick Christiaensz, stood ready to depart on the ship *Swarte Beer,* or *Black Bear,* for a journey to America. Though she did not know it at the time, she would never see her husband again; he would meet his end along the shores of the Hudson River, during fighting with the Native Americans he had hoped to profit from. By 1622, Marritgen would be struggling to regain her financial footing as a widow alone in Golden Age Amsterdam, one of the first, but far from one of the last, women widowed by Dutch North American ambitions. She did not describe her last glimpse of her husband. She might have waved goodbye from the docks, or, like many wives and children of men sailing to the East and West Indies, she could have headed up the steep steps of the Schreierstoren, or Weeper's Tower, at the edge of the harbor for one last look as the ship weighed anchor. Perhaps she traveled as far as the "pure sand-duned beach" at Den Helder to "say adieu, until we meet again" from the "weeper hook" as the ship slipped out into the North Sea from the island of Texel. However Marritgen and Hendrick chose to say goodbye, they were not alone in their parting. With some fifty thousand maritime workers venturing forth annually from Dutch harbors in the late seventeenth century, husbands and wives, brothers and sisters, parents and children took leave of one another time and time again (Figure 3).[1]

1. The Schreierstoren still stands, one of the few surviving buildings from early efforts to wall the growing city of Amsterdam in the fifteenth century. With its excellent view of the harbor and departing ships, the tower would be a perfect place to wave goodbye, and popular belief has long asserted that the name of the tower came from the weeping wives of VOC sailors, although this is doubtful. For a seventeenth-century poem depicting women and men

FIGURE 3 ◆ Leave-taking on the Dutch seashore. Engraving. From
Elias Herckmans, *Der zee-vaert lof, handelende vande gedenckwaerdighste
zee-vaerden.* . . . (Amsterdam, 1634), 211. This item is reproduced by
permission of The Huntington Library, San Marino, Calif.

This depiction of the painful farewells caused by overseas expansion
accompanied a multi-book verse history of seafaring that celebrated
the triumph of Dutch sailing in the Golden Age.

---

who traveled to Den Helder to wave farewell as ships left Texel and headed into the North
Sea, see E. Herckmans, *Der zee-vaert lof, handelende vande gedenckwaerdighste zee-vaerden.* . . .
(Amsterdam, 1634), 211–213 ("pure," 211, "say adieu," 212, "weeper hook," 213). For more on
the mishaps of the *Swarte Beer,* see Victor Enthoven, "Early Dutch Expansion in the Atlantic
Region, 1585–1621," in Johannes Postma and Enthoven, eds., *Riches from Atlantic Commerce:
Dutch Transatlantic Trade and Shipping, 1585–1817* (Leiden, 2003), 38. For an exploration of
one Dutch marriage across the seas, see Leonard Blussé, *Bitters bruid: Een koloniaal huwelijks-
drama in de Gouden Eeuw* (Amsterdam, 1997). For transatlantic marriage in a later period, see
Sarah M. S. Pearsall, *Atlantic Families: Lives and Letters in the Later Eighteenth Century* (Oxford,
2008). For a dysfunctional Spanish transatlantic marriage, see Alexandra Parma Cook and
Noble David Cook, *Good Faith and Truthful Ignorance: A Case of Transatlantic Bigamy* (Durham,
N.C., 1991). On the numbers of sailors departing, see Annette de Wit, "Zeemansvrouwen
aan het werk: De arbeidsmarktpositie van vrouwen in Maassluis, Schiedam, en Ter Heijde
(1600–1700)," *Tijdschrift voor sociale en economische geschiedenis,* II, no. 3 (2005), 60; Karel Davids,
"Maritime Labour in the Netherlands, 1570–1870," *Research in Maritime History,* XIII (1997),
41–71.

As the leader of a trading voyage to the coast of North America just ten years after Henry Hudson's exploration of the area, Skipper Hendrick Christiaensz clearly took part in building a transatlantic economy while working for the short-lived New Netherland Company as it extended Dutch commerce across the ocean. Yet, those left behind in Amsterdam, like his wife, also participated in empire building, though in perhaps less obvious ways. Marritgen's actions and choices, both when she readied her husband for his journey and when she sought to find her feet as a widow, aided the construction of these newly developing, cross-ocean connections.

For wives, sisters, cousins, and parents left behind in the Netherlands' maritime districts, overseas expansion happened at one remove. Their role in the creation of empire came through their relationships to others. Despite the vast reaches of time and space that separated them from kin who left Amsterdam on board company ships, those relationships did not perish. Instead, they persisted and sometimes grew stronger as people put them to use for personal and financial ends. Through their ties with travelers, Amsterdammers built and maintained crucial links between the home country and the world beyond.

Kin and family played an essential part in the creation of the Dutch empire at every level. Men and women far wealthier than Hendrick and Marritgen served as investors and directors of Dutch overseas trading companies, acting on behalf of their relatives. Kiliaen van Rensselaer (circa 1590–1643), one of the leading Amsterdam investors in the Dutch experiment along the mid-Atlantic coast of North America, provides a good example of this familial orientation. Losing his father at a young age, he nonetheless acquired the critical business skills needed to operate as one of the merchant princes of the Golden Age by learning the jewel trade from his late father's relative Wolfert van Bijler. Van Bijler developed such confidence in Kiliaen that he named the young man as one of the executors of his estate, over closer relations. Van Rensselaer went on to make a fortune in the jewel trade by partnering with his cousin and co-executor, Jan van Wely. He took care to keep the money in his extended family network by marrying within his kin group. Over the winter of 1615–1616, he successfully sought the hand of his "dearest cousin," seventeen-year-old Hillegond, the only child of the late Van Bijler's eldest brother and heiress to some twelve thousand guilders of her uncle's fortune. Van Rensselaer's family-based wealth allowed him to become one of the principal early investors in the WIC, and he bought shares worth more than eighteen thousand guilders in 1625. On the basis of this investment of family capital, he became a company director. After the death of Hillegond, he again married within his extended family, this time to Anna van Wely.[2]

Even though Van Rensselaer never crossed the Atlantic himself, he looked to the colony to ensure the continued position of his familial alliance within the social and economic elite. As a director, he participated in the company decision to allow major investors to become patroons within the colony, enabling them to set up heritable patrimonial estates along the Hudson. He appointed kin, such as his grandnephew Arent van Curler, to key positions of leadership over his patroonship, and he saw his nephew Wouter van Twiller chosen as director of New Netherland in the 1630s. He also attempted to legally convert his ownership of the patroonship into a fiefdom. Eventually, two of his sons, Jan Baptist and Jeremias, traveled to the colony and became resident patroons, establishing the family as one of the Hudson Valley elite for generations. Van Rensselaer's actions reflect the involvement of an entire family circle, not simply an individual, in creating overseas empire. From his acquisition of investment capital, to his management of the company, to his desire to establish a patrimonial estate, his extensive kinship ties formed the basis for empire.[3]

Yet actions by and on behalf of kin by people far below the social, economic, and political level of the elite also proved essential to the construction of empire. Those who worked the ships, supplied and prepared sailors' trunks, and looked after family inheritances across the ocean created thousands of overlapping transatlantic links. People like Marritgen and Hendrick did the work and endured the separations that made possible the seaborne expeditions that enriched men like Van Rensselaer. Each traveler, couple, or family taking part in these Atlantic voyages did so in dialogue with economic forces that manifested themselves in the personal, familial, and local

2. Janny Venema, "Searching for True Love: Letters from Kiliaen van Rensselaer," in Martha Dickinson Shattuck, ed., *Explorers, Fortunes, and Love Letters: A Window on New Netherland* (Albany, N.Y., 2009), 116–128 ("dearest cousin," 123–124, 126). Willem Frijhoff identifies Van Rensselaer's first wife as Van Bijler's daughter, not his neice, and his second wife as Jan van Wely's daughter; see Frijhoff, *Wegen van Evert Willemsz: Een Hollands weeskind op zoek naar zichzelf, 1607–1647* (The Hague, 1995), 614.

3. Ibid.; Donna Merwick, "A Genre of Their Own: Kiliaen van Rensselaer as Guide to the Reading and Writing Practices of Early Modern Businessmen," *WMQ*, 3d Ser., LXV (2008), 669–712; A. J. F. van Laer, trans. and ed., *Van Rensselaer Bowier Manuscripts: Being the Letters of Kiliaen van Rensselaer, 1630–1643, and Other Documents Relating to the Colony of Rensselaerswyck* (Albany, N.Y, 1908). Janny Venema proves that "even though" Van Rensselaer "worked as an individual, [he] did so as a member of a family and a business network"; see Janny Venema, *Kiliaen van Rensselaer (1586–1643): Designing a New World* (Hilversum, Netherlands, 2010), 13.

realities of their own experience. These families all had economic lives, in other words, that together formed the economy of the early modern Dutch Atlantic empire.

The Atlantic economy as families lived it offered both perils and opportunities. In their quest to survive, and perhaps profit from, transatlantic travel, Marritgen Wouters, Hendrick Christiaensz, and others depended on one another. Interpersonal bonds, based on face-to-face relationships, became key tools people used when they went abroad or when they had to endure in the absence of relatives and friends. Since immediate interactions, bonds of kinship, and connections within the local community joined men and women together, the ties people turned to in order to navigate the Atlantic economy depended on the work of women and men alike. Many of them never left Amsterdam, and most of them came from humbler backgrounds than Van Rensselaer, yet, together, all these people helped build the empire by enabling personal and familial economies to reach out across the ocean.[4]

Uncovering the work done by women and men tied by blood and marriage to those who sailed to Holland's North American colony reveals that the formal, large-scale economy of the WIC depended on a diffuse, small-scale system created and inhabited by individual actors in Amsterdam and abroad. By looking after the interests of their own families, people in Amsterdam and beyond crafted webs of economic affiliations. These webs not only helped families survive the Atlantic economy, they enabled and supported that economy. By forming the bridge between the personal finances of the individual or household and emergent international commerce, interlocking social connections provided the material for empire.

Maritime Amsterdam and Economic Networks

Dutch overseas expansion and trade rested on the actions of men and women, rich and poor, seeking to follow their own interests and the interests of their families as best they could. Yet the work done by the VOC and WIC was striking, then and now, for its size and complexity. Their extensive operations depended on the movement of a staggering quantity of capital, goods, and people through Dutch port cities. By the mid-1630s, thousands of cargo ships delivered some seven hundred thousand tons of goods to Amsterdam a year,

4. For the development of "trust networks" in support of English transatlantic trade that were "structured by family, place of origin, occupation, religion, or political convictions," see Nuala Zahedieh, *The Capital and the Colonies: London and the Atlantic Economy, 1660–1700* (Cambridge, 2010), 106.

and tens of thousands of maritime workers shipped out in the service of the major companies annually. Influential investors and company directors like Van Rensselaer were not the only ones to draw on and represent the interests of broader social networks. Women and men far down the social ladder also relied on and constructed such networks as they undertook the business of peopling company ships and caring for the imperial workforce passing through Amsterdam. Through lodging, innkeeping, and sexual services, they created debt systems that enabled them to keep company ships moving. Intimate ties and international finance comingled in the homes of Holland's harbor districts, as sailors' kin and maritime innkeepers kept men and money flowing across the Atlantic.[5]

Maritime Amsterdammers—those with intimate and family ties to people who worked the seas—took part in the overlapping businesses of moneylending, lodging, and procuring maritime laborers. Sailors worked hard when at sea, but they also had periods in port with little to do. Men putting in and those looking for work often arrived in Amsterdam broke, waiting to be paid or waiting to ship out, just at the moment when they most longed for some coins in their hands. Amsterdam women and men sought to make a profit by meeting the financial—and also the personal—needs of these waiting men. By using personal bonds to fulfill individual economic needs, Amsterdammers helped maintain the transatlantic system.

Sailors and soldiers needed to ready themselves for their voyages, but they had little cash to buy necessities. Things as simple as purchasing clothes would have to come from loans, backed by the only collateral many sailors had: their future wages, once they were sure of a ship, that is. Notary records abound with notes on their WIC pay. Gunner's mate Herbert van Didderen, for instance, promised to pay Willem Pietersz, a "clothes seller," forty-six guilders from his first wages, from "whatever place, be it on water or on land," he should happen to be. Although he had to leave the name of the ship blank, Willem Jansz van Borculo also banked on his future earnings as a midshipman sailing to New Netherland when he agreed to pay a woman named Annetgen Jans seventy guilders for expenses and loans "both for outfitting for the journey and other." The debt document functioned as a kind of speculative currency that the lender could then sell at a discounted rate to others. After all, should Willem Jansz die before he earned the seventy guilders he promised, Annetgen Jans would be out of luck, so she might well be willing to sell the debt for less cash immediately to someone willing to take

5. Merwick, "A Genre of Their Own," *WMQ*, 3d Ser., LXV (2008), 674.

a gamble on the sailor's survival. Although lending to sailors and soldiers was a complicated and risky financial venture, women and men alike in the oceangoing quarter of Amsterdam made a business of extending this kind of microcredit to departing sailors and soldiers.[6]

Lenders could take some steps to lessen their risks. In August 1663, Annetie Jans loaned twenty-four guilders to a New Netherland soldier. In this case, the man not only promised to pay out of his wages, he transferred to her the right to collect the first twenty-four guilders he earned directly from the WIC. In other words, the small portion of the soldier's wages advanced before he left Holland or available to relatives during his absence would be hers. Although departing sailors and soldiers desperate for supplies and short on cash doubtless suffered under the high rates and interest they paid for their "outfitting and other," lenders in the maritime community did make it possible for them to survive their episodes of penury in Amsterdam.[7]

Given that many of these soldiers and sailors lived in poverty and stood a chance of dying before they earned sufficient wages to pay the balance of their loans, such credit might well be seen as a sort of aid to those in need. The impoverished in Zwolle, for example, depended on borrowing, pawning, and buying with delayed payments to make ends meet. The needy looked to neighbors and others with whom they had close social connections for this kind of aid, and lenders likely provided it out of a sense of obligation to "their" poor. Perhaps women like Annetgen Jans, who loaned money to the down and out of Amsterdam's maritime community, felt a similar sense of obligation to the workers they helped clothe and supply. Yet the amounts sailors and soldiers owed often far exceeded their likely earnings, leaving them trapped in eternal debt and beholden to their bondholders.[8]

6. Debt acknowledgement, Dec. 6, 1631, Not. Arch. 945, 73v, Not. G. Selden, SA ("clothes seller"); Debt acknowledgement, May 12, 1654, Not. Arch. 1329, 31v, Not. H. Schaef, SA ("both for outfitting").

7. Debt acknowledgement, Aug. 27, 1663, Not. Arch. 2866, 44v–45, Not. B. Coornhart, SA. The Annetie Jans mentioned here is very likely the same Annetgen Jans who loaned money to Willem Jansz van Borculo nine years before, but the combination of this first name and patronymic is so common that it is difficult to be certain.

8. Ibid. For an analysis of the means by which VOC sailors' wages were made available to family and creditors, see Danielle van den Heuvel, "*Bij uijtlandigheijt van haar man": Echtgenotes van VOC-zeelieden, aangemonsterd voor de kamer Enkhuizen (1700–1750)* (Amsterdam, 2005). On aid and loans to the poor, see Hilde van Wijngaarden, *Zorg voor de kost: Armenzorg, arbeid, en onderlinge hulp in Zwolle, 1650–1700* (Amsterdam, 2000), 242–244. Ingrid van der Vlis has noted that "the poor had to be well-known in the neighborhood and to have a good name" to get credit. The maritime community might have functioned similarly, perhaps as another kind of neighborhood, where lenders felt they knew and wanted to aid their debtors; see Van der

Men waiting for wages or assignments needed to eat and sleep somewhere, in addition to finding cash for their outfitting. Again, many denizens of maritime Amsterdam, both male and female, eagerly helped themselves while helping this mobile workforce. Debts for living expenses tied up men's wages long before they ever earned them. Some sailors and soldiers stayed on in the houses of married sailors, paying for their costs on credit and often adding loans for outfitting on top. In January 1664, some six WIC soldiers bound for New Netherland appeared within two days of one another before the same notary to transfer part of their wages to "Pieter Hansz sailor" for "lodging, housing, food and drink, and money provided for outfitting." No woman's name appears in these particular debt documents, but it seems unlikely that a sailor alone did all that cooking for a group of hungry soldiers. Because official records often hide the joint work of a married couple under the husband's name, women's work went unmentioned but remains obvious nonetheless. In seventeenth-century Holland, sailors' wives who lived near the harbors could add to their income by providing lodging for men come to look for work at sea. Even though such family work is too easily overlooked, it had a crucial role in maintaining Amsterdam's sailing economy.[9]

Those who provided loans and housing formed bonds that served an important function in this mobile economy. In 1643, Warnar Francken van Woerden, who was both "just come home" from the sea and about to travel again to New Netherland aboard the *Swarte Raven* as supercargo, owed "Lyntien Bastiaens, wife of Jan [Jorichsz] Heen, living in the Bird of Paradise near the Exchange," a significant sum of 350 guilders for expenses "at her house and [for] money provided for his outfitting." He promised to pay

Vlis, *Leven in armoede: Delftse bedeelden in de zeventiende eeuw* (*A life in poverty: Living off charity in seventeenth-century Delft*) (Amsterdam, 2001), 243–244 (quotation, 243).

9. Debt acknowledgements, Jan. 11–12, 1664, Not. Arch. 1330, unpaginated, Not. H. Schaef (quotations); Manon van der Heijden and Daniëlle van den Heuvel, "Surviving Strategies of Dutch Seamen's Wives, 17th–18th Centuries," in Simonetta Cavaciocchi, ed., *Ricchezza del mare ricchezza dal mare: Secc. XIII–XVIII: Atti della "Trentasettesima Settimana di Studi," 11–15 aprile 2005,* Istituto internazionale di storia economica "F. Datini," Prato, Serie II, Atti delle "Settimane di Studi" e altri Convegni, XXXVII (Florence, 2006), 1113; De Wit, "Zeemansvrouwen," *Tijdschrift voor sociale en economische geschiedenis,* II, no. 3 (2005), 77. Taverns run by maritime families also served the sailors of eighteenth-century England; see David Cordingly, *Seafaring Women: Adventures of Pirate Queens, Female Stowaways, and Sailors' Wives* (New York, 2007), 6–7. On the tendency throughout early modern Europe for economic activity undertaken jointly by husbands and wives to appear under men's names only, see Darlene Abreu-Ferreira, "Work and Identity in Early Modern Portugal: What Did Gender Have to Do with It?" *Journal of Social History,* XXXV (2002), 859–887.

her out of his first wages, but, recognizing that IOUs like his often traded hands, he also mentioned that he would pay either her or whoever presented the document to him. A few days later, Warnar Francken came back before the notary again, this time to entrust Lyntien Bastiaens with the oversight of his own financial claims. He empowered her to collect 20 guilders of his past wages from his work aboard the *Salamander,* which had been arrested by a claimant. In addition, he authorized her to collect 13 guilders and 4 stivers' worth of credits in his account book owed him by three men, including at least one sailor.[10]

Since his account book, the proof of the debts owed him, still remained in possession of the WIC, Francken could not collect the money himself. The complicated nature of finances for sailors who were embedded in the debt-credit cycle, dependent on the sometimes slow WIC, and continually on the move led them to set up financial relationships with the women who remained behind in Amsterdam and cared for them when they were ashore. Lyntien Bastiaens, in this case, understood all about the complications of transatlantic finance; in addition to lodging and lending, she was also a skipper's wife. Warnar Francken's mobility meant that he would not be present in Amsterdam long enough to collect the debts that were endemic to the early modern European economy. Yet he needed money before setting sail again. Lyntien helped him square the circle, while also doubtless making a profit herself. Women like her helped keep the Atlantic economy moving at its most basic level by allowing skilled seamen like Warnar Francken to keep working in spite of the gaps and inefficiencies inherent in the early modern debt-credit economy.[11]

The financial importance of landladies and innkeepers gives a new twist to the significance of the household economy. Because men ashore in Amsterdam could be cut off from their own family networks, they created new ones centered around very different kinds of homes. As a result, the intimate ties of the household became intertwined with the international economy. With thousands of men setting sail each year aboard Dutch ships in the seventeenth and eighteenth centuries, many men needed lodging. Inns played a critical part in keeping this mobile population available and fit for work.

10. Debt acknowledgement, Mar. 21, 1643, Not. Arch. 1792, 230–231, Not. C. Vliet, SA (quotations); Empowerment, Mar. 24, 1643, Not. Arch. 1792, 256, Not. C. Vliet, SA; Civil marriage record, Aug. 13, 1633, DTB 441, 166, SA. Lyntien Bastiaens's husband's surname was given in the marriage record as Hoen.

11. Civil marriage record, Aug. 13, 1633, DTB 441, 166, SA.

Innkeepers combined the practices of lodging and loaning, thus establishing lasting financial ties and obligations with the seamen they housed. In March 1641, Willem Hots, an Amsterdam innkeeper, had debts recorded in both Dutch and French. As the foreign language documents attest, immigrants from other parts of Europe looking for work also needed a place to stay before they shipped out. Female innkeeper Catalin d'Acker made loans to seven WIC soldiers in March 1641, including loans to "Jan Linsi from Denen in Schottland, Willem (^Mowat or) Mood from Edenburg, and Jan Cambel from Sterlin, both also in Schotland" for forty-eight guilders each for expenses, cash advances, and "other." Although the notary had some trouble with the Scottish names and places, the document illustrates the multiethnic nature of the maritime world in Amsterdam. The companies' insatiable demand for labor made such foreign employees essential; tying both immigrant and local workers to Dutch ports was crucial to keeping Dutch ships staffed. Innkeepers did exactly that by binding sailors and soldiers to maritime Amsterdam through debt.[12]

To create that debt, some innkeepers and moneylenders also provided this motley crew of men ashore with the social and sexual activities sailors and soldiers infamously sought while on leave. When men acknowledged debts for both their "outfitting . . . and other," as midshipman Christiaen Marckwart did to the widow Lysbeth Joris, what exactly was the "other"?

12. Debt acknowledgement, Mar. 5, 1641, Not. Arch. 1335, 16v, Not. H. Schaef, SA (quotations). For an eighteenth-century Amsterdam female innkeeper who loaned money, see Anne E. C. McCants, "Petty Debts and Family Networks: The Credit Market of Widows and Wives in Eighteenth-Century Amsterdam," in Beverly Lemire, Ruth Pearson, and Gail Campbell, eds., *Women and Credit: Researching the Past, Refiguring the Future* (Oxford, 2001), 33–49. For more loans to foreign WIC workers, see Debt acknowledgements, March 1641, Not. Arch. 1335, 16–25v, Not. H. Schaef, SA. For a debt contract to D'Acker in French, see Debt acknowledgement, Jan. 29, 1641, Not. Arch. 1335, 6v, Not. H. Schaef, SA. D'Acker's name also appears spelled as Cathalina Dacree. French IOUs from soldiers in the same period were also made out in favor of innkeepers Philips de Potre and Charles Carré. On migration to maritime Amsterdam, see Sölvi Sogner, "Young in Europe around 1700: Norwegian Sailors and Servant-Girls Seeking Employment in Amsterdam," in Jean-Pierre Bardet, François Lebrun, and René Le Mée, eds., *Mesurer et comprendre: Mélanges offerts a Jacques Dupaquier* (Paris, 1993), 515–532; Lotte C. van de Pol, "The Lure of the Big City: Female Migration to Amsterdam," in Els Kloek, Nicole Teeuwen, and Marijke Huisman, eds., *Women of the Golden Age: An International Debate on Women in Seventeenth-Century Holland, England, and Italy* (Hilversum, Netherlands, 1994), 73–81. On the multiethnic background of long-distance sailors, see Jan Lucassen, "A Multinational and Its Labor Force: The Dutch East India Company, 1595–1795," *International Labor and Working-Class History*, no. 66 (Fall 2004), 12–39.

After all, the inns in Amsterdam had about as good a reputation as the men on leave themselves.[13]

The background to an incident that occurred in New Amsterdam all too plainly elucidates the sort of reputation enjoyed by the inns of Amsterdam. After relocating to the colony, Grietje Reyniers made herself infamous when she pulled up her skirts and invited the soldiers who were scolding her as a whore to kiss her backside. The sailors, however, doubtless thought they had good cause to taunt her as a whore. At least two New Netherlanders remembered an earlier trip to Amsterdam when they lodged "in the house of Pieter de Winter, tavernkeeper there, at whose house Griet Reyniers was a servant, who served . . . liquor." When Grietje reportedly dawdled in another room with some German soldiers, "her mistress went away and saw through a hole in the door that Grietje . . . had her petticoat upon her knees." Having been a waitress in an Amsterdam inn did Grietje no good in New Amsterdam.[14]

If inns had seedy reputations, a bit of wild behavior by sailors and soldiers ashore might not have seemed beyond the pale to seventeenth-century Dutch observers; however, if seamen were not careful, their personal conduct could have serious consequences. Although sailors ashore were known to live a bit large, Skipper Willem Cornelisz Oudemarkt found himself in trouble when some of his own men accused him of being so drunk he had to be helped back on board ship and of behaving in an unseemly manner with women in the taverns of New Netherland. Yet, at least one of his sailors denied the severity of these reports and defended his captain on the grounds that sailors considered such behavior normal and expected. "Although he on occasion also made merry like and with others," he explained, such "often happens with people who come ashore." Prostitution was seemingly an accepted facet of life in maritime quarters.[15]

At times, wives of the poorest sailors had no choice but to move into inns, bordellos, or common dwellings of shady reputations when their husbands

<hr/>

13. Debt acknowledgement, June 8, 1654, Not. Arch. 1329, 37v, Not. H. Schaef, SA (quotation). On depictions of soldiers and prostitution in Golden Age art and the argument that they were shown as intruders into the intimate space of the home, see Richard Helgerson, "Soldiers and Enigmatic Girls: The Politics of Dutch Domestic Realism, 1650–1672," *Representations,* LVIII (Spring 1997), 49–87.

14. Testimony, Mar. 21, 1639, in *Provincial Secretary,* I, 107 (quotations), Declaration, Oct. 13, 1638, 69. Variants of her name include Griet Reniers.

15. Testimony, Mar. 28, 1646, Not. Arch. 1293, 37v, Not. H. Schaef, SA (quotations). For differing interpretations of the captain's behavior, see Testimony, Oct. 11, 1644, Not. Arch. 1861, 436, Not. J. Steur, SA; Testimony, Oct. 14, 1644, Not. Arch. 1290, 1–3, Not. H. Schaef, SA.

went abroad, since their portion of their husbands' wages was too small to provide them with a decent roof over their heads, and even that had often already been pledged away to creditors. Some maritime wives lodged in the same dwelling in rented rooms where male travelers and colonists frequented one or more of the residents, perhaps as lodgers, perhaps as paying visitors. In 1645, Neeltgen Henricxdochter, wife of a boatman, and Ryckegen Douwes, wife of a sailor away in Greenland, both lived in rooms in a house on Brouwersstraat in Amsterdam. One day, Neeltgen was busy hanging up laundry in the loft when she heard New Netherland schoolmaster Adam Roelants berate Ryckegen as "a whore and pig." Adam Roelants was present on the stairs that day, Neeltgen explained, because he "hangs around and traffics by day and night with certain female persons [seeckere vrouspersoone], who also live in a Room above her." Something in those close quarters, though, caused tensions to explode, and he began to beat and defame Ryckegen, claiming to have lain with her three times in a shed. Neeltgen and another neighbor rushed to Ryckegen's aid. But, even days later, outside the courthouse, the schoolmaster continued his nasty screed, asserting in front of multiple witnesses that "when I (repeated here reverently) screwed her, I thought that I had a Young maid, but when I looked up, I realized that it was an ugly old whore." Adam Roelants's vicious physical and verbal attack constituted a violation of norms so severe that two of her neighbors came forward to defend her, in both body and reputation.[16]

The resulting deposition provides a window into the close living spaces of maritime women, where women with husbands aboard ship crowded in rented rooms and struggled to pay their way. Adam Roelants's outrageous insults do not prove that Ryckegen traded sex for money, but her housemates brought men into the house "day and night," showing that this sailor's

16. Testimony, July 25, 1645, Not. Arch. 1291, 112, Not. H. Schaef, SA (quotations). On seamen's wives and bordellos, see De Wit, "Zeemansvrouwen," *Tijdschrift voor sociale en economische geschiedenis,* II, no. 3 (2005), 76; see also Lotte C. van de Pol, "Prostitutie en de Amsterdamse burgerij: Eerbegrippen in een vroegmoderne stedelijke samenleving," in Peter te Boekhorst, Peter Burke, and Willem Frijhoff, eds., *Cultuur en maatschappij in Nederland, 1500–1850: Een historisch-antropologisch perspectief* (Heerlen, Netherlands, 1992), 179–218; Van der Heijden and Van den Heuvel, "Surviving Strategies," in Cavaciocchi, ed., *Ricchezza del mare ricchezza dal mare,* 1113. Danielle van den Heuvel quite rightly points out that, even though some seamen's wives certainly did move into brothels and work as prostitutes in their husbands' absence, they as a group do not seem to have been regarded as necessarily dishonorable at the time; therefore, seamen's wives should not be assumed to have been prostitutes; see Van den Heuvel, "*Bij uijtlandigheijt,*" 68, 93. For an example of a woman who signs away her share of her Brazil-bound husband's WIC wages to an innkeeper, see Debt acknowledgement, Sept. 28, 1641, Not. Arch. 1335, 91, Not. H. Schaef, SA.

wife, at the very least, lived close to the edge of prostitution. The boarding houses and inns that New Netherland travelers sought out when ashore in Holland were not sources of housing alone. They were places where maritime women themselves found lodging, and they might have needed occasional money from visitors to make ends meet. Travelers remained part of the maritime world when they climbed the stairways of such houses, relying on women to meet both their residential and sexual needs.[17]

For their part, male and female innkeepers did not always deny the reputations of their inns. Amsterdam tavern keeper Swaentgen Jans even testified on behalf of an aggrieved wife that her husband had lodged with her for six weeks with another woman, thus admitting that her establishment had been used for an adulterous affair. Some landladies and landlords undoubtedly saw sexual exchanges as a chance to extract yet more WIC wages from their customers. In fact, keeping an inn for sailors and acting as a madam were not that far apart in seventeenth-century Amsterdam.[18]

If sailors were not careful, they woke up from their hangovers owing more money than they had to hosts who had plied them with drink and women. Such indebtedness led to the occupation known as the *zielverkoper,* or soul seller, in which the holder of a sailor's debt "sold" him to a particular captain. As Lotte Constance van de Pol explained it in her study of prostitution in Amsterdam, the WIC and VOC both needed a constant stream of men so poor they had little choice but to risk their lives at sea, and prostitution was an important way of reducing young men to poverty. Foreigners or country

17. Testimony, July 25, 1645, Not. Arch. 1291, 112, Not. H. Schaef, SA. On public insults and the need for women to defend themselves against them, see Lotte van de Pol, *The Burgher and the Whore: Prostitution in Early Modern Amsterdam,* trans. Liz Waters (Oxford, 2011), 51–54.

18. Testimony, Nov. 12, 1631, Not. Arch. 945, 62v, Not. G. Selden, SA. For a discussion of the role of whorehouses in lodging sailors during the seventeenth century, see Lotte Constance van de Pol, *Het Amsterdams hoerdom: Prostitutie in de zeventiende en achttiende eeuw (Prostitution in Amsterdam in the seventeenth and eighteenth centuries)* (Amsterdam, 1996), 148–150. For female innkeepers, see A. C. M. Kappelhof, "Vrouwen buitenshuis in Breda en omgeving (1550–1650)," *Jaarboek van het Centraal Bureau voor Genealogie,* LVIII (2004), 61–62. On connections between accusations of public whoredom and wives of VOC sailors, see Manon van der Heijden, *Huwelijk in Holland: Stedelijke rechtspraak en kerkelijke tucht, 1550–1700* (Amsterdam, 1998), 259–264. On the complicated associations of madams with motherhood for their role in housing and caring for sailors, in addition to providing sexual services, in the later English-speaking world, see Paul A. Gilje, *Liberty on the Waterfront: American Maritime Culture in the Age of Revolution* (Philadelphia, 2004), 50. For the varied economic activities of seamen's wives, including lodging, in New England, see Daniel Vickers and Vince Walsh, "Young Men and the Sea: The Sociology of Seafaring in Eighteenth-Century Salem, Massachusetts," *Social History,* XXIV (1999), 17–38; Elaine Forman Crane, *Ebb Tide in New England: Women, Seaports, and Social Change, 1630–1800* (Boston, 1998), 103–105.

boys coming to Amsterdam for the first time lacked social connections with captains and had to rely on soul sellers for placement and, consequently, for the promise of wages that made it possible to borrow while ashore. For the VOC in the seventeenth and eighteenth centuries, "the majority of the soul-sellers were women," often the wives of seaman, often working officially under a husband's name. Soul selling, frequently based on debts for drink and prostitution in the inns, "was a family business, with the woman of the house usually in charge." The patterns of indebtedness seen among seventeenth-century New Netherland–bound sailors and soldiers endured, and seamen's wives continued to act as soul sellers in the Maas district into the eighteenth century. Although some men clearly came to trust and rely on honest landladies, others found themselves sold onto unpleasant or dangerous voyages. The amounts some sailors were obliged to pay vastly exceeded their monthly wages, meaning they would receive little or nothing for their years of work.[19]

Seedy and exploitative as they were, the innkeepers and soul sellers of Amsterdam had an essential function in the maritime economy. When sailors and soldiers came ashore, landladies and landlords supplied them with cash and met their immediate needs. As young, immigrant men arrived in Amsterdam looking for work aboard ship, they often had no money and no social contacts. Soul sellers provided them with a place to live, food, drink, companionship, and supplies, enabling them to prepare for their journeys before placing them on VOC and WIC ships. At the same time soul sellers exploited sailors' weaknesses, they helped staff the ships nobody wanted to

19. Marc A. van Alphen, "The Female Side of Dutch Shipping: Financial Bonds of Seamen Ashore in the 17th and 18th Century," in J. R. Bruijn and W. F. J. Mörzer Bruyns, eds., *Anglo-Dutch Mercantile Marine Relations, 1700–1850: Ten Papers* (Amsterdam, 1991), 125–132 (quotations, 128); Van de Pol, *Het Amsterdams hoerdom*, 139, 342. On the reliance of the companies on soul sellers and other intermediaries and creditors for labor recruitment, see J. Lucassen, "Zeevarenden," in L. M. Akveld, S. Hart, and W. J. van Hoboken, eds., *Maritieme geschiedenis der Nederlanden*, II, *Zeventiende eeuw, van 1585 tot ca 1680* (Bussum, Netherlands, 1977), 133–136. On women's role in soul selling, see De Wit, "Zeemansvrouwen," *Tijdschrift voor sociale en economische geschiedenis*, II, no. 3 (2005), 76–77; Van der Heijden and Van den Heuvel, "Surviving Strategies," in Cavaciocchi, ed., *Ricchezza del mare ricchezza dal mare*, 1113–1114; Van den Heuvel, "*Bij uijtlandigheijt*," 68–69. On soul selling and WIC employees headed for New Netherland, see Jaap Jacobs, *New Netherland: A Dutch Colony in Seventeenth-Century America* (Leiden, 2005), 51–54. For the suggestion that eighteenth-century English sailors were recruited for work on slave ships in similar ways, see Stephanie E. Smallwood, "African Guardians, European Slave Ships, and the Changing Dynamics of Power in the Early Modern Atlantic," *WMQ*, 3d Ser., LXIV (2007), 709. For the work of later, evidently mostly male, sailor-brokers or "crimps" in the English-speaking Atlantic, see Judith Fingard, *Jack in Port: Sailortowns of Eastern Canada* (Toronto, 1982).

sail on. Others acted as small-scale bankers and financial overseers for travelers. Thus, even though these peripatetic and seemingly rootless men might have had few social or financial resources in Amsterdam, the women they lodged with gave them essential financial ties, even as they exploited those connections for their own ends.[20]

Sailors' and skippers' wives helped keep overseas finances running and sometimes expanded on their duties to become financial operators in their own right. As they used their intimate ties to the sailing population for their own best interests, their financial activities in turn strengthened the ties binding the maritime world together, helping to fashion a community, albeit an odd, exploitative community, that reached out across the ocean. Maritime women and men relied on their personal and financial ties to one another to establish an economic network that allowed them to serve as a liaison between the personal economy of individual maritime workers and the large-scale economy of the WIC. Domestic and sexual services created debts that entangled sailors and soldiers with maritime women and men and helped the WIC staff its ships. Out of the face-to-face relationships formed in the dwellings and neighborhoods of Amsterdam's harbor quarter came an empire.[21]

20. Studies have identified a division in the maritime labor system of the Netherlands. Regional trading voyages and fishing ships were staffed locally, through social connections, whereas long-distance company ships (or "the external segment") relied on soul sellers and innkeepers to recruit casuals and strangers; see Karel Davids, "Maritime Labour in the Netherlands, 1570–1870," *Research in Maritime History*, XIII (1997), 41–71 (quotation, 62); Paul C. van Royen, "Mariners and Markets in the Age of Sail: The Case of the Netherlands," *Research in Maritime History*, VII (1994), 51. The division in recruitment strategies is clear; however, it would be a mistake to see the soul sellers and innkeepers as divorced from social networks. On the contrary, the recruiters were the means by which strangers and peripatetics were woven into maritime social and economic networks. Since these women were joined to the maritime world through their family and marital relationships, the companies need to be understood as relying on intimate and social networks to staff their ships, just as the fishing and regional vessels did. Yet, the way in which these men became part of maritime networks should not be romanticized. They earned less, worked longer voyages, and faced greater danger than regional sailors and fishermen, and the debt burden they accrued as a result of lodging and recruitment could be crushing. Nonetheless, neither should scholars ignore the way that landladies lent money for goods and managed finances for departing sailors. In addition to exploiting many workers, some innkeepers and recruiters might have also proved themselves a crucial resource for other sailors and soldiers.

21. For a call for maritime historians to pay more attention to gender and the relationship between mariners and port communities, see Daniel Vickers, "Beyond Jack Tar," *WMQ*, 3d Ser., L (1993), 418–424. As Vickers points out, understanding the relationship between sailors and their home communities promises to "deepen our understanding of the seafaring activities that built and maintained empires overseas" (423). For example, the fact that re-

Financial Agents and Personal Ties

Eventually, soldiers, sailors, and travelers left the houses and inns of maritime Amsterdam behind and took their place on board ships headed to New Netherland and elsewhere. With the chartering of the WIC in 1621, the number of Atlantic-bound ships rose, and increasing numbers of Amsterdammers followed in Marritgen Wouters's footsteps, waving goodbye to family, spouses, and friends sailing out across the Zuider Zee. As those ships began taking settlers to North America in 1623, more and more travelers needed someone to help them manage their newly transatlantic finances. They turned to their kin, immediate connections, and family. Ties within and between maritime families enabled people to negotiate the small-scale, informal, and grey economies that flourished in these years. Once the WIC changed its regulations to allow wider access to the beaver-skin trade in 1638, travelers used these same intimate networks to enter the transatlantic fur trade. Growing migration by middling families and the creation of a burgher population in New Netherland in the 1640s and 1650s caused an even wider range of travelers and Amsterdammers to become caught up in trading networks involving an ever greater variety of goods. Complex webs and financial instruments show that these networks developed into a functional Atlantic economy that ran in tandem with the economy of formal companies and larger interests. The structure of this new Atlantic economy paralleled that of the local early modern economy, from the participation of women to the reliance on face-to-face, personal systems of credit and trust. Thus, the intimate networks of travelers and Amsterdammers allowed for the development of a diffuse, participatory commercial economy that diversified the trade system beyond the large-scale merchant houses and equally helped establish the Dutch Atlantic empire.

When Amsterdammers and travelers waved goodbye to one another, the financial ties between them did not suddenly end; people continued to man-

---

cruitment and lending lay in the hands of women and men from the same neighborhoods and backgrounds as the maritime workers themselves likely militated against strong class identity among Dutch Atlantic sailors in the seventeenth century. The patterns of class-based antagonism between maritime workers and maritime capital that Marcus Rediker has identified on eighteenth-century English-speaking ships seems unlikely in an environment where household, neighborhood, and gender continued to mediate workers' relationships with their labor. See Peter Linebaugh and Rediker, *The Many-Headed Hydra: Sailors, Slaves, Commoners, and the Hidden History of the Revolutionary Atlantic* (Boston, 2000). Networks of relationships among people from the maritime quarter organized, mobilized, and prepared this workforce and were thus an essential element in building the Dutch early modern empire.

age their personal and financial lives together. The wealthiest travelers left behind families and kin, houses and partnerships, accounts and credits due. The poorest left crushing debts and needy family members. People had to find someone they could trust to represent them honestly and further family interests in their absence. Travelers most often turned to the very family members, kin, and intimate connections who waved goodbye from shore. Relatives and in-laws, parents and spouses, friends and neighbors were among those whom travelers counted on most. For instance, Wouter Jansz, a sailor going to "the Virginias" in the service of the WIC in 1627, asked his two uncles to oversee the inheritance due him from the estate of his wife's late grandmother. Both his financial capital and his financial representatives were drawn from among his close relatives.[22]

To enable their family, kin, and friends to act for them, sailors, soldiers, and settlers relied on legal empowerments to transform their personal bonds into powerful legal and economic assets. When Claes Jansz was about to embark for New Netherland in March 1648, he empowered Anna Jansz, his sister, to look after his affairs during his absence. He needed to choose someone he trusted well to have "oversight, authority, and administration" over the two houses he owned and rented out in Amsterdam. He authorized her to "make new leases with the present occupants or to rent the same to others, all as she shall find good and advisable." He also asked her to collect from anyone else who owed him money for any reason, "promising to hold good and valid all that by his . . . sister shall be done or transacted regarding this." Through the legal instrument of the empowerment, Anna Jansz became an important financial agent for her brother.[23]

Men sailing out from Amsterdam often trusted and relied on their wives above all others. Like all Dutch *huysvrouwen,* or housewives, maritime women formed essential partnerships with their husbands, and they had detailed knowledge of their seafaring spouses' interests and personal property. Marritgen Wouters, whose late husband had sailed as the *Swarte Beer's* skipper in 1619, could enumerate years later in precise terms every item she had packed for "her deceased husband, which he had taken with him in his Eastern chest on his journey to the Virginias." She recounted everything from his nine shirts, five of which were new, to his two "ear pillows," to over twenty-seven guilders in reals of eight. She demanded restitution for all of these items, and many more, from Skipper Adriaen Jorisz, who helped bring

22. Empowerment, May 7, 1627, Not. Arch. 721, 158, Not. P. Carelsz, SA.
23. Empowerment, Mar. 25, 1648, Not. Arch. 1690, unpaginated, Not. P. de Bary, SA.

her late husband's ship home from Zeeland. She was angry at having only received a few of her husband's possessions and but "eight english five-stiver coins." Her exact list shows that her husband's sea chest was very much an extension of the intimate space of the home, and she knew its insides as well as those of her own cupboards. Her husband's chest had great importance to her as the last remnant of their financial partnership. She expected that everything, every penny, would return, even if her husband did not. This kind of personal interest and intimate knowledge made wives ideal legal representatives.[24]

Strengthening the marital tie with an empowerment allowed families to circumvent legal restrictions on women and wives and enabled them, instead, to become powerful economic actors while their husbands were away. Before his departure to New Netherland in 1647, Jacob Claesz Berckman van Amsterdam followed a typical, broad formula when he authorized his wife, Aeltgien Dircxdochter, to oversee all his business and affairs with anyone, taking care to mention that she could "buy, sell, rent, and benefit fixed and real property." These kinds of documents changed a wife's position under the law. Like women in much of Western Europe, women in the early modern Netherlands lost their ability to act at law and make binding contracts when they married, at which point they came under the legal authority of their husbands. Through public proclamation, men could even prevent their wives from incurring debts for minor household affairs customarily permitted to all women. Empowerments, however, reversed the legal incapacities brought about by marriage, making it possible for women to appear in court, contract, and sue on behalf of husbands, brothers, and kin.[25]

24. Testimony/demand for payment, Oct. 24, 1622, Not. Arch. 691, 30v–31, Not. J. Warnaertsz, SA.

25. Empowerment, Apr. 19, 1647, Not. Arch. 1294, 48–48v, Not. H. Schaef, SA (quotations). See also, Empowerment, May 15, 1652, Not. Arch. 2279, V, 25, Not. J. de Winter, SA. On empowerments' centrality to seamen's wives' ability to act at law, see De Wit, "Zeemansvrouwen," *Tijdschrift voor sociale en economische geschiedenis*, II, no. 3 (2005), 71; Van den Heuvel, "*Bij uijtlandigheijt*," 72–76. On court petitions by VOC sailors' wives who lacked empowerments, see Van der Heijden and Van den Heuvel, "Surviving Strategies," in Cavaciocchi, ed., *Ricchezza del mare ricchezza dal mare*, 1103–1120. For commentary on the legal practices of the time, see Hugo Grotius, *The Jurisprudence of Holland*, trans. R. W. Lee, I (Oxford, 1926), 30–31. The use of empowerments to allow wives to act for absent husbands resembles the custom of female "deputy husbands" under English law in colonial America. People in Old and New Amsterdam seemingly likewise thought that "the wife could appropriately stand in" for an absent husband; see Laurel Thatcher Ulrich, *Good Wives: Image and Reality in the Lives of Women in Northern New England, 1650–1750* (New York, 1991), 33–50 ("deputy husbands," 35, "wife," 36). However, wives cannot be understood to have automatically stepped into that role. In

Given the centrality of debt and credit in the early modern European economy, empowered wives and relations played an essential part in sustaining Dutch economic life at home as more and more Amsterdammers undertook long distance travel. To serve the domestic and international economies, small businesses and artisanal shops had to continue operating even if the husband and proprietor went abroad. For example, bakers in port cities increasingly supplied not only local households but ships stocking up on stores before sailing to colonial ports. Thus, when Jan Tames, a baker on the High Street in Amsterdam, stood ready to travel overseas in 1638, he empowered his wife and a clerk to oversee not only his business affairs in general but "especially" to demand payment of fifty-five guilders for bread delivered to Skipper Willem Claesen, whose ship lay ready to sail "to the Virginias." Climbing on board every ship leaving Amsterdam for America were other men, like Jan Tames, who had establishments that needed to keep running without them or who similarly looked to expand their enterprises overseas.[26]

Women and men who stayed in Amsterdam and agreed to act as legal agents also provided the essential link between family and company. Sailors, soldiers, and company officials could usually only receive their WIC wages in Amsterdam itself, so travelers needed someone to collect their pay on their behalf if they or their families were going to be able to access that money before their next trip home. As Lubbert van Dincklagen prepared to sail to New Netherland on board the *Eendracht* in 1634 as New Netherland's *fiscaal*, or law enforcement officer, he chose to empower "Wÿngaertgen Aertsbrugh, wife of Jan Joosten, silversmith in Haerlem, his ... wife's niece" to collect his wages from the WIC. Surviving for years without access to their pay posed many obvious hardships for maritime workers as well as for their families

---

Dutch practice, wives needed empowerments to safely shed their legal incapacity. Departing men sometimes empowered other relatives instead, and men and courts sometimes refused to recognize wives as legal actors if they did not produce an empowerment. The best accounts suggest that this was also true in English colonial legal systems; see Terri L. Snyder, *Brabbling Women: Disorderly Speech and the Law in Early Virginia* (Ithaca, N.Y., 2003), 119–120. Snyder makes clear that a "deputy husband" was still a feme covert unless she received an empowerment. For growing hostility toward empowerments for seamen's wives in America at the turn of the nineteenth century, see Lisa Norling, "'How Frought with Sorrow and Heartpangs': Mariners' Wives and the Ideology of Domesticity in New England, 1790–1880," *New England Quarterly,* LXV (1992), 422–446.

26. Empowerment, Apr. 28, 1638, Not. Arch. 1022, 64, Not. S. van der Piet, SA. Although the empowerment mentioned Jan Tames's coming "voyage and absence," it did not state where he was headed.

at home. Aboard ship, men had access to the basic necessities of food and shelter, and they could seek day labor ashore or try to carry on some kind of petty trade as they traveled from port to port to meet their immediate needs. But empowering someone to collect their wages for them would let dependents, too, have access to the money or perhaps even the ability to send the money abroad. Thomis Jansz, a sailmaker destined for New Netherland in 1646, chose to tackle this problem by empowering his wife, Jannetgen Meelis, to collect nine hundred guilders plus interest he claimed from WIC administrators. In the absence of large institutions willing to serve customers of modest means, like the banks, postal services, insurance companies, and rail lines characteristic of much later colonial empires, these travelers relied primarily on those linked to them most closely by blood and marriage to enable them to survive both financially and personally.[27]

But collecting wages meant more than just linking family and company; at a broader level, such actions helped keep money flowing and the economy working within Amsterdam. Jacob Everts Sueijdhorst van Hamburg, for instance, empowered Bartel Goelits to collect his as-yet-unearned wages from the WIC for the journey he was planning to make "with God's help" to "New Netherland in the Virginias." In the wake of his wife's death, Jacob Everts clearly signed on for the voyage from a need to provide money for his child. The child was considered orphaned under Dutch law, and the city of Amsterdam had asserted oversight, demanding that the child's maternal inheritance of three hundred guilders be protected. Jacob Everts had to put that hefty sum on deposit. Without the cash in hand, he probably felt he had no choice but to leave his motherless child behind and earn wages by working for the WIC in its faraway colony. The departing widower charged Bartel Goelits with collecting every penny and depositing it with the local orphan chamber to satisfy the demand. Although this transaction might seem like a family problem, it had wider implications within the Dutch economy. Because of the requirement to protect children's debts by deposit, orphan chambers tended to be particularly solvent arms of city governments. The managers of the chambers used the cash that surviving parents deposited to make loans to individuals and, often, other branches of government, thereby earning interest for children while opening up family wealth to civic use.

27. Empowerment, Apr. 21, 1634, Not. Arch. 916, 118-118v, Not. B. Verbeeck, SA (quotation). Wÿngaertgen was listed as Lubbert van Dincklagen's "huysvrouws Nichte" and thus could have been either his wife's niece or her cousin. For Thomis Jansz, see Empowerment, Mar. 24, 1646, Not. Arch. 1646, unpaginated, Not. J. van der Hoeven, SA. See also Empowerment, Sept. 11, 1663, Not. Arch. 3186, 59, Not. H. Outgers, SA.

By enabling Bartel Goelits to collect his WIC wages as soon as possible and place them on deposit, Jacob Everts was also giving the city and burghers of Amsterdam immediate access to the money he was earning through his work in North America. In many small ways, empowerments permitted sailors' wages to circulate within the home economy during the years they were away.[28]

Travelers entrusted people beyond their immediate kin with the duty of maintaining their economic lives when they went abroad, drawing on a broad range of immediate personal ties. Maritime women made particularly helpful financial allies for travelers setting sail from Amsterdam. Though many migrants and sailors relied on their own kin in Amsterdam to act as their agents, not everyone had that option. Wives or mothers of other Amsterdam sailors stepped in to fill the breach. When Claes Claesen van Rotterdam, a sailor just returned from the East Indies, was about to leave again for New Netherland, he turned to the wife of his new captain, Anneke Jans van Amsterdam, to collect his VOC wages. Willem Gay, "born in Bristo in England and living in London," had served under at least three different Dutch captains by 1631. On the point of another departure that February, Gay still had wages due him, and he chose to empower "Lieutenant Gerrit Eycken or in his absence his wife Hilletge Wybrants" to collect his money for him and show him accounts "upon his return from wherever it shall have been." By acting as agents, maritime wives stood in the stead of missing or faraway kin.[29]

Often the ties between men and women in empowerments went unexplained. Mattijs Capito, the former supercargo of the WIC ship *Swol*, stayed in New Netherland after his service was up. He stood to receive more than 745 guilders in earnings, but he needed an agent in Amsterdam to collect it for him. He chose a woman he trusted, although she was apparently unrelated to him: "Sytje Harmans, residing at Amsterdam on the Nieuwesyts Achter Burghwal, next to the sign of 'The Gilt Pitcher.'" Capito did not say how he knew Harmans. Were they coreligionists, lovers, former neighbors, landlady and tenant, business partners, or perhaps just from the same hometown? Empowerments like these serve as a reminder of the subtlety of

28. Transport, June 14, 1632, Not. Arch. 788, 366, Not. J. Verhij, SA (quotations). On orphan chambers' finances, see B. S. Hempenius-van Dijk, *De weeskamer van de stad Groningen, 1613–1811* (Groningen, Netherlands, 1991), xv–xvi.

29. Empowerment, Feb. 25, 1631, Not. Arch. 945, 3v, Not. G. Selden, SA (quotations); Empowerment, Sept. 7, 1643, Not. Arch. 558a, 171, Not. J. Westfrisius, SA.

the social ties that bound Amsterdam society together. Although sometimes difficult to trace, social networks gave travelers access to a wide range of possible agents when they sought to manage their new transatlantic lives.[30]

The international social networks that people developed in the nascent Dutch empire helped Amsterdam women administer family property an ocean away, even among poor families whose holdings seem small enough to have fallen through the cracks. Annetgen Juriaensdochter, for instance, evidently worried about her sailor son away in the cold winters of New Netherland; perhaps they had lacked the money to outfit him fully before his departure. To send him a bundle of warm stockings, shoes, shirts, and cloth, she turned to someone she knew, Skipper Willem Reuwarts, sailing to New Netherland on the *Haring* in 1637. Yet, by the time the goods reached New Netherland, the skipper had died and her boy had already sailed away. Her property consequently fell into the hands of a stranger; the ship's steward took charge of the goods and sold them in New Netherland, saying he was doing so for the mother's profit. In 1640, however, several crewmates testified on the mother's behalf on their return to Amsterdam when they learned she had never received her money from the steward. Even with the death of the man she originally trusted, her goods were not without sympathetic oversight. A network of relationships among the maritime population kept watch over property as small as a bundle of socks.[31]

Maritime women similarly stood up for one another's families when they observed behavior that violated their own norms and expectations. When Anne Bouwessdochter, the "widow of the late Jan Jacobsz van Wieringen in his life skipper, sailing to the Virginias," sought testimony about her financial dealings with a hostile brother-in-law, she did not have to look far. Those able to give detailed accounts of her brother-in-law's various transactions with her and with themselves over the years included two other maritime women, "Annetgen Arents, wife of Willem Hontum, skipper, . . . and Dieuwertge Willemszdochter, wife of Claes Jansz, sailing as under-helmsman in east india." Annetgen Arents's testimony, in particular, reveals the family and community nature of fur trading in maritime Amsterdam. She remembered clearly counting out three hundred guilders to the brother-in-law in

30. Empowerment, Aug. 10, 1647, in *Provincial Secretary*, II, 470–471 (quotation, 471). For similar instances of men empowering women to whom their connection is unstated, see Empowerment, Sept. 8, 1648, in *Provincial Secretary*, III, 34–35, Empowerment, Sept. 9, 1648, 37–38, Empowerment, Aug. 14, 1649, 137–138.

31. Testimony, Mar. 27, 1640, Not. Arch. 1281, 33v, Not. H. Schaef, SA.

payment for "a certain quantity of otter pelts" he was selling on his brother's behalf and asking him, "What shall you do with this money (^will you send it to Jan Jacobsz . . . or put it at interest[?] Jan will be rich)." The brother-in-law did not elect either of her two good financial options, simply saying "Jan Jacobsz my brother has charged me that I shall keep it and give it back when he comes home."[32]

Yet he evidently did not give the money back to his brother like he said he would. Annetgen Arents recalled that Skipper Jan Jacobsz later said that his brother owed him "a remarkable sum of money for the sale of the otters," along with other money lent to him. Annetgen had reason to believe that the skipper spoke the truth when he complained about his brother. She explained that she knew of Skipper Jan Jacobsz's good character through the social ties among sea captains; she testified "that the aforementioned Jan Jacobsz has done well by her, the deponent's, husband." Her testimony provides a glimpse into the world of the women in oceangoing Amsterdam. Maritime women acted as full economic partners of their absent kin; they knew one another and one another's husbands personally; and they kept watch for violations of the trust-based, face-to-face financial system they depended on. The detailed knowledge that the women who testified showed of another woman's financial dealings with her own family reveal that a dense set of overlapping ties grew up among the women and families of the harbor quarter.[33]

As the tale of Anne Bouwessdochter's fight with her brother-in-law suggests, acting as agents for departed travelers quickly drew kin and spouses into the complicated realities of international trade, including the fur trade. Before 1638, the WIC held a monopoly on all beaver skins exported from New Netherland; therefore, the individual sale of furs in Amsterdam violated the law. Yet, despite the risks involved, the potential for substantial profits still tempted sailors, soldiers, and others to try sneaking furs into the home provinces. Thus, when Jan Baptist van Antwerpen, gunner's mate on the WIC ship *Nieuw Nederland,* stood ready to depart once more in 1632, he empowered his wife, Belitge Gerritsdochter, not only to look after family finances but also to deal with a case of illicit trade gone awry. In particular, he charged her "especially in order, by any manner of praying and supplicating, to pursue and to recover from the Honorable Lords Administrators of

32. Testimony, Feb. 13, 1630, Not. Arch. 756, 43, Not. N. Rooleeu, SA. Annetgen Arents's husband was most commonly called Willem Hontom; other variants include Hunthum and Hontoms.
33. Ibid.

the licensed West India Company all such 23 pieces of beaver furs as he . . . brought over from New Netherland," which had been confiscated.[34]

Jan Baptist and Belitge were not the only maritime family tempted by the grey market fur trade in the years before 1638. Skipper Dirck Corssen Stam, for instance, allegedly engaged in extensive fur smuggling with a maritime woman in 1637. Two women testified that they had heard tales about illicit fur trading when they went to Annetgen Ariens's home to fetch a piece of satin they had bought from her, only to find her away from the house. Annetgen's mother told them that her daughter had gone "a few days and nights to Monickendam, and had bought there from Dirck Corssen and the mates . . . around five thousand guilders of peltries and other goods that they had just brought with them from the West Indies." When the women expressed surprise at it, the gossipy mother added "that they should say nothing further about it because her daughter could get into trouble." She could indeed, for the hearers told the whole story to Kiliaen van Rensselaer in his capacity as a WIC director the very next day.[35]

The women gave the culprit's name as Annetgen Ariens, but it seems likely that it was in fact Annetgen Arents, wife of Skipper Willem Hontom, who had testified about buying otter pelts from the late skipper Jan Jacobsz's brother seven years earlier and who knew all about fur trading and the possibility of doing side deals with captains and mates. As a Hudson Valley skipper's wife, Annetgen Arents would have learned that seamen looking to avoid the prying eyes of Amsterdam's harbor would need to unload their questionable goods at Monnikendam before the ship made the last leg of its journey into Amsterdam. Part of the duties of maritime wives in the early years of Dutch colonization in North America, beyond rectifying their husbands' affairs and looking after family finances, was knowing the ins and outs of the illegal economy.

When their husbands and sons had no place to hide the evidence but in their own houses, members of maritime families could not help but be involved in shady dealings. Skippers, factors, and sailors employed by the large concerns that were part of the WIC sometimes wanted to do more than trade for their employers, but they needed help from the women of the maritime quarter if they wished to get away with it. In 1638, Stam made

34. Empowerment, Apr. 7, 1632, Not. Arch. 843, unpaginated, Not. J. Hoogeboom, SA.

35. Testimony, Nov. 20, 1637, Not. Arch. 1049, 214, Not. J. van de Ven, SA (quotations). Women in early modern Portugal similarly transgressed the law to maximize profit; see Darlene Abreu-Ferreira, "From Mere Survival to Near Success: Women's Economic Strategies in Early Modern Portugal," *Journal of Women's History*, XIII, no. 2 (Summer 2001), 58–79.

another voyage to "the English Virginias" and "Jemston" with his brother Arent acting as clerk and keeping books. Something must have been amiss with the books, however, because instead of taking them to the investors in the voyage, the Varleth brothers, the Stam brothers reportedly took them first "to the house of their mother." Next, the books went clandestinely to Dirck Corssen Stam's own house, where a witness heard his wife say that the books were there but that she was not supposed to say anything because they did not want it known that they were there. Such testimony suggests that, although not everyone could keep a secret, Amsterdammers knew perfectly well that some trading should not be mentioned.[36]

In 1638, however, the WIC finally decided that the advantages of attracting more investors and settlers by opening the trade outweighed the loss of their exclusive monopoly. Accordingly, they lifted all restrictions save a per-beaver tax on furs exported from New Netherland. Once the WIC legalized the exportation and sale of beaver skins by private individuals, even more travelers sought to take part in what maritime women already knew to be a profitable business and began sending home furs to the women and men left behind in Amsterdam. People in the developing empire of the 1640s turned to the same tools travelers had used from the WIC's beginning to manage wages and existing businesses: they looked to their intimate networks, strengthened by empowerments, to do the now legal work that Atlantic exchange demanded. Thus, when Henrich Cornelisz van Harmelen, about to depart on "his trip to New Netherland with the ship the *Valckenier*" in May 1649, chose to empower his "stepfather," Aert Aertsz Kaent, to clear up a case he had still outstanding against "Coenraet Leendertsz, furrier in Utrecht," he built on well-established precedents.[37]

At the simplest level, travelers in the wake of the 1638 opening of the beaver-skin trade shipped furs home to whatever family and kin remained in Europe. Small-scale operators in New Netherland sometimes asked sailors or officers leaving for Europe to take along a consignment of furs. Jelle Evertsz, for example, gave sixty-four beavers, two otters, and two squirrel-skin jackets to a boatswain in Manhattan, asking the sailor to deliver them

---

36. Testimony, Nov. 26, 1641, Not. Arch. 1501, unpaginated, Not. J. Oli, SA.

37. Empowerment, May 6, 1649, Not. Arch. 1296, 62v, Not. H. Schaef, SA (quotations). The WIC's decision to relinquish their monopoly on the beaver-skin trade was part of a broader change in WIC policy that year. Amsterdam shareholders also forced the company to open up its trade with Brazil and the Caribbean; see Jan de Vries and Ad van der Woude, *The First Modern Economy: Success, Failure, and Perseverance of the Dutch Economy, 1500–1815* (Cambridge, 1997), 401.

to his wife, Annetje Gerrits, when the ship reached home. Sailors and others in the WIC's employ served to connect families on both sides of the Atlantic, making it possible for individual traders to profit from transatlantic exchange.[38]

Such husband and wife teams allowed couples to turn marriages into colonial trading ventures. Before his departure for New Netherland in 1657, Sergeant Major Francois Fijn empowered not only his "dear wife," Barbara Mansfelt, but also her mother, Lysbet Mansfelt, to oversee all his current debts, credits, and affairs; to "receive all the goods and wares which shall be consigned and sent" from New Netherland; and to represent him against all parties before the commissioners of Amsterdam, as needed. Similarly, in 1660, Jan Evertsz sent over twelve beaver skins from New Netherland to his wife, Jannetge Jans, with specific instructions to deliver them to Lucas Lucasz van der Vliet for sale. Also in 1660, Adriaen Symonsz, a New Netherland *vrij handelaar,* or free trader independent of the WIC, purchased goods on credit and sent "three cases of peltries" back on consignment to his wife, trusting her to oversee repayment to his lender. Marriage thus became the basis for transatlantic business partnerships that enabled couples to cash in on the colonial economy without having any affiliation with the WIC.[39]

The strategy of relying on family, kin, and intimate connections even appealed to families with significant capital. Mistress Adriana Borchel knew that her husband had sent her a shipment aboard the *Graff* that included "three and thirty pieces of whole beavers, seventy pieces of half beavers, four and thirty partial beavers, seven otters and three more otters" all packed together, plus a case with 130 whole beavers, a small package with another 4 beavers, 330 pounds of tobacco, and a shipment of finished Virginia tobacco. However, when the ship docked at La Rochelle, France, in 1654, Adriana needed to invoke the substitution clause in her husband's original 1653 empowerment to appoint Sir Henrij ter Smitten, a La Rochelle merchant, to represent her there. Borchel's honorific title "Juffrouw," or "Mistress," and the extent of the shipment she was expecting mark her as higher status than many other empowered female fur traders. She had social connections with an established foreign merchant, too, which many sailors and even company officers lacked. But she and her husband nonetheless chose to use empow-

38. Empowerment, Dec. 14, 1648, Not. Arch. 1946, 859, Not. D. Doornick, SA.
39. Empowerment, Mar. 16, 1657, Not. Arch. 1853, 127v–128v, Not. N. Kruijs, SA ("dear wife"); Receipt, Oct. 23, 1660, Not. Arch. 2755a, [379], Not. P. van Buijtene, SA; Conveyance, Nov. 22, 1660, Not. Arch. 1362, 106, Not. H. Schaef, SA ("three cases").

erments to keep their American trading all in the family rather than hire agents. Their actions show that relying on marital bonds to participate in colonial trade appealed to would-be traders up and down the economic scale.[40]

Some Amsterdam women who were of merchant status, like Adriana Borchel, began modest trading ventures in their own names after the fur trade opened to all in 1638. Catharina Varleth, a woman from an Amsterdam merchant family, for instance, engaged in transatlantic trade and even entered into complicated overseas legal proceedings when she did not receive payment for more than three hundred guilders worth of goods taken to America for her. In 1641, she empowered Jan Cant, a departing traveler, to collect "from David Provoost, residing in the English Virginias, or in such place where he shall be found, all such money, returns, effects, and merchandise as he has with him on her behalf, and has taken with him from here in order to sell for her." In turning to Cant as her representative, she was not turning to a stranger. At the time, Cant was acting as the Virginia agent for Catharina's three brothers in their tobacco trading ventures. Thus, Catharina's higher status and extensive family ties gave her access to a representative she felt confident in trusting.[41]

Catharina Varleth's struggle to turn international networks to her advantage did not end with Cant's agency. Even though her empowerment was eventually passed on to "the Hon. Willem Kiefft, Commander in the Virginias, otherwise called the New Netherlands," Varleth had yet to collect five years later. This time, assisted by her brother Caspar Varleth, a prominent trader and eventual migrant to the colony, Catharina empowered another traveler to see to the matter on her behalf, noting that the goods had been entrusted to Provoost, "his housewife, and the same's brother" in three parts, as recorded in her account book. The agent chosen with her brother's help took the matter to court in New Netherland, where it was decided largely in her favor. Arbiters appointed by the council of New Netherland decided that Provoost should pay her some 623 guilders in return for money loaned and interest, although the 300 guilder debt for goods was left undecided because of lack of evidence and want of advice. However, to compli-

40. Empowerment, Jan. 15, 1654, Not. Arch. 2196, 53–54, Not. A. Lock, SA.

41. Empowerment, July 23, 1641, Not. Arch. 992, pt. 15, 73, Not. J. Bosch, SA (quotation). Variants of Catharina Varleth's first name include Catharin and Catryna; Varleth is sometimes given as Verlet or Verleth. On Cant's Virginia agency, see Agreement, July 20, 1641, Not. Arch. 1501, [83–84] unpaginated, Not. J. Oli, SA. For an example of the Varleth family's, and specifically Caspar's, early involvement in overseas trade to New Netherland, see Contract, Aug. 26, 1636, Not. Arch. 414a, 173–173v, Not. N. Jacobs, SA.

cate matters further, they ordered him to remit the money "by the ship *De Princes*," which sank on the return voyage, drowning around eighty New Netherlanders and travelers and destroying goods and financial records for many more. After some additional delay, two years later in 1649 Varleth finally had in hand a claim for 620 guilders on Provoost's WIC wages, although she observed that it was only part of a larger sum he owed her.[42]

Varleth's long fight to have her agreements fulfilled shows the challenges and potential of engaging in the independent overseas trade. Her claim was significant, illustrating the sizable cash resources she had at her disposal. Yet, even though she was from a family with considerable economic reach, she chose to send over goods with three departing travelers in ways that mimic the strategies of female and male traders far down the economic ladder. Her ability to appeal to a network of travelers to see to her affairs and her reliance on the support of her merchant brothers and their overseas contacts meant that she was not flying without a net. On the contrary, her extensive social and familial network with merchants tied to New Netherland provided her with the support to see her claims through.

As migration and trade to the colony rose at the end of the 1640s into the 1650s, an increasing number of Amsterdammers had similar social connections reaching across the Atlantic. People from many levels of society doubtless felt, like Varleth, that by sending goods to the Atlantic coast of North America, they would not be taking undue risks. As more intricate social networks developed, independent, international trade became more complex along with them, and a fully formed imperial economy emerged by the 1650s.

As the population of settlers grew, the variety of goods people thought might yield a profit grew, too. Beer provides a good example of the diversification of goods sent abroad as settlement expanded. Migrants heading to the colony in the 1650s and 1660s took along kegs, paid for with either cash or credit. The buying and selling of beer frequently took place between women. Abeltgen Jansdochter, whose husband was already in New Netherland in 1651, made an official IOU with "the honorable Henrick de Weer, beer wholesaler and deliverer," when she acknowledged that she and her husband owed 395 guilders for delivered beer, excise, and impost money. Yet she made clear that the debt was for beer delivered according to an account

42. Empowerment, Mar. 22, 1646, Not. Arch. 993, pt. 19, 12–12v, Not. J. Bosch, SA ("the Hon. Willem Kiefft"); Report of referees, July 17, 1647, in *Provincial Secretary*, II, 430–432 ("*De Princes*," 431); Transport, Mar. 6, 1649, Not. Arch. 1786, 138–139, Not. P. van Velsen, SA.

settled between "her, the appearer, and the wife of the aforesaid Henrick de Weer."[43]

The shipment of Dutch beer to the colony allowed the men and women who ran Amsterdam's wholesale and delivery businesses access to the world of independent transatlantic trade. To negotiate the transatlantic economy, they relied on the same tools that people used to manage finance and fur trading. Cornelia Wachters, the widow of an Amsterdam beer wholesaler and deliverer, empowered a New Netherland woman about to return to America to collect more than thirty-one guilders there from Jelles Douwes and his wife Hester for delivered beer and excise costs in 1655. The dependence on empowerments to turn face-to-face contacts into financial agents kept this particular transatlantic exchange entirely in the hands of women.[44]

Beer wholesalers who gave credit to departing travelers sometimes looked not just to make a profit but also to gain access to colonial goods. In 1656, for instance, Jan Andries van Berenberch's widow, a New Netherland resident, acknowledged a debt to a beer wholesaler and deliverer that included 230 guilders and two good elk-skin coats. As more Amsterdammers went abroad taking local trade and debts with them, the small-scale international economy began to closely resemble the credit-debt networks so common in early modern Europe.[45]

Yet beer wholesalers and their customers were not the only ones hoping to capitalize on expanding social networks among travelers to reach new markets. For women well used to doing retail business in Amsterdam, the growing population of Amsterdammers abroad offered attractive potential. The Honorable Tryntje Willems, a widow and "public business woman," sent over to New Netherland some 840 guilders' worth of linen with departing New Amsterdam merchant Nicolaes de Meyer on credit, with his promise to pay her "as soon as the ships that now currently are ready to depart to New Netherland shall have again arrived here in this city from there." As immigration increased in the 1650s, products like linen would become increasingly marketable in New Netherland, just as they were in Holland.[46]

43. Debt acknowledgement, Nov. 17, 1651, Not. Arch. 1346, 86v, Not. H. Schaef, SA (quotations). Account book practices also often obscured women's purchasing, not just women's retailing, in eighteenth-century America; see Ann Smart Martin, "Backcountry Women and Goods: Linking Local and Global Economies" (paper presented at the Thirteenth Berkshire Conference on the History of Women, Scripps College, Claremont, Calif., June 2–5, 2005).

44. Empowerment, Apr. 26, 1655, Not. Arch. 1305, 64, Not. H. Schaef, SA.

45. Empowerment, May 17, 1656, Not. Arch. 1306, 94v–95, Not. H. Schaef, SA.

46. Debt acknowledgement, Mar. 20, 1663, Not. Arch. 2290, pt. 4, 73–74, Not. J. de Winter, SA.

Such independent trade in goods sent over with Atlantic travelers mirrored the local economy of the Netherlands. Especially at the small scale, early modern European women managed to take part in, if not dominate, the local distribution of goods, even at times and places where they remained shut out of many other economic sectors. Having social connections to someone traveling abroad provided the chance for women to export the products they sold on the local market to the developing New Netherland *burgerij,* or urban citizenry. The widowed Mistress Anna Hustaerts decided to try her hand at international trade when she sent along a shipment of "lace and needlework" with Cornelis and Janneke Melyn to New Netherland in the 1640s for them to sell there on her behalf. When she did not receive payment, she was able to appeal to another departing traveler, fur trader Govert Loockermans. Hustaerts authorized him to collect "eighty-two guilders and sixteen stivers," the sum that she had expected these typical female crafts to yield. Similarly, in 1663, "the Honorable Mistress Elisabeth Cornelis van Buytene, wife of Johannes Ebel, living in Dordrecht, being a business woman and doing her own trade in lace," empowered the super-cargo of the *Bontekoe* to collect in America for forty guilders' worth of lace delivered to "Elsgen Jaspars van Amsterdam (^also) having been a business woman in lace." These female traders' reliance on debt and credit to sell fine needle goods and their appeal to social connections are of a piece with the workings of the local early modern European economy. With the migration of more women to the colony from the second half of the 1640s onward, some businesswomen found their partners, friends, and potential customers living abroad, making it possible for them to engage in the transatlantic economy growing outside the WIC.[47]

Larger numbers of travelers crossing the Atlantic made it possible for small-scale Amsterdam traders to find a range of potential representatives willing to look after their goods. Styntge Pieters, an Amsterdam widow, sent goods along with Harmen Reyndertsz to sell in New Netherland on her behalf. Later, she empowered another traveler named Willem Cornelisz, a "free settler" who lived and traded in the Delaware River area with the

---

47. Empowerment, Dec. 19, 1645, Not. Arch. 2026, 66, Not. S. van Nieulandt, SA ("lace and needlework"); Empowerment, Apr. 13, 1663, Not. Arch. 3177a, 100–101, Not. A. van Zurck, SA ("Honorable Mistress"). On seventeenth-century women's participation in trade within Europe, see Natalie Zemon Davis, *Women on the Margins: Three Seventeenth-Century Lives* (Cambridge, Mass., 1995); Merry Wiesner Wood, "Paltry Peddlers or Essential Merchants? Women in the Distributive Trades in Early Modern Nuremberg," *Sixteenth Century Journal,* XII, no. 2 (Summer 1981), 3–13.

confidence-inspiring nickname the "Rycke Vryer," or the "Rich Bachelor," to collect whatever goods and effects Reyndertsz still had in hand. Yet this second agent failed either to send her goods back to her "or to bring them over himself, notwithstanding that he himself was since here in this land." Styntge therefore turned to a third traveler, the financial overseer of the colony, Johannes de Decker, in 1662. She empowered this influential colonial official to collect the goods, make a settlement, and "to follow the orders" she would give him about how to dispose of her property. Clearly, sending goods abroad could be risky without a spouse or kin to look after one's interests. Yet, Styntge Pieters was still able to locate three different men from among the growing web of transatlantic travelers who agreed to manage her trade for her.[48]

Maritime women—the wives, mothers, and kin of seafaring men—had particular opportunities and needs to make use of these developing trading opportunities. Having access to and acquaintance with a large number of travelers and merchants, they were well placed to take part in overseas exchange. Jannetge Cloeck's husband, Skipper Barent Jochemsz, for instance, had traveled to and traded in New Netherland, but, by 1660, he had left the Atlantic to work for the VOC on a voyage to the East Indies. Jannetge, therefore, was left to look after the couple's American interests, including a number of debts still outstanding in New Netherland. Jannetge drew on the legal empowerment her husband made before his departure to authorize, in turn, at least four substitutes setting sail from Amsterdam to collect each and every guilder, from the 806 guilders owed on the account of New Amsterdam merchant Gerrit van Tucht to the 8 guilders due from New Netherlander Hans Hans Schaer for "six schepel of salt." Dense ties and a variety of goods shaped the marital property this maritime wife oversaw.[49]

The increasing complexity of transatlantic society and the development of complicated networks of personal relationships become clear when looking at what happened to legal empowerments like Barent Jochemsz's to Jannetge Cloeck. It was not always possible for individuals to empower someone they knew personally to act for them in all the faraway ports and colonies where they had claims. As more individuals crossed the Atlantic in multiple directions, legal empowerments themselves got passed on from

48. Empowerment, Dec. 7, 1662, Not. Arch. 1367, 101v, Not. H. Schaef, SA.
49. Empowerment, Jan. 28, 1664, Not. Arch. 3187, 27–27v, Not. H. Outgers, SA (quotation); Empowerment, Jan. 7, 1661, Not. Arch. 2756a, 53–54, Not. P. van Buijtene, SA; Empowerment, May 2, 1661, Not. Arch. 2757a, 563–564, Not. P. van Buijtene, SA; Empowerment, Jan. 23, 1662, Not. Arch. 2760a, 188–189, Not. P. van Buijtene, SA.

person to person, creating a system of "substitutes." For example, Thomas Swartwout empowered his wife, Hendrickje Barents, in 1653 to oversee the family's affairs while he was away. However, the following year, she herself stood ready to depart for New Netherland, so she passed the empowerment on to notary Cornelis Dircxsz Grijn. Relying on the "Clauso of Substitutie" her husband had included in his original empowerment, she charged Grijn with taking care of all unfinished business in her absence as well as renting out the couple's now-vacant house. In passing on her empowerment, Hendrickje generated a new string of relationships.[50]

Substitution clauses made it possible for empowered women to create complex international chains of personal ties, causing financial networks to expand to include towns and routes outside a claimant's web of personal acquaintances. Working as a soldier in Curaçao in the 1640s, Pieter Jansz van Gorcum had claims for his employment on the WIC's Zeeland office. However, he evidently did not know anyone traveling directly from Curaçao to Zeeland whom he trusted, so he empowered a woman in Curaçao named Jelletge Sybrantsdochter to collect his wages. She and her husband then sailed from Curaçao to New Netherland. There, her husband, acting as her legal representative, drew on the substitution clause to pass on the empowerment to Govert Loockermans, a New Netherland merchant traveling to Amsterdam in 1647. On his arrival in Amsterdam, Loockermans, for his part, transferred the empowerment to Jan Jansz, a sailor from Vlissingen in Zeeland, "who shall also sail back with him [Loockermans]" to New Netherland. Thus, Jelletge Sybrantsdochter was but one part in a long train of face-to-face relationships that worked to keep this soldier connected with his financial life in the fatherland. Travelers' financial representatives, like Jelletge, not only drew on preexisting personal connections, they also worked as active and conscious agents of travelers, building new social networks to help them tame the vast distances of the Atlantic.[51]

50. Empowerment, June 6, 1654, Not. Arch. 2281, pt. 3, 72, Not. J. de Winter, SA.

51. Empowerment, Mar. 13, 1647, Not. Arch. 1294, 34, Not. H. Schaef, SA (quotation). This system of substitutes bears similarities to the systems of credit and trust that David Hancock describes among English merchants; see Hancock, *Citizens of the World: London Merchants and the Integration of the British Atlantic Community, 1735–1785* (Cambridge, 1995). Like empowerments, bills of exchange and letters of introduction also allowed merchants to extend their economic activity beyond the circle of their own personal acquaintances. In the case of substitutions in empowerments, the beneficiaries of these growing networks of trust sometimes came from within the merchant class, like Hancock's Englishmen, but could also come from far below it. A soldier for the WIC was unlikely to have the financial or social capital to benefit from a bill of exchange, but substitute representatives could and did act on behalf of

As a result of the new social and economic networks developing among Atlantic traders, it is possible that some people found themselves pulled into the transatlantic economy unexpectedly. Debt and credit were common in the local economy, and every time an Amsterdammer went abroad, they took their debts along with them. In 1656, an Amsterdam widow named Saertje Symons had to empower a helmsman on the ship *Vergulde Beer* when her debtor Marritgen Joris moved abroad with her husband before paying Saertje back some two hundred guilders. Saertje did not make clear the origins of this debt, although she mentioned it was the remainder of a larger sum. Perhaps she had knowingly lent outfitting money or sent goods along with Marritgen Joris, or perhaps Marritgen had simply left town without warning. Either way, Saertje had entered the transatlantic credit economy, relying on a personal empowerment to collect on what had once been a face-to-face transaction.[52]

While some might have been drawn into trade accidentally, many others took part in Holland's growing independent transatlantic economy intentionally by forming complicated financial instruments. Bottomry loans, in which the lender took on the risk of the sea in exchange for higher interest rates, offered women and men the potential for big profits, but only if they were willing to take a gamble. From the borrower's perspective, bottomry functioned as a sort of loan and insurance combined. Those seeking loans to buy goods agreed to repay not only the capital but very high interest rates. In return, if the goods were lost at sea or damaged before reaching America, the lender held the risk. For Amsterdam women of means who looked to make money from overseas trade but had no plans to travel abroad, bottomry loans proved an attractive way to enter international trade networks. Mistress Lodewÿna Poppendams and a male partner, for instance, went in together to loan eight hundred guilders to an Amsterdam shoemaker about to depart to New Netherland. The eight hundred guilders' worth of "goods, wares, and merchandise" had already been loaded on the ship *Bever* on behalf of borrower Jan Evertsz when the notary drew up the official contract in 1661. In this case, Evertsz promised to pay 25 percent interest. Poppendams and her partner stood to make a tidy sum if all went well.[53]

---

such maritime workers. Empowerments, however, traveled ahead of or beyond the principal, rather than with him or her. In other words, rather than taking a letter of introduction on their travels, substitutes carried empowerments to places the principal was unable to visit.

52. Empowerment, Dec. 12, 1656, Not. Arch. 1898, 361, Not. F. Uijttenbogaert, SA.

53. Bottomry contract, Mar. 11, 1661, Not. Arch. 2756b, 488–489, Not. P. van Buijtene, SA.

However, the risk of lending on bottomry was significant. Another shoe-maker stood bond for Evertsz in the event of nonpayment, but Poppendams and her partner took on all the hazards of the sea, from the time the ship sailed from "this city of Amsterdam, to the Manathans in New Netherland and from there after trading is done back to this City, until the anchor has fallen." If the ship was lost or the goods damaged underway, it would be solely Poppendams's and her fellow lender's problem. In the end, it was not the dangers of the ocean voyage that threatened their potential profits, it was the market itself. A year later, Poppendams did receive "some peltries and bear hides to sell for the highest price" from Evertsz's wife, Annetgen Hendricx, in fulfillment of the bottomry debt, but, by 1664, the furs re-mained unsold "as a result of the low price of the same" on the Amsterdam market. Evertsz's wife and the shoemaker who stood bond on his behalf therefore agreed that Poppendams should hold on to the furs as long as she saw fit, in hopes that eventually the price would rise enough to pay back the principal and interest on the loan. As the independent trade to North America grew more complicated in the 1650s and 1660s, bottomry debts went far beyond the informal "sending over" of a few items for sale by other Amsterdammers.[54]

Not everyone who used bottomry instruments to enter the independent trade across the ocean came from high-status backgrounds like Mistress Poppendams. Normally, the trading companies permitted sailors to take along small amounts of goods for sale in their sea chests, yet not all sail-ors had the capital to buy such goods before they set out. Middling-status Amsterdammers willing to lend on bottomry capitalized on sailors' oppor-tunities. Sailor Jochem Martens Went, for instance, received two hundred guilders' worth of "merchandise" on bottomry from "Jannetje Douwes, wife of Lourens Pietersen, bed seller." Though Jannetje took on significant risk by agreeing to loan on bottomry, Went agreed to pay her "two percent per month for bottomry money for the peril and chance of the Sea." Since the voyage "from this city, to New Netherland . . . and from New Netherland to the English Virginias and from there back again to . . . this city of Am-sterdam" could easily take a year, Jannetje could expect to earn a handsome profit.[55]

54. Ibid. ("this city"); Testimony, Jan. 9, 1664, Not. Arch. 2768a, 59–60, Not. P. van Buijtene, SA ("some peltries"). On bottomry in Amsterdam from 1585 to 1680, see S. Hart, "Rederij," in Akveld, Hart, and Van Hoboken, eds., *Maritieme geschiedenis der Nederlanden*, II, 121–132.

55. Bottomry contract, Nov. 26, 1645, Not. Arch. 1746, 617, Not. J. Spithoff, SA (quotations). On the use of bottomry contracts by men trading on the small scale, see Jacobs, *New Nether-*

Some women taking part in the new Atlantic economy managed to build on opportunities for profit making, like that Jannetje Douwes identified, to create strong positions as international traders. For older maritime wives and widows, particularly, a lifetime spent as a part of the independent small-scale economy sometimes gave them significant and far-flung interests across the Atlantic. In 1662, Helena Jacobs had to rectify the international affairs left hanging by the death of her husband, Adriaen Bloemmaert, a longtime captain for the VOC and WIC, onetime New Netherland resident, and former "quartermaster of the Castle Del Mina in Guinea." To collect "from every and all of her debtors in New Netherland," Helena turned to Pieter Tonneman, about to set sail as New Amsterdam's chief legal officer, and "Skipper Claes Bordingh, who also lives in New Amsterdam." To deal with her interests in the slave trade, she looked to "the Honorable Pieter Lanck, skipper, about to depart to the coast of Guinea" to collect the twenty-four "slaves that her . . . aforementioned late husband . . . left in the hands of . . . Christiaan Planck," clerk in Elmina. What her agent should do with these slaves, she did not say. As a widow, she now inhabited a different legal category than she had as a wife. Her period of legal incapacity was over, yet she retained a widespread network of social and economic ties among the maritime population, despite her skipper husband's death. It would be up to her to decide the fate of these unnamed slaves, whom she had never seen. Her actions show just how important it is to understand the construction of empire and its painful consequences, not as something done by abstract or large-scale forces, but rather as something built by men and women making individual choices to pursue their own interests by exploiting their social and economic connections.[56]

---

land, 67–69. Many sailors likely lacked sufficient capital to purchase even small quantities of goods up front. As Van der Heijden and Van den Heuvel attest: "Soldiers and sailors were the poorest rewarded occupational groups in the Dutch Republic; their earnings were two or three times less than the salaries of common labourers ashore"; see Van der Heijden and Van den Heuvel, "Surviving Strategies," in Cavaciocchi, ed., *Ricchezza del mare ricchezza dal mare,* 1110.

56. Empowerment, Mar. 23, 1663, Not. Arch. 1603, 40–40v, Not. A. Loefs, SA ("quartermaster"); Empowerment, Oct. 3, 1662, Not. Arch. 2290, pt. 2, 30, Not. J. de Winter, SA ("the Honorable Pieter Lanck"). Helena Jacobs's name also appears as Juffrouw Helena Blommerts, or Bloemmaerts. On Dutch involvement in the slave trade, see Johannes Menne Postma, *The Dutch in the Atlantic Slave Trade, 1600–1815* (Cambridge, 1990); P. C. Emmer, "De slavenhandel van en naar Nieuw-Nederland," *Economisch- en sociaal-historisch jaarboek,* XXXV (1972), 94–147.

By making such choices, some women created new legal identities that allowed them to escape legal incapacity even during their husbands' lives. One such woman was Annetgen Arents, the wife of Skipper Willem Hontom, who had been active in colonial trade at least since 1630, when she had testified about the otter pelts disputed by Anne Bouwessdochter and her brother-in-law. Annetgen built on her role as a skipper's wife to become a merchant in her own right, and her career even outlasted that of her husband. By 1652, Annetgen Hontoms, as she now called herself, by then perhaps near fifty years old, made out an empowerment to a ship's carpenter who was traveling to New Netherland to collect goods from various people who owed her there. She made clear that the debts were to her, mentioning that her husband was retired (he was an "oudtschipper," or "old skipper," now, no longer a *schipper*) and that "she, the appearer, [was] a public business woman" who did "public trade."[57]

Being a public businesswoman, Annetgen had legal abilities that far exceeded those of most wives. Even with an empowerment, most wives under Roman-Dutch law had limited legal capacity and remained wards of their husbands. Their sphere of legal action was confined to the range covered by the empowerment, and in general they had no ability to create an estate or business separate from joint marital property. Not so for public businesswomen, however. They had the ability to act on their own. As Hugo Grotius, the preeminent jurist of Golden Age Holland, explained, "Nowadays, a married woman, engaged in public commerce or business, can indeed contract in all matters pertaining to that commerce or trade." Consequently, Annet-

---

57. Empowerment, Dec. 18, 1652, Not. Arch. 1302, 294v, Not. H. Schaef, SA (quotations). The changing way in which Annetgen Arents Hontoms's name appears provides a corrective to a misunderstanding in colonial American historiography about New Netherland women's naming practices. Linda Briggs Biemer, while helpfully pointing out women's economic activities in the colony, argued that the tendency for Dutch women to not always appear under their husbands' last names signaled "the independent treatment" of women in Dutch law and culture; see Biemer, *Women and Property in Colonial New York: The Transition from Dutch to English Law, 1643–1727* (Ann Arbor, Mich., 1983), x, 3 (quotation). However, this analysis conflates patronymics and surnames and misses the correlation between surnames and high status. Notaries identified Annetgen Arents, when younger, in terms of her first name and patronymic without any surname, sometimes followed by a reference to her husband's identity ("wife of"). When she was older and her social status had risen, notaries included her husband's surname, although with an "s" added, indicating the genitive case: Hontom's wife, in essence. Yet it is only in this later period that the documents note her legal independence as a *koopvrouw*. Surname usage, therefore, was not indicative of a woman's legal capacity or independence. Also, notaries' and secretaries' choices might or might not have reflected how a woman would have chosen to identify herself.

gen Arents Hontoms would have had all the freedom she needed to pursue her fur-trading activities.[58]

Female traders gained their status through a combination of community acceptance and spousal permission. Annetgen and other businesswomen referred to themselves both as "openbare koopvrouwen" and as "bekende koopvrouwen." They were both "public businesswomen" and "well-known businesswomen." There is a certain circularity to the title: Annetgen was allowed to do business because it was well known that she did business. Indeed, she had done so for more than twenty years. Thus, she had used the trading networks of the maritime community to build a new and very different legal identity for herself, even as her trading activities allowed her to help build the networks that created an empire.

Women like Annetgen Arents Hontoms show that Amsterdam's transatlantic intimate networks produced an Atlantic economy by giving people the ability to look after their financial interests and property in the newly expanding world. These networks grew as individuals took action on behalf of those far away and engendered new connections where none had existed before, binding people together around common interests and personal ties. Skippers, sailors, and their wives cooperated with one another, took advantage of one another, and shared a sense of how the Atlantic economy

58. Grotius, *Jurisprudence of Holland*, trans. Lee, I, 30-31 (quotation). I have made minor modifications of Lee's translation on this point based on the accompanying Dutch transcription. For women and Dutch law, see Ariadne Schmidt, *Overleven na de dood: Weduwen in Leiden in de Gouden Eeuw* (Amsterdam, 2001); Schmidt, "Vrouwen en het recht: De juridische status van vrouwen in Holland in de vroegmoderne tijd," *Jaarboek van het Centraal Bureau voor Genealogie*, LVIII (2004), 26–44; Heleen C. Gall, "'European' Widows in the Dutch East Indies: Their Legal and Social Position," in Jan Bremmer and Lourens van den Bosch, eds., *Between Poverty and the Pyre: Moments in the History of Widowhood* (London, 1995), 103–121; Kappelhof, "Vrouwen buitenshuis," *Jaarboek van het Centraal Bureau voor Genealogie*, LVIII (2004), 45–67; Danielle van den Heuvel, *Women and Entrepreneurship: Female Traders in the Northern Netherlands, c. 1580–1815* (Amsterdam, 2007), 23–24, 56–69; David E. Narrett, *Inheritance and Family Life in Colonial New York City* (Ithaca, N.Y., 1992), 42–44. These newer studies contradict some statements about supposedly lenient Dutch law in New Netherland in Biemer, *Women and Property in Colonial New York*, esp. x, 75–76. For the experiences of women with the law in seventeenth-century English colonies, see Mary Beth Norton, *Founding Mothers and Fathers: Gendered Power and the Forming of American Society* (New York, 1996); Marylynn Salmon, *Women and the Law of Property in Early America* (Chapel Hill, N.C., 1986). For an analysis of the advantages and disadvantages of the similar status of feme sole traders under English law, see Marjorie K. McIntosh, "The Benefits and Drawbacks of *Femme Sole* Status in England, 1300–1630," *Journal of British Studies*, XLIV (2005), 410–438; for feme sole and other women traders in colonial America, see Patricia Cleary, "'She Will Be in the Shop': Women's Sphere of Trade in Eighteenth-Century Philadelphia and New York," *Pennsylvania Magazine of History and Biography*, CXIX (1995), 181–202.

ought to work that derived from established tools and patterns. Using old techniques in a new environment, kin and social groups in Amsterdam and beyond together fashioned an informal, diffuse, small-scale economy. Maritime Amsterdam represented a melding of both long-distance and immediate forces. As intimate ties formed networks, an Atlantic empire emerged that was a familiar place even for those who never left shore.[59]

Conclusion

The people who lived, worked, and traded in seventeenth-century Amsterdam were an unusual kind of early modern colonial entrepreneur. The merchant leaders of the Netherlands, many of whom commissioned portraits from the leading artists of the Golden Age, including Rembrandt and Frans Hals, have formed the enduring image of seventeenth-century Dutch traders. In their portraits, these stolid members of the mercantile elite sit, almost majestically ranged, in their snug black waistcoats and tall beaver felt hats. Together, these men ruled the Netherlands' municipalities during this period, and some of these paintings still hang in buildings that once housed the great monopolies and exchanges of the Golden Age. Abraham van den Tempel's depiction of the merchant and WIC director Abraham de Visscher captures the image of burghers grown stout through the profits of overseas trade (Figure 4). His rich clothing and comfortable girth point to his wealth, while the family crest of three mermaids at the top right corner of the painting leaves little doubt that his family money came through the relationship between people and the ocean in maritime Amsterdam. Yet a fuller picture of early Atlantic empires requires that faces like De Visscher's be joined by the other faces of seventeenth-century international trade. Bakers and bed-sellers' wives, shoemakers and sailors, too, wagered their own futures and savings in cross-ocean trade. In so doing, they turned to personal connections, to the immediate ties of kin and neighborhood, to transform the Atlantic Ocean into an economic network that greatly resembled their neighborhood economies.

Tracing the development of this international network reveals the stages of empire formation in the early modern Dutch Atlantic. At the most basic level, maritime Amsterdammers created financial webs that ensnared

59. On the sense of belonging created by the ownership of both land and personal property, which aided the creation of Dutch communities in eighteenth-century South Africa, see Laura J. Mitchell, *Belongings: Property, Family, and Identity in Colonial South Africa (An Exploration of Frontiers, 1725–c. 1830)* (New York, 2009).

FIGURE 4 ✦ *Abraham de Visscher (1605–1667), koopman te Amsterdam en bewindhebber van de West Indische Compagnie.* Attributed to Abraham van den Tempel (1622–1672). Circa 1650–1667. Oil on canvas. 127 × 100 cm. Bequest of J. Balguerie-van Rijswijk, Rijksmuseum, Amsterdam

maritime workers in debt, enabling them to supply the WIC and VOC with the workforce those companies needed. From the first, wives, parents, and kin took responsibility for overseeing the financial lives of travelers and smoothing the connection between the family economy and the WIC. Through their endeavors, family members in Amsterdam helped create the transatlantic financial connections that underlay the nascent empire. The transatlantic networks that travelers and those left behind built also gave people a way to enter the fur trade as independent actors, especially after the WIC opened fur exports to all in 1638. When migration increased from the late 1640s on, that independent economy would become more complex and more diversified. In the 1650s and 1660s, fully formed intimate networks sustained a mature Atlantic empire.

The "merchants" who built this trade likely rarely resembled the black-waistcoated urban elites painted by Van den Tempel and others. Instead, some of these merchants were women, whether they were widowed "Mistresses" trying to expand their lace dealing to new markets or soldiers' sisters seeking to do what they could to help their families stay afloat. The ordinary soldiers, sailors, and settlers who worked and took passage on Amsterdam ships bound for America created and upheld this trade, outside the purview of the merchant princes who controlled the WIC. Kiliaen van Rensselaer and his peers acted as representatives of their families as they built the WIC, but the kin networks they used and supported through this large-scale mercantile activity need to be seen alongside the family networks of thousands of other women and men in Amsterdam and beyond. People up and down the social scale similarly extended their family economies overseas along with the ships that set sail from Texel. As personal ties developed into increasingly dense transatlantic intimate networks, people from all walks of life took part in the new trading opportunities and bore the burdens of the many separations this new overseas commerce demanded.

When Marritgen Wouters waved goodbye to her skipper husband for the last time in 1619, she was just one of many family members left behind. Yet the friends, neighbors, and family who stayed ashore did not cease to be a part of the lives of those who worked the ships and peopled the outposts of Dutch colonial ventures. The actions they took to secure their relationships with those at sea and those beyond the seas built the Dutch Atlantic empire, one family at a time.

CHAPTER TWO

"She Is Now Already at Sea"
Extending Ties, Creating Empire

 On March 30, 1663, the ship *Roseboom*, under Skipper Pieter Reyersen, set sail from Texel on a return voyage to Manhattan in the company of the ship *Hoop*. They set out with 125 souls aboard, but the very first day they had to unload the body of "a woman . . . who had died in Texel." The loss of one passenger, however, was made up before the end of the journey by the birth of another. On April 21, the keeper of the ship's journal noted that "a woman delivered a young son," although he later corrected himself by crossing out "son" and writing in "daughter." The ship finally arrived at Manhattan on a misty, still day in early June. As they sailed "inside the Sand Point," the ship's chronicler penned, "the Lord God be praised for a completed journey." A relatively short, easy passage nonetheless saw the death of one woman, the motherhood of another, and the birth of a little girl.[1]

The presence of women and the continuation of family life at sea was not limited to the *Roseboom*. Whether they traveled as maidservants, single women seeking their fortunes in trade and marriage, daughters of merchant families, or wives accompanying cargoes of goods, women took their place on board the many Dutch ships connecting the ports that ringed the Atlantic. In other words, women did more than provide an economic anchor for mobile men, as Marritgen Wouters did when her husband sailed from Amsterdam in 1619. Other women took part directly, by stepping aboard themselves, in the new floating world that Dutch ships created. Through their travels and the family ties they maintained, these women did important work building the Dutch Atlantic empire. Dutch vessels kept both women and men in motion within a dynamic Atlantic world.

---

1. Log of two trips to Holland and return, Oct. 10, 1660–June 1663, Miscellaneous Manuscripts, Ships—Dutch, NYHS.

Mobility allowed women and men, regardless of their background or economic resources, to create a variety of personal and economic networks. The poor moved around the ocean as the employees of companies, patroons, and wealthy families. Middling-status families booked passage on their own. Members of the merchant class traveled themselves or employed kin to do their bidding abroad. Some travelers would experience all three patterns over the course of their lives, as changing opportunities and economic circumstances left the boundaries of class and status porous. The ability to cross the ocean several times en route to multiple destinations enabled people at all levels of society to build a series of constantly shifting links between Europe and the Americas. These complex journeys, performed by women and men up and down the social scale, produced intricate webs of connections radiating in all directions.

What kept these far-reaching, delicate patterns strong was intimacy. Familial, immediate, and interpersonal associations defined these relationships as intimate, making them durable enough to do the work people needed to survive or cash in on the Atlantic economy. Participants in the Dutch Atlantic world, both male and female, particularly relied on cross-gender alliances to solidify their long-distance networks. Marriage formed one of the primary institutions structuring international trade and finance for small and large actors alike. Traders and merchants deliberately interwove the personal and the economic, invoking the intimacy of gendered family and affective ties to construct networks capable of sustaining overseas exchange. The Dutch Atlantic economy, therefore, depended on the actions, presence, and relationships of both women and men who created and maintained social, personal, and intimate ties.[2]

2. In the wake of the work of Laurence Stone on England, scholars sometimes suggest that emotion and affect were not an essential component of early modern marriage and family in Europe, but family relationships in the seventeenth-century Netherlands were clearly understood to ideally contain an affective dimension; see Luuc Kooijmans, "Liefde in opdracht: Emotie en berekening in de dagboeken van Willem Frederik van Nassau," *Holland, historisch tijdschrift*, XXX (1998), 231–255; Judith Hokke, "'Mijn alderliefste Jantielief': Vrouw en gezin in de Republiek: Regentenvrouwen en hun relaties," *Jaarboek voor vrouwengeschiedenis*, VIII (1987), 73. See also Willem Frijhoff, "Liefde in Holland: Inleiding," *Holland, historisch tijdschrift*, XXX (1998), 191–195. As the Reformation made marriage a public matter, leading to a de-emphasis on reproduction as the sole purpose of marriage, Manon van der Heijden writes that "marital love became the most important object of marriage. Love and companionship were to be the bond that kept men and women together"; see Van der Heijden, "Punishment versus Reconciliation: Marriage Control in Sixteenth- and Seventeenth-Century Holland," in Herman Roodenburg and Pieter Spierenburg, eds., *Social Control in Europe*, I, *1500–1800* (Columbus, Ohio, 2004), 55–77 (quotation, 57). For expressions of feeling in the courtship letters

The constant mobility of New Netherland's many sojourners, sailors, and settlers made it possible for people to keep connections alive despite the distances that divided them. Far from being inimical, mobility and intimacy proved mutually reinforcing, as people relied on the movement of individuals within their networks to continually rebuild Atlantic links. It mattered that some of these mobile individuals were female. The meetings and partings of women and men allowed travelers to reaffirm the familial and economic bonds that underlay their intimate relationships. People created new marriage ties as they passed from place to place and formed new affiliations with fellow sojourners on docks and in ports around the Atlantic. As people continually reshaped their intimate networks, their relationships traced a fluid map of imperial ties.[3]

As people traveled the Atlantic, constituting and renewing their personal and economic connections, they created, not one kind of transatlantic network, but several. Differences in the density of ties, the economic reach of participants, and the role of family led to the development of distinct patterns of relationships. At the simplest level, marriage allowed men and women to enter small-scale trade and build economic lives. More complex networks among middling folk supplemented the marital bond with extensive ties of family, guild, and neighborhood. Networks backed by greater capital wove elite kin groups together with formal power structures. Each kind of network, in turn, supported and enabled particular strata of economic activity. Bonds of marriage, family, community, and clan made the formation of all kinds of transatlantic connections possible.

Intimate attachments and family ties built the economy of empire from the ground up. Personal relationships between men and women across the social spectrum created economic links between the colony and homeland.

---

of Kiliaen van Rensselaer, patroon and WIC director, see Janny Venema, "Searching for True Love: Letters from Kiliaen van Rensselaer," in Martha Dickinson Shattuck, ed., *Explorers, Fortunes, and Love Letters: A Window on New Netherland* (Albany, N.Y., 2009), 116–128. Venema shows that Van Rensselaer, writing in 1615, had "ideas about marriage as a social, religious, and economic partnership for which he considered love, reason, discretion, and fairness important ingredients" (118). Thus, New Netherlanders sometimes referenced affective bonds to invoke family connections.

3. On the Dutch Atlantic empire, see Johannes Postma and Victor Enthoven, eds., *Riches from Atlantic Commerce: Dutch Transatlantic Trade and Shipping, 1585–1817* (Leiden, 2003). For an excellent survey of the nature of the Dutch empire in the Indian Ocean, see Kerry Ward, *Networks of Empire: Forced Migration in the Dutch East India Company* (New York, 2009), 1–48. See also Femme S. Gaastra, *The Dutch East India Company: Expansion and Decline* (Zutphen, Netherlands, 2003); C. R. Boxer, *The Dutch Seaborne Empire: 1600–1800* (New York, 1965).

In a kind of phoretic symbiosis, poor men and women used the income and mobility offered by employment with the WIC to gain entrance into the Atlantic economy through modest trading ventures while also providing the labor that allowed those ships to move in the first place. As a result of their movement around the Atlantic basin on company ships, they sometimes formed the most important relationship needed to participate in this new economy—marriage. Putting this most intimate of ties to work through mobility, they not only made the beginnings of an economic life, they also created the small-scale, overseas economy. Families of middle means, with links to the officer class of the WIC and the skills and resources necessary to break into the artisanal class, used mobility, too, to allow wives and husbands to complete the transatlantic economic circuit. They parlayed their WIC pay and status into credit, making it possible for them to become active in the independent fur trade and to establish artisanal businesses on American shores. Marriage and mobility enabled a few of them to enter the lowest ranks of the merchant class. Their dense economic networks fostered a system of trade and finance parallel to formal companies and provided the basis for settler society in the Hudson Valley. For those with even greater economic reach, family connections mingled inseparably with the contracts that underlay the large-scale merchant companies that were a part of the WIC. Gendered marriage and kin associations functioned both practically and rhetorically to allow families to extend their economic webs and solidify their elite status.

Family shaped empire in different ways for all of the diverse people taking part in the Dutch Atlantic economy. Women's activities and gendered family relationships proved essential to building this economy by facilitating the various forms of mercantile and financial exchange that grew up outside, beside, and within the formal confines of the company. Through the development of intimate networks that spanned the seas, people from all levels of society extended the early modern European economy across the Atlantic Ocean.

Personal Ties and Maritime Workers' Mobility

Just as the ocean is never at rest, the people who sailed the Atlantic kept ceaselessly in motion. The farewells waved to those in the Schreierstoren did not mean that people who sailed out of Amsterdam left behind a Europe they never expected to see again. People often made not just one passage but several, trading one port for another as circumstances or choice demanded.

In each new port, travelers made new connections but also worked to keep old ones alive. Dynamic transatlantic ties, sustained by individual travelers and colonists, created networks that were at once personal and economic. The extreme mobility of the Dutch Atlantic would make it possible for people up and down the social scale to maintain transatlantic connections and take part in cross-ocean trade. For those on the lower rungs of the social and economic ladder, the jobs and ships of the WIC proved essential to their ability to enter into the Atlantic economy. Through their personal relationships, soldiers, sailors, and their kin constructed new lives for themselves while developing unique individual strategies that helped build the nascent imperial economy.

When people set sail from Amsterdam to the West, they wove a complicated web from one port to another, made up of the old relationships they took with them and the new ones they formed along the way. Instead of traveling to and fro between two points, ships very often sailed in circular patterns. Sailors and sojourners setting forth on Skipper Gerrit Jansz van Dyck's ship in 1655, for instance, expected to travel "to the Bight of Guinie, the Caribbean islands and New Netherland, and finally returning again to this city of Amsterdam." Dutch involvement in the shipment of slaves from Africa drew ships like this south to present-day Ghana and Angola as well as other ports along Africa's Atlantic coast. To sell those slaves, Dutch skippers sailed to Portuguese and Spanish ports from Brazil to Colombia on the South American mainland and to English, French, and Dutch outposts across the Caribbean islands and along the North American coast. Sometimes voyages outside the Dutch empire had the sanction of foreign imperial powers, but most often skippers simply relied on local demand for slaves and the informal tolerance accorded by local officials.[4]

4. Transport, Sept. 8, 1655, Not. Arch. 1704, 725, Not. P. [de Bary], SA (quotation). The WIC became an official subcontractor for the Spanish *asiento,* or slave trading contract, in 1662, but demand encouraged significant illegal trade to Spanish and Portuguese America before that time; see Henk den Heijer, "The West African Trade of the Dutch West India Company, 1674–1740," in Postma and Enthoven, eds., *Riches from Atlantic Commerce,* 160–162; Wim Klooster, *Illicit Riches: Dutch Trade in the Caribbean, 1648–1795,* Koninklijk Instituut Voor Taal-, Land-en Volkenkunde, Caribbean Series, no. 18 (Leiden, 1998). For slave-trading destinations, see Johannes Menne Postma, *The Dutch in the Atlantic Slave Trade, 1600–1815* (Cambridge, 1990), 27; Ernst van den Boogaart and Pieter C. Emmer, "The Dutch Participation in the Atlantic Slave Trade, 1596–1650," in Henry A. Gemery and Jan S. Hogendorn, eds., *The Uncommon Market: Essays in the Economic History of the Atlantic Slave Trade* (New York, 1979), 353–375; Emmer, "The Dutch and the Making of the Second Atlantic System," in Barbara L. Solow, ed., *Slavery and the Rise of the Atlantic System* (Cambridge, 1991), 75–96.

The varied circuit of seventeenth-century Dutch ships reflected the widespread pattern of Dutch economic involvement throughout the Atlantic. The Dutch commercial empire and its free-trade ideology meant that New Netherland was just one stop in a wide array of ports. In 1642, for instance, a skipper from Delftshaven took his ship *Propheette Salomon* from Madeira to "Badstoen in Nieuw Nederlant" with a shipment of wine, as his crewmen later explained at his request. Although the skipper and his sailors evidently paid little heed to the imperial boundaries that placed Boston in New England, they were perfectly clear about which ports would allow him to sell goods for a profit. The sailors, soldiers, and colonists on Dutch ships frequently followed even more complex trajectories than the ships themselves. Edward Agerd, a WIC soldier from London, came ashore in New Amsterdam in 1642, looking for a way to collect the wages that he had earned during his service on Curaçao. He chose to empower William Harley "[from] Middlesex," who stood ready to depart for Holland to secure them for him. Comrades such as Agerd and Harley split up midway through their circles around the Atlantic, dividing their time between more than one WIC ship and stopping over ashore in multiple and unexpected places.[5]

5. Testimony, Mar. 30, 1643, ONA 95, 178/289, Not. J. van Aller Andriesz, GAR ("Badstoen"); Empowerment, Aug. 5, 1642, in *Provincial Secretary*, II, 58–59 ("[from] Middlesex," 58). William Harley's name is given in the document as Willem Harle. Because the demand for sailors increased at a greater rate than the population throughout the seventeenth century, many foreign sailors worked Dutch merchant vessels during this period. But outsiders could have found it difficult to find places on the smaller ships making safer, shorter, and well-paid journeys to European ports or fishing spots. Foreign sailors were more likely to find work on WIC or VOC ships. Before the 1720s, approximately 25 percent of VOC crews were born outside the Netherlands; see J. Lucassen, "Zeevarenden," in L. M. Akveld, S. Hart, and W. J. van Hoboken, eds., *Maritieme geschiedenis der Nederlanden*, II, *Zeventiende eeuw, van 1585 tot ca. 1680* (Bussum, Netherlands, 1977), 132–133; Jan de Vries, "The Population and Economy of the Preindustrial Netherlands," *Journal of Interdisciplinary History*, XV (1985), 668–669. About half of the male labor market in the core provinces in the republic period drew on foreign workers; see Jan Lucassen, "A Multinational and its Labor Force: The Dutch East India Company, 1595–1795," *International Labor and Working-Class History*, no. 66 (Fall 2004), 12–39. Documentation makes it difficult to assess WIC sailors, but there is no reason to assume rates were significantly different from the VOC. The ethnic diversity of sailors on company ships serves as a reminder that strategies used by WIC and VOC sailors could very well have prevailed among sailors working the ships of other imperial powers, such as Harley and Agerd's home country of England. Willem Usselincx might have been the loudest voice among the pamphlet press upholding the virtues of free trade on an international level; he had a special interest in the West Indies and the New World. See [Willem Usselincx], *Vertoogh, hoe nootwendich, nut ende profijtelick het sy voor de vereenighde Nederlanden te behouden de vryheyt van te handelen op West-Indien....* ([1608]).

Such itineraries were commonplace, and travels did not necessarily end just because people decided to try their hands as settlers, even for those at the lower rungs of economic life. Soldiers and sailors became colonists for a time, only to take to the sea again later. Cornelis Barentsz van Amsterdam followed this kind of mixed trajectory before finally returning to Amsterdam in 1642. He "shipped out as gunner with the ship *De Griffien* to Curaçao, from there passing on to *De Neptunus,* on which he went to New Netherland" before traveling back to Amsterdam aboard the *Eyckenboom.* His journey around the Atlantic evidently took so long that his very identity came into question. When he returned to Amsterdam, he needed some proof that he was "the same person as Cornelis Barentsz as above and no other." He found two travelers willing to testify that they knew him from their time in New Netherland, with one witness saying he had known Barentsz "already more than six years." Similarly, Jan Jans, commonly called Jan de Wael, spent more than eight years in Brazil and New Netherland as a cooper in the service of the WIC before heading home in 1647, only to drown when the ship *Prinses* sank off the Welsh coast. "Fished from the water" shortly after death, this Rotterdammer was buried near Swansea, as two survivors who "knew him very well" later testified. Such long and complicated journeys show the blurry line between traveler and settler. For Jan de Wael and those like him, New Netherland represented just one stop among many on a sojourn around the ports of the Dutch Atlantic that often lasted until death.[6]

Sex was not a barrier to this kind of mobility, even for those with few economic resources. Women sailed the seas as well, following the same complicated and mixed trajectories as men. Often, women traveled as a result of their connections to spouses and kin who went abroad as WIC employees. Bielke Harmans, whose husband had left Holland in 1646 as a soldier under Peter Stuyvesant bound for Curaçao and then New Netherland, appears, at first, to be the typical Amsterdam wife of a poor soldier, a man who had shipped out only when forced to by dire necessity but who presumably expected to return to the wife he left behind in Europe. She had only to wait in Amsterdam and scrape by as best she could without him. However, before his departure, he borrowed some ninety-seven guilders, almost certainly because he could not afford to outfit himself as a soldier otherwise. By 1648, with the semiannual rent day looming a month and a half away and no money on hand, Bielke chose to leave off waiting and become a traveler

6. Testimony, Apr. 9, 1642, Not. Arch. 1285, 52, Not. H. Schaef, SA ("shipped out"); Testimony, Oct. 23, 1647, ONA 392, 76/135, Not. J. Delphius, GAR ("Fished").

herself. She transferred the scanty two months' wages that she could collect from the WIC per year in her husband's absence to an Amsterdam master mason who assumed the debts for rent and her husband's outfitting. After a year and a half on her own, she was "intending and resolved to leave in order to join her aforesaid husband in New Netherland."[7]

Bielke's options might have been bleak—other women left behind by husbands working for the WIC and the VOC found themselves forced to resort to public charity—yet, marriage to a company employee abroad provided her with a lifeline that single poor women might not have had access to. As her case shows, having a husband employed at sea did present some women with an "out," giving them a way to escape the trap of urban poverty at home. Because a husband's potential future company wages could afford wives access to credit, marriage was a key to survival for many maritime women. Being poor with little to live on meant that women from seagoing families had little to leave behind if they chose to follow their husbands or family members overseas. As a result, the marital tie between husbands and wives often proved stronger than the local ties binding people to Amsterdam, pulling men and women alike out of their hometowns and onboard the ships sailing the Atlantic. Though women like Bielke struggled on the ragged edges of poverty, overseas voyages occasionally opened up new possibilities in the world beyond Amsterdam. By doing their best to take the escape offered by those Atlantic ships, Bielke and her fellow sojourners shaped this newly expanding world in perhaps unexpected ways.[8]

7. Debt acknowledgement, Mar. 12, 1648, Not. Arch. 1342, 15, Not. H. Schaef, SA (quotation). On the financial arrangements allowed by the VOC for paying small portions of wages to sailors' wives, see Danielle van den Heuvel, *"Bij uijtlandigheijt van haar man": Echtgenotes van VOC-zeelieden, aangemonsterd voor de kamer Enkhuizen (1700–1750)* (Amsterdam, 2005). Rotterdam's VOC wives received only ten to thirty-five guilders per year on average, far less than it would have taken to support one person, let alone a family; see Manon van der Heijden and Van den Heuvel, "Surviving Strategies of Dutch Seamen's Wives, 17th–18th Centuries," in Simonetta Cavaciocchi, ed., *Ricchezza del mare ricchezza dal mare: Secc. XIII–XVIII: Atti della "Trentasettesima Settiman di Studi,"* 11–15 aprile 2005, Istituto internazionale di storia economica "F. Datini," Prato, Serie II, Atti delle "Settimane di Studio" e altri Convegni, XXXVII (Florence, 2006), 1112. On the resulting poverty of WIC and VOC seamen's wives in Delft, see Ingrid van der Vlis, *Leven in armoede: Delftse bedeelden in de zeventiende eeuw (A life in poverty: Living off charity in seventeenth-century Delft)* (Amsterdam, 2001), 193–197.

8. Van der Vlis, *Leven in armoede*, 193–197; Annette de Wit, "Zeemansvrouwen aan het werk: De arbeidsmarktpositie van vrouwen in Maassluis, Schiedam, en Ter Heijde (1600–1700)," *Tijdschrift voor sociale en economische geschiedenis*, II, no. 3 (2005), 75–76; Van der Heijden and Van den Heuvel, "Surviving Strategies," in Cavaciocchi, ed., *Ricchezza del mare ricchezza dal mare*, 1110–1112. The need to provide help for seamen's wives and families was a common problem throughout the Atlantic world; see Ruth Wallis Herndon, "The Domestic Cost of

Even the poorest maritime Amsterdammers found means to cross the oceans in the wake of their family members. Sailors' and soldiers' wives sometimes managed to convince the WIC to allow them to set sail without paying any cash for their passage, deducting the money from their husbands' wages instead. Among the passengers traveling to the colony in 1655 could "be found the wife (named Seytie Wouters) and child of one Frans Allart, midshipman in service of the Company." WIC administrators reminded New Netherland authorities to subtract the cost of their passage in Allart's account book, since "the Company here has undertaken to pay it to the ship owners." Catarina Everstyn, wife of drummer Hendrick Jansen Sluyter, made the journey "with their two children (the one being a suckling and the other 3½ years old)" on similar terms in 1654, as did Magdalena Hendricx, wife of carpenter Jan Engelburcht, and her five children. Though getting credit at home in Amsterdam could be difficult, WIC policies made it possible to follow husbands and kin abroad even when cash was short.[9]

It might seem self-evident that poverty would limit the number of passages family members made, but it was certainly not always true that poor people only succeeded in crossing the Atlantic once. When families came to join a soldier or sailor husband in the Americas, the pattern of migration did not necessarily end. By 1661, Jonas Willemsz van Amsteldam, a former soldier in New Netherland, had returned to Amsterdam, but he was preparing to ship out again, this time for Africa. Typical peripatetic soldier? No

Seafaring: Town Leaders and Seamen's Families in Eighteenth-Century Rhode Island," in Margaret S. Creighton and Lisa Norling, eds., *Iron Men, Wooden Women: Gender and Seafaring in the Atlantic World, 1700–1920* (Baltimore, 1996), 55–69.

9. Directors to Peter Stuyvesant and council, May 24, 1655, NYCM, XII, 20, fol. 1, NYSA ("be found"); Directors to Stuyvesant and council, July 30, 1654, NYCM, XII, 9, fol. 2, NYSA ("two children"); Directors to Stuyvesant, July 7, 1654, in Charles T. Gehring, ed. and trans., *Correspondence, 1654–1658*, NNDS, XII (Syracuse, N.Y., 2003), 23. WIC directors repeatedly debated how much the company should promote immigration and population growth, but, by the 1650s, wives traveled on credit regularly. Higher-status women, such as Catharyna van Werven, wife of Long Island minister Johannes Polhemius, used this tactic as well (Directors to Stuyvesant and council, June 14, 1656, NYCM, XII, 39, fol. 3v, NYSA). In 1656, the practice of giving free passage on credit became official policy for the middling classes, when company directors resolved that "all craftsmen and farmers, who can show that they will be able to earn their living, shall receive on loan free passage there with their wives and children"; see Resolution, Mar. 9, 1656, Extracts from the Register of Resolutions of the WIC, New Netherland Papers, Bontemantel Collection, Rare Books and Manuscripts Division, NYPL. Even unmarried women could sometimes receive free passage. "Anneken de With, widow, and her three daughters" all traveled gratis about a month after the resolution was passed; see Resolution, Apr. 3, 1656, Extracts from the Register of Resolutions of the WIC, New Netherland Papers, Bontemantel Collection, Rare Books and Mss. Div., NYPL.

doubt. Yet, before heading for Guinea, he acknowledged a debt of seventy-eight guilders as "remainder from the larger sum for board and passage for him, his wife, and her brother on the . . . ship the *Gulde Bever* on the journey here" from North America. He might have been a peripatetic, but he traveled around the Atlantic in good company. Husbands and wives, together with children and other kin, might cross and recross the ocean a number of times. By taking out credit against soldiers' and sailors' wages, families of WIC workers turned employment into a resource, enabling them to become mobile throughout the Atlantic world. Whether that mobility in the end allowed them to escape poverty is unclear, but the opportunity to travel at least opened up prospects for trade and work abroad that differed from those available to Amsterdam's urban poor.[10]

That wives, kin, and in-laws succeeded in following WIC sailors and soldiers back and forth across the seas shows that, for those among the maritime poor, marriages and families persisted, even in the face of long and complicated itineraries. Yet, in addition to maintaining already established relationships, people also created new intimate and family bonds during their journeys. Just as family relationships enabled people to travel, travel itself led to the formation of new marriages. For some, making new personal and economic connections, particularly ties of marriage, might have been the point of traveling to begin with. Because so many men of marriageable age shipped out from Amsterdam as soldiers and sailors, some women in Holland found it hard to marry. Without marriage, economic survival for women was difficult. Unless a poor or middling woman wed, she could only be a member of someone else's *huysgezin,* or household, not the manager of her own, and her possibilities for social and economic advancement remained slim. The low pay servant women earned made marriage an appealing option to many, and the colonies often had an overabundance of young men. This imbalance was even more pronounced on the ships traveling between colony and homeland. Thus, when a single or widowed woman crossed the seas, she might have been hoping to improve her odds of finding someone she could marry.[11]

10. Debt acknowledgement, Dec. 31, 1661, Not. Arch. 1330, unpaginated, Not. H. Schaef, SA (quotation). For an example of a woman who lived a stunningly mobile life as she followed family members across the Atlantic and Indian Oceans throughout the British Empire during a later period, see Linda Colley, *The Ordeal of Elizabeth Marsh: A Woman in World History* (London, 2007).

11. De Vries, "Population and Economy," *Journal of Interdisciplinary History,* XV (1985), 668–670; Danielle van den Heuvel, *Women and Entrepreneurship: Female Traders in the Northern Netherlands, c. 1580–1815* (Amsterdam, 2007), 19; Lotte Constance van de Pol, *Het Amsterdams*

New Netherland employers certainly feared that young servant women would do exactly that, and masters and mistresses included restrictive, sometimes vindictive, antimarriage clauses in the servitude contracts they made with the young Amsterdam women they hired as maids and paid to bring across the seas. Many settled for obliging their maids to repay "the freight and board" of bringing them over, as Annetgen Gerrits agreed to do if she married within her three years of service. Others demanded that all wages be forfeited or that servant women who married pay a fine. In 1639, Clara Matthys's master, Jonas Bronck, insisted that, if she married before her time expired, she would have to pay back her wages, the expenses of her own passage, plus "the cost . . . of sending someone else there," in addition to any other expenses, damages, or interest. Employers' frustrations are perhaps understandable. To find a new maidservant to replace Clara if she married, Bronck would have had to hire one on his next trip to Amsterdam or empower someone else willing to do so on his behalf, taking the gamble, sight unseen, that the woman would suit.[12]

The long delays such a change would entail might force a family to hire locally to find help for a mistress, and African women, among others, certainly did do paid and unpaid work within burgher households. Yet, the continuing demand for such domestic workers, as suggested by New Netherland burgher families' repeated calls for increased supplies of slaves, indicates that finding such help might not have been easy. Locking a young Amsterdam woman into a contract for several years probably seemed like the more expedient option. While policy makers saw the continued importation of young women as a benefit to the colony, individual employers' interests were to keep maids in their own homes as long as possible. Employers' fears that such young women would find a way to escape their bondage through marriage illustrate just how important women's work was to nascent burgher households, and the demand for such servant women led to continued female mobility across the Dutch Atlantic.

Perhaps unsurprisingly, new relationships began before ships even reached America, despite all employers did to prevent them. When a gunner on the *Brant van Troyen* approached New Netherlander Andries Hud-

hoerdom: Prostitutie in de zeventiende en achttiende eeuw (*Prostitution in Amsterdam in the seventeenth and eighteenth centuries*) (Amsterdam, 1996), 108.

12. Servitude contract, Apr. 29, 1653, Not. Arch. 1349, 48v, Not. H. Schaef, SA ("freight and board"); Servitude contract, Apr. 28, 1639, Not. Arch. 1555, 591–593, Not. J. van Oli, SA ("the cost").

den during one transatlantic crossing on behalf of a friend with an offer to "reimburse him for the passage, [board] and other expenses which he had incurred for Maddelena Michiels," a maidservant, he got an angry response. "Hudden answered . . . [that] I should take away the cow and the calf also and that he did not wish to have any whore in the house." Though beginning a relationship too quickly might not do one's reputation any good, a woman on board a ship full of eager young men knew she had decent odds of finding one she could live with, if she survived her time at sea. Women of limited means, like Maddelena, used employment to become mobile, but they used that mobility to escape employment by getting married. Marriage to a sailor, for a single servant woman, was not simply a matter of having a romantic seaborne adventure; instead, it was about creating a relationship essential to her ability to survive and rise economically. Women's opportunities to use intimacies formed during their travels to improve their economic status angered their would-be employers but shows quite clearly the connection between marriage and economic standing for seventeenth-century women, even in the most mobile of contexts.[13]

Women who formed new associations with one another and with sea-going men as they traveled wove an intricate network of personal relationships that stretched from ship to ship and port to port. Complicated testimony in 1645, based in large part on what had been heard through word of mouth, by Skipper Lourens Cornelisz van Catwijck detailed the adventures of three such women at sea. He reported that he met two *vrouspersonen,* or female people, "the one named Jannetgen Willems commonly known as Pretty Bride, and the other being the wife of the honorable Mte. Jacob who in that time [worked] as surgeon in the service of the . . . Company," in Curaçao and that these two women told him that "they along with one other

13. Declaration, June 1639, in *Provincial Secretary,* I, 190–191 ("reimburse," 190–191, "Hudden answered," 191). For a survey of young female servants' experiences in Holland that indicates Hudden's concerns about a whorish maid might have been widely shared, see Derek Phillips, *Well-Being in Amsterdam's Golden Age* (Amsterdam, 2008), 79–93. On the stereotype of servants as lustful husband hunters, see Marybeth Carlson, "A Trojan Horse of Worldliness? Maidservants in the Burgher Household in Rotterdam at the End of the Seventeenth Century," in Els Kloek, Nicole Teeuwen, and Marijke Huisman, eds., *Women of the Golden Age: An International Debate on Women in Seventeenth-Century Holland, England, and Italy* (Hilversum, Netherlands, 1994), 87–96. Hudden's suggestion that Maddelena was already pregnant seems to have reflected his own stereotypes and his anger about losing his maid so quickly; because the story was retold before a notary, hearers evidently thought it slanderous rather than a simple statement of fact. On ministers' apparent toleration of pregnant brides in seventeenth-century Amsterdam, see Herman Roodenburg, *Onder censuur: De kerkelijke tucht in de gereformeerde gemeente van Amsterdam, 1578–1700* (Hilversum, Netherlands, 1990), 255–257.

named Sijtge Pieters . . . had sailed out from [Amsterdam] with the ship *St. Jacob* . . . destined for Brazil, where they were also sailing." Though he first identified one of the women as the wife of the surgeon, he was evidently referring to a time before she married. Underway, the ship put in at the island of Saint Vincent for supplies, where the three single women met a gunner named Cornelis de Boer from the ship *Barquelange.* Sijtge Pieters and the gunner quickly married at sea. A new tie among the three female voyagers and a new marriage, therefore, grew out of these women's travels.[14]

Rather than ending these women's adventures, marriage came in the middle of their voyage; mobility continued to shape their lives after marriage, just as it had before. After Sijtge Pieters's shipboard union, "the same three female people sailed to Curaçao . . . without husbands." At Curaçao, the other two women married also. The skipper then went on to explain that he set sail from Curaçao with one pair of the newlyweds, Jannetgen Willems and her husband, with the intention of returning to Holland. But hostile winds kept them idled too long, and the ship experienced "an absence of victuals underway," causing a change in plans. Putting in at Bermuda, the skipper left the newlyweds there and went on to Manhattan. After almost two months in New Netherland, he stood ready to try the passage to Holland again, and, this time, Sijtge Pieters, whom he had already heard so much about, came on board with her husband, Cornelis de Boer. How they had traveled from the Caribbean northward, he did not say. Once at sea, Sijtge became ill: "He found underway that the same Sytgen became very miserable with the *morbum gallicum*" and that she refused to see the ship's surgeon, "who [could] have cured her of it," so that the room where she stayed "stank so very foully that he . . . could not bear it therein." Sick as she was, Sijtge still lived when the ship finally reached Amsterdam. Sometimes sick and sometimes hungry, these three hearty women nonetheless took their place alongside men aboard the ships sailing the Dutch Atlantic, and, as they did so, they all changed their status from single to married.[15]

This skipper's testimony provides an intriguing glimpse of the ways in which the fluidity of the Atlantic shaped private life, even as personal relationships helped shape the culture of Atlantic mobility. The men and

14. Testimony, Oct. 9, 1645, Not. Arch. 1291, 193, Not. H. Schaef, SA. Jannetgen Willems is also called Jannetgen Willemsdochter; her nickname in Dutch is *Schoonbruyt.* The skipper did not know the name of the surgeon's wife. Sijtge Pieters was also called Sytgen in this document.

15. Ibid. The illness referred to here was probably syphilis; see M. de Vries et al., *Woordenboek der Nederlandsche taal* (The Hague, 1882–), s.v. "pok."

women aboard the Netherlands' Atlantic ships lived in a stunningly mobile and dynamic world. Amsterdam, Recife, Bermuda, New Amsterdam—all the ports of the Atlantic stood open to them, even if they did not always fully control where they went. They bounced from one port and one ship to another, as the new ties they formed underway pulled them in new directions. Far from being inimical to married life, travel and marriage went hand-in-hand. However, the work and family lives of those who initiated their unions at sea would be defined, for a time, by the ship, not the home. Yet, even without the house that made a family a huysgezin, marriage remained a central part of seventeenth-century Dutch social and economic strategies. Sometimes wives traveled with their new husbands, and sometimes they traveled without them, just as these three women sometimes stuck together and sometimes separated.[16]

Travel as a woman had plenty of risks. In addition to the physical and medical hazards of life at sea that everyone endured, servant women afloat faced potential exploitation of their new master-servant relationships. A poor single woman might have felt she had scant protections at sea or on foreign shores. Doubtless being one of a few single women aboard a ship full of men would have been daunting or even physically threatening. Maritime travel for women was hardly unproblematic, and indeed it is testimony to just how bleak prospects were for poor women alone in seventeenth-century Amsterdam that setting sail, with all its obvious perils and unpleasantness, sometimes seemed preferable to staying ashore.[17]

16. In addition to coming aboard as passengers, women might have occasionally sought work on board while disguised as men, but they seem to have either been very rare or very rarely discovered. See L. Koelmans, *Zeemans lexicon: Woord en woordbetekenis bij Michiel de Ruyter* (Zutphen, Netherlands, 1997), s.v. "vrou persoon," for an example from 1653: "Today Captain Pyeter Bytter van Amsterdam brought 2 female persons on board to the Lord Admiral, who had hired themselves on as men." Female sailors who avoided discovery have to be understood as extremely successful performative men. Slave ships also, of course, contained female as well as male slaves, and African women served alongside men as "guardians" appointed by the crew to keep watch over other slaves; see Stephanie E. Smallwood, "African Guardians, European Slave Ships, and the Changing Dynamics of Power in the Early Modern Atlantic," *WMQ*, 3d Ser., LXIV (2007), 679–716 (quotation, 679).

17. Amanda Cathryn Pipkin points out that Jacob Cats, the preeminent moral poet in seventeenth-century Holland, referred to rape as an ever-present fear for all women, showing that it was a culturally recognized category of violence, which means that female travelers could well have sensed danger aboard ship; see Pipkin, "Every Woman's Fear: Stories of Rape and Dutch Identity in the Golden Age" (Ph.D. diss., Rutgers University, 2007), 1. For rape on a VOC ship, see François Pelsaert, *Ongeluckige voyagie van het schip Batavia....* (Amsterdam [1663?]), 14, 38. Rape was prosecuted extremely rarely, appearing in the church court records of Amsterdam only nine times between 1578 and 1700; see Roodenburg, *Onder censuur,* 302.

Rather than waiting, destitute and deserted, in home ports, some women from the maritime quarter or from families of those who worked the ocean clearly preferred facing the risks of transatlantic travel. And doing so often allowed them to form the intimate connection most crucial to their economic survival: marriage. Although life at sea is often imagined as the archetypal male world, such was not the case in the seventeenth-century Dutch Atlantic; ships carried European women and men alike, meaning that marriage and intimacies between women and men formed a part of shipboard life.[18]

The rarity of legal action may suggest that women surrounded by men, such as those aboard ship, might have felt that they had few protections against sexual assault. Yet, it is important not to dehistoricize rape or to assume that white women must have perceived it as a more likely threat aboard seventeenth-century ships than ashore simply because of the numerical predominance of men. Indeed, the crowded conditions onboard, where one's screams probably would have been overheard, might have felt "safer" to seventeenth-century Dutch women than life alone in a rented Amsterdam room or as a servant working in the confines of a male employer's house. Among the few cases of rape in Amsterdam church records are those of Maria van der Horst, a young single woman living alone, and two maidservants whose mistresses were not at home and whose cries, therefore, went unheard. On these cases and the centrality of the unheard cry in seventeenth-century ideas of rape, see Roodenburg, *Onder censuur*, 303–305. On the assumption by male employers, including Jacob Cats, that servant women were sexually available, see Phillips, *Well-Being*, 89.

18. Some writers continue to depict the seagoing world as a predominantly male world based on homosocial male bonds. Paul A. Gilje, for instance, elegantly reveals the interconnections between sailors and maritime women ashore but suggests that in the eighteenth and nineteenth centuries, American women and men in the maritime world lived in "separated sphere[s]," if not exactly separate ones; see Gilje, *Liberty on the Waterfront: American Maritime Culture in the Age of Revolution* (Philadelphia, 2004), 34, 59 (quotation). In nineteenth-century America, the maleness of shipboard life was so commonly culturally assumed that part of the appeal of shipboard work to black men was the possibility of living a "manly life" at sea; see W. Jeffrey Bolster, "'To Feel Like a Man': Black Seamen in the Northern States, 1800–1860," *Journal of American History*, LXXVI (1990), 1178 (quotation). For the British Atlantic of the eighteenth century, Jeffrey D. Glasco acknowledges the importance of competing concepts of gender and ideas of masculinity to class identity among sailors, but his investigation of "the impact of gendered divisions between men in the shipboard homosocial environment" is predicated on the maleness of ships; see Glasco, "'The Seaman Feels Him-self a Man,'" *International Labor and Working-Class History*, no. 66 (Fall 2004), 42 (quotation). The model of male ships versus female seashore does not fit with the patterns of the seventeenth-century Dutch Atlantic. Viewing seafaring men in the context of their kinship and neighborhood ties to maritime communities and maritime women can help disrupt the tendency to depict all seafarers on Atlantic-borne ships as (exclusively male) deracinated proto-proletarian workers and can remind us that "the Hobbesian world of oppressed Jack Tars serving in ocean-going factories existed alongside locally based, family-run coasting vessels operated along the lines of family farms, with a wide array of labor arrangements in between"; see Michael J. Jarvis, "Maritime Masters and Seafaring Slaves in Bermuda, 1680–1783," *WMQ*, 3d Ser., LIX (2002), 604 (quotation).

Together, marriage and mobility enabled some maritime women to break into the world of small-scale colonial trade. Female travelers and their soldier and sailor husbands often acted as business partners, adding a transatlantic aspect to the financial union of marriage. When "Laurens Jans sailor and Annetje Cornelis, spouses living on the Manathans in New Netherland," were preparing to sail home to America from Amsterdam in April 1655, both signed a debt acknowledgement for 120 guilders for "merchandise" loaded in the ship *Bontekoe*. The couple agreed to pay it "from New Netherland with the first ship [sailing] around next All Saint's day," or, failing that, they would be liable for interest of "twenty per cent per year, beginning next All Saint's day." This loan was a significant risk for the couple, but, by borrowing on credit, they had the chance to participate in the overseas economy through trade, not just through Laurens Jans's work aboard ship. It is very unlikely that Annetje Cornelis could have taken out such a loan to buy trade goods as a single unemployed woman unless she had access to significant collateral that went unmentioned in the contract. Her husband's wages provided the lender some assurance that the capital and interest might be recoverable if the goods failed to appear on the "first ship." As married yet mobile women, Annetje and other wives at sea gained access to credit and trade by building on their husbands' employment.[19]

Over time, marriage and mobility allowed some maritime women with limited means to carve out niches for themselves that offered financial stability or perhaps, at best, a means to rise economically. One woman's itinerant life in the 1640s points to the way mobility and family provided the basis for economic survival or even success. Geertge Nanningsdochter, a thirty-year-old widow in Amsterdam in 1641, decided to try her luck as a colonist in the private patroonship of Rensselaerswijk. She did not go abroad alone, however, but took along her son, daughter, and a maidservant. Her first connection to New Netherland was a servitude contract she signed with the patroon of Rensselaerswijk, yet, at the same time, the contract reiterated preexisting family bonds by binding her along with her children and servant. Her choice to sign the contract shows the contradictions of her economic status. Her contract bound her as a dependent of Kiliaen van Rensselaer's family, and she needed their resources to make the journey across the Atlantic. Only by drawing on the capital of a high-status family, whose patriarch was one of the principal directors of the WIC, was Geertge Nanningsdochter able to become mobile. But, her widowhood and the fact that she had a maidservant

19. Debt acknowledgement, Apr. 15, 1655, Not. Arch. 2054, 142v, Not. J. Hellerus, SA.

of her own suggest that she had perhaps not always been without means. Her journey abroad had the potential to allow her to regain her footing financially or, alternatively, to fix her in the position of a contract laborer.[20]

On her arrival, Geertge Nanningsdochter almost immediately formed new intimate ties in New Netherland. Both she and her servant, Jannetje Theunisz, benefited from the many marriage options there, and, in December 1641, very shortly after their arrival, both married on the same day. Geertge Nanningsdochter quickly began building a new huysgezin as the wife of Abel Henricxsz Riddenhaes; just over nine months after their wedding, the couple baptized a baby boy. Despite the roots she was creating in the colony, she did not stay long. By the summer of 1644, again a widow at thirty-three, she set about selling the house and lot she inherited along the East River and preparing to return to Holland. Even after her departure, however, her financial connections to the colony persisted. Once she returned to Amsterdam, she had to empower another widow-traveler, Susanna Rudolvin, to oversee the sale of her Manhattan property a second time when the first buyer defaulted. Though she struggled to capitalize on her property from across the ocean, her time as a married woman in New Netherland had left her with an important financial asset.[21]

Geertge Nanningsdochter's transatlantic adventures do not end there. Her continued travel serves as a reminder of the mobility of women's lives in the seventeenth century, both geographically and in terms of their economic status. By 1646, she began to ready herself for another Atlantic crossing. Her preparations show how familial connections among travelers enabled small-scale, long-distance exchange. Her eldest son, then eighteen years old, had bound himself to serve the WIC and stood ready to depart for New Netherland aboard the *Prinses* in July 1646. His mother intended to go with him. Assisted by a fellow traveler also headed to New Netherland, the mother and son contracted to borrow one hundred guilders from an Amsterdam widow for "outfitting for this journey and other." Having experienced New Netherland's trading economy before, Nanningsdochter knew the benefit of taking along goods on credit. Although half the sum could be collected out of her son's WIC wages, the other half she promised to repay at the first opportunity in "wares or transferred accounts" sent home from New Nether-

20. Servitude contract, July 11, 1641, Not. Arch. 1054, 67v–68, Not. J. van de Ven, SA.

21. Samuel S. Purple, ed., *Records of the Reformed Dutch Church in New Amsterdam and New York: Marriages from 11 December, 1639, to 26 August, 1801*, Collections of the New-York Genealogical and Biographical Society, I (New York, 1890), 11; Deed, Aug. 2, 1644, in *Provincial Secretary*, II, 243–244; Empowerment, Oct. 17, 1644, Not. Arch. 1862, 451, Not. J. Steur, SA.

land. This deal shows that she used a male family member's WIC wages as the basis for credit, as did many poorer Atlantic travelers. Yet she had also learned during her previous journey how the transatlantic economy worked. She knew that "wares and transferred accounts" shipped across the ocean through personal networks provided handsome returns, and that she took half the debt on herself suggests she was not without economic resources, even though her son signed on as a low-level, low-paid WIC employee.[22]

Geertge Nanningsdochter and her son set sail aboard the *Prinses* in its trip first to Curaçao and then on to North America as part of the historic journey that took Governor Stuyvesant to North America for the first time. Following the pattern she had established before, Nanningsdochter created new personal bonds in the colony in short order after her arrival. In July 1647, she married for the third time, to Claes Jansz Kust. The following June in New Amsterdam, Geertge and Claes baptized their first son, named for his father, with her eighteen-year-old daughter from her first marriage standing by as one of the witnesses. They would have at least one more son, Johannes, a few years later. Though she had traveled incessantly in the 1640s, Geertge nonetheless managed to create a widening circle of family in New Netherland. Her travels suggest the ways in which financial and familial concerns alike lured even women of modest means to make the trip across the ocean multiple times. Each time that women crossed the ocean, they established new connections, both economic and familial, that served to continually recreate and renew the links between colony and homeland.[23]

Geertge profited from her travels and the connections she formed. Her marital adventures did not end with her wedding to Kust. Widowed again at forty-two, she took to ship once more—although, this time, she only went as far as the upriver communities of Fort Orange and Beverwijk. There, she resisted the duplicitous advances of Rut Arentsz, who offered her a ring for sex with the dubious promise to make it all legal later, choosing instead to marry Willem Bout. Together, the pair had many financial advances and reverses, but they took part in the beaver-skin trade with the nearby Mohawks, operated a mill, tapped liquor, and generally lived the diverse, productive life of colonists who had managed to establish themselves economically. She built

22. Debt acknowledgement, July 21, 1646, Not. Arch. 1340, 69v, Not. H. Schaef, SA. The deal went awry, and the pair soon stood ready to depart without having received their promised loan, but they very well might have received it by the time they embarked.

23. Purple, ed., *Marriages*, 14; Thomas Grier Evans, ed., *Records of the Reformed Dutch Church in New Amsterdam and New York: Baptisms from 25 December, 1639, to 27 December, 1730*, Collections of the New York Genealogical and Biographical Society, II (New York, 1901), 24, 33.

these varied activities on the marriages she formed and the mobility she repeatedly chose. She drew on the resources of patroon and company to cross the ocean, and, each time she did, she married once more and continued improving her economic status.[24]

The lives of women like Geertge Nanningsdochter illustrate how extensively personal life in the early modern period could be transformed by the mobility of the Atlantic world. Family not only persisted despite the vast distances that separated people but also grew out of the experience of travel itself. Old relationships stretched across the ocean, hope of future ties drew people across the seas, and new intimacies were born aboard ships. Seeing these connections reveals how people at the lower end of the social ladder shaped and made use of the Atlantic economy. Lacking the capital to become investors in overseas merchant companies, they participated in the imperial economy more directly, through the movement of their own bodies rather than the movement of their money. They achieved this mobility by going into the service of the WIC or wealthy families. Male soldiers and sailors together with their female kin and companions embodied the mobility of the Dutch Atlantic empire. They sustained this economy not only through their work at sea and on land but also by becoming functional economic actors themselves through marriage. Company wages provided the basis for credit, enabling women and men to remain mobile and to enter transatlantic trade through small ventures. For some, the boundaries of status proved porous enough that they were able carve out economic spaces for themselves, if not rise economically, as Geertge Nanningsdochter did. Trading on the possibilities offered them by the larger-scale entities of company and patroonship, these maritime workers and travelers built a separate small-scale

24. Rut Arentsz's ill intentions are suggested by the fact that he might have pulled the same ruse on another woman. Geertge Nanningsdochter told her story in court only after Rut called that woman a whore and refused to marry her. By 1655, she appeared in court as Bout's wife; see Court minutes, Feb. 18, Mar. 4, Apr. 29, 1653, Aug. 26, [1655], Sept. 20, Nov. 30, 1655, in Charles T. Gehring, ed. and trans., *Fort Orange Court Minutes: 1652–1660*, NNDS, XVI, pt. 2 (Syracuse, N.Y., 1990), 44–45, 53, 207, 209. On the couple's tavern keeping, see Janny Venema, *Beverwijck: A Dutch Village on the American Frontier, 1652–1664* (Hilversum, Netherlands, 2003), 304. On the need to engage in diverse economic activities to survive as a fur-trading family in Beverwijk, see Martha Dickinson Shattuck, "Women and Trade in New Netherland," *Itinerario*, XVIII, no. 2 (1994), 40–47. Such strategies of mixed economic activities were also practiced in one similarly sized North Holland town in the same period; see A. Th. van Deursen, "The Trades in the Village of Graft," in Elisabeth Paling Funk and Shattuck, eds., *A Beautiful and Fruitful Place: Selected Rensselaerwijck Papers*, II, trans. Charles Forceville (Albany, N.Y., 2011), 17–25.

economy that connected Atlantic ports together through the intimate bonds of marriage and family.[25]

Independent Networks and Families of Middle Means

Men and women with somewhat greater economic reach than soldiers, sailors, and maidservants also participated in the Atlantic economy based on their own mobility. People of officer and artisan status had more access to credit and family wealth than the often young, single men and women of the maritime poor. Yet, they, too, lacked the capital to become major participants in large-scale companies and partnerships. As middling-status women and men sought to engage in trade and establish businesses in the Americas, they worked to create a financial and mercantile system of their own to help them manage money and goods across the ocean as they operated outside the formal structures of the WIC. Such individuals likewise came to rely on marriage as one of the primary systems for sustaining their independent trade, but they also had wide circles of social connections to draw on. Dense intimate networks among middling families provided the structure and mobility people needed to turn new transatlantic associations to their personal, and familial, advantage. As they pursued their collective interests, these women and men helped structure the Dutch commercial empire in North America.

25. For the idea that the Atlantic world, because of the male social environment aboard ship, instead nourished the origins of class consciousness, see Peter Linebaugh and Marcus Rediker, *The Many-Headed Hydra: Sailors, Slaves, Commoners, and the Hidden History of the Revolutionary Atlantic* (Boston, 2000), 143–173. A brief historiographical discussion of this depiction's inappropriateness for the VOC, which was the largest European employer before the 1750s, can be found in Lucassen, "A Multinational and its Labor Force," *International Labor and Working-Class History*, no. 66 (Fall 2004), 30, which concludes that the persistence of older ritualized protest goals shows that Linebaugh and Rediker's idea of class consciousness is not a good fit for Dutch workers in the Indian Ocean. Women's role in the Dutch Atlantic, both ashore and afloat, suggests the need to go a step farther and to question the extent to which even employees aboard large ships belonging to a major company, such as the WIC, that sailed long-distance voyages should be seen as separate from the world of kinship, community, and patrimonial networks. Gendered social and economic roles could continue aboard Dutch Atlantic ships because of the presence of even a few women aboard, and economic and social ties often linked sailors to their own families and to the wives of their skippers and officers ashore. Geertge Nanningsdochter and others show that, at least for the seventeenth-century Dutch Atlantic, early modern social and economic patterns of identity and behavior, with kinship, gender, and status at their heart, seem far more likely to have prevailed than the class-based ones suggested by Linebaugh and Rediker.

Because middling-status families brought more capital and resources into their overseas lives, travelers seem to have created more complex networks of social and economic contacts than did many of their poorer shipmates. Rather than relying primarily on immediate family connections, middling-status sojourners and colonists developed broader networks that united communities. The families who took part in the Dutch attempt to colonize and establish plantations in Brazil, for instance, set up networks of financial and personal connections with one another that survived transplantation to New Netherland as the Dutch were gradually militarily displaced from the Pernambuco area. As former settlers of Brazil moved on to other parts of the Atlantic, the economic and personal alliances they initiated in South America persisted. In 1655, for instance, the WIC ordered Governor Stuyvesant to give up his attempt to exclude Jews from New Netherland, citing the Brazilian background of some Jewish would-be emigrants. In light of the many Jewish losses in Brazil, administrators argued, exclusion ran contrary to reason and justice; they therefore granted the petition of a group of Portuguese Jews to travel to and trade with New Netherland. Together, these migrants formed a community that took part in local and transatlantic trade.[26]

Indeed, links between the Jewish community of Amsterdam and former Brazil colonists persisted long after the Portuguese recapture of Recife. The Dutch Reformed minister Johannes Polhemius and his wife, Catharyna van Werven, had lived in Pernambuco in the early 1650s, before returning to Amsterdam and later moving on to Long Island. While in South America, they lent the substantial sum of more than fifteen hundred guilders to a fellow colonist and then used that note to themselves obtain credit from Amsterdam merchant Abraham Cohen. Not until 1661, years after the couple had originally created these financial links, did Cohen receive payment and

---

26. Directors to Peter Stuyvesant and council, Apr. 26, 1655, NYCM, XII, 18, fol. 1, NYSA. For an analysis of the networks within and beyond the Atlantic Jewish population, see Wim Klooster, "Communities of Port Jews and Their Contacts in the Dutch Atlantic World," *Jewish History*, XX (2006), 129–145. Noah L. Gelfand argues that New Netherland's Jews represented several disconnected families, not a community, although he admits that Amsterdam Jews "were able to develop family networks" within the Dutch Atlantic; see Gelfand, "Jews in New Netherland: An Atlantic Perspective," in Shattuck, ed., *Explorers, Fortunes, and Love Letters*, 39–49 (quotation, 43). Jewish ties to Amsterdam reflected the fact that the city was one of the few places, even in the Netherlands, where they could live freely and practice their faith; see Lotte van de Pol, *The Burgher and the Whore: Prostitution in Early Modern Amsterdam*, trans. Liz Waters (Oxford, 2011), 44–45. On the importance of social networks among "minority religious groups" in providing credit and support for English Atlantic trade in ways that were even "more effective than family networks," see Nuala Zahedieh, *The Capital and the Colonies: London and the Atlantic Economy, 1660–1700* (Cambridge, 2010), 108 (quotations).

give them a receipt, finally closing the circle of debt that had tied them all together. Though the couple had moved from pillar to post during Polhemius's long career as a colonial minister, their financial bonds persisted in their new residence. For many in the Dutch Atlantic, the very mobility that might seem at first glance to have been so destabilizing ironically provided the connections that people used to structure their economic lives. The financial and commercial relationships that travelers of moderate means built with one another formed a thick economic transatlantic network that allowed them to stay bound to one another even as they continued to travel—together and separately—around the Dutch Atlantic.[27]

Just as people of limited means traveled incessantly around the Atlantic basin, so, too, did those of middling status. Married and single, female and male, these travelers moved around the ocean on the ships worked by their poorer compatriots. Yet, they were more likely to sail at their own expense, rather than as an employee or dependent of a master, company, or patroon. Their ability to book passage gave them the chance to take a larger cargo of goods along with them when they sailed. Perhaps a desire for marriage motivated single women of this station in life to take to the sea, just as it likely did for would-be maidservants, such as Maddelena Michiels. However, their ability to couple such journeys with trading ventures made their travels fulfill two goals at once. When Engeltjen Joppe, "single woman," planned to travel from Amsterdam in Holland to "Amsterdam in New Netherland" in 1659, she treated the journey as a business proposition. She contracted to take around one thousand guilders' worth of goods with her, payable when the ship Trouw returned home, at an interest rate of 22 percent. The size of her loan indicates a difference of scale between her and a servant like Maddelena and suggests she had access to significant economic resources. Travel, initiated for whatever reason, gave middling-status women the chance to trade.[28]

Just as the unmarried Engeltjen Joppe had assets in her own name, many married women of the artisanal and middling levels of Dutch society likewise had access to family resources and small businesses that husbands overseas sometimes sought to tap. A wife's business potentially provided a husband with the credit needed to survive in the cash-poor Atlantic economy.

27. Receipt, Mar. 25, 1661, Not. Arch. 3098, 71–72, Not. H. Rosa, SA. On the continuing role of Netherlandish traders in Spanish and Portuguese America after the fall of Dutch Brazil, see E. Stols, "No hay más Flandes en o tempo dos flamengos in koloniaal Amerika," De zeventiende eeuw, XXI (2005), 11.

28. Bottomry contract, Jan. 15, 1659, Not. Arch. 2206, 90–92, Not. A. Lock, SA.

Tomas Davitzen, husband of Claesje Gerritsz, an Amsterdam egg dealer, wrote a bill of exchange he expected her to pay on his behalf while he remained in New Netherland. His unusual, pleading address draws on letter-writing conventions and suggests that he hoped a hyperbolic reminder of their spousal tie would further his economic claims.

> Honorable, virtuous, dear wife, Claesje Gerritsz, egg merchant,
>
> You shall please pay my bill of exchange for the sum of one hundred fifty guilders within eight days of seeing this to the Honorable Rieuwert Jans or the shower of this,
>
> done in New Netherland, on the 26th of June, 1660.
>
> (was signed) Tomas Davitzen.[29]

Davitzen's appeal to marital obligation in this case fell flat. When Rieuwert Jans presented Claesje with the bill in Amsterdam in 1663, she merely replied "that she had nothing to do with this bill of exchange" and refused to pay. The legality of her refusal was far from clear. Although courts considered marital property to be a community of goods, husbands, under normal circumstances, were recognized as the sole managers and guardians of marital estates. That even her husband, however, referred to her status as an egg dealer suggests she might have been known as an *openbare koopvrouw*, or public businesswoman, and, as such, her earnings might have been deemed

---

29. Insinuation, July 11, 1663, Not. Arch. 2884, 435, Not. W. van Veen, SA (quotation). Davitzen addressed Claesje with the formal form of "you." Would-be merchants needed to acquire credit to trade both domestically and overseas, forming a challenge throughout Europe in the early modern period. London's individual merchants addressed this problem in the second half of the seventeenth century by building networks that shared credit, cost, and information, enabling them to outperform chartered companies in part by diversifying goods sold; see Zahedieh, *Capital and the Colonies*. Small-scale economic actors of middling status in Holland lacked the capital needed to get access to developing formal capital markets yet had goods valuable enough to act as collateral. Consequently, they frequently resorted to the pawn shops of Amsterdam, in addition to trading on their local status to receive shop credit, strategies unavailable to those below them on the economic ladder and unneeded by those above them; see Anne E. C. McCants, "Goods at Pawn: The Overlapping Worlds of Material Possessions and Family Finance in Early Modern Amsterdam," *Social Science History*, XXXI (2007), 213–238. Families of this status attempting to break into Dutch international trade combined the creation of networks with the use of personal property and small-scale businesses as collateral. On the Dutch early modern economy generally, including the shortage of cash and the importance of credit, see Jan de Vries and Ad van der Woude, *The First Modern Economy: Success, Failure, and Perseverance of the Dutch Economy, 1500–1815* (Cambridge, 1997); Violet Barbour, *Capitalism in Amsterdam in the 17th Century* (Ann Arbor, Mich., 1963).

immune from a husband's debts. Local courts tended to be inconsistent, but, whatever the legality of the situation, the existence of the bill of exchange to begin with shows that her husband had successfully gotten credit in New Netherland based on her economic status. Rieuwert Jans immediately made a formal demand for payment in the presence of a notary, signaling his intention of pursuing his claims in court. Like it or not, middling-status women like Claesje had access to assets that husbands might seek to put to use in the credit-based Atlantic economy.[30]

Not all wives of middling status were as reticent as Claesje Gerritsz to join in the transatlantic credit economy. In some debt contracts, wives put their own property at risk, along with their husbands'. Warnaer Wesselsz and Anna Elisabeth Masschop, who had determined to travel to New Netherland from Amsterdam in 1653, for instance, jointly placed all their "furniture, clothes, and jewels as they ... have here in this city" under special mortgage to Skipper Herman Cranen, with the understanding that if they died while underway or before returning to Amsterdam, he would sell it all to recover what the couple owed him, provided he also use the money to pay back Wesselsz's mother for what they owed her. Similarly, Siboult Rieuwertsz and Annitie Mulders, another married pair traveling together to New Netherland, backed their debt of one hundred guilders with the interest that Annitie claimed was due her as a mother from her late first husband's inheritance to their son. Married women of middling status often had assets, either as a part of marital community property or because of their own family ties. Their willingness to put these resources to use as collateral granted couples access to the credit needed to take part in Atlantic exchange. Whether such actions resulted in profit or in the loss of their property would depend on the vagaries of international markets for New Netherland goods like beaver skins. But their ability to draw on these resources illustrates the web of economic and familial connections that middling-status couples relied on as they established a financial system that allowed them to participate in overseas trade.[31]

Unable to hire factors to represent one end of transoceanic businesses yet able to afford occasional passage for themselves and their goods, mar-

30. Insinuation, July 11, 1663, Not. Arch. 2884, 435, Not. W. van Veen, SA (quotation). Claesje Gerritsz did not explain why she thought she was not legally obliged to pay. On married women's legal status and strategies used to avoid paying husbands' debts, see Van den Heuvel, *Women and Entrepreneurship*, 56–69.

31. Contract, May 9, 1653, Not. Arch. 1838, 218–219, Not. N. Kruijs, SA (quotation); Debt acknowledgement, Dec. 9, 1656, Not. Arch. 1840, [580–581], Not. N. Kruijs, SA.

ried couples of the artisan class and officer corps often traveled the ocean separately to create continuing circuits of exchange. New Netherlander Jan Evertsz Bout, bound for the fatherland from New Amsterdam in 1649, had utter confidence, no doubt born of experience, in his wife's ability to manage family finances in the dynamic Atlantic context. Bout empowered his wife, Tryntie Symons d'Witt, who would remain behind in New Netherland, "to demand and receive in his absence all such debts, cash and goods as may be due him here at the Manhatans, or elsewhere; also to satisfy and pay all that he may owe here or elsewhere and further in his absence to act as if he . . . were present." Before his departure, the couple also made a joint will that showed their close financial and personal cooperation. Being "of fairly advanced age," the pair made each other the full heir of all but a small sum, to the exclusion of all their blood relations, "in return for the love and fidelity shown to each other." This couple's careful preparation for separation shows that they knew the dangers of ocean travel, but they relied on the spousal tie between them to form the basis for transatlantic economic prosperity. By acting as partners, husbands and wives from the middle rungs of the social ladder better seized the opportunities of colonial trade; indeed, they recognized that their most intimate connection, with one another, represented the best tool they had to negotiate the mobility demanded by colonial realities.[32]

Because of people's constant movement and the separation of spouses that often ensued, middling wives in both America and Europe needed to know a great deal about the complex economies of a number of Atlantic

32. Empowerment, Aug. 19, 1649, in *Provincial Secretary*, III, 160 ("to demand"), Will, Aug. 19, 1649, 158–160 ("fairly advanced," 158). The empowerment was a necessary step; one should not assume that wives were able to act at law when husbands were away without one; see Van den Heuvel, *Women and Entrepreneurship*, 57; Susanah Shaw, "New Light from Old Sources: Finding Women in New Netherland's Courtrooms," *De halve maen*, LXXIV (2001), 9–14; De Wit, "Zeemansvrouwen," *Tijdschrift voor sociale en economische geschiedenis*, II, no. 3 (2005), 71. Acting as an agent was a common activity for New Netherland women. Of the eighty-four women who appeared in court in an eight-year period in Beverwijk, Martha Shattuck has counted sixty-six identifiably married women. Of those, fifteen acted as agents for absent husbands; see Shattuck, "Women and Trade in New Netherland," *Itinerario*, XVIII, no. 2 (1994), 44. Although local practice clearly allowed women to sometimes act at law in New Netherland without showing a written empowerment, at other times courts denied such women standing. The rates of women in court decreased at the end of the seventeenth century under English rule, but the limitations on their legal abilities during marriage were serious enough that one should avoid concluding that "the Dutch female occupied an exalted position"; see Sherry Penney and Roberta Willenkin, "Dutch Women in Colonial Albany," *De halve maen*, LII, no. 2 (Summer 1977), 8 (quotation).

port towns, and they depended on fellow travelers to provide them with that information. Given their husbands' frequent travel and the fluidity of the Atlantic world, financial survival obliged wives to wear many hats. Geertruyt Willems, for instance, had a husband who had spent the early 1630s in America but, by 1639, had sailed for the East Indies, leaving her behind in Amsterdam. Managing the family estate in his absence required her to seek formal testimony from a New Netherlander in Amsterdam on the value of her husband's farm there, including prices of livestock in the early 1630s. Geertruyt had to be able to prove, for instance, that a mare might have sold for two hundred guilders, whereas a pound of butter had fetched six stivers. Like many colonial farm wives, she needed to know the worth of butter versus pork fat on the local market, but the mobility of the Atlantic transforms the picture by making her an Amsterdam agent of the international economy. As husbands and wives moved around the Dutch Atlantic world, middling families could accumulate a range of property in various local economies. The wives in these economic partnerships not only needed diverse economic competencies, they also needed a host of fellow travelers, neighbors, kin, and social connections willing to provide information and support.[33]

The mobility of men and women around the ocean enabled families to keep track of property through verbal news networks. Travelers on board every ship carried not only goods but also information. The stories they told renewed the bonds of kin, trade, and property between those in far-flung reaches of the Dutch Atlantic. Since sailors often switched ships mid-route, someone who had been in a particular colony, or heard the news from someone who had, could well be aboard any ship arriving in Holland. In 1634, the Dutch seafarer and author Elias Herckmans described the shore at Den Helder, across from the island of Texel, as a place "where so many seamen land" and where one "hears so many strange tidings." The spoken transatlantic news network worked so efficiently that at least one Amsterdam investor felt letters did not need to cover events in New Netherland at all. Seth Verbrugge wrote to his cousin and American factor Govert Loockermans that he should not fill his missives with colonial updates. Verbrugge admonished that he could always learn about "the state of the country" from the "skipper and passengers" aboard New Netherland ships. The information these

33. Testimony, Mar. 3, 1639, Not. Arch. 1187, 2, Not. J. de Vos, SA. The testimony does not state when or if Geertruyt Willems ever lived in New Netherland herself.

travelers relayed to those waiting on shore had both personal and financial consequences.[34]

Tryntge Pietersz of Amsterdam, whose husband, Abraham Jacobsz, had gone to Fort Orange in New Netherland as a carpenter, heard the story of her husband's death through two returning travelers. The two testified that, beginning in September 1653, they had "had very good and familiar knowledge" of Tryntge's husband in Fort Amsterdam and that they knew for certain that he "was drowned there, on the Catskill, nine miles from the Fort Orange." However, they not only gave the widow news of her husband's death, they also testified before a notary at her request that they had been

34. E. Herckmans, *Der zee-vaert lof, handelende vande gedenckwaerdighste zee-vaerden....* (Amsterdam, 1634), 211 ("where so many"); [Seth Verbrugge] to Govert Loockermans, Mar. 26, 1648, Loockermans Correspondence, folder 3, doc. 2, NYHS ("state of the country"). Most studies of imperial communication have focused on documents; see David Cressy, *Coming Over: Migration and Communication between England and New England in the Seventeenth Century* (Cambridge, 1987), esp. 213–234; Ian K. Steele, *The English Atlantic, 1675–1740: An Exploration of Communication and Community* (New York, 1986). Expanding English commercial and administrative ties to India depended on voluminous scribal and printed documents; see Miles Ogborn, *Indian Ink: Script and Print in the Making of the English East India Company* (Chicago, 2007). A letter-writing revolution around 1700 allowed individual families to stay connected, personally and economically; see Sarah M. S. Pearsall, *Atlantic Families: Lives and Letters in the Later Eighteenth Century* (Oxford, 2008). These letters helped create the British Atlantic, as individuals pursued their own interests through written exchanges while collectively building the larger structures of empire; see Konstantin Dierks, *In My Power: Letter Writing and Communications in Early America* (Philadelphia, 2009). Yet, even in the eighteenth-century British Empire, the spoken word often preceded written documents; see Steele, "Time, Communications, and Society: The English Atlantic, 1702," *Journal of American Studies*, VIII (1974), 1–21. Verbal and written networks overlapped in the Netherlands; see Jeroen Blaak, *Geletterde levens: Dagelijks lezen en schrijven in de vroegmoderne tijd in Nederland, 1624–1770* (Hilversum, Netherlands, 2004), esp. 293–298. For those of middling status and below, who lacked formal factors and might not have been literate, spoken transatlantic networks served as the primary form of financial communication. Traces of these ephemeral, face-to-face interactions survive in the notarial archive. Women and men who heard news from travelers sometimes found it expedient to convert voices into ink by paying notaries to record testimony, especially since peripatetic speakers might soon sail away. These spoken communications served similar functions to eighteenth-century British letters. Although people relied on these oral networks in pursuit of particular familial interests, by initiating these essential communication structures, they created economic exchange systems and built empire. Though Dierks reserves the term "empire" for the more administratively unified political constructs of the 1700s, oral communication systems, existing even among those below the literate classes, allowed for the creation of the Dutch commercial system in the seventeenth century. If "much of the historical geography of empire is the history of ship-borne communication," then understanding the function of the spoken words carried aboard ships, alongside writing, can help reveal the geography of early modern empires; see David Lambert, Luciana Martins, and Miles Ogborn, "Currents, Visions, and Voyages: Historical Geographies of the Sea," *Journal of Historical Geography*, XXXII (2006), 479–493 (quotation, 486).

present "when [her] aforementioned husband's goods were publicly sold there." Such testimony was the first step for the widow in making financial claims on the WIC and her deceased husband's debtors, so, for Tryntge, news from abroad signaled a new phase in both her familial and economic life. Travelers bearing stories of those far away kept an eye on the transatlantic property of middling-level families and helped encode news about that property in written form so that it could serve economic purposes.[35]

Husbands and wives not only depended on a network of social connections to manage their overseas property, spouses also provided a crucial financial resource for the broader Dutch transatlantic community. The unity of marital finances across the ocean provided a way for others to transfer funds from colony to homeland. When Gerrit Jansz Klinckhamer provided some 205 guilders in board and cash to Pieter Heyn in New Amsterdam in 1649, for instance, he did not expect to be repaid in America. Rather, he stipulated that Heyn pay the sum to his wife, Geertien Abrahamsz, who lived in De Rijp, Heyn's own hometown in the Netherlands. Loans repayable to a spouse abroad functioned as an effective way for couples to transfer money across the ocean. That Klinckhamer's wife lived in the hometown of another New Amsterdam resident provided an important opportunity for the couple to renew the financial link between them. The immediacies of neighborhood brought into play in the transatlantic setting thus presented husbands and wives with a way to stay connected. Conversely, the tie between a husband and wife represented a financial asset for the wider Atlantic population. Since the WIC paid wages in Holland and beaver skins were turned into cash there as well, travelers were often cash-poor in America but expecting wealth at home. By contracting a debt with a husband in New Amsterdam payable to a wife in Europe, Heyn illustrated how the financial aspect of marriage acted as an important economic resource for others. Transactions like this renewed the economic bonds between spouses, while at the same time enabling transatlantic financial connections.[36]

Given the central role spousal bonds played in managing the economic life of families as well as wider communities, it makes sense that gossip and

35. Testimony, Aug. 25, 1655, Not. Arch. 2055, 113, Not. J. Hellerus, SA (quotations). Wives of VOC sailors similarly depended on news brought by returning sailors and travelers; see Van den Heuvel, "*Bij uijtlandigheijt*," 81–84. On one Rotterdam widow's attempt in 1650 to achieve economic stability by using a notary to transform stories heard through social networks into documents, see Douglas Catterall, "Drawing Lives and Memories from the Everyday Words of the Early Modern Era," *Sixteenth Century Journal*, XXXVI (2005), 651–672.

36. Bond, July 19, 1649, in *Provincial Secretary*, III, 119–120.

news telling put a premium on keeping marriages in order. Sometimes travelers, unaware of the effectiveness of these verbal networks, sought to use the fluidity of the Atlantic world to sever tethers to the past in favor of new lives abroad. For example, Jan Pietersz, skipper of the ship *Fortuyn,* tried to leave his married life behind when he crossed the Atlantic. On a trip from Barbados to Boston, two of his sailors claimed that he became engaged to a woman named Belitie, who was traveling as a servant of the former director of Rensselaerswijk, Arent van Curler, and his wife. The two married in Boston, the sailors reported, which they knew for certain since they themselves received invitations to and attended the June wedding. With this marriage, Belitie seemed to be using the geographic mobility provided her by her employer to achieve economic mobility by changing her status from a low-paid servant to a skipper's wife. No one knew at the time, however, "that the aforementioned Jan Pietersz still had a wife living in the fatherland." Indeed, when the two sailors returned to Holland in January 1650, they met that very wife, Niesge Gerrits, and went before a notary at her request to tell all that they knew. In the personal, face-to-face social world of maritime Amsterdam, the encounter between the skipper's wife and a wedding guest was probably inevitable. The skipper perhaps thought that, by putting an ocean between himself and his spouse, he had escaped the marriage and all of the legal and financial baggage that went with it, but the sailors' testimony reveals his misunderstanding. The news networks that spanned the seas put an emphasis on marriage and family ties, which often formed the basis for transatlantic trade and finance, making anonymity a scarce commodity.[37]

When wives of this class moved around the ocean themselves, they not only assumed a lack of anonymity, they actively traded on their husbands' names and positions as officers and business owners. Their ability to get credit hinged on their status as the wives of craftsmen and officers. When Jannetgen Jans prepared for her journey to New Netherland in 1648, she proudly told the notary that she did so as the "wife of Jurrien Andriess, who sailed out in 1646 as Constable with the Yacht the *Groote Gerrit* in service of the West India Company here, and who is now skipper on the ship *de Liefde,*" and who also served under Governor Stuyvesant on his historic 1646

---

37. Testimony, Jan. 14, 1650, Not. Arch. 1093, 54, Not. J. van de Ven, SA (quotation). On formal and informal monitoring and punishment of marriage abuses, including bigamy, see Manon van der Heijden, "Misdrijf en zonde: Sociale controle van huwelijksgedrag in Holland tijdens de Vroegmoderne Tijd," *Tijdschrift voor sociale geschiedenis,* XXVII (2001), 281–308; Van der Heijden, "Punishment versus Reconciliation," in Roodenburg and Spierenburg, eds., *Social Control in Europe,* I, 55–77; Roodenburg, *Onder censuur,* 305–309.

journey to the colonies. Borrowing 146 guilders for her "outfitting" aboard the merchant ship *Valckenier,* Jannetgen promised to repay the amount by the end of the coming September "with goods, that she shall send from New Netherland." Her trading activity reflected her strong identity as a maritime officer's wife, as shown by her detailed recitation of her husband's past postings and current status. She went on to stake her portion of her husband's WIC wages as collateral for the debt, thus employing a strategy that would have been familiar to poorer soldiers' and sailors' wives who relied on their husbands' WIC employment to get passage to the colony. For her, trading grew out of her preexisting relationship to the maritime world through her officer husband.[38]

Some middling-status women traveled repeatedly between the colony and the homeland to pay off earlier contracts and make new ones so that their families could continue to profit from colonial trade. During their journeys, they sometimes helped the families of other artisans and officers look after their overseas interests as well. When Marritgen Damen first departed to join her husband, Henrick Andriesz, a freeman in New Netherland, in 1651, she left behind a complicated financial and family network. In addition to empowering a "hide seller" in Amsterdam to collect her late first husband's wages "as well from the East as the West India Companies," Marritgen also left her children by her first marriage and their estate in the hands of their guardians and their aunt. But Marritgen's crossing to New Netherland in 1651 was just the first of many, it would seem; by 1655, she was again in Amsterdam, ready to depart once more for the colony. On this voyage, Marritgen agreed to act as an agent for an Amsterdam widow and beer wholesaler, who sought to collect some thirty-one guilders for delivered beer and costs from "Jelles Douwes distiller in New Netherland" and "his wife Hester." Traveling wives, therefore, helped create a small-scale financial system that aided traders working outside the formal construct of a company, even as they went about their own business. By continually renewing contacts between Europe and the Americas, their travels provided creditors and lenders with a support network when borrowers failed to pay; such actions made colonial trade safer and more feasible for small-scale, independent commerce.[39]

38. Debt acknowledgement, Mar. 28, 1648, Not. Arch. 1342, 20, Not. H. Schaef, SA.

39. Empowerment, Mar. 18, 1651, Not. Arch. 1300, 43–43v, Not. H. Schaef, SA ("hide seller"); Empowerment, Apr. 26, 1655, Not. Arch. 1305, 64, Not. H. Schaef, SA ("Jelles Douwes"); Empowerment, Nov. 4, 1655, Not. Arch. 1305, 112, Not. H. Schaef, SA. The documents suggest, though they do not state, that Damen went to the colony without her children. By

Although women were willing to act as agents for others, they primarily crossed the ocean in service of their own family's economic interests. In Marritgen's case, she and her husband lived at Fort Orange, the heart of New Netherland's fur-trading country, and they both took part in the beaver-skin economy there. To profit from their fur trading, they cooperated as financial partners to export pelts to Amsterdam. By 1662, Marritgen had returned to Amsterdam again, this time accompanied by her husband. Together they declared themselves fully satisfied and gave a full receipt to "Mr. Gerrit Barentsz Kours, merchant here," for the three account books he kept of the "trade, which he has done and performed for them here since the year 1656 and thereafter, until [March 29, 1662], inclusive." In total, the couple received more than 870 guilders in hand from the merchant for that business. Such sums were beyond the reach of the maritime workers and maidservants who sailed alongside them. Marritgen's repeated ocean crossings need to be seen in the context of the family trading business that she was helping to build. Her mobility, her tie to her spouse, and her social connections with others of her status constituted an economic network that ran parallel to that of the WIC.[40]

Carrying out this kind of transatlantic business required skills. Women who wanted to establish their families in the ranks of middling-status traders needed to be able to negotiate the world of account books and contracts, as Damen successfully did. Illiteracy on the part of either a husband or wife made it difficult for small-scale actors to become large-scale traders. Some illiterate New Netherlanders turned to officeholders and administrators in order to use writing to support their family's economic ties. In 1662, Teunis Tomasz van Naarden appeared before the *burgermeesteren* of New Amsterdam "as he has heard that Burgomaster Paulus Leendersen has received a letter from his (Teunis') wife" and he wanted to know "what she writes." The mayors told him that, "whereas she owes, as he knows, 300 to 400 fl. to

---

1668, however, her daughter identified herself as a New Netherlander, so at some point her children joined her there; see Receipt, Oct. 20, 1668, Not. Arch. 1520, unpaginated, Not. J. Oli, SA. Marritgen and her husband went into the beer business themselves, buying a brewery with equipment in Beverwijk; see Conditions of auction, Dec. 11, 1656, in *Fort Orange Records,* II, 15–16, Surety for purchase, Dec. 11, 1656, 16–17; see also Conveyance, Feb. 10, 1657, 33–34.

40. Receipt, Apr. 3, 1662, Not. Arch. 2289, pt. 4, 45–46, Not. J. de Winter, SA (quotations). Marritgen sued "the wife of Jan Martensen" for fourteen and one half beavers in 1659 in the Fort Orange court; see Court minutes, Dec. 9, 1659, in Gehring, ed. and trans., *Fort Orange Court Minutes,* 472. For Damen in the context of the fur-trading town of Beverwijk, see Shattuck, "Women and Trade in New Netherland," *Itinerario,* XVIII, no. 2 (1994), 46.

several parties, he should send over enough beavers to pay these debts, and if he wishes her with him, he is to come." Although he was illiterate, Teunis Tomasz asked to have the letter and to have it read to him. Whether his wife wrote the letter herself or had someone write it for her, she found an ingenious way to communicate with her husband over great distances about both personal and financial matters. Doing so required her to turn to the more formal structures of New Netherland's administration, where literacy was a precondition for office and thus a resource high-status men possessed, even if her own husband did not. An ability to negotiate the world of writing independently was one of the skills women and men would need if they were to take full advantage of the opportunities offered by mobility.[41]

The failure to keep a clear written account of trading activities, for instance, bedeviled one New Amsterdam wife, Grietje Maes, when she tried to move into retail trade. Maes, who could "not read nor write," maintained that she had not been fully paid by Jacob Cohn for nails she had sold him, so she tried to place an arrest on his goods. However, Joost Goderus, keeper of the city scales, found that his books did not support Maes's position, and she faced prosecution for her actions. When the court asked her if she had any proof "that she had traded something more with the Jew, [she] answere[d] no, and that she cannot write." Maes was surrounded by text. The man from whom she had bought the nails wholesale showed his own "little account book," which he offered to affirm by oath; the keeper of the city scales had his written record; and Cohn supported his position in a letter that recorded the spoken details and insults he had faced over the nails. But this world of ink was closed to Maes, and, without an account book of her own, the court overturned her attempt to seize Cohn's goods. Moving into retail trading required skills that she did not have.[42]

Maes had similar struggles when she tried to carry on transatlantic trade on her family's behalf. In February 1661, Maes was in Amsterdam planning to return to her husband in New Netherland with 360 guilders' worth of beer to sell. She had a notary draw up a contract with Amsterdam merchant Augustyn Bouccaerdt, who promised to deliver twenty oxheads of beer to the ship *Vergulde Bever* on which Maes had booked her passage back to New

41. Minutes, Mar. 17, 1662, in Berthold Fernow, trans. and ed., *Minutes of the Orphanmasters Court of New Amsterdam, 1655–1663; Minutes of the Executive Boards of the Burgomasters of New Amsterdam; The Records of Walewyn van der Veen, Notary Public, 1662–1664* (New York, 1907), 131–132 (quotations). On the way illiterate people managed to participate in letter exchanges in the English Atlantic, see Cressy, *Coming Over*, 217–221.

42. Minutes, Aug. 20, 27, 1658, CMNA, II, 286, 292, NYCMA (microfilm).

Netherland. She promised to repay the capital plus 22 percent interest when the ship returned to Amsterdam. Her partner was obviously skittish, insisting that Maes find someone to cosign the contract. In response, she turned to one "Sir Eldert Verwer van Diemen," who promised to pay if she defaulted. However, Grietje failed to have her cosigner actually sign the contract itself, giving Bouccaerdt grounds to pull out of the agreement. A month and a half later, Bouccaerdt had yet to deliver the beer, and he refused to do so until she "gave him satisfaction" by providing an adequate cosigner. Otherwise, he threatened to hold her responsible for all risks and costs "of leakage, accidents, and also cellar rent" caused by keeping the beer in storage since their original agreement. Clearly at a loss, Greitje's only response to his new demand was to cry out, "What do you want me to do?" By the end of April 1661, Grietje's ship was ready "with God's help to depart for New Netherland [and] to set sail with the first good wind," but she still had no beer to take home. She issued a formal protest for fulfillment of the contract and for damages caused by the delay. Whether she succeeded in collecting the beer before departure is unclear, but her struggle itself is illuminating. Many other traveling wives managed to conduct their family's business successfully, but Grietje Maes struggled repeatedly. She could not negotiate the world of writing, either in an account book or a contract, and that disability limited her capacity to expand her family's economic reach and to climb into the ranks of retail merchants and overseas traders.[43]

If a woman had the necessary skills, her mobile economic activity helped her family build on employment with the WIC to establish itself within the colonial artisanal class. A dedication to navigating not only the ocean but the Atlantic financial system allowed some wives to carve out a new economic status for themselves and their families. Traveler and wife Janneken Jans van Leeuwarden discovered the hard way that the mobile life required fortitude and gumption. Janneken, a Friesland native, had moved abroad to live with her husband, Reinholt Reinholts, in Brazil sometime in the 1640s. While there, her husband loaned around one hundred guilders to Tomas ten Have van Deventer, clerk of the garrison's books and later a lieutenant. Ten Have died in 1648 before repaying, but Reinholt nonetheless still had a claim to present to the WIC offices to collect the sum out of the deceased officer's wages. Thus, when Reinholt's wife prepared to sail back to Amsterdam from

43. Contract, Feb. 12, 1661, Not. Arch. 2676, 189–190, Notary J. van Wijningen, SA ("Sir Eldert Verwer"); Demand, Mar. 30, 1661, Not. Arch. 2676, 241, Notary J. van Wijningen, SA ("gave"); Demand, Apr. 21, 1661, Not. Arch. 2840, 355–356, Notary D. Danckertsz, SA ("with God's help").

Recife on her own in 1650, he entrusted the written debt agreement to her. However, underway, Janneken's ship, the "frigate the *Wildeman*, . . . being come to England at the Isle of Purbeck, sank on 15 April last, shortly before midnight." Although Janneken and some others survived, the "ship and goods and around fifty souls [were] lost and drowned." Among the merchandise and documents lost was the proof of the loan to Ten Have. Despite her harrowing experience, Janneken still saw to her husband's financial claim when she reached Amsterdam. She sought out testimony from the former Recife notary public who had drawn up the original debt as well as from the official "comforter of the sick" there, both of whom had also been aboard the *Wildeman,* about the circumstances, so that she could still try to collect from the wic. No matter what she felt about her narrow escape from death, Janneken clearly understood that survival required staying afloat financially, too, and she did what she could to repair the damage that the shipwreck had caused.[44]

Though the dangers of transatlantic travel must have been all too clear to Janneken and Reinholt, they continued to see their future as tied to overseas trade and colonization; transatlantic travel remained a crucial part of their lives. In 1654, Reinholt was back in Amsterdam, having given up on Brazil, but he nonetheless readied himself to depart for New Netherland. Unfinished family business in Holland, however, meant that the couple had a significant unpaid claim of some 1150 "Kaiser's guilders" from "their Cousin Rinck in Leeuwarden." Leaving Janneken behind with an empowerment to settle the family business, Reinholt sailed for the Americas once again. Putting wealth that came from kin networks to work was essential if Janneken and Reinholt were to profit from their colonial adventures. The couple did not intend for Janneken to stay behind in the Netherlands forever, though. One year after her husband's departure, Janneken, too, prepared to depart for New Netherland. She had evidently settled the matter with "Cousin Rinck," but she had yet to collect for a claim the pair had on the wages "of one Adriaen Jans van Gendt, former soldier," which remained in the hands of a solicitor. To help create a network capable of forwarding the family interests while both of them lived abroad, Janneken turned to an Amsterdam shoemaker, Hendrick Kerckman, a member of the same guilded profession as her husband. Associations of guild and craft, therefore, stretched across

44. Testimony, Aug. 8, 1650, Not. Arch. 560, 146–146v, Not. J. Westfrisius, SA. The destruction of WIC records makes it difficult to know if Janneken managed to collect the debt, but the testimony of two such reliable witnesses would have gone far toward establishing her claim.

the ocean when needed. As members of the artisanal class, she and her husband had a dense web of social connections to draw on when they traveled.[45]

In addition to putting this guild relationship to work in overseeing a preexisting financial claim, Janneken used the connection with Kerckman to build a new transatlantic trading business. The shoemaker she entrusted before her departure in 1655 did more than simply collect an outstanding debt for the couple; he also became their Amsterdam representative in international trade. Just over three years later, Janneken returned to Amsterdam once again, while her husband remained behind working at his craft in New Netherland. Janneken gave Kerckman a receipt for having satisfactorily settled the accounts he maintained "from a certain commission and factorship done by him for and on their behalf since June 1655 until today, inclusive." Kerckman had sold "wares and merchandise sent by them from New Netherland to him," earning the couple more than 376 guilders. Janneken thus remade a preexisting tie into something new and different, into a reliable international economic relationship.[46]

As an expression of the transatlantic trading business she constructed, Janneken began to assert a legal identity that reflected the reality of her remarkable economic activities and shows how much things had changed for her and her husband since her days as the shipwrecked wife of a company employee. Although Janneken made clear that Kerckman had traded for the

45. Empowerment, June 16, 1654, Not. Arch. 561, pt. B, 69, Not. J. Westfrisius, SA ("Kaiser's"); Empowerment, May 10, 1655, Not. Arch. 1305, 74, Not. H. Schaef, SA ("Adriaen Jans"). Janneken's experience points out that, even though women were usually excluded from guild membership, guilds could still provide a basis for relationships that formed part of a woman's social capital, enabling her to engage in other areas of the economy. Scholars have emphasized the role of guilds in limiting early modern women's economic participation; see Van den Heuvel, *Women and Entrepreneurship*, 132, 175–176, 271–272; Sheilagh Ogilvie, "How Does Social Capital Affect Women? Guilds and Communities in Early Modern Germany," *American Historical Review*, CIX (2004), 325–359. For a brief overview of the exclusion of women from most guilds and the complications these policies could raise, see Maarten Prak, "Moral Order in the World of Work: Social Control and the Guilds in Europe," in Roodenburg and Spierenburg, eds., *Social Control in Europe*, I, 176–199, esp. 189–193. Yet Janneken offers a different perspective; she turned for credit to a connection within the shoemaker's guild, which related to the craft her husband practiced ashore, not the mercantile activities the couple carried out across the seas. No guild existed for transatlantic beaver-skin traders. If one had, it would have likely limited the ability of women, particularly married and single women, as opposed to widows, to take part in the trade. Therefore, a guild tie aided Janneken's economic activity precisely because the guild did not pertain to that activity but, instead, represented part of her larger social network.

46. Receipt, Nov. 6, 1658, Not. Arch. 1358, 103, Not. H. Schaef, SA.

married pair—giving a receipt based on an oral empowerment from her husband for trade done on "their" behalf—her independent travel around the Atlantic led her to carve out a legal status for herself somewhat different than that of a wife, just as she helped her family climb within reach of the lower ranks of the merchant class. Janneken began to name herself as a merchant or female trader, equal to the male merchants who sailed alongside her. She asserted to the notary that she not only had a verbal empowerment from her husband but that she "was also known to be a Businesswoman." Janneken thus concluded the family's transatlantic trade as a publicly recognized koopvrouw, giving a receipt on behalf of both "her and her aforementioned husband."[47]

In other words, just as her willingness to travel had allowed her to act as an agent of her family in the transatlantic economy, the traveling and trading that she did in turn allowed her to assert the legal status of a merchant woman. Given the legal restrictions on women and the limited sources of credit available to them, public recognition and trust was key to a woman's ability to operate successfully in business. Women in seventeenth-century Zwolle, for example, were forced to seek poor relief because they had lost public trust and credit after taking people's money for goods and then losing it. Janneken followed the opposite path. She overcame many obstacles and continued to meet her obligations, fulfill her contracts, and settle her debts; her success allowed her to claim trust, credit, and a new legal and economic status for herself and her family. Just as women helped transform social webs into transatlantic networks, participation in those networks could transform the status of such women and their families.[48]

Janneken's legal position and family status had been shaped by her colonial adventures, and she had no intention of turning her back on the international fur-trade economy, despite her presence in Amsterdam. Just a few months later, in January 1659, she began preparing for her return trip to Manhattan. Before she left Amsterdam, Janneken hired two men to work for her husband in his shoemaking business in New Netherland, promising to

47. Ibid.
48. On the difficulties of getting credit as a woman, see Anne E. C. McCants, "Petty Debts and Family Networks: The Credit Markets of Widows and Wives in Eighteenth-Century Amsterdam," 33–49, and Laurence Fontaine, "Women's Economic Spheres and Credit in Preindustrial Europe," both in Beverly Lemire, Ruth Pearson, and Gail Campbell, eds., *Women and Credit: Researching the Past, Refiguring the Future* (Oxford, 2001), 17. On the need to seek charity after losing access to credit, see Hilde van Wijngaarden, *Zorg voor de kost: Armenzorg, arbeid, en onderlinge hulp in Zwolle, 1650–1700* (Amsterdam, 2000), 242.

pay them their yearly wages "in good merchantable Beavers, or other goods and wares, according to the market price there and above that also to pay the value of twelve stivers in wampum each week." Once more asserting a financial capacity that reflected her activities as an international trader, she placed "her own person and goods," as well as her husband's, as bond for fulfillment of the contract. The trade she carried out, then, allowed her to support the growth of the couple's artisanal business in the colony. Janneken Jans's story is one of a person both transformed and transforming. Her travel and trade not only changed her legal and economic self but also helped create and sustain new transatlantic connections, weaving a network out of the many overlapping allegiances and claims that made up the Atlantic economy.[49]

As travelers turned the Atlantic Ocean into a network of relationships, mobility offered opportunities along with risks. Both women and men participated in creating and sustaining these transatlantic webs as well as putting them to work for economic ends. In doing so, their intimate networks transformed both the Atlantic and the people themselves. International exchange depended on these transitory and constantly changing ties. As they booked passage around the ocean, members of artisan and officer families fashioned networks out of their personal, kin, and social ties. They then used these networks to build an economic system of finance and exchange that would let them enter the Atlantic trade system, even though they lacked the capital to be a part of the WIC or form independent merchant houses. This system functioned because of the active participation of women. By putting their personal resources to use to establish credit, by managing family property when their husbands traveled, and by crossing the Atlantic to keep capital and goods moving, women from families of middling means helped create an independent economy that ran in tandem with the formal imperial system.[50]

---

49. Service Contracts, Jan. 2, 9, 1659, Not. Arch. 1359, 1v, 8, Not. H. Schaef, SA.

50. Some middling families in the eighteenth-century British Empire were similarly mobile. For these families, "their horizons were very wide, but they were ultimately contained within the limits defined by the expanding and contracting British Empire"; see Jacob M. Price, "One Family's Empire: The Russell-Lee-Clerk Connection in Maryland, Britain, and India, 1707–1857," *Maryland Historical Magazine*, LXXII (1977), 165–224 (quotation, 167). To a certain extent, the same could be said for earlier Dutch families, whose travel was shaped by the ships on which they could most easily secure passage, those of the WIC and VOC. Yet, the presence of Dutch women and men in many English colonies and cities during this same period and the broad reach of Dutch ships beyond WIC-run ports suggest "contained within" is not the best language to describe the relationship between middling families' mobility and

Merchant Families' Formal and Informal Ties

Just as intimacy shaped the personal and economic networks belonging to the people of worker and artisan status who sailed to and from New Netherland, so, too, it shaped the networks belonging to backers of larger-scale economic activities. Kinship infused both the WIC and the largest merchant houses operating in the beaver-skin trade. Differences in the status and economic strength of the people who created these networks, however, made these personal relationships function in very distinctive ways from those belonging to the men and women who worked the seas and scrambled to pay for passage to and from the colony. Yet, marriage still remained a key component of this more formal level of overseas trade and was especially valued for its ability to foster alliances among merchants and factors, patrons and clients. Wives mattered to economic networks both for the goods they carried and for the kinship bonds they strengthened. For people with significant financial capacity, familial and economic ties came together through the medium of ink in material texts to build the structure of companies. As larger-scale economic concerns stretched out across the ocean, gendered family intimacies served a symbolic and practical function, providing the strength needed to keep nascent transatlantic mercantile connections together.

Higher-status families had access to a key tool that the poorest travelers sometimes lacked: written communication. As a component of the larger structures of company and administration, ink enabled family ties to become even more efficient economic links for the burgher elites who ran merchant houses and participated in colonial governance. Because written documents had both personal and economic ramifications, colonists of merchant status treated them as vital resources.

Conflicts over who had the right to family letters drew wealthy colonists into court. One of the central bones of contention in the bitter dispute that took place in New Netherland in 1656 between Maria Varleth and her brother-in-law Joost van Beeck was the ownership of particular family papers. After the death of her husband, Johannes van Beeck, in the Peach War of 1655, Maria's brother-in-law challenged her status as widow and heir, claiming that since Johannes and Maria's marriage had been performed in New England without family permission, she was not a legal widow. In ad-

---

the formal empire. It is more helpful to think of these families as living in a world with many parallel lines and points of contact with the formal Dutch empire but not entirely contained within it.

dition to the ownership of slaves, trade goods, and tobacco, Varleth and her brother-in-law fought most rancorously over who was the rightful heir to letters and written documents.[51]

The Varleths represented one of the most influential kin groups associated with New Netherland. As the daughter of Amsterdam silk merchant Caspar Varleth, Maria belonged to a family that formed part of the burgher elite of Holland's politically and economically dominant city. Accordingly, her extended family participated in the expansion of consumption characteristic of the Golden Age. Abraham Varleth assembled a small collection of paintings by some of the leading artists of the period, including Hendrick Cuyper, Aert van der Neer, and Dirck Stoop. Her uncle, Pieter Varleth, himself a merchant in Amsterdam, served as a director of the WIC, and his name carried power and respect not only in Amsterdam but throughout the Netherlands. In 1636, two of the Varleth brothers, Caspar and Daniel, invested in the trade to the Hudson Valley, paying a substantial twelve hundred guilders to own a tenth-part share in the voyage of the ship *Rensselaerswyck*, which was to carry settlers to New Netherland and trade for furs and tobacco along the coast. Thus, they operated at a larger scale than most travelers and settler families; they had more money to invest and chose to channel that investment through the formal structure of a company.[52]

51. On the role of parental permission in establishing the legality of marriage, see J. Th. de Smidt and Heleen C. Gall, "Recht en gezin," in G. A. Kooy, ed., *Gezins geschiedenis: Vier eeuwen gezin in Nederland* (Assen, Netherlands, 1985), 37–39. Even jurists remained unsure if the ability of parents to deny minors permission to marry was absolute. See also Van der Heijden, "Punishment versus Reconciliation," in Roodenburg and Spierenburg, eds., *Social Control in Europe*, I, 57. Varleth and her brother-in-law also disputed the funeral expenses. On the importance of funerals to maintaining honor, see Van de Pol, *Burgher and the Whore*, 48. On the importance of written documents and account books to seventeenth-century Dutch mercantile concerns, see Donna Merwick, "A Genre of Their Own: Kiliaen van Rensselaer as Guide to the Reading and Writing Practices of Early Modern Businessmen," *WMQ*, 3d Ser., LXV (2008), 669–712.

52. For a discussion of Varleth family ties, see Jaap Jacobs, *New Netherland: A Dutch Colony in Seventeenth-Century America* (Leiden, 2005), 298. Abraham Varleth was a near relative of the New Netherland branch of the family, and he baptized his first son, Casparus, with Francina, Maria's sister, acting as a witness, for whom he also named one of his daughters; see Doopregistier, Apr. 9, 1653, June 23, 1655, and Oct. 30, 1658, DTB 65, 117, and 141; 94, 432, accessed July 15, 2013, https://stadsarchief.amsterdam.nl/archieven/archiefbank/indexen/doopregisters/zoek/index.nl.html. For the inventory of his paintings, see Inventory 1151, Apr. 22, 1660, Montias Database of 17th Century Dutch Art Inventories, Frick Collection, accessed July 15, 2013, http://research.frick.org/montias/browserecord.php?-action=browse&-recid=2352. For evidence that Pieter Varleth's name commanded respect for his ties to the WIC beyond Amsterdam, see the legal empowerment given him by a canon's widow in Utrecht to rectify a debt her husband had stood bond for before the WIC (Empowerment, Mar. 5, 1639, Not. Arch.

When one branch of the Varleth family decided to move from trading with to living in North America around 1650, they likewise did so with access to more resources than the migrants who came as soldiers, artisans' wives, or servant girls. Since posts in Holland's monopoly companies frequently remained within families, Pieter Varleth's position no doubt played a role in securing Maria's brother, Nicolaes Varleth, his influential post in New Netherland as a *commies,* or administrator, for the WIC. Nicolaes managed to trade on his position and connections to extend his family's social network through marriage. In the same year as Maria's dispute with her brother-in-law, Nicolaes married Anna Stuyvesant, sister of the colony's governor. Recognizing that the marriage made him part of the Varleth family, Governor Stuyvesant aided his new kin in powerful ways, such as when he intervened on behalf of Judith Varleth in 1662, when she found herself accused of witchcraft in the English settlement at Hartford. Asking English officials there to heed the request of Nicolaes, "me Brother in lawe (being necessitated to make a second voyage for ayde his distressed sister Judith Varleth . . .)," Stuyvesant made his family relationship clear. Marriage also extended the family's reach to Virginia through connections to the German merchants and planters Augustyn Hermans and George Hack. Family associations ensured that the Varleths arrived in New Netherland with powerful social and economic capital, and marriages in the colonies promised to stretch their network and economic reach even further.[53]

The Varleth women did much more than simply act as brides for economically influential men. In this extended merchant-class clan, women still undertook important duties as managers of finances and transatlantic representatives, just as they did among their poorer neighbors and fellow

34-4, 34, Not. C. van Vechten, Utrechts Archief). He was also respected by a late skipper's family in Rotterdam, for whom he collected the dead man's WIC wages, a process that could ordinarily take quite some time (Empowerment, Jan. 15, 1646, ONA 416, 259, Not. J. E. van der Heul, GAR). For an early trade contract, see Contract, Aug. 26, 1636, Not. Arch. 414, 173-173v, Not. N. Jacobs, SA. For a discussion of the organization and financing of the 1636 voyage, see Oliver A. Rink, *Holland on the Hudson: An Economic and Social History of Dutch New York* (Ithaca, N.Y., 1986), 197.

53. Peter Stuyvesant to the Deputy Governor and Court of Magistracy in Hartford, Oct. 13, 1662, New York-Connecticut Correspondence, 1662-1731, BV New York State "C," NYHS (quotation). For the Varleth's connections to Hermans and Hack by marriage, see Christian J. Koot, "The Merchant, the Map, and Empire: Augustine Herrman's Chesapeake and Interimperial Trade, 1644-73," *WMQ*, 3d Ser., LXVII (2010), 613, though the exact family ties are misidentified—Nicolaes was a sibling of the brides, not their father. He also appears in Dutch records as Augustijn Heermans.

travelers. For example, in 1656, Caspar Varleth empowered his niece, Janneken Varleth, to act as his agent in Amsterdam, and Catharina Varleth traded actively to North America from her home in the Netherlands. But the alliances within the merchant class that women created through marriage coincided with their direct actions as traders and agents.[54]

Maria's fight to step into her late husband's position within the Van Beeck family and to gain access to his letters reflects the interplay of trade and marriage for women of Holland's merchant class. Marriage allowed the Varleth family to expand their economic resources by bringing other merchant families, ideally with a place in the formal avenues of power, into their intimate network, and these Amsterdammers regarded affinal ties to be just as binding as those of blood. For example, Caspar Varleth looked to affinal kin to find an agent in Amsterdam when he departed from there "with his family to live in New Netherland" in 1650. He chose to empower father and son Francois and Pieter Heybloom, two Amsterdam businessmen, to look after his interests in his absence. Although not Varleth's blood relatives, they were his in-laws; eight years earlier, Pieter Heybloom had married Caspar's daughter, Francina. Varleth authorized the pair to look after family matters, including inheritances due from his late brother and sister. But he also expected them to take on the responsibilities arising from the complexities of colonial trade, and he made specific mention of debts still owed him from Brazil. Caspar showed tremendous faith in the Heyblooms' economic abilities, fully confident that they would be able to manage "all his . . . business and affairs . . . in his name." Having kin he trusted in this way, even those related through his daughter's marriage, not blood, kept Caspar's intricate transatlantic finances in order, ensuring that he and his family started life in New Netherland on firm financial footing.[55]

Maria's marriage, like that of her sister, Francina, had implications for the economic reach of her family, and her fight for the letters needs to be seen in that context. Asserting control over the late Johannes van Beeck's commercial estate required knowledge of consignments, debts, and credits. That knowledge lay recorded in ink, in the pages of account books and family letters. Whoever retained possession of those pages had a huge advantage in taking Johannes's place within familial and trade networks. Maria found herself summoned to court by her brother-in-law's ally, merchant Cornelis

54. For Caspar's reliance on Janneken, see Empowerment, July 13, 1656, Not. Arch. 1949, 215, Not. D. Doornick, SA. See Chapter 1 on Catharina Varleth.

55. Empowerment, Aug. 14, 1650, Not. Arch. 1947, 519–521, Not. D. Doornick, SA (quotations); Civil betrothal records, Aug. 2, 1642, DTB 458, 128, SA.

Schut, who sued for the return of the "large books regarding the Cargoes sent to him in the year 1652 and 1653," which he had handed over to Johannes before his death. In his written complaint to the court, Schut admitted that he had received an extract taken from the books from "her brother Verleth," but he explained that only the person in possession of the whole book could carry on the trading business successfully. Schut wanted access to the books "because of the many goods she must still have by her as in this book they are not recorded sold, and also that she has received the debts which are recorded debited in the first book and now the debtors say that they have already paid, and also in order to oversee accounts from this aforesaid book." In other words, as the widow and the holder of the books, only Maria knew which goods remained unsold, debtors came to Maria with payment, and only Maria could balance the accounts. As long as she had the books, she held the family business in her hands. Joost van Beeck took the liberty of sending the court written approval of Schut's suit, saying that the books also contained records of private transactions and adding that, as Johannes's brother, "we request to have all of the books." By using the word "we," Joost subtly tried to suggest that he spoke as the representative of the Van Beeck family. He would have to fight with Maria, however, if he wanted to be the one to take over Johannes's commercial connections. In his assault on her position, he focused on attacking her access to the written word.[56]

While the case with Schut remained ongoing, Maria found herself facing another affront from her brother-in-law. This time, she was the one who took the matter to court, "complaining . . . about Joost van Beeck, that he took her letters that arrived from the *patria* in the ship the *Gelderse Blom* and that belong to her husband the late Jan van Beeck." Asking not just for the

---

56. Court minutes, Feb. 7, 1656, CMNA, I, 499, NYCMA (microfilm) (quotations). Taxed at the highest rate, Schut was one of the wealthiest residents of New Amsterdam in 1655; see Jacobs, *New Netherland*, 332. Maria's expectation that she would step into her late husband's place was likely not unusual for high-status women, who held a "reasonably independent position" during widowhood and took on more responsibilities in the business world; see Hokke, "'Mijn alderliefste Jantielief,'" *Jaarboek voor vrouwengeschiedenis*, VIII (1987), 73 (quotation). Widows often also needed to find some way to continue supporting their children, and if Maria lost control of the merchandise her late husband imported and exported, she probably would have had few options. On widowhood as the motivation for entering paid work as a midwife, see Hilary Marland, "Catharina Schrader (1656–1745): Een bijzondere vroedvrouw of vrouw van haar tijd?" in Monique Stavenuiter, Karin Bijsterveld, and Saskia Jansens, eds., *Lange levens, stille getuigen: Oudere vrouwen in het verleden* (Zutphen, Netherlands, 1995), 105–117. On trade as a source of support for unmarried women in early modern England, see Pamela Sharpe, "Dealing with Love: The Ambiguous Independence of the Single Woman in Early Modern England," *Gender and History*, XI (1999), 209–232.

return of the letters but also for "judgment and justice for the violence," she explained that he had taken the letters "out of the hands of Claes van Elslant and had opened the same." Doing so had left Maria out of the loop; she had never had a chance to read the letters herself. Joost tried to mitigate the violence of the theft by explaining, perhaps not very gallantly, that "his wife had taken a certain two letters, addressed to Johannes van Beeck, and that the same were opened by her and read by him." However he acquired the letters, they represented a key familial and commercial tie. Joost admitted in court that the letters included "a letter from his brother Nicolaes van Beeck and a letter from his brother-in-law Poulus Jellesz with a Consignment of some goods from Nicolaes van Beeck." In fact, when he was forced to deposit the letters with the secretary for safe keeping, they were found to contain much more than that. In addition to the two letters were "a general Cargo; a record of Consignment; [and] a price currant." Though he confessed that he had "no particular obligation or empowerment" from his family to take and open the letters, he refused to return them. He argued that "neither the letters nor the goods sent with them belong to Maria Verleth, because the marriage was never declared legal, but rather he is the heir." Joost sought to usurp Maria's position as Johannes's widow within the commercial network of the Van Beeck family, and he did so by questioning the legitimacy of her marriage in order to deny her access to crucial letters and documents.[57]

The possibility that the New Netherland court might delegitimize Maria's marriage into the Van Beeck family posed a serious threat to her attempt to create an important familial alliance and held the potential to stain her honor and bastardize her child. The Van Beecks traded tobacco on behalf of some members of the Varleth clan, and marriage should have tied the two trading families even more tightly together. Drawing on the mobility of the Atlantic world and the transgression of boundaries by colonists and travelers alike, Maria somewhat spuriously asserted in response to the challenge to her marriage that she was "no burgher here, but a foreigner, and that [she was] an inhabitant and burgher in Herfort in New England." She undoubtedly made this claim to avoid having guardians appointed over the estate by the orphan's court, as was required of all widows and widowers resident in New Amsterdam. Her residency claim came in response to Joost van Beeck's demand, when she sued him about the letters, "that there may be guardians appointed" over Johannes's estate. Maria Varleth would undoubtedly have known that as the nearest male relative on the side of the deceased, Joost

57. Court minutes, Feb. 7, 1656, CMNA, I, 502, NYCMA (microfilm).

stood a very good chance of being appointed guardian and that she would be required to hand over account books as part of settling the estate. Indeed, he was initially appointed guardian, which may explain why Maria defied the orphan court's first summons, claiming that she had some errands to do instead. Joost ended up declining the guardianship, but Maria's defiance nonetheless needs to be seen in light of her desperate struggle to maintain her position within family commercial networks by holding on to the letters and documents that enshrined that position on paper.[58]

The new network of connections Maria's marriage represented took physical form through words scrawled in ink on paper. When she fought to retain her late husband's letters, she fought to retain her own status and the economic reach of the Varleth family. In the end, New Amsterdam society did accept her as a legitimate widow and her child as Johannes van Beeck's legal heir, inscribing her name as a widow in the records of the orphan chamber and writing her daughter's name in the baptismal registry with one of the members of New Amsterdam's municipal court acting as witness. The court pointed out that, since her marriage had been performed by churchly authorities and had never been nullified, she, not Joost van Beeck, was the presumptive heir to the letters.[59]

58. Court Minutes, Feb. 7, 8, 1656, CMNA, I, 502, 505, NYCMA (microfilm) (quotations); Orphan's Court Records, Nov. 9, 16, 1655, Jan. 20, 24, 1656, Orphan Masters' Records, Records of New Amsterdam, NYCMA (microfilm, NYSL); Koot, "The Merchant, the Map, and Empire," *WMQ*, 3d Ser., LXVII (2010), 614. It is unclear from the records whether Maria ever did submit to having the estate inventoried by the guardians. Although Dieneke Hempenius-van Dijk has asserted for Friesland and Groningen that "if a widow or widower was left behind with minor children, he or she would immediately become the guardian of these children simply by operation of law," such was decidedly not the case in New Amsterdam, where no woman, including any mother or grandmother, was appointed by the orphan's court as guardian; see Dieneke Hempenius-van Dijk, "Widows and the Law: The Legal Position of Widows in the Dutch Republic during the Seventeenth and Eighteenth Centuries," in Jan Bremmer and Lourens van den Bosch, eds., *Between Poverty and the Pyre: Moments in the History of Widowhood* (London, 1995), 93 (quotation). For New Amsterdam's practices, see Susanah Shaw Romney, "Intimate Networks and Children's Survival in New Netherland in the Seventeenth Century," *Early American Studies*, VII (2009), 270–308.

59. Orphan's Court Records, Nov. 9, 1655, Orphan Masters' Records, Records of New Amsterdam, NYCMA (microfilm, NYSL); Evans, ed., *Baptisms*, 39. On the position held in 1655 by the baptismal witness, Johannes Nevius, see Jacobs, *New Netherland*, 490. For the court's declaration of Maria as presumptive heir, see Court minutes, Feb. 8, 1656, CMNA, I, 505, NYCMA (microfilm). Joost van Beeck tried to appeal this decision, and the pair ended up in court again repeatedly. Since aspects of these intertwined cases got referred to arbiters, whose decisions did not always get recorded in the court minutes, it is not possible to determine who came out the winner overall. It seems clear, though, that Joost's attempt to oust Maria entirely from her familial and commercial position failed.

Her next marriage, in 1658, to Paulus Schrick, allowed her to extend her family's status once more. Schrick drew on the Varleth family's alliance with Governor Stuyvesant to use the formal structures of authority to safeguard family interests. When he sought to protect and rectify the Varleth family estate in the Connecticut River valley after Caspar's death, he traveled to Hartford with a letter of recommendation in his pocket from Stuyvesant, his "brother-in-law." Maria's struggles show that, for families of this status, ink and blood intermingled to determine the shape of family commercial concerns. Formal channels of power and commerce intertwined with marriage, kin, and clan as members of merchant families sought to hold their place in transatlantic family businesses. Marriage made people kin, and ink put that kinship to economic use.[60]

A glimpse inside some letters exchanged among another merchant family, the Verbrugges, shows the interweaving of formal structures and family ties and suggests the key symbolic work done by gendered tropes of family intimacy within those relationships. Seth and Gillis Verbrugge ran the largest merchant house operating in New Netherland. Although smaller-scale traders had to rely on unpaid family, kin, and friends within their social network to help them operate both halves of transatlantic businesses, the Verbrugges owned the largest of only four formal companies trading in the colony that employed factors for a considerable period of time. Yet they did not seek to hire from outside; instead, marriage and kin networks kept employees safely within the family. Before Govert Loockermans became the Verbrugges' primary factor in the 1640s, he had previous experience in the colony that would have made him a knowledgeable and well-connected representative regardless of whose kin he was. He had served the WIC in New Netherland since 1633 and rose to become company clerk by the time he left in 1639. Yet, he was also a relative, tied by marriage to the Verbrugge clan through his 1641 wedding to Adriaentje Jans. As the niece of Gillis Verbrugge and widow of the merchant Jan van de Water, who had died on a voyage "to the Virginias" in the late 1630s, she linked this former WIC employee to a capital-rich Atlantic merchant family at the same time as the Hudson Valley trade was fully opening to private trading companies. It is unclear which came first: his marriage or his commercial connection to the family. Such economic and

60. Peter Stuyvesant to court of magistrates, Hartford, June 9, 1663, New York–Connecticut Correspondence, 1662–1731, BV New York State "C," NYHS (quotation). On Schrick's status, see Jacobs, *New Netherland*, 298.

familial unions strengthened each other in the web of ink that kept them connected across the ocean.[61]

In the letters between Loockermans in America and the Verbrugge family in the Netherlands, familial and economic concerns intermingled constantly. Though their business experienced reverses as well as successes, both sides took care to ease any potential strain on their relationship caused by the ups and downs of trade by invoking their familial connection to one another, especially through references to Loockermans's wife, who remained in Holland. In modern-day terms, their relationship was not even all that close, filtered through marriage rather than blood, but letters from the Verbrugges and their coinvestors nonetheless began with an affectionate address to "Cousin" Govert Loockermans. What affection lay behind such terms, if any, can only be imagined, but the invocation of family served to remind Loockermans of his obligations to the merchant clan he had joined through marriage.

To one letter addressed to Loockermans in the late 1640s, Seth Verbrugge added a personal postscript, seeking to draw on the mutuality of kinship among traders to benefit another member of his network of relatives. Apologizing for not writing at greater length, Seth went on to ask a special favor: "I bid you to please be somewhat helpful," Seth wrote, to "the young man Johannes de Peyster coming over on our ship" since he was, Seth explained, "my wife's Uncle's Sister's son," who could perhaps be put to work in the store. Lest Loockermans forget what was due to kin, Seth stressed their family relation to one another in his closing, "my little wife greets you from her heart, your affectionate cousin, Seth Verbrugge." By adding the diminutive to his word for wife—calling her his *vroutie* rather than his *huysvrouw*—Seth Verbrugge signaled Loockermans's intimate standing within the family and renewed the bonds of kinship that underlay even the formal economic relationship between investor and factor. Of course, employing De Peyster would have hardly been a sacrificial act of charity on the part of the Verbrugge trading company; he had previous experience in the silk shop and had proven himself a good servant, faithful to the company and family. De

61. On Adriaentje Jans's family ties, see Testimony and empowerment, May 25, 1639, Not. Arch. 1280, 69v–70, Not. H. Schaef, SA (quotation). Her first name also appears as Ariaentge. On the size of the Verbrugge concern and the number of companies employing factors, see Jacobs, *New Netherland*, 69–70. On Verbrugge family connections, see David William Voorhees, "Family and Faction: The Dutch Roots of Colonial New York's Factional Politics," in Shattuck, ed., *Explorers, Fortunes, and Love Letters*, 132.

Peyster's connection with the family, though distant by today's standards, had enabled him to acquire experience and skills that made him a valuable asset. Through his words of affection and deliberate reference to familial ties, Seth sought to make sure Loockermans found a way to make use of those skills.[62]

The gendered language of family intimacy served an important symbolic and practical function in the letters, creating a sense that transatlantic empire was merely a web of kin despite its formal commercial entities. References to wives run throughout the official correspondence between the Verbrugges and Loockermans. In December 1647, Loockermans not only mentioned that Stuyvesant's wife gave birth to a son in October, he also reported that "[our] Jacob Hap is to marry a widow (^with three Children) . . . a pious woman[;] I hope that he will now lay aside his old ways and take up a Godly life." Earlier that year, in August, Loockermans combined family and financial news when he mentioned that eighty guilders of the two hundred he sent over should be given to his wife, "by way of a dress for Cousin Angeneetgen, who is to marry Montannie, a steady person." The inclusion of personal news, the intermingling of family and trade, and the reiteration of words of affection for the readers and their wives served as a reminder that personal ties could not be separated from the economic ones that the letters were ostensibly about. In particular, the connection with Agnieta Gillis promised to provide the family with an alliance within the formal lines of administrative power in the colony. Her betrothed, Johannes La Montagne, served as a member of the colony's governing council from 1638 until 1656, in addition to acting as a diplomat in negotiations with Munsee and Mohawk groups. He would be an important man for any fur-trading family to call kin. Buying her a wedding dress would not just be a loving gesture from kin—it would be a prudent renewal of a potential business connection. The inclusion of women in these men's business letters affirmed the familial bonds reinforcing financial ties reaching across the ocean.[63]

62. Seth Verbrugge and company to Govert Loockermans, [1647], Loockermans Correspondence, Box 1, doc. 1, NYHS (quotations). On the importance of the language of affect to hierarchical and patrimonial relationships in early modern France, see Arthur L. Herman, Jr., "The Language of Fidelity in Early Modern France," *Journal of Modern History*, LXVII (1995), 1–24. On emotion among high-status Dutch families, see Hokke, "'Mijn alderliefste Jantielief,'" *Jaarboek voor vrouwengeschiedenis*, VIII (1987), 45–73.

63. Govert Loockermans to Gillis Verbrugge, [Dec. 21, 1647], Loockermans Correspondence, folder 2, doc. 7a, NYHS ("[our] Jacob Hap"); Loockermans to Verbrugge, Aug. 2, 1647, Loockermans Correspondence, folder 2, doc. 4, NYHS ("by way of a dress"). In A. J. F. Van Laer's notes accompanying these documents, he identifies the couple as Agnieta Gillis, widow

News of Loockermans's own wife also permeated the letters, and references to her acted to ease commercial strains in difficult economic times. The discussion of Loockermans's wife served as a tool for each side to get what they wanted out of their business partnership. Loockermans's letters to his "very dear Uncle and Cousins" consistently stressed his desire to have his wife come over to New Netherland from Holland. In one letter to Gillis Verbrugge, he noted, "I should have also written to my wife, but I hope that she is now already at sea." However, the Verbrugges emphasized the impossibility of such a request, even while they sought to renew the affection between the married pair in their own letters. Johannes Verbrugge tried, in 1648, to explain the issue at length, stressing the willingness but physical incapacity of Loockermans's wife to undertake such a journey. Johannes explained "that she does not know what she should do on the one hand she wishes indeed that she was with you on the other she cannot because of her poor health" and the difficulties of "going over the sea with the 3 children." Johannes acknowledged the pain of separation, saying that he "wish[ed] indeed that you had some camphor with you in order to dampen a little the rising of the flesh." Johannes perhaps sought to mitigate any alienation Loockermans might feel from the family because of the dispute by closing with well-wishes from "all our kin particularly your mother: and my father and mother and [your marÿ luls] and all the little offspring."[64]

Loockermans, for his part, stressed that his requests for his wife reflected his dedication to business. He cited promises he had made repeatedly to the former colony director Willem Kieft, Governor Stuyvesant, and Stuyvesant's wife that his wife would join him in America. Her presence would have indicated to political leaders that Loockermans was committed to the long-term economic success of the colony and was not just a sojourner seeking to make a quick guilder for his employers. Just as the writers used family to strengthen a business connection, Loockermans used an appeal to business matters to strengthen a personal request.[65]

of Arent Corssen Stam, and Johannes La Montagne. On La Montagne's positions, see Jacobs, *New Netherland*, 489–490. On gift giving to brides, see Irma Thoen, *Strategic Affection? Gift Exchange in Seventeenth-Century Holland* (Amsterdam, 2007), 107–114.

64. Govert Loockermans to Gillis Verbrugge, [1647], Loockermans Correspondence, Box 2, doc. 2, NYHS ("very dear"); Loockermans to Verbrugge, [Dec. 21, 1647], Loockermans Correspondence, folder 2, doc. 7a, NYHS ("I should have"); Johannes Verbrugge to Loockermans, Mar. 24, 1648, Loockermans Correspondence, folder 3, doc. 1, NYHS ("that she does not").

65. Govert Loockermans to the investors, [1648], Loockermans Correspondence, folder 3, doc. 3, NYHS.

The question of where Loockermans's wife should live might have been a site of tension between investors and factor, but the continual discussion of it served as an occasion for the repeated renewal of both economic and personal bonds. In fact, Seth Verbrugge often sought to create an impression of continued intimacy between the married pair in his letters—for example, in one letter he noted, "Your little wife has charged me to write to you that when you want stockings that you should mention the color too[;] she is strong and healthy." However, he did not think the obligations of husbands to wives were at odds with a commitment to business. When Seth heard rumors that "she bid you come home in her letter," he wrote Loockermans saying that he "hope[d] you shall be wiser, and please not to listen to such counsel." Rather, he beseeched Loockermans to remember the "contract we have made together," and to keep in mind that men in trade were often "2 or 3 Years, even more, absent from their wives[;] one must strike while the iron is hot." Though Verbrugge and Loockermans shared a family tie, when push came to shove, Verbrugge reminded Loockermans that there was also a contractual dimension to their connection. In the service of family economic interests, business contracts trumped even marriages. As Seth Verbrugge himself put it, "about the trade, that goes to our hearts." Formal, written agreements structured the way high-status merchant families worked.[66]

Despite Seth's assurances to Loockermans regarding his wife's good health, it was not long before the Verbrugges had to break the news of her death, saying that the investors asked only that he sell the remaining merchandise before coming home. Loockermans, in response, used his long separation from his late wife as a way to defuse his employers' dissatisfaction with his fur trading. Writing to his "beloved uncle and all the kin and investors," Loockermans acknowledged receipt of the letters "containing the sorrowful tidings" of the "death of my well beloved wife." Going on to discuss the scarcity of deer hides and the high prices everyone had to pay for beavers, Loockermans put what he saw as the incomprehensible "discontent with my service" by the investors in the context that "I have had to abandon my dear and well beloved wife who I was not allowed to take with me who now the good Lord has pleased to take to His eternal kingdom." Lest financial concerns prompt the investors to look elsewhere for a factor, Loockermans reiterated that theirs was a familial, as well as a business, relationship. Because the business remained in the family, Loockermans's

66. Seth Verbrugge to Govert Loockermans, Aug. 12, 1647, Loockermans Correspondence, folder 2, doc. 5, NYHS ("Your little wife"); Verbrugge to Loockermans, [Mar. 26, 1648], Loockermans Correspondence, folder 3, doc. 2, NYHS ("she bid you").

appeal for empathy doubtless hit home; the link between kin and trade was clear to all, and the intimacies of family sustained both. His language about his love for his wife served a practical function to strengthen the relationship between factor and employer at a rocky financial moment. Loockermans used material text, in the form of a letter, to remind the Verbrugges that their relationship was familial as well as contractual and that dismissing him would ignore the sacrifices he had made at the Verbrugges' behest. For those at the very highest level of New Netherland's economic scale, business and family were one and the same.[67]

The Verbrugges had the capital to establish a formal company, something that was beyond the reach of most of New Netherland's immigrants and sojourners. Yet, the formal structure they built remained thoroughly infused with the intimate networks that would-be traders up and down the social scale employed. Loockermans was able to secure his status through a combination of marriage and trade, and the Verbrugge-Loockermans clan as a whole used marriage to extend their reach throughout the merchant class and into the realm of officeholders, just as the Varleths did. Loockermans's sister, Anna, wed merchant Oloff Stevensz van Courtlandt, and his sister-in-law married into the wealthy and powerful Van Couwenhoven family. The three brothers-in-law served together as members of the "Nine Men," who advised the governor and council in the late 1640s, and they went on to dominate New Amsterdam's municipal government after it formed in the 1650s. By the time of Govert's death in 1671, his estate made him New York's wealthiest merchant—not bad for a man who came to the colony at age sixteen as a cook's mate.[68]

67. Loockermans to the investors, Aug. 24, 1649, Loockermans Correspondence, folder 4, doc. 6, NYHS (quotations); Gillis Verbrugge and investors to Govert Loockermans, [1649], Loockermans Correspondence, folder 4, doc. 2, NYHS. Loockermans referred in his reply to "alde vrinde ende reeders"; while "vrienden" in modern Dutch refers to friends, in the seventeenth century it was also commonly used as a synonym for relatives ("bloetverwanten"). Thus, I have translated it here as kin. On friendships as relationships of mutual obligation, see Willem Frijhoff and Marijke Spies with Wiep van Bunge and Natascha Veldhorst, *Dutch Culture in a European Perspective*, I, *1650: Hard-Won Unity*, trans. Myra Heerspink Scholz (Assen, Netherlands, 2004), 215–219.

68. Willem Frijhoff, "Govert Loockermans (1617?–1671?) en zijn verwanten: Hoe een Turnhoutenaar zoch wist op te werken in de Nieuwe Wereld," *Taxandria, Jaarboek van de Koninklijke geschied—en oudheidkindige kring van de Antwerpse Kempen*, LXXXII (2011), 5–68; Declaration, Nov. 11, 1639, *Provincial Secretary*, I, 244. For more on Loockermans, see Voorhees, "Family and Faction," in Shattuck, ed., *Explorers, Fortunes, and Love Letters*, 130–132. On the Nine Men, see Jacobs, *New Netherland*, 143, 488–489. On economic and social fluidity in the colony, see Shattuck, "Women and Trade in New Netherland," *Itinerario*, XVIII, no. 2 (1994), 40–49. On economic mobility based on the gradual acquisition of farmland, see the discussion

As elite families with access to financial, intimate, and social capital beyond the reach of maritime workers or even artisans, the Verbrugges, Loockermans, Varleths, and others enjoyed resources not available to all. Whereas those trading on the small scale sometimes had to rely solely on oral transoceanic news networks, these higher-status families turned to ink—in the form of letters and contracts—to help them organize their transatlantic trade. They signed contracts, wrote letters, kept account books, and made use of the administrative structures and offices of private companies, the WIC, and the colonial government. Yet, that formality did not run counter to gendered ties of family and kin. Instead, the empire of the written word grew out of and remained essentially entwined with the intimate empire of family. Men and women of the merchant class used marriage to construct their economic networks, just like men and women all the way down the social scale. Their marriages had the potential to unite powerful networks of commercial connections, however, and communications in the form of paper and ink added a formal dimension to their family commerce. Their intimate networks melded with and created the formal structures of company and administration, even as they continued to look to marriage, intimacy, and the women in their families to profit from Dutch overseas ventures.[69]

Conclusion

The travelers who worked the seas between Amsterdam and North America hoped to profit from the ships sailing ever farther from the Netherlands. By grabbing the ship's lines and hoisting themselves aboard, they made a very direct and bodily investment in the success of those overseas ventures. But

---

of Cosyn Gerrits/Gerritsen in Firth Haring Fabend, *A Dutch Family in the Middle Colonies, 1660–1800* (New Brunswick, N.J., 1991), 6–7. Though Loockermans's climb up the economic ladder was dramatic, as a cook's mate he would have been considered an underofficer, above a common sailor in both rank and pay; see Lucassen, "Zeevarenden," in Akveld, Hart, and Van Hoboken, eds., *Maritieme geschiedenis der Nederlanden*, II, 136–138.

69. For the strategy of interweaving kin networks with political and company offices in the Netherlands in the Golden Age, see Julia Adams, *The Familial State: Ruling Families and Merchant Capitalism in Early Modern Europe* (Ithaca, N.Y., 2005); Adams, "Principals and Agents, Colonialists, and Company Men: The Decay of Colonial Control in the Dutch East Indies," *American Sociological Review*, LXI (1996), 12–28. On the interweaving of kinship networks, company, and politics among seventeenth-century La Rochelle families active in the trade to New France, see J. F. Bosher, "Research Note/Note de Recherche: The Lyon and Bordeaux Connections of Émmanuel Le Borgne (c. 1605–1681)," *Acadiensis*, XXIII, no. 1 (Autumn 1993), 128–145.

plenty of other Netherlanders, whose feet never traded the solid cobble-stone streets for the heaving deck of a ship, hoped to turn overseas trade to their advantage as well. They did so, not by putting their bodies at risk, but by venturing their money. They became shareholders in the wic, which, along with the voc, was one of the earliest publicly traded concerns in Europe. Interestingly, these armchair imperialists shared one of their key tools of investment with travelers up and down the economic scale. Their investments represented, not the actions of individuals alone, but the engagement of their intimate networks of family and kin.

Those who invested in the wic did so as members of families. The purchase of shares drew on the resources of kin networks, and inheritance made those shares the property of networks of family members, not just a single investor. This meant that women took an active role in determining who owned pieces of the wic. In one heated inheritance battle in Rotterdam, two women had to figure out how to divide ownership of wic shares. Aeltgen Cornelisdochter, widow of Franchois Dawes, who had died in England, struggled to split her late husband's estate with her stepdaughter, Elisabeth Franchois Dawes, herself a widow of a man who had died in the East Indies. The two women finally came to terms, dividing the wic shares fifty-fifty. Other, presumably less contentious, family members chose to continue keeping wic shares together under common management. After the death of Leendert Willemsz Starcken and Mayken Michiels in 1633, the husbands of their three daughters apportioned their joint estate equally. However, the three men, Pieter Ariensz van der Werff, married to Annetje Leenderts, Huybert Jansz van de Weteringh, married to Cornelia Leenderts, and Jan Lambertsz Vermase, married to Lisbeth Leenderts, did not split everything. Instead, they continued to hold in common some account books, obligations, annuities, and shares in the wic. Ownership of the company, divided by design among shareholders, was in fact divided among many networks of kin groups and families throughout the Netherlands. Participants in empire who stayed safely at home nonetheless took part in the new economy on behalf of their spouses, families, and kin.[70]

Even at the most removed level of overseas expansion—the investment of shareholders in the official monopoly companies—the formal economy rested on and supported intimate ties of family and marriage. For people who took part in Dutch Atlantic expansion more directly, family and over-

70. Arbitrage settlement, Jan. 14, 1643, ONA 458, 74/159, Not. L. van Zijl, GAR; Contract, June 30, 1633, ONA 321, 67/159, Not. A. van der Graeff, GAR.

seas trade intertwined even more. Rather than living their lives within the walls of the family home, these men and women ventured abroad, keeping their relationships strong through their own mobility. Their travels and their connections to one another ensured that family would persist across the ocean, and these relationships became the basis for their economic activities. These networks also created some of the first systems of transatlantic trade.

The existence of these crucial networks, and women's importance in building them, show the need to look more closely at women and gender to understand how early modern imperial economies developed. Dutch women of the Golden Age once remained little-known stereotypes, labeled as busy housewives with a close eye on every guilder. Actually, women in the Netherlands operated in a complicated legal environment with restrictions similar to those placed on female traders throughout Western Europe.[71]

Written expressions of customary law delineated limits on married women's ability to contract and trade comparable to, though in detail distinct from, the complex legal status known in England as coverture. Daily custom

71. For a typical depiction of Dutch women, see Simon Schama, *The Embarrassment of Riches: An Interpretation of Dutch Culture in the Golden Age* (New York, 1987). For critiques of this image, see Els Kloek, "De geschiedenis van een stereotype: De bazigheid, ondernemingszin en zindelijkheid van vrouwen in Holland (1500–1800)," *Jaarboek van het Centraal Bureau voor Genealogie*, LVIII (2004), 5–25; D. Christopher Gabbard, "Gender Stereotyping in Early Modern Travel Writing on Holland," *Studies in English Literature, 1500–1900*, XLIII (2003), 83–100. The debate over early modern women's roles, which is increasingly complicated by Dutch politics, has led some scholars to make strong statements about female economic capacity; see Tine de Moor and Jan Luiten van Zanden, *Vrouwen en de geboorte van het kapitalisme in West-Europa* (Amsterdam, 2006). A more moderate assessment argues that "women in the sixteenth and seventeenth centuries received more opportunities to trade and to lead their lives independently"; see Manon van der Heijden, Elise van Nederveen Meerkerk, and Ariadne Schmidt, "Terugkeer van het patriarchaat? Vrije vrouwen in de Republiek," *Tijdschrift voor sociale en economische geschiedenis*, VI, no. 3 (2009), 26–52 (quotation, 29). See also Schmidt, "Vrouwen en het recht: De juridische status van vrouwen in Holland in de vroegmoderne tijd," *Jaarboek van het Centraal Bureau voor Genealogie*, LVIII (2004), 26–44. Anne McCants demonstrates instead women's restricted access to credit and continuing economic constraints; see McCants "Petty Debts and Family Newtorks," in Lemire, Pearson, and Campbell, eds., *Women and Credit*, 48. See also, Jan de Vries, *The Industrious Revolution: Consumer Behavior and the Household Economy, 1650 to the Present* (Cambridge, 2008), 81. Women disproportionately sought poor relief, showing their limited economic opportunities; see Van Wijngaarden, *Zorg voor de kost*. The segmented labor force kept women's wages low; see Elise van Nederveen Meerkerk, "Marktwerking of discriminatie? Spinlonen van mannen en vrouwen in de zeventiende-eeuwse Nederlandse textielnijverheid," *Tijdschrift voor sociale en economische geschiedenis*, VI, no. 1 (2009), 53–79. Women's economic and legal capacity might have even declined during this period; see Fontaine, "Women's Economic Spheres," in Lemire, Pearson, and Campbell, eds., *Women and Credit*, 17. Conditions worsened particularly for seamen's wives; see De Wit, "Zeemansvrouwen," *Tijdschrift voor sociale en economische geschiedenis*, II, no. 3 (2005), 60–80.

and local court practice probably allowed women greater flexibility than the formal writings of jurists would suggest—in the Netherlands and elsewhere. On the ground, in daily practice, women—single, married, and widowed— played critical roles in the Dutch economy at home and abroad, but they did so without heading formal companies, acting instead informally as members of their families.[72]

As women like Maria Varleth, Janneken Jans van Leeuwarden, and Geertge Nanningsdochter helped build a new imperial economy, they used tools and worked within constraints common to their contemporaries throughout Europe. Indeed, the development of colonial overseas trade might have offered many women unique opportunities. No guild prohibited their access and the rise of a burgher society in New Netherland opened up a growing market for traditional female products, like needlecrafts. Women took advantage of the new opportunities afforded by transatlantic shipping by forming intimate relationships, particularly marriages, that allowed their familial and local economies to expand overseas. The kinds of intimate networks they created varied with their social background and economic

72. At the very end of the seventeenth century, some widows began to head merchant companies with overseas interests; see Van den Heuvel, *Women and Entrepreneurship*, 232–263. Yet, this late and limited participation leads Van den Heuvel to declare that the Golden Age of seventeenth-century Holland was no golden age for women in business. Amy Louise Erickson argues that English women's economic activity was not prevented by coverture but, rather, that coverture forced families to become accustomed to complex financial instruments, thus paving the way for capitalism. The relative freedom of unmarried English women to invest also encouraged capital markets; see Erickson, "Coverture and Capitalism," *History Workshop Journal*, LIX (Spring 2005), 1–16. Although Erickson clarifies the differences between coverture and the tradition of guardianship practiced in continental Europe, the tendency to engage in complex legal and financial practices so that women could operate legally and economically was by no means limited to England. It is important to keep in mind that, in the Netherlands, even though marriage was usually regarded as a community of goods, under normal circumstances the husband alone had the ability to manage marital property, making the legal position of married women not as different from women under coverture as Erickson suggests. Furthermore, my research indicates considerable participation of Dutch women in small-scale business and finance. Yet, she does draw critical attention to the question of how women's complex economic practices related to the development of capitalism, and her focus on the limitations on women economically and legally in the areas where capitalism first emerged, rather than on a supposed unusual permissiveness, points in a fruitful direction and serves as a corrective to arguments that exaggerate early modern European women's economic and legal capacities (such as De Moor and Van Zanden, *Vrouwen en de geboorte van het kapitalisme*). A similarly complex relationship between women's legal and economic status and transatlantic credit existed in Spain; see David A. Norton, "Global Home Economies: Understanding the Spanish Economic System on a Local Level" (paper presented at the Thirteenth Berkshire Conference on the History of Women, Scripps College, Claremont, Calif., June 2–5, 2005).

standing, but these connections proved essential to the imperial economy at every level. Looking at women's actions and the function of gendered relationships among worker, middling, and merchant families thus reveals the crucial role of intimacy in building the economy of this early modern empire.[73]

With the establishment of the intimate tie of marriage, the mobile men and women who worked the seas employed the resources of the WIC and wealthy families and companies for their own purposes, fostering a small-scale trade system that existed in symbiosis with large-scale operations. By putting their dense familial and social networks to use through the cooperative travel of husbands and wives, middling-status families created a financial and trade system that operated alongside merchant companies and enabled an artisan and burgher class to take root in the American colony. Wealthy kin groups used marriage and the gendered discourse of family to solidify their hold over and profit from formal companies and to support formal agreements and material texts. Individual activities, personal interactions, and private networks maintained by women built this empire from the ground up.

In quest of economic survival and prosperity, people fashioned multiple forms of intimate networks. Every economic level, however, saw the imbrication of family and trade. Private interests—small and large, familial and economic—facilitated and accommodated formal imperial efforts. By manipulating social bonds to advance their own interests, individuals si-

73. On the debate over the effects of guilds on early modern women's economic participation and the argument that Dutch guilds formed "no obstacle," see Ariadne Schmidt, "Gilden en de toegang van vrouwen tot de arbeidsmarkt in Holland in de vroegmoderne tijd," *De zeventiende eeuw*, XXIII (2007), 160–178. For the opposite view, see Van den Heuvel, *Women and Entrepreneurship*, 132, 175–176, 271–272; Ogilvie, "How Does Social Capital Affect Women," *AHR*, CIX (2004), 325–359. In practice, locality and economic sector shaped women's opportunities and their experiences of guilds and networks; see Van den Heuvel, *Women and Entrepreneurship*, 267–277. For a study of one Dutch town, see A. C. M. Kappelhof, "Vrouwen buitenshuis in Breda en omgeving (1550–1650)," *Jaarboek van het Centraal Bureau voor Genealogie*, LVII (2004), 45–67. For a classic description of the situation of women under French law that shows its overwhelming similarity to Roman-Dutch practice, see Jean Brissaud, *A History of French Private Law*, trans. Rapelje Howell, Continental Legal History Series, III (Boston, 1912), 144–153. On the tools that seventeenth-century French women used to negotiate these restrictions and survive economically, see John Cashmere, "Sisters Together: Women without Men in Seventeenth-Century French Village Culture," *Journal of Family History*, XXI (1996), 44–62; Julie Hardwick, "Women 'Working' the Law: Gender, Authority, and Legal Process in Early Modern France," *Journal of Women's History*, IX, no. 3 (Autumn 1997), 28–49; Zoë A. Schneider, "Women before the Bench: Female Litigants in Early Modern Normandy," *French Historical Studies*, XXIII (2000), 1–32.

multaneously created the economic empire of the Dutch Atlantic. Clusters of people, closely tied to one another through marriage and kinship, enabled the integration of the imperial structure. The constant mobility and inconstant human beings that constituted this set of early modern transatlantic connections formed a continually changing shape. Intimate networks transformed the Atlantic from an impassable gulf, separating people from those with whom they had their closest ties, into a web of connections, keeping families bound with intimate ties to possibilities just over the horizon.

CHAPTER THREE

◆ ◆ ◆

"Not Altogether Brotherly"

Elusive Intimacy between Natives and Newcomers

 As many of the travelers sailing the Atlantic on Dutch ships clambered ashore in the Hudson Valley, they faced a new world and a new set of challenges. If Janneken Jans van Leeuwarden and her contemporaries were to survive—if they were to do better than that and actually profit from their colonial ventures—they would have to determine what kinds of relationships they needed and wanted with the people who were already there—the Mohawk, Mahican, Munsee, Susquehannock, Shinnecock, Montauk, and other Native American villagers, whose own social networks already covered the mid-Atlantic coast in a web of personal and economic ties. Meeting people, trading with people, and sorting out what manner of associations one desired with those people would shape the ways both locals and newcomers negotiated the changing circumstances of life introduced with the arrival of Dutch ships. Just as people trading across the Atlantic relied on their personal connections, people trading throughout the mid-Atlantic region depended on face-to-face relationships, including those reaching across lines of culture and community, to make their way in the new conditions created by Dutch colonial expansion.[1]

1. Most of the indigenous villagers living south of the Mahicans and Mohawks along the shores of the Hudson during the Dutch period are now discussed by scholars as part of the Munsee people, although they also had extensive bonds with their neighbors in the Delaware Valley who are regarded today as Delaware / Lenape. Dutch-language documents from the time, however, do not refer to these people by any collective name; instead, they treat each group of villages separately or refer to all Native people by the catch-all term "wilden." Even when documents quote sachems directly, village and regional terms still serve to identify people, not a collective term such as Munsee, suggesting that such labels may be anachronistic and should be used with care. The term "Algonquian" will be used here to refer to all Munsee, Unami, and other Algonquian-language-speaking peoples living on Long Island and in the Hudson and Delaware Valleys, and the term "Munsee" will be used only for those groups in the mid-Atlantic region who are believed to have spoken the Munsee language; see Ives

Complexities and contradictions characterized interactions among these very different peoples. As sojourners disembarked in America for the first time, no single pattern governed their encounters with their new indigenous neighbors. From Guyana to southern Africa to Sumatra, Dutch dealings with local people varied greatly; relations were distant, violent, exploitative, intimate, and everything in between. At the Cape of Good Hope, for instance, servants of the VOC quickly became embroiled with the Khoekhoe people in violence over land. These early hostilities identified the Khoekhoe as outsiders, whereas the later integration of Khoekhoe families as (often unpaid) workers on settler farms signaled their newly colonized status and initiated a period of much more intense contact. In contrast, combat between Javanese polities and the Dutch in Batavia developed into a multifaceted and complex situation after the establishment of a lasting peace, when Javanese villagers moved into the Batavian hinterland. A similarly diverse array of relationships existed across the various empires in North America at the time the Dutch arrived, from forced proximity in New Mexico to uneasy watchfulness in Virginia to mutual exchange in New France. The interplay between colonists and Native people in the Hudson Valley depended, not on any single established precedent, but rather on what people thought about and wanted from one another.[2]

Goddard, "Delaware," in William C. Sturtevant, ed., *Handbook of North American Indians*, XV, *Northeast*, ed. Bruce G. Trigger (Washington, D.C., 1978), 214–216.

2. Ad Biewenga, *De Kaap de Goede Hoop: Een Nederlandse vestigingskolonie, 1680–1730* (Amsterdam, 1999), 105–108, 211–212; Robert Ross, "Khoesan and Immigrants: The Emergence of Colonial Society in the Cape, 1500–1800," in Carolyn Hamilton, Bernard K. Mbenga, and Ross, eds., *The Cambridge History of South Africa*, I, *From Early Times to 1885* (Cambridge, 2010), 168–210. For a comparison of southern Africa and North America, see Carmel Schrire and Donna Merwick, "Dutch-Indigenous Relations in New Netherland and the Cape in the Seventeenth Century," in Lisa Falk, ed., *Historical Archaeology in Global Perspective* (Washington, D.C., 1991), 11–20. On the East Indies, see Hendrik E. Niemeijer, *Batavia: Een koloniale samenleving in de zeventiende eeuw* ([Amsterdam], 2005). On North American patterns, see James F. Brooks, *Captives and Cousins: Slavery, Kinship, and Community in the Southwest Borderlands* (Chapel Hill, N.C., 2002); Melanie Perreault, "'To Fear and to Love Us': Intercultural Violence in the English Atlantic," *Journal of World History*, XVII (2006), 71–93; Susan Sleeper-Smith, *Indian Women and French Men: Rethinking Cultural Encounter in the Western Great Lakes* (Amherst, Mass., 2001). This variety of interactions serves as a reminder to avoid Parkmanesque ascriptions of settler-Native relations to the national character of various colonizers; see Francis Parkman, *The Jesuits in North America in the Seventeenth Century: France and England in North America, Part Second* (Boston, 1898), 44. On the continuity of European approaches to Native Americans, despite national and imperial divides, see John A. Dickinson, "French and British Attitudes to Native Peoples in Colonial North America," *Storia Nordamericana*, IV (1987), 41–56.

What people seemed to want most during the first two-thirds of the seventeenth century in the mid-Atlantic was trade. Just like all early modern people, New Netherlanders and Mohawks, Munsees, Lenapes, Shinnecocks, Mahicans, and Susquehannocks managed to trade by forming face-to-face ties with one another. As Henry Hudson's and other Dutch-sponsored ships began nosing around the mid-Atlantic coastline in 1609, tense and tenuous exchanges of Dutch goods for Munsee, Montauk, Mahican, and Mohawk food, beads, and beaver skins sustained annual trade expeditions. With the arrival of full-time residents, first a few soldiers and traders in forts followed by settler families and slaves in the mid-1620s, the yearly, shoreside meetings began to develop into daily trade. By the 1630s, settlers and Mohawks, Mahicans, and Munsees living upriver around Fort Orange, the heartland of the beaver-skin trade, came together often to swap goods, furs, and food. Mahican villagers, for their part, welcomed the Dutch and tried to act as good hosts, developing particularly close ties with the residents of the Rensselaerswijk patroonship on the eastern shore of the Hudson, where they "lived near the farm households." Close contact was so important that, in the 1640s and 1650s, extensive trade with Mohawk and Mahican neighbors came to define the seasonal rhythms of the town of Beverwijk, and people flooded into town in the summertime to participate in the fur trade. Settlements began to proliferate by the late 1650s, expanding at the initial strongholds at Fort Orange and Manhattan and developing on western Long Island and midway up the Hudson at Esopus. Daily exchanges of food, drink, and firewood, along with the key trade goods of wampum and beaver skins, took place at every one of these settlements. A true interpersonal economic network united villagers throughout the region. Trading brought people together.[3]

3. Shirley W. Dunn, *The Mohicans and Their Land, 1609–1730* (Fleischmanns, N.Y., 1994), 127 (quotation). See also Oliver A. Rink, *Holland on the Hudson: An Economic and Social History of Dutch New York* (Ithaca, N.Y., 1986); Allen W. Trelease, *Indian Affairs in Colonial New York: The Seventeenth Century* (Ithaca, N.Y., 1960); Donna Merwick, *Possessing Albany, 1630–1710: The Dutch and English Experiences* (Cambridge, 1990), 68–133. It remains unclear how unusual day-to-day interactions between Europeans and Native Americans were in early America. Far more attention continues to be paid to diplomatic relationships than local ones. Some inland Native American groups, like the Cherokees, clearly managed to participate in diplomatic and commercial exchange in the 1600s without experiencing extensive daily contact; see Tom Hatley, *The Dividing Paths: Cherokees and South Carolinians through the Era of Revolution* (New York, 1995), 32–33. Yet, coastal Native groups served as intermediaries during this period and might have been a visible presence in Carolina towns. Works on diplomacy and warfare have suggested that in some regions, like eighteenth-century Pennsylvania, peoples remained divided by a no-man's-land; see James H. Merrell, *Into the American Woods: Negotiators on the*

Yet vast distances continued to separate colonists and Native peoples, and these divisions frequently resulted in violence. Localized fighting broke out almost as soon as Dutch ships began arriving regularly in the 1610s. Serious wars erupted quickly and repeatedly once settlement began in the mid-1620s, most often, though not exclusively, between colonists and Long Island and Hudson River Munsee-speaking groups. The Dutch participated in attacks on the Mohawk as early as the summer of 1626, just two years after the first Dutch families arrived. Conflict with the Raritans exploded in the early 1630s, only to be followed by further armed clashes and individual murders from 1639 to 1641. Dutch troops staged organized attacks against a collection of downriver Munsee towns in 1643. Tensions once again became deadly in the lower Hudson Valley starting in 1649 and extending into the early 1650s, culminating in the Peach War, which took place primarily on and around Staten Island, in 1655. Midway up the Hudson River, at Esopus Creek, Munsee-speaking villagers and recent settlers ambushed and harried one another throughout 1658 and 1659, with an organized assault by Dutch soldiers following in 1660. A shaky period of truce ended in full-scale war once more in 1663. Individual incidents of bloodshed, sometimes deadly, took place throughout the mid-Atlantic region before, during, and after these dates.[4]

Pennsylvania Frontier (New York, 2000). Yet, Alison Duncan Hirsch shows widespread "social connections" among European, African, and Native people there that only disappeared with later violent westward settlement; see Hirsch, "Indian, *Métis,* and Euro-American Women on Multiple Frontiers," in William A. Pencak and Daniel K. Richter, eds., *Friends and Enemies in Penn's Woods: Indians, Colonists, and the Racial Construction of Pennsylvania* (University Park, Pa., 2004), 63–84 (quotation, 84). David L. Preston demonstrates that the "'village world'" saw extensive face-to-face encounters even in times of crisis; see Preston, *The Texture of Contact: European and Indian Settler Communities on the Frontiers of Iroquoia, 1667–1783* (Lincoln, Neb., 2009), 7. Daniel H. Usner, Jr. has shown that studying the local trade in daily necessities can reveal a host of such contacts, and this chapter relies on his formulation of the "frontier exchange economy"; see Usner, *Indians, Settlers, and Slaves in a Frontier Exchange Economy: The Lower Mississippi Valley Before 1783* (Chapel Hill, N.C., 1992). The challenge posed by Usner's work has not been sufficiently explored for English colonies, obscuring when and where face-to-face contact was common.

4. Paul Otto organizes this violence into what he calls the First, Second, and Third Munsee Wars; see Otto, *The Dutch-Munsee Encounter in America: The Struggle for Sovereignty in the Hudson Valley* (New York, 2006), 116–118, 142, 149–152. This periodization helps categorize the violence; however, these labels can suggest that this often localized fighting united all Munsee-speaking people against the Dutch throughout the region, which was never the case. For a timeline of conflicts involving Munsee villagers, see Robert S. Grumet, *The Munsee Indians: A History* (Norman, Okla., 2009), xix–xxxi.

Murderous as they were, these conflicts tended to remain local. Neither all settlers nor all their Native American neighbors, nor even all their Munsee-speaking neighbors, ever united in concert against one another. Likewise, neither the fur trade nor the local trade in consumables was ever seriously disrupted. The coexistence of warfare and economic interdependence among the peoples of the Hudson area makes it difficult to make sense of New Netherland. Some historians explain trade and violence by arguing that the Dutch attacked the Munsees but accommodated the Mohawks because they mistakenly assumed that the Dutch traded only with the latter. Such an easy association falls apart when the extensive trade the Dutch carried out with the Munsees in furs and consumables is viewed alongside the comparatively gradual growth of the trade in furs with the Mohawks. Nor did the Dutch characterize the Munsee as a single group; rather, they interacted with Munsee-speakers as a series of separate peoples based in independent villages. Donna Merwick argues for a chronological explanation of violence based on cultural change among Dutch settlers, who at first "wanted . . . peaceful encounters" centered around trade but eventually "betrayed" those ideals and sought farm land instead, a shift that culminated in the vicious Esopus wars between 1658 and 1663. Yet, the intense intermingling of peaceful and violent interactions throughout the Dutch period belies any attempt to draw a clear chronological distinction between an era of peaceful trade followed by a period of violent farming. If the scale of violence grew over time, so, too, did the scale of daily trade interactions.[5]

To explain why close contact resulted in increasing peace or increasing violence in a particular colonial setting, the nature of day-to-day interactions needs to be carefully explored. Indeed, it was the very closeness among peoples, brought about and encouraged by trade, that encouraged the climate of violence. Over time, people in the mid-Atlantic region established a series of connections among their villages that brought people together daily. Ris-

5. Donna Merwick, *The Shame and the Sorrow: Dutch-Amerindian Encounters in New Netherland* (Philadelphia, 2006), 3 (quotations). Paul Otto similarly notes change over time in Dutch-Munsee interactions but alternately dates increasing conflict over land to 1638, much earlier than Merwick; see Otto, *Dutch-Munsee Encounter*, 106, 165–166. Scholars need to be wary of assuming that close, daily contact led to peace. David Preston believes daily contact on the edges of Iroquoia shows how people, "for a time, coexisted and created mutually beneficial relationships"; see Preston, *Texture of Contact*, 18. Alison Hirsch goes further, adding a gender dimension and arguing that "social connections—relationships in which women were integral" sustained peace and that "as long as women remained deeply involved at every level of social interaction, there was peace"; see Hirsch, "Indian, *Métis*, and Euro-American Women," in Pencak and Richter, eds., *Friends and Enemies*, 84 ("social"), 65 ("as long as"). Yet, close

ing settlement in the 1640s and 1650s drew villages nearer, fostering regular patterns of exchange. But if the distances between them gradually narrowed, people also pushed one another away, both subtly and aggressively. As they came to realize just how much they disliked and mistrusted one another, proximity had deadly results. New Netherland's final years, from 1658 to 1664, culminated both in catastrophic fighting and a growing emphasis on the centrality of face-to-face exchange among settlers and locals.

The shape of social networks and individual intimacies explain this coexistence of trade and violence. A duality developed in the face-to-face relationships that underlay the exchange networks people built in the mid-Atlantic region. Despite their ties to one another, settlers and Native Americans continually struggled with their use of personal associations to negotiate the challenges of cross-cultural interactions. Even though extensive and varied contacts reached among colonial and indigenous villages, bringing people together within the realms of hearth and home and forcing them to share intimate details, people's interactions with one another usually stopped short of friendship. Settler and Native communities stayed geographically distinct and encounters remained fraught with tension.

In spite of the challenges they posed, personal ties remained the best way to cement the trade people needed. Therefore, individuals repeatedly sought one another out, even though they judged each other harshly. A remarkable pattern of daily cross-cultural interactions thus nurtured the consistent outbreaks of violence. Although people in the mid-Atlantic region developed a highly effective, widespread set of interpersonal economic networks, their failures to form intimate connections meant those networks did little to staunch the bloodshed that resulted as people lived closer together. Indeed, they might have heightened the antipathies that drove such violence. Though people met one another again and again, though they called one another friend and brother, the distances between them persisted. Those

---

contact also provided the breeding ground for strong antipathies. As Peter Silver explains, "Almost nothing about the history of the early modern middle colonies suggests that this hopeful view of contact between groups is true. With few exceptions, living together made the different sorts of people there feel frightened of one another's intentions"; see Silver, *Our Savage Neighbors: How Indian War Transformed Early America* (New York, 2008), xix. William A. Starna argues that the proximity that resulted from Hudson-area land purchases in the Dutch period explains the higher level of violence and conflict between the Dutch and the Munsees as opposed to the Dutch and the farther-off Mohawks; see Starna, "The Native-Dutch Experience in the Mohawk Valley," in Martha Dickinson Shattuck, ed., *Explorers, Fortunes, and Love Letters: A Window on New Netherland* (Albany, N.Y., 2009), 27–38.

distances constituted the boundary between communities, a boundary that only fragile and temporary bridges crossed.[6]

Getting to Know One Another, 1609–1630

In September 1609, Henry Hudson and his men laboriously explored the maze of bays, islands, and waterways that hid from view the river valley that would eventually become the heart of Dutch colonization in North America. As they carefully made their way past shoals and inlets, they repeatedly encountered local men and women, drawn to the shore to see what the visitors might have to offer. The journal of Robert Juet, one of the ship's officers, makes clear that neither side quite knew what to make of the other. Friendly exchanges gave way, in the dark of a rainy night, to deadly fighting. On September 5, locals and newcomers seemed to interact peacefully. According to Juet, "many of the people came aboord" and the ship "rode very quiet" at night. Yet, the next day, when five sailors went out to reconnoiter, they "were set upon by two Canoes, the one having twelve, the other fourteene men. The night came on, and it began to rayne, so that their Match went out; and they had one man slaine in the fight, which was an English-man, named John Colman, with an Arrow shot into his throat." Friendliness and deadly hostility alternated as people crossed the water to meet one another. These conflicting reactions continued even when people managed to trade peacefully. On September 11, Juet noted, "the people of the Countrey came

6. Intimacy in this context should be understood to refer to enduring immediate relationships in which affect and proximity were key components. They spanned the range from friendship to parenthood, fictive kinship, romantic partnerships, and many other ties. See Gwenn A. Miller, "'The Perfect Mistress of Russian Economy': Sighting the Intimate on a Colonial Alaskan Terrain, 1784–1821," in Ann Laura Stoler, ed., *Haunted by Empire: Geographies of Intimacy in North American History* (Durham, N.C., 2006), 300, on the need to consider "other close relationships—of learning, living, and labor" alongside sexual encounters in studies of intimacy and empire. In the case of seventeenth-century Dutch interactions in the mid-Atlantic region, sexual encounters existed, but close relationships such as Miller describes remained very rare. On the use of intimate kinship metaphors across the Northeastern colonial frontier, see William N. Fenton, *The Great Law and the Longhouse: A Political History of the Iroquois Confederacy* (Norman, Okla., 1998); Francis Jennings, *The Ambiguous Iroquois Empire: The Covenant Chain Confederation of Indian Tribes with English Colonies from Its Beginnings to the Lancaster Treaty of 1744* (New York, 1984); Merrell, *Into the American Woods*; Daniel K. Richter, *The Ordeal of the Longhouse: The Peoples of the Iroquois League in the Era of European Colonization* (Chapel Hill, N.C., 1992); Richard White, *The Middle Ground: Indians, Empires, and Republics in the Great Lakes Region, 1650–1815* (Cambridge, 1991). These works all establish that language of friendship, kinship, and brotherhood reflected specific Native American expectations about the duties that such relationships entailed.

aboord of us, making shew of love, and gave us Tabacco and Indian Wheat, and departed for that night; but we durst not trust them." Thus, "love" and distrust mingled from the outset in meetings between Natives and newcomers along Long Island and the Hudson River. When they sailed away, Juet recorded that they left behind both new friends who were "very sorrowfull for our departure" and the bodies of newfound enemies, shot and hacked to death with the sailors' guns and swords.[7]

Drawn together by a mutual desire for the things, knowledge, and power they offered one another, newcomers and Native people would try again and again over the next several decades to make these interactions work. Despite outbreaks of murderous hostility, people throughout the region came to know—and sought to be known to—one another. During this early period, people turned to personal ties to provide stability and protection from the volatile reactions of love and fear Juet described. These relationships came in many forms, from brief interactions to sustained partnerships. Because European traders often made short, annual trips and used violence to get what they wanted, many of these relationships remained tense and tenuous at best. But, as the Dutch developed a year-round presence, starting with the creation of a permanent trading post later called Fort Orange in 1614 followed by the establishment of settlements in 1624, these personal associations became both more sustained and more complex. Vulnerable settlers and sojourners needed trading ties to gain access not only to furs but also to daily necessities like food. People tried to initiate relationships to foster trade, but the fragile nature of those contacts kept the region explosive. By the 1640s, the area reached the boiling point. Getting to know one another proved a necessary but painful strategy for newcomers and Natives alike.[8]

Although a contemporary chronicler of Hudson's voyage explained that "there were never yet any ships or Christians in this area" before Hudson's arrival, the Native inhabitants of the region already understood perfectly

7. Robert Juet, *Juet's Journal: The Voyage of the "Half Moon" from 4 April to 7 November 1609,* ed. Robert M. Lunny (Newark, N.J., 1959), 28 ("many"), 29 ("were set upon"), 30 ("people"), 34–35 ("very sorrowfull," 34).

8. The kinds of things, knowledge, and power the numerous actors in this complex zone of cultural interaction looked for varied. Whereas whites wanted moneymaking items (furs and wampum) and daily necessities, indigenous traders desired a variety of manufactured trade goods as well as exotic food and drink. Everyone hoped to gain knowledge about one another's trade goods. Dutch traders, especially, needed cultural, political, and geographic information that could aid their trade. Some Native traders might have viewed the newcomers and their unusual goods as a source of spiritual power, whereas Europeans pursued the power to claim territory. Multiple and varied desires, then, drove these diverse groups together.

what Europeans and their trade goods meant. Rumors of visitors to the Chesapeake and the Saint Lawrence bearing strange goods had traveled through the villages of the East Coast long before Hudson ever sailed within hailing distance of their shores, and items brought to the coast by European fishermen had made their way far inland to Haudenosaunee communities before 1600. By the time Juet made his notes, Long Islanders were well acquainted with the idea of trading with sailors plying the Atlantic coast. The French presence to the north made Mohawks in particular acutely aware of the potential power and clear dangers Europeans and their trade goods offered. Samuel de Champlain had recently participated in an attack on Mohawks, and his use of firearms had left them "astonished." Mohawks hearing about the arrival of Dutch-sponsored ships knew the importance of having their own European trading partners to counter the alliance of the French with their northern enemies.[9]

This context explains why Juet and his fellow sailors repeatedly met people willing to trade as Hudson's ship sailed upriver. "This day the people of the Countrey came aboord of us," Juet wrote, "seeming very glad of our comming, and brought greene Tabacco, and gave us of it for Knives and Beads." Juet admired their "Skinnes of divers sorts of good Furres" and remarked that "they desire Cloathes, and are very civill." These savvy locals already knew just what to offer and what goods to ask for in return. The most noted aspect of the seventeenth-century mid-Atlantic economy—the exchange of beaver skins, beads, cloth, and trade goods—made its appearance with the very first Dutch-sponsored ship to wend its way up the Hudson River. But how and whether people would be able to sustain their newfound trading relationships with one another remained in question.[10]

Dutch traders and sailors needed the goodwill of the indigenous people they met. Regardless of their ships' guns and the seeming safety of their anchorages offshore, crews could find themselves outnumbered and overwhelmed if fighting erupted. Skipper Hendrick Christiaensz perished in one

---

9. Joannes de Laet, *Beschrijvinghe van West-Indien*, 2d ed. (Leyden, 1630), 101 ("ships or Christians"); H. H. Langton and W. F. Ganong et al., eds. and trans., *The Works of Samuel de Champlain in Six Volumes*, 6 vols. (Toronto, 1925), II, 95–100 ("astonished," II, 99). For the original French, see [Samuel de Champlain], *Les voyages de la Nouvelle France occidentale, dicte Canada. . . .* (Paris, 1632), 151. On this attack, see Fenton, *Great Law*, 243. European goods, such as glass beads, begin appearing at Iroquois archaeological sites after 1580, and fragments of Basque copper brought by fishermen to the Saint Lawrence are present from 1550 onward; see William Engelbrecht, *Iroquoia: The Development of a Native World* (Syracuse, N.Y., 2003), 133–137.

10. Juet, *Juet's Journal*, ed. Lunny, 28.

such incident in the sixteen-teens on board his ship *Swarte Beer* in an attack that only five crew members survived. Just as critically, Dutch visitors also remained dependent on indigenous people to feed them and restock their supplies for the trip home. Indeed, Juet mentioned food exchanges much more often than he mentioned furs in his journal. "They have great store of Maiz or Indian Wheate," he noted following his very first interaction with local people. Before leaving the Hudson River, Juet and his fellow travelers were offered currants, "Indian Corne," beans, oysters, pumpkins, grapes, and "a great Platter full of Venison." Hudson, in turn, not only had "two old men" and four women "dine with him," he also treated "some of the chiefe men of the Countrey" to "so much Wine and Aqua vitae, that they were all merrie." Trading alcohol for food, in addition to exchanging trade goods for furs, would always remain a key part of Dutch traders' strategies.[11]

Even though European traders relied on the protection and support of local people, interactions still threatened to go disastrously awry when people met as strangers. The story of Skipper Willem Jorisz Hontom and his crew's attempts to trade along the mid-Atlantic coast in 1620 demonstrates just how thoroughly things could fall apart. When Hontom's ship first arrived "in the Virginias," the crew failed to establish any workable interactions with the Native Americans they encountered. Although they stayed there "a long time and sought to do honest trade," they found to their dismay that "the *wilden*" there would not trade with them. After giving up and setting sail for home, they decided to give it one last try along the Long Island coastline.[12]

This time, the crew had better luck, when "some wilden came on board there, to whom they showed every friendship, in order to move the same to trade." Realizing that their would-be customers might simply paddle away and knowing that if they failed again they would have to return to Amsterdam with their chests full of unsold goods, the crew tried to use "friendship" as a means to facilitate trade across the cultural divide. When the crew had spoken awhile with their guests, the Long Islanders asked that the ship "wait yet one day or two, that pelts should come out of the country." Long Island's Montauk, Shinnecock, and other Algonquian villages specialized in

11. Ibid., 28–34 ("great store," 28, "Indian Corne," 31, "Platter," 33, "two," 34, "chiefe men," 32). On Hendrick Christiaensz, see Jaap Jacobs, *New Netherland: A Dutch Colony in Seventeenth-Century America* (Boston, 2005), 36; Testimony/demand for payment, Oct. 24, 1622, Not. Arch. 691, 30v–31, Not. J. Warnaertsz, SA.

12. Declaration, Aug. 14, 1620, Not. Arch. 200, 625–626v, Not. J. Bruijningh, SA; this translation relies on the typescript transcription made by Simon Hart held by the SA.

wampum production and fishing, with little direct access to the large numbers of beavers on the mainland, so, if Hontom and his men wanted pelts, they would have to be patient.[13]

Hontom and his crew waited one day, then two, and then three, when, finally, "one of the wilden came on board with ten or twelve pelts, which the same, so it seemed, sought to trade." Yet, the Dutch traders' "friendship" was wearing thin, just as their Native partners were beginning to let their own suspicions surface. "Although they showed and presented him [their guest] out of the chest that stood above, certain axes and other wares, so he let it be known that he had no desire for the goods therein, demanding that someone should fetch other axes and wares out of the hold of the ship." Previous experience with other traders had obviously taught this man never to trust that the goods the Dutch brought out first were the best. The absence of any real acquaintance with or knowledge of Hontom and his crew meant he had little reason to change his view.[14]

Without relationships born of any personal connection, the time that Hontom and his men had spent trying to get furs from the Long Island traders suddenly seemed likely to have been wasted. As the sailors began to fear that their potential trading partners were not friends but deadly enemies, trust completely broke down. According to the sailors' testimony, while some of the crew went below decks to bring up the goods demanded by their choosy guests, others left the ship to haul in the anchor, and still others lay in their cabins asleep. Just then, a number of Long Islanders who had been in the vicinity "came on board with an appearance of friendship." However, that friendliness soon dissipated when they went into the hold and began demanding that the factor open all the chests, "totally differently than they had normally traded other times." Based on previous tales of trade on the

13. Declaration, Aug. 14, 1620, Not. Arch. 200, 625–626v, Not. J. Bruijningh, SA (quotations). On wampum production on Long Island, see George R. Hamell, "Wampum: Light, White, and Bright Things Are Good to Think," in Alexandra van Dongen et al., "One Man's Trash Is Another Man's Treasure": The Metamorphosis of the European Utensil in the New World (Rotterdam and Williamsburg, 1995–1996), 41–51; Lynn Ceci, "Tracing Wampum's Origins: Shell Bead Evidence from Archaeological Sites in Western and Coastal New York," in Charles F. Hayes III, Ceci, and Connie Cox Bodner, eds., Proceedings of the 1986 Shell Bead Conference: Selected Papers, Rochester Museum and Science Center, Research Records, no. 20 (Rochester, N.Y., 1989), 63–80; Ceci, The Effect of European Contact and Trade on the Settlement Pattern of Indians in Coastal New York, 1524–1665 (New York, 1990); Elizabeth Shapiro Peña, "Wampum Production in New Netherland and Colonial New York: The Historical and Archeological Context" (Ph.D. diss., Boston University, 1990).

14. Declaration, Aug. 14, 1620, Not. Arch. 200, 625–626v, Not. J. Bruijningh, SA.

coast, the factor began to fear that they were trying to get at the knives, "in order to kill him and the others." Slamming the chest shut, he ran to the skipper to tell him "the intention" of the visitors, and the skipper called the crew together to force all the guests but "four of the most principal ones" off the ship. As the four men stood surrounded by strangers on the deck of a foreign ship, they were in grave danger of becoming casualties of trade. Other indigenous men aboard Dutch ships had faced captivity, mutilation, and murder, so the danger was very real. In this particular encounter, mutual antipathies got the upper hand.[15]

Through conversation and overt conciliatory gestures, the four men managed to pull themselves back from the brink. Hontom's sailors reported that after the violent expulsion of the other visitors, they began "making peace and treating with them." The Long Islanders reestablished cordiality by giving the crew "some beads," and "they parted from each other on friendly terms." The "beads" that restored friendship with Hontom and his crew were wampum, valuable polished shell beads fashioned into belts by skilled Long Island artisans. At once a powerful diplomatic symbol and a valued trade good, wampum provided the basis for Long Islanders' exchange with inland groups who used it for sacred ritual purposes. Dutch traders quickly adapted to local uses of wampum and came to regard it first as a trade item that afforded access to furs and later as a form of currency in exchanges with colonists and Native villagers alike, from Long Island to the Delaware Valley. Thus, while the Dutch sailors saw these beads as restitution for attempted "thievery," the four Long Island men meant the gesture quite differently.[16]

From one side of this unfortunate encounter, the incident looked like a criminal attempt by savages on the lives and goods of the crew; from the other, it appeared like a brutal kidnapping of guests held by force until they paid ransom in sacred wampum. Each side had ample reason to fear and mistrust the other, and such fears made cross-cultural encounters explosive and risky. Testimony about Hontom's voyage illustrates the danger and instability of attempts to trade without personal ties. Trade demanded communication and trust; in effect, it demanded some kind of relationship, some kind of "friendship," capable of reaching across the wide cultural and linguistic chasms that yawned between Amsterdammers and Long Island Algonquians.[17]

15. Ibid.
16. Ibid.
17. Ibid. See also Otto, *Dutch-Munsee Encounter*, 60.

The danger nervous traders and sailors like Hontom's men posed did not stop Native people from approaching ships to trade. As Nicolaes van Wassenaer, a seventeenth-century chronicler of the Dutch during their Golden Age of overseas trade, would explain in the 1620s, even though the "various nations" who lived along the Hudson made fearsome enemies, "when they have seen the ships one or two times, or have traded with us, they are all Friends." To signal peaceful intentions, women joined in the groups visiting Dutch ships. As Van Wassenaer observed regarding indigenous traders who came south from Canada, "if they bring along the women, that is a sign, that they come in friendship, if they come to visit the Yachts without them, everyone must be on their guard."[18]

Whatever strategies indigenous men and women used, going onboard a Dutch ship remained risky. When European traders did not get what they wanted, they frequently resorted to force. In 1622, a leader of the "Sickenanes, [who lived] between the Brownists, and the Hollanders" found himself imprisoned by "Jaques Elekes ... on his Yacht," and he was only released after paying a large ransom in wampum. Already by 1622, Dutch traders understood that getting access to furs often hinged on their ability to first access wampum made by Algonquian women. In this instance, the trader more commonly known as Jacob Eelkens evidently decided that ransom would yield more wampum than exchange. But, some clever Dutch traders looking for an advantage over their competitors changed the equation by going ashore themselves and visiting indigenous towns, making themselves vulnerable and thereby signaling their own peaceful intentions.[19]

Traders operating out of Fort Orange had the chance to outcompete their shipbound competitors by building ongoing, face-to-face connections with local village leaders. Van Wassenaer described Pieter Barentsz, for example, as one of the most successful traveling traders of the 1620s. Van Wassenaer pointed to Barentsz's local relationships as the key to his profits. In his trav-

18. [Ni]colaes van Wassenaer, *Historisch verhael alder ghedenck-weerdichste geschiedenissen....*, 21 vols. (Amsterdam, 1622–1635), VI, 144 ("various"), XII, 39 ("if they bring"). For indigenous uses of women in diplomatic negotiations in Texas, see Juliana Barr, *Peace Came in the Form of a Woman: Indians and Spaniards in the Texas Borderlands* (Chapel Hill, N.C., 2007).

19. Van Wassenaer, *Historische verhael,* XII, 39 (quotations). Eelkens had been present at the earlier ransom incident on Hontom's ship in 1620; see Simon Hart, *The Prehistory of the New Netherland Company: Amsterdam Notarial Records of the First Dutch Voyages to the Hudson* (Amsterdam, 1959), 54–55. For more accusations against Eelkens and the violent confinement and murder of a Mohawk leader during trade with Hans Jorisz Hontom, see Interrogation, July 14, 1634, Not. Arch. 1040, 20–21, Not. J. van de Ven, SA. See also Dunn, *Mohicans,* 83; Merwick, *Possessing Albany,* 166.

els outside Fort Orange, Barentsz had learned to speak the languages of "all the Nations nearby." Van Wassenaer explained that Barentsz "visits all the Peoples in a shallop, and trades with them in friendship." These personal trading relationships enabled Barentsz to make "an accord" with the very man formerly imprisoned by Jacob Eelkens. When approached in friendship, the man promised Barentsz "to trade with no one other than with him." By visiting his hosts in their own homes and villages, Barentsz found a way to counteract the bitter distrust left by shipboard Dutch traders willing to use brutal tactics.[20]

The advent of settlement in 1624 made it possible for a greater number of European men and women to begin following in Pieter Barentsz's footsteps and start building so-called friendships with locals for the purposes of trade. In September 1626, WIC secretary and factor Isaac de Rasière wrote his superiors about his trip to Manhattan in 1626 to assure them of his efforts to secure and expand the trade with the Mohawk, Susquehannock, and Munsee inhabitants of the Hudson and Delaware River regions. The key to his strategy was establishing what he called "vrientschap," or "friendship," with all the surrounding groups. He noted that a group of thirty or forty "Minquaes" (Susquehannocks) had recently visited him, "seeking friendship with us," and that "I in turn showed as much friendship as possible," which led the visitors "to ask that a sloop or small ship be sent to them when the trading season comes." Continuous presence allowed De Rasière to connect the present and the future through personal interactions in a way not possible for visiting traders.[21]

Year-round settlement and the increased contact it brought did not fully stabilize relationships; in many ways, it simply increased the number of interactions capable of giving offense. De Rasière worried that if he was unable to oversee the interactions of other traders with local groups to ensure that "the nations are treated well," there would be "discontent." Better to treat everyone properly, "each according to their condition and humors," he asserted, to "keep them always in devotion." His friendly approach, however, was a matter of policy, not personal inclination. For his own part, he remained wary. "In sum, these people must, like children, be maintained with caresses . . . one must be familiar with them and lead them to believe

---

20. Van Wassenaer, *Historische verhael,* XII, 39–39v ("all the Nations," 39v, "an accord," 39).

21. Isaac de Rasière to WIC Directors, Sept. 23, 1626, in A. J. F. van Laer, ed. and trans., *Documents Relating to New Netherland, 1624–1626, in the Henry E. Huntington Library* (San Marino, Calif., 1924), 192–193 (quotations, 192); Records of the WIC, 1624–1626, HM 548, Huntington Library, San Marino, Calif.

that one trusts them a great deal, and meanwhile be on guard." Trust was more strategy than reality.[22]

However much friendliness might have been feigned, settlers quickly formed relationships with their indigenous neighbors, even threatening to leave WIC traders out of the loop. In the early years before 1638, settlers were required to sell any beaver skins they bought to WIC representatives, but they used their own contacts with their Native neighbors to buy furs and wampum at the source and drive a hard bargain with the company. De Rasière wanted to pay only one guilder for each beaver skin bought from colonists, but he had such a hard time acquiring sufficient furs on his own account that he soon had to pay more. Regarding the trade, he observed in 1626, "it goes very badly here; whatever there is, it is taken by the families [colonists]." Women fur traders particularly bedeviled him; "the wife of Wolfert Gerritsz" van Couwenhoven refused his bid of three and a half guilders for two otters, demanding five. Although he first tried to stick to his guns, when "the wife of Jacob Lourissz, smith," made a counter offer, he was forced to meet the price. De Rasière clearly felt frustrated, but he should not have been surprised to find female traders driving such shrewd bargains. Women in the colony took an active part in the exchanges of furs and wampum that moved those goods from Native American hands to WIC ships, just like *huysvrouwen,* or wives, in Amsterdam participated in the small-scale exchanges that drove the sale of colonial products there.[23]

The early settlements continued to depend on Native Americans not just for access to the furs that promised profit but also for wampum. Wampum was precious because it provided means to obtain furs, but it also secured the necessaries of life. Thus, even though De Rasière desperately hoped to beat out French and English competition by stocking Fort Orange with "a thousand ell of wampum" in the winter of 1626, he nonetheless found himself forced to sell twenty pounds of it to hungry "families" at one guilder per pound. He had to do it, he explained, "because they complain so much about the victuals." With it, "they buy from the wilden maize, fish, and so forth." To eat, settlers had to exchange their European currency for the quickly developing, Native-produced medium of wampum. De Rasière sent samples of the white and dark strung beads to Amsterdam in the hope that it could be manufactured there and sent back in bulk to the colony "as they are greatly

22. De Rasière to WIC Directors, Sept. 23, 1626, in Van Laer, ed. and trans., *Documents Relating to New Netherland,* 201–203, 212–213 ("nations," 200, "discontent," 203, "each," 200, "keep," 203, "In sum," 212).

23. Ibid., 216–219 ("it goes very badly," 216, "wife of Jacob," 219).

sought and there are no more here." But, in the end, if settlers and traders wanted access to wampum and the food and furs it enabled them to purchase, they had to adapt to local economic realities and meet the demands of indigenous villagers.[24]

As their contact with indigenous neighbors increased, De Rasière and others in the early settlements hungrily saw the bounty of local villagers' food production. De Rasière noted the skill with which Algonquian women and men cooperated to manage fishing in the springtime. "In April, May, and June," they spend their time fishing, he wrote; " they catch [fish] with a net that they weave from wild hemp that the women and old men spin from the thread, very beautifully. . . . The biggest fish is a sort of white salmon, which tastes very good." He perceived that gender played a role in the distribution and consumption of this fish, with women taking charge. This observation suggested to De Rasière that the fish might be an aphrodisiac, of sorts: "It appears, that [the oil in this fish's head] makes them luxurious [unchaste], since one often sees, that he, who gets some when he goes fishing, has given the same to the women when they come back, which they take good care of." Settlers evidently not only acquired the fish from their neighbors, they also acquired the gendered ideas about its effects. De Rasière remarked that "our folk also give witness" to the white salmon's sexual powers, as they, too, experienced the same results when they ate a great deal of it. Whatever the supposed consequences of eating this fish, Dutch purchasers clearly understood that its capture resulted from the work of women and men together. Women and older men prepared the nets, younger men managed the nets during the fishes' spring run up the Hudson, and women alone handled and processed the catch. The food so desperately needed by settlers and traders was in women's hands. The wife, De Rasière observed, "provides the daily bread, for herself and her husband." The maize and bean hills they relied on required "a great deal of work," and it was "the women [who] must carefully watch over" them. Thus, the New Netherlanders who traded goods or wampum for locally caught fish and corn realized from the earliest days of settlement that they depended on the work of women and men alike.[25]

24. Ibid., 226–227, 232–233 ("thousand," 227, "families," 232). An "el" was a unit of measure roughly based on the length of a person's underarm, from body to fingertip; with local variations, it comes to just under seven hundred millimeters. See M. de Vries et al., *Woordenboek der Nederlandsche taal* (The Hague, 1882–), s.v. "el."

25. De Rasière to Samuel Blommaert, [1628], in A. Eekhof, "De 'memorie' van Isaack de Rasière voor Samuel Blommaert, Het oudste Hollandsche bericht betreffende Nieuw-Nederland en New Plymouth, de kolonie der 'Pilgrim Fathers,'" *Nederlandsch archief voor kerkgeschiedenis*,

By the mid-1620s, Dutch residents, who needed trade to survive and succeed, had learned that women also helped anchor long-distance trade. In his account of New Netherland's Native peoples, Van Wassenaer gave a somewhat confused description of the interweaving of polygamy with trade in Northeastern Native communities. "It is very common with them that a Man buys and has many Wives, but not in one place, if he journeys five or six miles, he finds another wife who will also take care of him, eight or ten miles further he finds again another household, and so on, traveling through the Land buying up peltries." De Rasière further claimed that a woman whose husband strayed sexually complained to the village sachem, who allowed the wife to take every last possession and stitch of clothing from her husband as she chased him out of the house as naked as "Adam" himself. Whether these ethnographic descriptions were wholly accurate is beside the point; they demonstrate, instead, that Dutch traders and settlers, who increasingly sought to form relationships with indigenous villagers in order to trade successfully, believed that, in addition to controlling the food they so desperately needed, women also played an important role in the fur trade and regulated key resources within their marriages.[26]

In part, this better knowledge of women's crucial work came from the increasing contact newcomers had with Native people in their own villages. In the 1630s and 1640s, some Dutch traders took their desire to secure trading ties through personal relationships yet further by becoming guests within intimate spaces of indigenous villages and homes. Journeying far from shoreline strongholds, they forged their way upstream and overland, into the heart of Native communities. Despite the questionable behavior and odd ways of these outsiders, Mohawks, Mahicans, Munsees, and Algonquian Long Islanders made them welcome, often choosing to tolerate their presence, inviting them to reside with them for a time in their own attempts to solidify trading partnerships. These wandering traders, known in Dutch as *boslopers,* depended on the kindness and support of their hosts as they shared their longhouses or wigwams with them.

As they took them in, fed them, protected them, and guided them on their way, indigenous villagers got to know boslopers on a deeply personal

n.s., XV (1919), 268–270 ("April," 268, "appears," 268–269, "our folk," 269, "provides," 270). See also J. Spinoza Catella Jessurun, *Kiliaen van Rensselaer van 1623 tot 1636* (The Hague, 1917), vii–viii.

26. Van Wassenaer, *Historisch verhael,* VI, 145v ("very common"); De Rasière to Blommaert, [1628], in Eekhof, "De 'memorie,'" *Nederlandsch archief voor kerkgeschiedenis,* n.s., XV (1919), 271 ("Adam").

level. The journal of Harmen Meyndertsz van den Bogaert, who traveled to various Mohawk and Oneida towns in 1634–1635, shows that his hosts struggled with his alien culture, even as his presence and dependence allowed them to strengthen their trading networks. After his long, cold voyage that winter, Van den Bogaert had learned enough of the Mohawk tongue to make a brief wordlist. The words he recorded testify to the intermingling of economic and personal concerns within the confined spaces of the longhouses where he stayed. In addition to practical words needed for travel ("the creek," "to the north") and trade ("beaver," "axes"), he also included words of a highly personal nature ("vagina," "excrement," "sweat"). That he acquired and used such vocabulary during his stay is a reminder that he and his hosts got to know one another on a remarkably familiar basis.[27]

The curiosity was mutual, as Mohawk and Oneida men, women, and children got to see these strange outsiders firsthand. The packed quarters of a winter longhouse gave everyone a chance to have a closer look at Van den Bogaert and his companions. In the longhouses, he reported, "we caused much curiosity in the young and old. . . . They pushed one another into the fire to see us. It was almost midnight before they left us. We could not do anything without having them shamelessly running about us." Shame or distance found little place in settings such as this. Sitting together around longhouse firesides, visiting boslopers and their hosts learned all about one another's ways, habits, and bodies.[28]

The villagers who played host to Dutch traders did not view their interactions with their guests as a one-off visit. Instead, they hoped to use the nascent relationships they formed with visiting traders as bridges that would enable them to cross cultural distances again and establish better patterns for subsequent trade. One Onondaga leader who met with Van den Bogaert "asked [him] earnestly to visit his country in the summer." Oneida leaders sought promises about the amount of wampum that would be paid per beaver skin in the future, complaining that "we have to travel so far with our pelts and when we arrive we often find no cloth, no [wampum], no axes,

27. Gunther Michelson, "Wordlist," in Harmen Meyndertsz van den Bogaert, *A Journey into Mohawk and Oneida Country, 1634–1635,* ed. and trans. Charles T. Gehring and William A. Starna (Syracuse, N.Y., 1988), 51–65 ("creek," 58, "north," 62, "beaver," 53, "axes," 52, "vagina," 56, "sweat," 60). For the original manuscript version of this journal, see Van den Bogaert, Memorial, 1634–1635, Huntington Manuscripts 819, Huntington Library. The translation, however, is indispensable, not only for the excellent annotation of the journal but also because Michelson has correlated Van den Bogaert's original transcriptions with current Mohawk and Oneida words and phrases.

28. Van den Bogaert, *Journey,* ed. and trans. Gehring and Starna, 7.

kettles or anything else; and thus we have labored in vain." Although Van den Bogaert would make no price guarantees, the Oneida council suggested that a mutual agreement regarding acceptable standards of trading behavior would be advantageous to both sides. "You must not lie," the council implored, "and come in the spring to us and bring us all an answer. If we receive four hands [length of wampum per beaver], then we shall trade our pelts with no one else." For those who treated with Van den Bogaert and his companions, the future loomed larger than the present. For Van den Bogaert, making good on the intimate knowledge and personal relationships he had formed during his journey would depend on his ability to maintain long-term ties with his Mohawk and Oneida friends. Among the few complete phrases included in Van den Bogaert's wordlist are those that stressed the ongoing and personal nature of trading relationships. "When shall you return," "I shall fetch it," and "I know them well" complimented phrases like "in the spring," "yesterday," and "tomorrow." Such phrases and words allowed him to voice his ideal of personal trading ties persisting over time. Both sides expressed the hope that these lasting personal ties would serve as guideposts for further interactions and trade.[29]

However much Van den Bogaert and his hosts expressed optimistic visions of a shared future, the journal shows that the relationships boslopers formed in their travels remained fraught. Mohawk and Oneida speakers repeatedly expressed disdain for what they saw as the tendency of Dutch people to take without giving. Van den Bogaert and his companions were made very aware of these attitudes when they were berated by their hosts. Though one Osquage man called the itinerant trader "his brother and good friend," other Oneidas and Mohawks spoke differently. Van den Bogaert noted that when they arrived at one Oneida town, "one of the councillors came to ask me what we were doing in his country and what we brought him for gifts. I said that we brought him nothing, but that we just came for a visit. However, he said that we were worth nothing because we brought him no gifts. . . . And this councillor derided us as scoundrels." Van den Bogaert and his companions struggled to keep their own tempers in check. When the boslopers were once again scolded as scoundrels, "Willem Tomassen became so angry that the tears ran from his eyes." But power constraints forced the men to put up with their hosts' criticisms. As Van den Bogaert commented, "had they had any malicious intentions, they could have easily grabbed us with their hands and killed us without much trouble." Brothers and good

29. Ibid., 19 ("asked"), 15 ("we have to travel"), 16 ("You must not lie"); Michelson, "Wordlist," ibid., 57, 61–62 ("return," 61, "fetch," 62, "spring," 61, "yesterday," 57).

friends? Perhaps in metaphor, but, in reality, the ties between boslopers and their indigenous hosts seem considerably more mixed.[30]

Despite the continuing dependence of settler communities on the trade in food and furs, and despite the better cross-cultural knowledge, Native people's visits to settler towns remained just as tense as boslopers' trips to Native communities. As people came to know one another better, strong antipathies formed from bad memories of past meetings. In 1633, the Mohawk headman Saggodryochta traveled to Fort Orange to trade. However, rather than sell his skins, he packed them up again and left immediately when he saw Hans Jorisz Hontom, the brother of Willem Jorisz Hontom who had taken the four Long Island men captive in the 1620s. Several years before, Hans Jorisz, like his brother, had also resorted to kidnapping and extortion when he held a Mohawk man for ransom aboard his ship. But, rather than release the man when the ransom was paid, he emasculated and killed him. Seeing Hontom in Fort Orange once more, Saggodryochta complained that he was a scoundrel and left the Dutch settlement at once. Over time, Hontom's reputation had the power to drive traders clear out of town.[31]

Native men and women not only disliked many of the people they encountered in Dutch settlements, they also faced disrespect and abuse when they arrived in towns bearing food and goods. Even though Native American traders were central to New Amsterdam's markets, some of the newcomers preferred simply taking their goods to forming relationships with the people carrying them. In 1639, an unnamed Native woman visiting New Amsterdam suffered an attack at the hands of a Dutch sailor who threw her down and drew a knife "to cut the belt which [she] had around her waist." Wearing wampum belts had strong political, religious, and social meaning for Long Island Algonquians, and they highly prized the wampum women made from shells in the wintertime. As one Dutch observer explained, they "string it, wearing it on the neck and hands, making belts from it, which the women wear in their hair and the men on the body." That this visitor wore belts of wampum suggests she was of high status, but that did little to protect her from the greedy sailor. The colony's mobile population of sailors and sojourners ensured that there would always be someone who cared more about grabbing loot than about establishing lasting trading relationships. New Netherland's economy drew Mohawk and Algonquian women traders

30. Van den Bogaert, *Journey*, 7 ("brother"), 13–14 ("one," 13, "Willem," 14).

31. Examination of Bastiaen Jansz Krol, June 30, 1634, in A. J. F. van Laer, ed. and trans., *Van Rensselaer Bowier Manuscripts: Being the Letters of Kiliaen Van Rensselaer, 1630–1643, and Other Documents Relating to the Colony of Rensselaerswyck* (Albany, N.Y., 1908), 302–304.

into settler towns, but Dutch antipathies toward them meant that they did not always receive good treatment when they got there.[32]

Mistreatment of the indigenous women who came to settler communities to trade reflected a persistent gender-based denigration of them by immigrant men. By the end of the 1630s, continuing close contact combined with the persistence of these attitudes culminated in laws prohibiting intimate sexual relationships across cultural lines. In 1638, the colony's governing council outlawed sexual intercourse with "heathens, blacks, or other persons" along with "mutiny, theft, false testimony, slanderous language and other irregularities." Most of these relationships, especially if they were temporary and took place in Native villages, doubtless went unmentioned and, perhaps, even unknown within the Dutch community, but some men found their activities brought to light as a part of legal proceedings. A few men faced prosecution after 1638, although, in most cases, their sexual activities were just one of many offenses mentioned in witness testimony, suggesting that men who transgressed only the law's sexual proscriptions might have avoided legal penalties. For instance, in 1639, WIC corporal Hans Steen faced testimony from seven of his men about his misbehavior. In addition to having had a Native woman spend the night in his bunk under the same blanket, Steen supposedly hid a keg of brandy and stole company gunpowder. So his temporary demotion and condemnation to ride the wooden horse can only partly be attributed to his forbidden sexual relationship in the guardhouse. But, the interlude received mention from five of the seven deponents, showing that sexual relationships with Native American women had come to seem scandalous in many Dutch minds. The mounting presence of indigenous women and men in settler towns made intimate relationships increasingly possible, but legal and social prohibitions intensified at the same time.[33]

32. Declaration, June 18, 1649, in *Provincial Secretary,* I, 177 ("to cut"); De Rasière to Blommaert, [1628], in Eekhof, "De 'memorie,'" *Nederlandsch archief voor kerkgeschiedenis,* n.s., XV (1919), 269 ("string it").

33. Ordinance, Apr. 15, 1638, in *Council Minutes,* I, 4 (quotations). For a comprehensive discussion of sex between Native women and traders in New Netherland, see Jacobs, *New Netherland,* 394–396; for a briefer discussion, see Otto, *Dutch-Munsee Encounter,* 139. Jan Platneus and Jacob van Leeuwen were both mentioned in court proceedings for their adulterous sexual activities with local women; see Jacobs, *New Netherland,* 396. On Platneus, see Minutes, Oct. 3, 1641, in *Council Minutes,* I, 122. For Steen, see Trial, Apr. 7, 1639, 43–45. See also the demotion of Nicolaes Coorn, Dec. 2, 1638, 33–34. For a brief synopsis of the patroon Kiliaen van Rensselaer's condemnation of interracial sex, see Matthew Dennis, *Cultivating a Landscape of Peace: Iroquois-European Encounters in Seventeenth-Century America* (Ithaca, N.Y., 1993), 165. Van Rensselaer, however, made his remarks from afar in the Netherlands.

The Dutch were not alone in their negative impression of their neighbors. Munsee villagers did not think very highly of colonists, either. Indeed, the continuing dependence of settlers on food produced by Munsee women made colonists very aware of the danger posed by Native peoples' growing antipathy toward them. Colonists realized that the very women and men they relied on to provide them with food did not like being near them very much. In particular, New Netherland settlers had the habit of letting their pigs and cattle roam "in the Forest," where they uprooted Native women's maize hills, on which everyone depended. The trade in bulky consumables encouraged people to live in adjoining communities, but, when villages grew up too near one another, conflict frequently resulted. In 1640, the colony council worried that the "great damage" done by roaming beasts would make corn "dear in the autumn and our good people [would] suffer want." Even more dangerous than high prices and scarcity was the possibility that Native villagers would "be induced to remove and to conceive a hatred against our nation." Being too close might have seemed scandalous, but being too far apart threatened the colonists with destruction. Colonists were ordered to fence their animals or hire shepherds to watch over them.[34]

Though food dependence in this case encouraged colonists to try to behave like somewhat less repellant neighbors, in the end, participation in daily exchange did not lead to more peaceful cross-cultural relationships.

34. Contract, May 4, 1649, Not. Arch. 1089, 8–9v, Not. J. van de Ven, SA ("in the Forest"); Ordinance, May 9, 1640, in *Council Minutes*, I, 73–74 ("great damage," 73). Pigs ran free in Holland as well; see Peter G. Rose, "Dutch Foodways: An American Connection," in Donna R. Barnes and Peter G. Rose, eds., *Matters of Taste: Food and Drink in Seventeenth-Century Dutch Art and Life* (Syracuse, N.Y., 2002), 18. On conflict over free-ranging stock, see Otto, *Dutch-Munsee Encounter*, 109; James Homer Williams, "Great Doggs and Mischievous Cattle: Domesticated Animals and Indian-European Relations in New Netherland and New York," *New York History*, LXXVI (1995), 245–264. On conflicts over animals in general, see Virginia DeJohn Anderson, *Creatures of Empire: How Domestic Animals Transformed Early America* (New York, 2004); William Cronon, *Changes in the Land: Indians, Colonists, and the Ecology of New England* (New York, 1983); Neal Salisbury, *Manitou and Providence: Indians, Europeans, and the Making of New England, 1500–1643* (New York, 1984). Long Island Algonquian villagers began raising stock in the later years of the 1600s, particularly cattle, but they seem to have not yet begun doing so during the Dutch period. On Native stock raising in the Northeast, see David J. Silverman, "'We Chuse to be Bounded': Native American Animal Husbandry in Colonial New England," *WMQ*, LX (2003), 511–548. The introduction of stock changed the landscape of Long Island, too, as grazers reduced forest cover and increased grasslands, so their presence challenged indigenous subsistence strategies in multiple ways; see Glenn Motzkin and David R. Foster, "Grasslands, Heathlands, and Shrublands in Coastal New England: Historical Interpretations and Approaches to Conservation," *Journal of Biogeography*, XXIX (2002), 1569–1590.

Quite the opposite. A desire to reorient the food trade along lines more advantageous to the colony underlay New Netherland's first major war with neighboring Munsee-speaking villagers. In 1639, the colony council resolved to demand an in-kind "contribution" from local villages near Manhattan, payable in furs, maize, or wampum. Any nation not inclined to make such a payment "in a friendly way" would be urged or coerced into cooperation. Although the council justified this demand based on the costs of building a fort and supporting soldiers who ostensibly protected indigenous towns, such a claim would have likely struck any Algonquian villagers who heard it as laughable. With less than fifty soldiers at the time, Fort Amsterdam hardly represented a formidable installation, and indigenous villagers probably saw those soldiers as more apt to be aggressors than protectors. Yet, Director Willem Kieft's subsequent designs to enforce this contribution proved anything but a laughing matter. Kieft's unexpected attempt to "force them to give their Corn for nothing" sparked bitter fighting beginning in 1640, when colonial forces burned the village of Raritan in a bloody massacre. Despite some colonists' criticisms of this conflict, attacks continued through the summer of 1643. Proximity and dependence in the 1630s bred vicious violence, not greater friendship.[35]

In 1645, sachems representing at least a dozen Munsee towns in the lower Hudson and eastern end of Long Island came to the chamber of the governing council in Fort Amsterdam, on Manhattan, and concluded a formal peace. Their agreement sought to end the killings that had plagued the region since Kieft's attempt to claim a tribute in corn. Oratam, Sesekemu, Willem, Pacham, Pennekeck, Mayauwetinnemin, and Aepjen did not even raise the possibility of making such a payment, focusing instead on establishing mutual promises for the punishment of killers. In addition, they strove to define how each side would visit the other. They agreed that no one from their towns would be "allowed to come with arms to the houses of the Christians on this island of Manhatans." In return, they solicited promises from the council that no colonist be permitted to "come to them with guns," unless accompanied by a local villager who provided fair warning of peaceful intentions. The council called all the settlers on the island to come to the council and hear the terms themselves. Together, then, the various participants in the daily exchanges and cultural encounters of the lower Hudson

35. Resolution, Sept. 15, 1639, in *Council Minutes,* I, 60 ("contribution"); David Pietersz. de Vries, *Korte historiael, ende journaels aenteyckeninge, van verscheyden voyagiens in de vier deelen des wereldts-ronde* (Hoorn, 1655), 161 ("force"). On the paucity of WIC soldiers and Kieft's War, see Jacobs, *New Netherland,* 54–55, 134–139.

region tried to hash out how they would interact in the future. Even with the brutal experiences of the attacks of recent years, neither side seemed to envision the possibility of not meeting at all. That they would visit one another's homes was simply an assumption all sides carried into the negotiations. They only sought to find a way to distinguish who came to trade and who came to kill.[36]

The debacle of Kieft's War and continuing conflicts about his leadership eventually led to his departure from the colony and the installation of a new leader, Peter Stuyvesant, in 1647. On his arrival, Stuyvesant strove to assure the survival of the costly colony by reaffirming peace throughout the mid-Atlantic region. Though he declined Munsee sachems' request for full compensation for the bloodshed as being "entirely too much," he did offer them a present as a renewal of their mutual "alliance and friendship." He wanted the various village headmen to understand that Kieft, the "old Sachem," had gone away. He, the new sachem, claimed he only wished for the Dutch and indigenous peoples of the region to live in peace as "good neighbors." With the war over and the practice of face-to-face trade reestablished, it was clear by the time Stuyvesant appeared that the colony was not going to go away. The new administration initiated a period of growth, and new settlers and traders flooded into the region, from Long Island to the Delaware Valley. People had learned that getting to know one another was difficult—perhaps even deadly—yet necessary to support the trade everyone wanted. But, whether these newcomers were capable of acting like the good neighbors that Stuyvesant promised remained to be seen.[37]

Building Economic Networks

After Stuyvesant's arrival in 1647, the colony experienced more than a decade of growth that reshaped the mid-Atlantic region. New Netherland expanded geographically, with new towns inhabited by both Dutch and English settlers springing up on Long Island, an increasing number of farms and villages taking shape along the Hudson, and, eventually, the reincorporation of the Delaware River area in 1655. The reach and strength of the colony's trading connections similarly expanded. Mohawks became far more important in the Fort Orange fur trade, and their contacts with residents at the settlement called Beverwijk became more frequent. Yet, the

36. Minutes, Aug. 30, 1645, in *Council Minutes*, I, 279 ("allowed"), 280 ("come").
37. Minutes, Aug. 26, 1647, ibid., 430–431 (quotations, 431).

continuation and strengthening of the trade in daily consumables with indigenous groups throughout the region was equally crucial. Food, drink, and firewood moved between all the villages of the area in ever-more-complex patterns as people developed their individual trading relationships into vast trade networks. Chains of marketing and connection joined people together in a single web of exchange, even as they continued to regard one another with suspicion and sometimes failed to live with one another in peace.

In spite of Stuyvesant's public renunciation of Kieft's War, memories of violence and a legacy of mistrust doubtless made people dubious about accepting would-be traders into the hearts of their communities. Yet, attempts to trade without such close contact remained explosive. Meetings at designated spots, in between settler and Native communities, remained meetings between strangers, where fear and distrust easily descended into violence. In 1647, three Dutch traders testified to a near outbreak of hostilities at "the usual trading place" with the Raritans, the Munsee villagers who had suffered so much during Kieft's War just a few years before. Bloodshed was only averted because, "at the opportune moment, God the Lord sent a violent storm of wind, thunder, lightning and hail stones." Everybody ran for cover and deserted the trading post. For the most part, close, personal exchanges in the midst of people's towns and homes, not meetings in the woods, formed the normal pattern from the end of Kieft's War through the Dutch period.[38]

As the former minister at Rensselaerswijk, Johannes Megapolensis, explained in 1651, "We live between [the Mohawks and the Mahicans], and they, coming to us from their Country . . . show us every friendship." During the summer months in particular, Native men and women were a regular sight in upriver households and on the streets near Fort Orange. Reverend Megapolensis explained that the Rensselaerswijk residents did not worry about allowing Mohawks to sleep in their houses during trading season. "Although they are so cruel against their Enemies," he wrote, "they are so very amicable towards us, that we have no fear of them; we go with them into the Forest, we meet each other sometimes one or two hours from all houses, but we think no different than if we had encountered a Christian; they also sleep by us in the room before our beds. I have even had 8 at the same time that were lying sleeping on the floor before my bed, for that is their manner, that they just lie down on the naked Earth, with just a stone or wood under their heads." Living cheek to cheek in small settler houses meant that people got a

38. Declaration, June 17, 1647, in *Provincial Secretary*, II, 409–410 (quotations, 409).

close look at one another's habits and had to trust each other a great deal. By choosing to visit settlers' spaces, Mohawks and other locals did more than just exchange anonymity for the beginnings of mutual acquaintance, they also built widespread trade networks with settler towns and villages.[39]

Native American men and women's visits to settler towns enabled both sides to gain powerful cultural and economic knowledge of one another. One Mohawk headman, Agheroense, for instance, communicated with and translated for Rensselaerswijk residents "because [he] very commonly trafficked with the Christians" and also spoke "all the key Indian or *Wildese* languages" in the region. Based on this linguistic ability gained through trade, he was able to act as an intermediary, negotiating peace between lower-Hudson Munsee speakers and the Dutch in 1645. Dutch hosts learned to talk to their guests as well. Though Megapolensis admitted that he found it difficult to produce a comprehensive grammar of the Mohawk language that took proper account of all the tenses and parts of speech, he and his visitors came to understand one another well enough to discuss serious matters about their beliefs, not just basic matters about exchange. When an "old Wife came to our house" one day, he understood her retelling of her origin myth and her theories about the differing origins of Europeans perfectly. Visiting enabled better communication and greater cultural exchange by the 1650s.[40]

An understanding of languages, however, was only the beginning of the economic knowledge visitors gained by spending time in colonial towns. By living side by side with Dutch residents, visiting indigenous traders learned about the merchandise offered for sale and the volume of pelts being purchased. For example, when a fire broke out in the gunpowder stored in "part of the house of Adriaen van Alckmaer" in August 1651, two Dutch traders and "two wilden" were unable to escape the flames that would consume both trade goods and beaver skins. Testimony about this tragic fire reveals just how closely buyers and sellers lived in New Netherland: goods, gun-

39. Johannes Megapolensis, "Kort ontwerp, vande Mahakuase Indianen. . . . ," in *Beschrijvinghe van Virginia, Nieuw Nederlandt, Nieuw Engelandt, en d'Eylanden Bermudes, Berbados, en S. Christoffel. . . .* (Amsterdam, 1651), 44–47 ("We live," 45, "Although," 46, "amicable," 47).

40. Adriaen van der Donck, *Beschryvinge van Nieuw-Nederlant. . . .* (Amsterdam, 1656), 29 ("because"); Megapolensis, "Kort ontwerp," in *Beschrijvinghe van Virginia*, 48 ("old Wife"). The phrase Megapolensis used to describe this woman, "een oudt Wijf," points more to advanced age than marital status and, in some usages, could be disparaging, suggestive of a gossiping or quarrelsome woman. His intention might have been to dismiss the myths she related as "old wives tales." On Agheroense, see Jon Parmenter, *The Edge of the Woods: Iroquoia, 1534–1701* (East Lansing, Mich., 2010), 64–65.

powder, furs, fur traders, and Native American traders all crowded together in a rented room. Visitors to settler homes not only got to know their hosts, they also got a good look at their hosts' goods and furs. Therefore, getting to know their trading partners very closely by coming into their towns and homes would remain a key strategy for Native Americans wishing to sell furs and goods throughout the Dutch era.[41]

Visitors demonstrated their commitment to the face-to-face economic network each time they made their way to a colonial town. Not everyone would have found walking and paddling to New Netherland towns an easy journey. People often crossed long distances through the territory of neighbors who might not welcome them. Communication barriers, time lost to travel, dangers of the voyage, and the instability of market prices among many other problems all provided logical reasons for would-be traders not to make the trip. Adriaen van der Donck, a prominent settler, colonial promotor, and author, reported on the challenges of travel faced by one Iroquois man, who, "accompanied by his Wife and Child, with about sixty Beaver pelts, came to sail the [Mohawk] River, during the spring, when the current ran at its fullest, intending to sell his pelts among the Netherlanders." Overwhelmed by the fast-moving river, his "little ship" went down, killing his family and ruining his goods. Despite this tragedy, the man returned to trade thereafter, telling his story "often" and coming to know Van der Donck "very well." Even those who knew the risks of travel all too well made the journey to meet and form lasting trading ties with their new neighbors.[42]

As people moved back and forth among the various villages of the region, the crucial paths and waterways became a sort of shared space. Immigrant traders and settlers often traveled in narrow canoes guided by skilled Native paddlers. The canoes and boats, "some very large," made by Mohawk craftsmen from hollowed trees impressed Megapolensis when he lived at the settlement of Rensselaerswijk. "I have many times sat and traveled" in one such Mohawk canoe "with 10, 12, and 14 people" the minister explained, adding that colonists regularly used a "wooden canoe gotten from the Indians, in which one can easily ship 200 schepel of wheat." To get around on their own, settlers needed to learn how to handle these tricky watercraft on the woodlands' swift-moving streams, but not everyone was up to the challenge. Jacob Jansz Schermerhoren sued, for instance, when hapless Marten Herpertsz upset "a canoe, in which were about 30 schepels of corn and a *mudde*

41. Testimony, Jan. 6, 1652, Not. Arch. 1099, 23v–24, Not. J. van de Ven, SA.
42. Van der Donck, *Beschryvinge*, 10.

of beans, which were thereby spoiled and perished through his carelessness." Travel would go more smoothly if traders convinced or hired local paddlers to pilot their canoes for them.[43]

In turn, Dutch sail craft plied the Hudson in the warmer months, harnessing the winds to connect downriver and upriver communities. Mohawks looking to travel downriver to New Amsterdam or Munsee villagers seeking to head north to Fort Orange often found it easier to hitch a ride on the larger Dutch yachts and sailboats working the river during season than to paddle the whole way themselves. When eight Mohawk headmen stopped by New Amsterdam in 1661 on their return from a diplomatic mission to the Delaware River area, where they had acted as intermediaries in peace negotiations between the Susquehannocks and neighboring tribes, they sailed north from New Amsterdam in "a Yacht to Fort Orange."[44]

Increasing numbers of ferries also came to crisscross the Hudson both north and south, as settlements spread out from the initial forts at Manhattan and Fort Orange to Long Island and both shores of the river. Upriver at Rensselaerswijk, ferries formed the principal connection between the farmers on the east bank and the outpost and community on the west bank, at Fort Orange. Leaders of the patroonship made sure that these ferries would carry Mohawks and Mahicans as well as settlers and slaves. In 1642, a lease with settler Hendrick Albersen granted him not only a farm and house lot but also exclusive right to operate a ferry from his place along Beaver's Kill, provided he give passage "for such . . . Christians and Indians as the Lord Patroon or his representative there" required for free. Long Island ferry operator Egbert van Borsum carried so many "soldiers, English, and Wilden over and back" that the colony council granted him payment for the use of his "boat and men." Van Borsum did not do the ferrying work himself, however, but relied on an African ferryman to take people to and fro. Africans, English, Dutch, and Native Americans all crowded side by side, not always happily or comfortably, but together nonetheless, onboard the growing number of ferries traversing the Hudson. Moving around by boat for the purposes of regional exchange meant depending on the skill and willingness of people from different cultures and backgrounds, whether that was the

---

43. Megapolensis, "Kort ontwerp," in *Beschrijvinghe van Virginia*, 47 ("some very large"); Court minutes, Dec. 23, 1653, in Charles T. Gehring, ed. and trans., *Fort Orange Court Minutes, 1652–1660*, NNDS, XVI, pt. 2 (Syracuse, N.Y., 1990), 72 ("30 schepels"), xl–xli. A "schepel" measures just over three quarters of a bushel, and a "mudde" is about three bushels.

44. Minutes, Apr. 7, 1661, NYCM, IX, 579, NYSA.

skill of Van Borsum's African ferryman, the skill of a Native canoeist, or the skill of a Dutch yachtsman.[45]

People traveling by watercraft and foot carried a wide range of goods with them. A look at what they hawked and peddled shows that trade in New Netherland comprised much more than beaver skins. Mainstays included food, drink, firewood, clothing, wampum, manufactured goods, and gunpowder, alongside furs. Munsee women bought mattocks and hoes to sow their fields. Settler women bought finely decorated bags, called *notas*, that indigenous women used to carry their wampum, grain, and fish to market. Mohawk men bought coats off Dutch traders' backs. Goods passed among villages again and again. In one instance, a settler man bought a coat back again once it had been remade into "a *wiltse* coat," reversing the standard pattern of the fur trade by paying a *"wilt"* in beavers. Who knows what this Long Island man bought with his beavers, but a wide range of manufactured goods and everyday consumables stood on offer at any of the settler towns and homes he chose to visit.[46]

45. Contract, June 7, 1642, Not. Arch. 1062, 108, Not. J. van de Ven, SA ("Christians and Indians"); Petition, [June 15, 1662], NYCM, X, pt. 1, 151–152, NYSA ("soldiers"); Complaint, Apr. 17, 1657, NYCM, VIII, 522–523, NYSA. For more on the varied work done by members of New Amsterdam's African population, see Chapter 4.

46. For the settler's purchase of the coat, see Court case, Jan. 22, 1658, NYCM, VIII, 653, NYSA (quotations). For a succinct list of goods commonly traded, see Otto, *Dutch-Munsee Encounter*, 138. See also Margriet de Roever, "Merchandises for New Netherland: A Look at Dutch Articles for Barter with the Native American Population," 73–93, and Alexandra van Dongen, "'The Inexhaustible Kettle': The Metamorphosis of a European Utensil in the World of the North American Indians," both in Van Dongen et al., *"One Man's Trash,"* 115–170. Since many of the items purchased by settlers were consumables like food and firewood, few clear traces of the trade appear in the archaeological record. Nan A. Rothschild argues that a paucity of goods of Native American manufacture in Dutch sites indicates "the social distance that excisted [sic] between Dutch settlers and the indigenous peoples," but extensive contact would have been necessary to carry bulky items of daily consumption between Native and settler homes; see Rothschild, "Social Distance Between Dutch Settlers and Native Americans," ibid., 189–201 (quotation, 193). If we take the example of firewood, William Cronon argues that "a typical New England household probably consumed as much as thirty or forty cords of firewood per year, which can best be visualized as a stack of wood four feet wide, four feet high, and three hundred feet long," representing more than an acre of forest; see Cronon, *Changes in the Land*, 120. By 1626, New Amsterdam already had thirty houses; thus, according to Cronon's rates, the colony was consuming some nine hundred to twelve hundred cords annually in the earliest years of settlement. On New Amsterdam settlement in 1626, see Jaap Jacobs and Martha Dickinson Shattuck, "Beavers for Drink, Land for Arms: Some Aspects of the Dutch-Indian Trade in New Netherland," in Van Dongen et al., *"One Man's Trash,"* 95–113. Even if New Netherland households for some reason consumed less wood than their English neighbors and even though Native woodcutters were not the only source

Many of these traders carried food with them on their voyages along the region's waterways and pathways. Colonists in the 1650s continued to count on food produced in indigenous villages as part of their own diets. Colonial farmers expanded their fields and increased their own harvests, but the food trade did not dwindle. Rather, the number of hungry mouths seeking to buy food raised in indigenous villages multiplied. That Native farmers, harvesters, and hunters were able to meet that growing demand should not be a surprise. Both Algonquians' and Iroquoians' long history of abundant food harvesting within the local environment made them essential producers of such critical staples as corn, venison, and fish.

Colonists and slaves from the Old World found it more difficult to hunt, fish, and farm in the cold Northern woodlands than the people who had grown up there. Haudenosaunee maize farmers in the seventeenth century grew three to five times more grain per acre than European wheat farmers using plow agriculture. In addition, very few European immigrants had any real hunting experience. Therefore, colonists depended on local villagers to do their hunting for them. Settlers often remarked that their Mohawk neighbors were "tremendous experts at catching Deer." They sought to persuade local hunters to trade game for the food and goods that they had to offer. As Megapolensis explained in 1651, "In the years before I came here, there were so many turkeys and deer, that they came near the houses and pig pens to graze, and they were then caught in such numbers by the Indians, that they sold one deer to the Dutch for one bread, for one knife, even for one Tobacco pipe, but now one must ordinarily give 6 or 7 guilders for one good deer." Even when wild animals were so abundant that they came practically to settlers' doorsteps, they struggled to catch them themselves— fortunately, local Mohawk, Munsee, and other hunters proved willing to trade. As animals became rarer in the vicinity of colonial towns and farms— and as Native hunters became more adept at negotiating Dutch monetary

---

of firewood, the potential size of the firewood trade alone could have led to extensive contact among Native Americans and settlers, though the material evidence of that trade quickly went up in smoke. On hoes (dissels), see De Rasière to Blommaert, [1628], in Eekhof, "De 'memorie,'" *Nederlandsch archief voor kerkgeschiedenis*, n.s., XV (1919), 270. On decorated bags known as *notas*, see Gehring, ed. and trans., *Fort Orange Court Minutes*, 252. On their use to carry dried fish, see Megapolensis, "Kort ontwerp," in *Beschrijvinghe van Virginia*, 47. On their use to carry wampum, see Treaty, July 10, 1663, NYCM, X, pt. 2, 203, NYSA. Notas remained appealing to English settler women—appealing enough to steal—even after the Dutch period ended; see Court minutes, May 5, 1667, *Minutes of the Town Courts of Newtown, 1656–1690*, Transcriptions of Early Town Records of New York (New York, 1940), 74. For a trader's sale of a coat off his back, see Van den Bogaert, *Journey*, 22.

systems—settlers like Megapolensis found themselves paying more for the foods they desired.[47]

Megapolensis might have grumbled about prices in the 1650s, but, in general, settler buyers paid up and made a profit in turn. Game formed the basis for networks of exchange, as settlers resold Native catches to one another. Adriaen van der Donck noted that colonists bought turkeys "when they are at their best from the Wilden for often ten stivers a piece, and among the Christians one typically gave a *daelder* or so," leaving those Dutch retailers with a very tidy twenty stiver (200 percent) profit. Moving locally hunted game through settler communities made for good business, even if everyone could see that buying a family's meat directly from the indigenous men and women who hunted and prepared it would stretch budgets farther. Women and children took part in these retailing chains, transporting food from one kitchen to another. When Marritie Trompetter sold a fish for three guilders and eleven stivers, Maria de Truy's "meisje," or girl, carried the money from one kitchen to the other—or at least she would have if she had managed to avoid dropping it in the water. Women played a particularly important role in shipping food from Manhattan and Long Island upriver to Fort Orange,

47. Megapolensis, "Kort ontwerp," in *Beschrijvinghe van Virginia,* 47 ("tremendous"), 43 ("In the years"). See also the translation included as Johannes Megapolensis, Jr., "A Short Account of the Mohawk Indians," in Dean R. Snow, Charles T. Gehring, and William A. Starna, eds., *In Mohawk Country: Early Narratives about a Native People* (Syracuse, N.Y., 1996), 38–46. Susan Sleeper-Smith assesses the variety of food production in the Native Northeast; see Sleeper-Smith, "Agrarian Landscapes: Indian Women and the Making of an Indian World in the Great Lakes" (paper presented at the *WMQ* / EMSI Workshop, "Women in Early America," Huntington Library, San Marino, Calif., May 26–28, 2011). On the intensive agriculture and diverse gardening practices in the Eastern Woodlands, see William E. Doolittle, "Agriculture in North America on the Eve of Contact: A Reassessment," *Annals of the Association of American Geographers,* LXXXII (1992), 386–401; R. Douglas Hurt, *Indian Agriculture in America: Prehistory to the Present* (Lawrence, Kan., 1987), 33–35. For evidence that Iroquois agricultural yields exceeded those of European plowed grain fields, which explains why the food trade persisted even as settlers established their own farms, see Jane Mt. Pleasant, "The Paradox of Plows and Productivity: An Agronomic Comparison of Cereal Grain Production under Iroquois Hoe Culture and European Plow Culture in the Seventeenth and Eighteenth Centuries," *Agricultural History,* LXXXV (2011), 460–492. For an early look at women's roles in Iroquois agriculture, see Joan M. Jensen, "Native American Women and Agriculture: A Seneca Case Study," *Sex Roles,* III (1977), 423–441. On the origins and variety of hunting, fishing, gathering, and cultivation practiced by the Iroquois, see Engelbrecht, *Iroquoia,* 9–34. On the management of forests to encourage fruit and nut trees while expanding forage lands for deer, see Marc D. Abrams and Gregory J. Nowacki, "Native Americans as Active and Passive Promoters of Mast and Fruit Trees in the Eastern USA," *Holocene,* XVIII (2008), 1123–1137. For comparisons of indigenous and European farming practices in the Northeast, see Carolyn Merchant, *Ecological Revolutions: Nature, Gender, and Science in New England* (Chapel Hill, N.C., 1989); Cronon, *Changes in the Land.*

where chronically high food prices made for an advantageous market. One Breuckelen widow, Teuntie Straetsmans, evidently lived almost entirely on the profits of the garden crops she sent north to her sister. Servants, huysvrouwen, settlers, and people of every description moved food and drink from home to home, inside and between settler towns.[48]

Food, closely tied as it is to the life of families and communities, drew both genders and all generations into networks of production, exchange, and consumption. Women and men cooperated in growing and preparing food, both in Native and in settler villages. Thus, the buying and selling of food relied on the work of all and brought a diverse group of people together. For instance, corn, the staple grain crop for Northeastern Algonquian and Iroquoian peoples alike, depended on the combined work of both women and men. Men did much of the heavy work of clearing the corn fields, while women did much of the planting. The elderly and children helped to watch the fields and scare away hungry deer and birds as harvest approached. Women then ground the grain by hand into flour for use, most often, as "porridge, which . . . is called *Sapaen*." Adriaen van der Donck explained that "one can scarcely go into any Indian's or Wilden's house at any time of the day, where such porridge is not being eaten." Boiled maize became so common in all the houses throughout the region, in fact, that Native travelers expected to find it wherever they went. "When they visit us or each other," Van der Donck continued, "their first question . . . is about it." Porridge had long been a staple of the evening meal in the Netherlands, so colonists took to this local version, adding milk to make it their own. Produced through the cooperative work of kin groups and villages and consumed within the intimate confines of settler homes, the "Indian Wheate" Robert Juet had noted in 1609 remained a key component of cross-border trade and eating patterns, even as the Dutch colony grew in its last two decades (Figure 5).[49]

48. Van der Donck, *Beschryvinge*, 40 ("when they are at their best"); Demand and answer, Nov. 9, 1654, CMNA, I, 261, NYCMA (microfilm) ("meisje"). De Truy's name is given here as D'Truwe. "Meisje," like the word "maid" in English, could be a term applied to a servant girl or a daughter. For Straetsmans, see A. P. G. Jos van der Linde, ed. and trans., *Old First Dutch Reformed Church of Brooklyn, New York: First Book of Records, 1660–1752*, NYHMD (Baltimore, 1983), 51, 75. On high food prices in Fort Orange, see Martha Dickinson Shattuck, "A Civil Society: Court and Community in Beverwijck, New Netherland, 1652–1664" (Ph.D. diss., Boston University, 1993); Janny Venema, *Kinderen van weelde en armoede: Armoede en liefdadigheid in Beverwijck/Albany (c. 1650–c. 1700)* (Hilversum, Netherlands, 1993), 23–30. See also Susanah Shaw Romney, "Intimate Networks and Children's Survival in New Netherland in the Seventeenth Century," *Early American Studies*, VII (2009), 270–308.

49. Van der Donck, *Beschryvinge*, 55 (quotations). On the role of the food barter trade, alongside the fur trade, in giving Ojibwa women food producers access to cross-cultural

FIGURE 5 ✦ Novi Belgii, Quod nunc Novi Jorck vocatur. . . . Detail. From
Arnoldus Montanus, *De Nieuwe en onbekende weereld* (Amsterdam, 1671). This item
is reproduced by permission of The Huntington Library, San Marino, Calif.

These images, taken from a number of earlier prints and maps of North America,
show that, even after New Netherland's demise, Dutch people continued to
associate indigenous residents of the greater Hudson Valley with abundant
food production, including the processing of corn, fishing, and hunting.

Food did not simply move between indigenous and settler villages in one direction—Native Americans purchased food in addition to selling it. As early as the 1630s, the idea of selling food to indigenous inhabitants had formed a part of the plans of the proprietor of Rensselaerswijk. Kiliaen van Rensselaer instructed his underlings to sell any extra "milk, butter, cheese and further all kinds of grain and root crops" to either "Christians" or their Mahican and Mohawk neighbors, whoever offered the patroon the highest price. In the end, local people did prove eager buyers for some of the exotic new foods the newcomers provided, particularly for fine Dutch baked goods and bread. Megapolensis noted the Mohawk taste for baked goods when he remarked that, in the early years, Mohawks so prized Dutch bread that the exchange of a single loaf for a deer had seemed a fair trade. That bread then made the journey home to indigenous towns and villages. When Van den Bogaert traveled in Mohawk country in the 1630s, he ate "a piece of wheat bread from an Indian who had come from Fort Orange" the day before. Other hungry buyers chose sweeter fare. One customer in Beverwijk was evidently so excited about the cake he bought from Jochem the Baker's maid, Anneken, that he forgot his notas full of wampum on the counter when he left. Over time, more and more settlers began trying to produce baked goods for Native American customers. Volkertie Juriaense, a baker's wife in the Fort Orange area, went so far as to build a bark house on her lot to accommodate visiting Mohawk and Mahican traders in 1652. Indeed, the trade in baked goods became so extensive in the 1650s that grain prices rose and some settlers complained that they could not get good bread.[50]

Soaring prices eventually prompted controversy between bakers and burghers. So many baked goods flowed across the border that the colony council feared that bakers neglected settlers, focusing instead on their beaver-rich

exchange, see Bruce M. White, "The Woman Who Married a Beaver: Trade Patterns and Gender Roles in the Ojibwa Fur Trade," *Ethnohistory*, XLVI (1999), 109–147. On colonists' consumption of *sapaen*, see Rose, "Dutch Foodways," in Barnes and Rose, eds., *Matters of Taste*, 23–24; Peter G. Rose, "A Taste of Change: Dutch Foodways in the New World," in Van Dongen et al., *"One Man's Trash,"* 203–213.

50. Instructions to Rutger Hendricksz van Soest, *schout,* and the council of the colony of Rensselaerswijk, July 20, 1632, in Van Laer, ed. and trans., *Van Rensselaer Bowier Manuscripts,* 208–212 ("milk," 211); Megapolensis, "Kort ontwerp," in *Beschrijvinghe van Virginia,* 42; Van den Bogaert, *Journey,* 21 ("piece"); Court minutes, Feb. 12, 1658, in Gehring, ed. and trans., *Fort Orange Court Minutes,* 355. Given how much settler women coveted these bags, it is perhaps not surprising that Anneken denied that the customer had left it behind. See ibid., 10; Jacobs and Shattuck, "Beavers for Drink," in Van Dongen et al., *"One Man's Trash,"* 105–106. For a bill of sale for a Beverwijk house that similarly had an "Indian house next to it," see Conditions for sale, 1659, in *Fort Orange Records,* I, 103–104 (quotation, 103).

Mohawk and Munsee neighbors. In February 1653, after receiving petitions from residents, the council forbade "the baking and sale to the Indians of white bread and cake." The issue sparked a flurry of petitions and complaints from all sides. Bakers wanted to control access to their profession to keep out the competition who continued to bake for Mohawk and Munsee customers while official bakers were shut out by the regulation. They complained that some "single bachelors," without the community ties that a *huysgezin,* or household, provided, baked goods "in order to sell them to the wilden, and without suiting the burghers, and when the [trading season] is over, they do other business." In contrast, they claimed that the regular bakers were at a disadvantage because "we promise to suit the Burghers and residents the whole year through," which put them very much "behindhand." It should not be a surprise that men and women in colonial towns would have eagerly seized on the possibility of baking for the Native American market. Unlike manufactured trade goods from overseas, baked goods allowed settlers to trade, even if they lacked the ability to import wares from Amsterdam.[51]

Competing interests among colonists escalated the tension. Although some settlers rushed into baking as a way to gain entry into regional trade, other settlers complained that a lack of enforcement of the new rules allowed bakers to continue favoring Native over settler customers, just as they had before. Indeed, the local court did nothing to prosecute Jochem the Baker or his maid, Anneken, when they sold forbidden cake in 1658, focusing instead on the mysterious disappearance of the customer's notas. Settlers complained that "the petitioners find and have daily experienced that the bakers do not act in good faith in the matter of baking bread for the burghers, but bolt the flour from the meal and sell it greatly to their profit to the Indians for the baking of sweet cake, white bread, cookies, and pretzels, so that the burghers must buy and get largely bran for their money." Some bakers, in other words, likely avoided the ban on serving Native customers by selling the sifted flour and letting Native American women do their own cooking. Northeastern Native women had long made cakes and

51. Gehring, ed. and trans., *Fort Orange Court Minutes,* 41 ("baking and sale"), 45, 110; Petition and Order, Oct. 10, 24, 1656, NYCM, VIII, 243–244, NYSA ("single bachelors"). See also Simon Middleton, "'How It Came That the Bakers Bake No Bread': A Struggle for Trade Privileges in Seventeenth-Century New Amsterdam," *WMQ,* 3d Ser., LVIII (2001), 347–372; James Homer Williams, "Cultural Mingling and Religious Diversity among Indians and Europeans in the Early Middle Colonies" (Ph.D. diss., Vanderbilt University, 1993), 85; Peter G. Rose, "Bread: Staff of Dutch Life in the Old and the New World," in Shattuck, *Explorers, Fortunes, and Love Letters,* 91–101; Janny Venema, *Beverwijck: A Dutch Village on the American Frontier, 1652–1664* (Hilversum, Netherlands, 2003), 287–290.

bread using corn flour. "Sometimes adding dried blueberries or raspberries, other times pieces of deer fat, then steeping the whole in lukewarm water," they shaped, wrapped, and baked the dough "under the ashes." Substituting white flour purchased from Dutch bakers for cornmeal would have made for a tasty change. Whoever was doing the preparation—single bachelors, rule-bending bakers, or Mohawk and Munsee cooks—baked goods from bread to cookies clearly attracted Native customers. The many voices raised on various sides of the issue illustrate that the sale of food was a serious business for all concerned.[52]

The food trade in the 1650s was the basis on which much of the other trade and economic activity in the region was built. Settlers' need for food grown by indigenous villagers forced them to trade whatever their Native neighbors demanded. Contraband cookies were not the only illegal goods settlers resorted to selling. People from every indigenous group in the vicinity were interested in buying firearms, for instance, even though various New Netherland laws forbade their sale and Stuyvesant continually sought to assure neighboring English colonies that no firearms trade existed. Yet, in 1653, the WIC directors in Amsterdam lamented that food dependence had prevented the enforcement of such laws. They sympathized that Stuyvesant, "upon the petition of those of Fort Orange and Colonie Rensselaerswijck, has had to wink at the placard concerning contraband goods." They begged him, at least, to ensure "that not a larger quantity of munitions is sold to the Indians through such connivance than each one needs for the provision of his household and with which to pursue a livelihood." They worried that the robust though illegal trade had already "provided all too many" weapons to indigenous traders and that "this savage and barbarian nation" could "turn these weapons against us," involving the company in yet another costly war. Even so, colony officials simply had to give in to pressure from allies to supply weapons and ammunition as part of treaty negotiations. In addition, individual settlers might have recognized that guns used for hunting could also provide the very game they hungered for. And they faced daily pressure from their would-be trading partners who had the power to force settlers to trade on their own terms. If guns were what Native traders wanted, settlers could

52. Petition, Mar. 17, 1654, in Gehring, ed. and trans., *Fort Orange Court Minutes*, 109–110 ("petitioners find"); H. H. Langton and W. F. Ganong et al., eds. and trans., *Works of Samuel de Champlain* (Toronto, 1932), IV, 304–305 ("Sometimes," IV, 305); [Champlain], *Les voyages de la Nouvelle France*, 286. On women's baking, see Engelbrecht, *Iroquoia*, 80. Most scholars have assumed that it was the bakers who made the cookies and pretzels, but Mohawk, Mahican, and Munsee women all had the skills needed to transform the flour into appetizing treats themselves.

either provide them or be shut out. Three New Netherlanders reported just such a threat to the governing council in July 1647. They claimed that they "all underst[ood] . . . the language of the Minquas [Susquehannocks]" and had been entrusted with a message to the council by "two chiefs of the Minquas, named Aqariochquo and Quadickho." The two leaders claimed that the governor of New Sweden, Johan Prins, had promised that the Swedes "could sell them powder, lead and guns enough, but that the Netherlanders, being poor, could not do so." Though the two sachems reported that they nonetheless refused to allow the Swedes to build their desired trading house, the warning was clear to any settler seeking to buy food.[53]

Similarly illegal was the sale of alcohol. Yet, like baked goods, drink was a desirable trade good that could be made by colonists in New Netherland, in addition to being imported from Holland. Repeated ordinances outlawed the sale of both large and small amounts of liquor to indigenous visitors and villagers beginning in 1643, but there is ample evidence that sales continued despite these prohibitions. Disobeying the laws potentially had serious consequences, but authorities were clearly willing to "wink" if such sales were part of the food trade, just as they did at weapons sales. New Amsterdam innkeeper Nicolaes Terhaer found himself hauled before the New Amsterdam court in 1654 for repeatedly selling liquor to Munsee visitors, even during the Sunday sermon. Terhaer denied that he had such serious business ties to the liquor trade, but he admitted that the face-to-face food economy had drawn his family into alcohol trading on a small scale confessing "that his wife had said to him that she had traded a *kan* of beer for a fish with the *wilde,* along with ½ *mutsje* brandy to which she had also added water." How else was his wife to get the food she needed to feed her huysgezin? Just eight months earlier, the WIC directors in Amsterdam had been forced to admit that the cessation of trade with New England owing to the Anglo-Dutch War (1652–1654) threatened the colony with a shortage of "meat or bacon" and that it behooved the colonists not to overindulge in "grain and other victuals" for the time being. Perhaps this context of scarcity worked to excuse the swapping of drink for fish. Although Terhaer found himself barred

<hr>

53. WIC Directors to Stuyvesant, June 6, 1653, 208 ("upon the petition"); Testimony, July 13, 1647, in *Provincial Secretary,* II, 426–427 ("all underst[ood]," 426–427, "two chiefs," 427); Peter Stuyvesant to Governor Theophilus Eaton, May 28, 1648, in Charles T. Gehring, ed. and trans., *Correspondence, 1647–1653,* NNDS, XI (Syracuse, N.Y., 2000), 31–32; Propositions made by the Mohawks, Nov. 19, 1655, in *Fort Orange Records,* I, 83–85; Propositions to the Maquas, Sept. 24, 1659, in Gehring, ed. and trans., *Fort Orange Court Minutes,* 458; Jacobs and Shattuck, "Beavers for Drink," in Van Dongen et al., *"One Man's Trash,"* 99.

from tapping beer, which threatened to devastate his innkeeping operation, on petition the authorities lifted the ban, allowing him to return to business as usual.[54]

By the mid-1650s, then, colonial towns and villages were ever more tightly tied to their neighboring indigenous villagers, whether those were Mohawks and Mahicans at Beverwijk and Fort Orange; Munsees near Manhattan; or Shinnecocks, Montauks, and others on Long Island. Colony leaders recognized this interdependence even as they worried that the colony continued to be at the mercy of people they considered savage. Nor did indigenous villagers have a particularly positive view of the settlers, despite the close trading connections drawing people together. Local criticism tended to focus on Dutch immorality, with particular emphasis on settlers' inability to be generous. Indeed, Mohawk disapproval of Dutch behavior remained so obvious and widespread that settlers could not help but be aware of it. In 1654, the court at Fort Orange recognized that "to renew the old alliance and friendship" between the Mohawks and the Fort Orange settlement, it would have "to send a present." Eleven settlers heeded the call, sending wampum, kettles, axes, and powder to assuage Mohawk criticism of high prices and greediness. Though they hoped to profit from their donations when the Mohawks made their customary present in return, these settlers' actions show they knew of their neighbors' criticisms. Mohawks had made doubly sure they had gotten the message by killing cattle. Yet, just the next year, Mohawk diplomats complained that Dutch hosts "did not entertain them in such a manner as they entertained us when visiting their land" and lamented that continual Dutch demands for payment for services to Mohawk visitors was "not altogether brotherly." Notwithstanding the close ties and constant contact, indigenous men and women had serious reservations about their new neighbors' conduct, and they openly expressed their concerns.[55]

54. Court minutes, June 8, 1654, CMNA, I, 240, NYCMA (microfilm) ("that his wife") (For a translation, see *RNA*, I, 207–208); WIC Directors to Peter Stuyvesant, Nov. 4, 1654, in Charles T. Gehring, ed. and trans., *Correspondence, 1654–1658*, NNDS, XII (Syracuse, N.Y., 2003), 30 ("meat"). On regulations, see Jacobs, *New Netherland,* 208. For a brief summary of repeated regulations (not always enforced) of the alcohol trade, see Jacobs and Shattuck, "Beavers for Drink," in Van Dongen et al., "*One Man's Trash*," 98–101. A "mutsje" was a small measure used for hard alcohol, which varied by time and place. A "kan" was larger, the typical measure for a draught of beer, later standardized at a liter; see M. de Vries et al., *Woordenboek,* s.v. "kan," "mutsje."

55. Call for presents, July 17, 1654, in Gehring, ed. and trans., *Fort Orange Court Minutes,* 146 ("to renew"); Propositions made by the Mohawks, Nov. 19, 1655, in *Fort Orange Records,* I, 83–85 ("did not entertain," 84).

These mutual negative attitudes explain how easily the region slipped into violence, even as the economic network linking people together grew stronger. The colony changed shape and geopolitical position significantly in 1655 when Governor Stuyvesant led a successful campaign against Swedish outposts in the Delaware Valley, reasserting a Dutch claim to the area that had preceded the formation of the Swedish company (in part by disaffected Dutch merchants) in 1638. Yet right in the midst of Stuyvesant's campaign, when the soldiers remained absent, deadly violence erupted at Manhattan. In September, a large group of canoes with perhaps near a thousand Native Americans aboard approached Fort Amsterdam. Who they were, exactly, was unclear. Some thought they came from the east, from Long Island and the Connecticut Valley. Some thought they were Susquehannocks, or perhaps Munsees backed by Susquehannocks. Still others thought Mohawks, Mahicans, or people from even further north numbered among the group. Evidently, Dutch settlers remained inept at distinguishing one people from another, despite daily trade and years of contact. Regardless of their identity, shots rang out before day's end in the first exchange of the Peach War.

From the beginning, the settlers had worried about the intentions behind their guests' visit. Though the visitors claimed they were on their way to fight an engagement with indigenous groups to the north, perhaps the Narragansetts, the inhabitants of Fort Amsterdam could not help but wonder whether they had also come to redress their grievances against Dutch settlers. In the aftermath, blame for the incident focused on Hendrick van Dyck, a former leader of forces in Kieft's War who had recently shot an indigenous woman gathering peaches from what he claimed was his tree — hence the name Peach War. And, Van Dyck did, indeed, sustain wounds that day. Perhaps the visitors disliked the Dutch decision to dislodge the Swedish and sought to draw the soldiers back from the Delaware Valley by creating a diversion. Perhaps they simply came to trade, and the nervous interim leaders let their prejudices and fears panic them. No matter who the visitors were or what purpose drew them to Manhattan, the fragile peace unraveled.[56]

Within days, several colonial settlements along the Hudson and on Staten Island smoldered in ruins, with animals slaughtered, somewhere between fifty and a hundred settlers killed, and many others taken hostage. Colony officials responded by furiously going on the offensive, spreading the blood-

56. Grumet, *Munsee Indians*, 70–72; Cynthia J. van Zandt, *Brothers among Nations: The Pursuit of Intercultural Alliances in Early America, 1580–1660* (New York, 2008), 179–186.

shed further. Yet, throughout the war, colonists struggled with their anomalous position: though they longed to attack their "barbarian" neighbors, in the end, they depended on them. In November 1655, colony officials debated whether to continue military action or to move toward reconciliation. Cornelis van Tienhoven strongly desired to press on with the fighting, calling it "just and necessary," yet, he remained unsure about proceeding without direction from higher authorities. "In the meantime we must dissemble," he argued, "though it be disagreeable." Johannes La Montagne, even more of a realist, stated that it mattered little whether the war was justified or not, "since we do not have the strength to pursue the war." Lacking superior military force, "it necessarily follows that we must keep quiet until we acquire it; meanwhile we should not trust to [sic] much in the Indians." In other words, strategic necessity alone forced New Netherlanders in 1655 to pursue friendship rather than war. Proximity was something to be borne, owing to necessity, and friendship was the guise needed to sustain that proximity until circumstances altered.[57]

The Peach War, therefore, dwindled away just as inexplicably as it began. Fighting never spread beyond the immediate downriver region. By December, the worst of the battles had ended, and, by the following March, Hudson Valley and Long Island indigenous leaders met with Stuyvesant to hammer out terms for reconciliation. The daily face-to-face exchanges that had long marked the region resumed even before the formal peace was established.

Nevertheless, the Peach War made colonial leaders look warily at the vast web of interpersonal interactions that sustained the regional economy. Even during the war, individual relationships and patterns of exchange persisted in ways that worried the colony's leaders. The colony council griped about settlers who continued to travel to indigenous villages, fearing that "through the sailing to and fro to the Wilden many false reports and rumors are caused both among us and among the Indian Nation." The council forbade anyone "of whatever quality he happens to be to sail over by boat or Canoe or any other watercraft whatever it may be called nor by any other means to have communication or discussion with" indigenous neighbors.[58]

---

57. Remonstrance to the States General, [October / November 1655], in *Council Minutes*, II, 120–123 ("barbarian," 122), Response to Stuyvesant's proposals, Nov. 10, 1655, 143 ("just"), 140 ("since"). On the care of surviving stock rounded up on Staten Island in 1655, see Orphan's Court Records, Jan. 10, 1655, Orphan Masters' Records, Records of New Amsterdam, NYCMA (microfilm, NYSL).

58. Ordinance, Oct. 18, 1655, NYCM, VI, 107–108, NYSA. For another translation, see Gehring, ed. and trans., *Council Minutes*, II, 101–102.

Such concerns persisted even as the war drew to a close. Stuyvesant and his councillors began to try to find a way to keep Native Americans out of the intimate spaces of settlers' homes, yet without disrupting trading ties. In December 1655, the colony council gave instructions to Jan Paul Jacquet, the new vice director of the Delaware River settlement, encouraging him to "make a bark house outside the fort as lodging" for visiting Susquehannocks and Lenapes rather than allowing "them to spend the night" inside the fort, "which should also be taken to heart by the inhabitants." Council members understood the importance of good relationships with these traders, ordering Jacquet to "associate with the natives with all due civility," in recognition that some sort of hospitality had to be provided for visitors "so that they are given less reason to complain." They trusted local Lenape and Susquehannock people so little, however, that the council cautioned him to "be on guard against them." Be courteous, but watch your step.[59]

To Dutch leaders, warfare seemed more natural than friendship. The city council of New Amsterdam worried in March 1656, just as the formal truce with downriver Munsee headmen was in the works, that resuming peacetime social contact would only make the colony vulnerable to renewed attack. They suggested that colonists should follow the example of their neighbors in New England and Virginia by keeping greater distance between themselves and Native Americans. English settlers had learned the hard way, having "had to suffer at various times great Massacres as did we here last 15 September under the guise of friendship and having come as friend in their houses and towns." They petitioned the colony council to pass laws prohibiting the kind of social interactions in the heart of settler homes that characterized the trading network people had built. They requested that the council "should make an order that from now on no wilden may come into this city other than to a place that Your Honors ordain for them to sell their goods. Excepted representatives of chiefs. Also that no burghers nor outside people shall receive them in their houses, nor lodge them." The war had shown that friendships could not be trusted.[60]

Munsee villagers clearly had similar anxieties. Some suspected that ending the conflict with the Dutch would only put them at risk of future attack and that individual friendships offered little basis for peace. One Wiechquaeskeck man named Joseph said as much in January 1656, as the

59. Provisional Instructions, [December 1655], Gehring, ed. and trans., *Council Minutes*, II, 160.

60. Petition, Mar. 3, 1656, CMNA, I, 522, NYCMA (microfilm). For alternate translations, see *RNA*, II, 51; Gehring, ed. and trans., *Council Minutes*, II, 256.

fighting was drawing to a close. Joseph had close relationships with European settlers, having been "a good friend of [Adriaen] Van der Donck, and [who] had taken care of his cows for some time." In addition, Joseph had had enough contact with Connecticut settlers that he spoke English comfortably. Despite these long-term friendships and contacts across cultural lines, Joseph apparently held little hope or even desire for a peaceful end to the Peach War. He noted that his people "had not begun" the war and feared that peace would only make them vulnerable to additional violence. When questioned by Connecticut authorities about "whether they intended to make peace with the Dutch," Joseph answered that "the Dutch would not keep the peace and that for this reason they were not of a mind to seek or make peace." Joseph indicated that holding on to Dutch captives offered the Wiechquaeskeck their only protection, "knowing full well and understanding that the Dutch would have to leave them in peace as long as the prisoners were among them." Although Joseph expressed doubt in the military ability of his people to defeat the Dutch or even protect themselves from attack, his mistrust of Dutch intentions made him doubt peace even more. Based on his years of contact and trade, this Wiechquaeskeck man placed little faith in his Dutch neighbors.[61]

Though Joseph feared his neighbors generally, colony leaders focused on one aspect of social interactions that they felt particularly needed prohibition: drinking and alcohol sales. The city council bemoaned "how by our nation the insolence of the Wilden is daily seen with great sorrow and shame, which they commit within this city both through drunkenness as otherwise." They called on Stuyvesant and his council to renew the ban on alcohol sales and to bring it into execution. Indeed, in the wake of the war, Stuyvesant and the council did seem to direct new energies toward the control of the alcohol trade and the social interactions with colonists that the sale of drink both reflected and encouraged. In 1656, the colony council decried that "many drunken wilden walk through the streets, without it being certainly found out, up to now, where they acquire the drink in violation of the ban." Council members also suspected that "the wilden are made wise and informed about many things." Though the council admitted it had no proof of guilt, it recorded that "many . . . complaints and presumptions fall upon Jan Dircksz and his wife." Such rumors seemed justified by the "uncommon correspondence the wilden have, and consistently have had" with

61. Paper presented to the council, Jan. 26, 1656, in Gehring, ed. and trans., *Council Minutes,* II, 204–205 ("good friend," 204, "Dutch would not keep," 204–205, "knowing," 204).

the couple in their home. On the sole basis of these reports, the council decided to privately warn off Jan and his wife and run them out of the colony. In the end, however, the minister convinced the council to let a reprimand suffice, and they were allowed to remain in their home. Perhaps authorities preferred settlers like Megapolensis who, while boasting that he hosted Mohawks in his home, complained "they are very sloppy, and messy, they do not wash their face nor their hands, but let it all sit on that yellow skin, and look like Pigs." Such dual desires and reactions—a desire for proximity and the goods that came with it mixed with dislike, or even disgust—were more comfortable than the suspicious friendliness of Jan Dircksz and his wife.[62]

What the council sought to control, in actions against people like Jan Dircksz and his wife, was the small-scale exchange of alcohol that often went along with drinking and talking together. Although the sale of kegs of hard liquor, especially brandy, certainly did take place in New Netherland, settlers and locals had created a small-scale trade in a wide range of drinks. Facing prosecution in 1656 were "Erick Michiels a Finlander and Cornelis Martensz a Swede" who had given "beer to the wilden as a gift." However, they did so in ignorance of the law on their first arrival in the colony, and only in small measure, so they escaped punishment. As newcomers, the two would have been eager to build the relationships of exchange that they would need if they were to participate in the regional economy—buying a few people a beer doubtless struck them as a good way to make friends and trading partners among their new neighbors.[63]

The magistrates of Beverwijk singled out this kind of exchange when they petitioned the colony council in 1656 for help fighting the alcohol trade. They claimed that "the smuggling of beer and wine . . . to the wilden is committed more and more," despite its illegality. The magistrates lamented that "nothing else can be expected than the ruin and destruction of this land" if the small-scale trade continued to grow. As evidence of the danger, they cited the case of "Willem Albertsen (alias) the crazy farmer [malle boer]" who received a deadly injury "due to the aforementioned smuggling, which he himself committed." No doubt Albertsen's case particularly galled the magistrates because they had to pay townswomen for his board and care out of charity funds. Albertsen evidently dealt in beer and wine by the glass, not brandy by the vat. Though the nature and origin of his injury is unclear,

62. Resolution, July 1, 1656, NYCM, VIII, 54–55, NYSA ("how by our nation"); Megapolensis, "Kort ontwerp," in Beschrijvinghe van Virginia, 47 ("sloppy").

63. Order, July 31, 1656, NYCM, VIII, 101, NYSA.

rowdy disturbances and even fights were relatively common when social drinking, by either settlers or their Mohawk, Mahican, and Munsee visitors, got out of hand. To avoid the expense of caring for casualties, the magistrates sought the colonial government's help in staunching the slow but constant flow—glass by glass—of alcohol to Native customers.[64]

Yet, this kind of exchange was as much a part of social life as it was trade. Jan Martensz de Wever, for instance, found himself hauled before the Beverwijck court in 1658 when "two Indians who were lodging there" were seen drinking "small beer" served by either Jan, "his wife, his maid, or someone else" from "a pewter pint measure." Rather than serious trade, however, this sounds more like typical socializing in a lively household. Just days later, the town officer complained "that several times he has found people in the defendant's house, drinking, both after the ringing of the bell and during divine service" without including the complaint about sales to Indians. Clearly, De Wever's place was an abode of rowdy drinkers, but only some of the time were those visitors Mohawks or Mahicans.[65]

Indeed, the increasing attempts to enforce alcohol laws might have had the ironic effect of making personal knowledge of even greater importance to buyers and sellers. To avoid arrest, you needed to know and trust those to whom you sold beer and brandy. In 1657, Susanna Janssen no doubt thought she was safe when she waited until her other guests had left before selling "three pints of beer, brandy, French and Spanish wine, mixed together" to Kanigeragae, a Mohawk man who showed up twice at her house one evening with a beaver skin in hand. Unfortunately for Susanna, he was working undercover for Fort Orange officers, and she found herself threatened with a crushing five-hundred-guilder fine. The illegality of the liquor trade made

64. Petition and resolution, Aug. 14, 1656, NYCM, VIII, 147–149, NYSA (quotations). The petition refers to further testimony describing the incident, but the testimony is no longer attached. The town provided alms for the boarding and care of Willem Albertsen in 1656; see Venema, *Beverwijck*, 322, 339, 349. Pierre Esprit Radisson, who traveled with a group of Mohawks on a trading voyage to the Dutch in 1653, wrote that the visitors drank "the hollanders" wine until "they fought with swords among themselves"; see Radisson, *Voyages of Peter Esprit Radisson, Being an Account of His Travels and Experiences among the North American Indians, from 1652 to 1684*, ed. Gideon Scull (Boston, 1885), 79 (quotations); Radisson, "Voyages of Pierre Esprit Radisson," in Snow, Gehring, and Starna, eds., *In Mohawk Country*, 62–92, esp. 89. Dutch drinkers also thought alcohol an excuse for violent behavior. For a victim of violence by a Dutch drinker, we need look no further than the *Malle Boer* himself, who had a knife drawn on him by Jacob Theunisz outside Jan Martensz de Wever's tavern a few years after his earlier injuries; see Minutes, Feb. 22, 1658, in *Fort Orange Records*, I, 99.

65. Court minutes, Feb. 8, 12, 1658, in Gehring, ed. and trans., *Fort Orange Court Minutes*, 353–355 ("two," 354, "several times," 355). See also Venema, *Beverwijck*, 92.

relationships between buyers and sellers across cultural lines even more complex and placed a high premium on personal trust.[66]

Prosecuting this kind of small-scale alcohol exchange brought authorities up against the complicated web that united social interactions, alcohol trading, and the all-important food trade. In the summer of 1656, the colony prosecutor found Michiel Tadens, a resident of New Amsterdam, at his house in Pearl Street "in his back little kitchen with a pipe of tobacco in company with a wilt who had a half-mutsje of strong waters in the hand, drunk almost empty." Tadens dismissed as unjust gossip the subsequent charge that he regularly sold liquor, explaining instead "that this wilt the day before had brought him some fish, which he did not want any money for, and thus he gave him that sop as a gift." Tadens, in his explanation of what the *fiscael* saw, gave voice to the complex interlinking of the social and the economic in the daily encounters that made up the regional exchange economy. Sharing a glass and a pipe suggested something more than just trade, and Tadens hoped to excuse himself by depicting the relationship as primarily a social exchange, part of a gracious thank-you for a generous gift of food. He also chose to name the kind of drink he gave his guest a "soopjen," a word suggestive more of a sustaining mix of wine or beer and bread than of hard liquor. In Tadens's description, this was a friendly meal, not an illegal booze sale. Tadens later faced a stiff penalty for his actions after his drinking partner told the prosecutor that he had never brought a fish to the house and that he had paid for the liquor with wampum beads. Yet, eating, drinking, and smoking together obscured the lines between trade and daily life, making control of the alcohol trade in the wake of the Peach War ultimately unsuccessful.[67]

Even at the larger scale, smuggling alcohol and the everyday food trade went hand in hand. Jacob Wolphertsz van Couwenhoven and Pieter Laurensen, two prominent longtime New Amsterdam residents, escaped a charge of liquor trading when they explained that they had journeyed to a Munsee village to buy venison, not to sell brandy. One evening, when Captain Marten Cregier made a diplomatic visit to the Navesink in 1663, he caught the pair on board a sloop off the coast of Staten Island. Cregier clearly suspected that the two men were engaged in liquor smuggling. However, Van Couwen-

66. Court minutes, Aug. 1, 20, 1657, in Gehring, ed. and trans., *Fort Orange Court Minutes*, 323–325, 328 (quotation). It is not clear if the court imposed the entire fine sought by the officer. See also Jacobs, *New Netherland*, 208–211.

67. Minutes, July 25, 1656, NYCM, VIII, 85–87, NYSA (quotations); Minutes, July 31, 1656, NYCM, VIII, 105–106, NYSA; M. de Vries et al., *Woordenboek*, s.v., "sop."

hoven calmly replied that "they went to trade for venison." Although Van Couwenhoven had previously been tried for selling "five vats" of "strong waters" to the Navesink, the court accepted his explanation that he intended to buy food, not sell alcohol. The extensive, daily contact among villages, which sustained the food economy of the mid-Atlantic region, made it easy for liquor dealers to excuse their visits to their neighbors.[68]

Indeed, attempts to enforce alcohol laws reveal entire networks of social and economic exchange that tied Native and settler villages together. In 1656, officials charged "Willem Hoffmeyr, born in Brazil, aged about twenty years," the stepson of baker Jochem Wesselsz and a baker himself, with selling beer. Hoffmeyr's confession illuminates the network of face-to-face connections that traveling for the alcohol and food trades encouraged. Hoffmeyr admitted to trading alcohol with villages north of Beverwijk several times, first in a canoe with two half barrels. The second time, he "sailed up the river and sold and peddled the beer among the Indians . . . and what is worse, had it sold and peddled for him by one Indian to other Indians." Officials saw his creation of a network of exchange as an even more serious offence than his entrance into the intimate spaces of Mohawk villages to trade. By initiating a network of resellers, Hoffmeyr was building what looked to officials like a business, rather than just casually exploiting momentary opportunities. Hoffmeyr's network of economic and personal relationships, likely formed through his background in baking, proved hard for him to resist. When released on bail for these charges, he allegedly had "not hesitated the same day to admit a drunken Indian to his house and contrary to expressed prohibition and warning of the court to pour out or sell beer to them." Young Hoffmeyr's case illustrates the reciprocal visiting and the network of retailing that the food and drink trades produced in the Hudson Valley. Such webs of connection, based on extensive day-to-day meetings among a wide range of people, sustained the colony but allowed for types of exchange that colony leaders did not always desire.[69]

Even the arms trade, which in the wake of the Peach War should perhaps have posed some very obvious dangers, proved tough to uproot. In August 1656, the governing council of New Netherland decried the continued smuggling of arms, despite laws to the contrary. The council sought to tighten arms regulations because both "Inhabitants and Neighbors" of

68. Journal, Dec. 6–11, 1663, NYCM, X, pt. 2, 431–434, NYSA ("they went"); Charge, May 4, 1662, NYCM, X, pt. 1, 125–126, NYSA ("five vats"). Marten Cregier also appears as Kregier.

69. Court minutes, Oct. 6, 1656, in Gehring, ed. and trans., *Fort Orange Court Minutes*, 253 (quotations). See also Venema, *Beverwijck*, 284–285.

New Netherland had complained about the continued sale of arms "as well to Christians as Indians, some not only presuming that the Director General and Council connive with the violators, but even publicly declaring that the Director General and Council ... have made free the importation and trade in Contraband." In response, the council renewed its ban on the importation "of any kind of Munitions of War" and ordered that all ships bound up the Hudson had to pass by New Amsterdam for inspection.[70]

Just two weeks after the August 1656 order, the council had to investigate Lieutenant Dirk Smith, a military officer of standing and longtime WIC employee, on suspicion of importing weapons. Smith admitted to selling a few guns, although he claimed he had prior permission from WIC officials in Holland. However, his oath to having done no more trade in arms was contested. Perhaps unwisely, Smith pointed to the ubiquity of the contraband arms trade as his primary defense. He claimed that he had been told by others "that, in the case of the wilden, every one was free to trade what was his, and [he] took the opportunity to acquire some beavers toward the lessening of [his] debts." Other colonists doubtless also noticed that selling guns would allow them access to the beavers they needed to "lessen their debts." Indeed, Smith suggested that the trade was rampant, even among the colony's upper crust, by both men and women. Before he had sold any guns, Smith had checked with a former corporal about the legality of weapons dealing. The man had responded wryly that "Pieter Cocqs and the *Juffrouw* from The Hague" had sold ten guns themselves. Since "they are doing their trade with [guns]," the corporal reasoned, "why should we then not be able to sell one gun?" Smith complained to the council that he had never expected to be arrested for the sale, "since so many guns are sold here to the wilden" and when "in the south they sell [guns] to the wilden by whole shipment." Smith was convicted, released from WIC service, and ordered out of the colony, but, in the end, he petitioned for and received pardon. Perhaps the vacated punishment was tacit admission that his arguments rang all too true.[71]

70. Ordinance, Aug. 11, 1656, NYCM, VIII, 135, NYSA; the document is badly damaged, and this translation comes from one made by E. B. O'Callaghan before the 1911 New York State Library fire, checked against what remains of the original; see O'Callaghan, ed. and trans., *Laws and Ordinances of New Netherland, 1638–1674* (Albany, N.Y., 1868), 236–238 (quotations, 236).

71. Sentence, Sept. 12, 1656, NYCM, VIII, 172–174, NYSA ("that, in the case"); Examination, July 31, 1656, NYCM, VIII, 104, NYSA ("Pieter Cocqs"); Charge and defense, Aug. 30, 1656, NYCM, VIII, 158–161, NYSA. "Juffrouw" was an honorific term accorded to women of high status, but not high enough to have a gentry title. Smith was not the only colony official

Maybe gun and alcohol sales could have been controlled, but only if the intense daily interactions among settler and indigenous men and women that fostered those sales had somehow been eliminated. Ultimately, such interactions were far too fundamental to the regional economy and the nature of the colony itself to consider their limitation. On the contrary, when changing trade patterns in 1657 threatened to leave settler towns and households out of the loop, colony leaders acted to protect the broad-based system of exchange that had come to characterize New Netherland. Although itinerant Dutch boslopers and annual sojourners had traded in the colony since its earliest days, as time passed and settlement increased, settlers came to fear that Native Americans would no longer come into their towns to trade if boslopers went to them. Therefore, laws passed in the later 1650s and 1660s sought to make it much more difficult for itinerant traders to operate. In 1657, the civic leaders of New Amsterdam, for instance, gave a predatory cast to their description of traveling traders in their petition to the colony council when they requested the formation of burgher rights and the exclusion of all but residents from trading there. The visiting "Scots," as Dutch speakers called roving merchants regardless of their ethnicity, would have to pay extra taxes or be excluded from trade. The city councillors requested the new regulations because "the Scots who sail yearly to and fro with the ships from the fatherland," on arriving in New Amsterdam, "mostly depart immediately to the Fort Orange or elsewhere without being willing to sell their goods and, having done their business, go away again at the first opportunity."[72]

The New Amsterdammers found itinerant traders to be "highly prejudicial" to "dese goede gemeente," or "this good community." They appealed to Dutch norms of municipal privileges, noting that in the city of Dordt "the Scots merchants are not permitted, to pass through that place, without having paid the staple-right." The governor and council acceded to the request, citing the special importance of towns in a military border zone. Referencing the First Anglo-Dutch War and the Peach War, they justified the new ordinance in light of the burghers' efforts "in the last national quarrel with the neighbors, as also in the sad and unexpected *rencontres* with the natives" as well as in consideration of the many burdens New Amsterdam faced as "the principal frontier and capital." Though WIC officials in Am-

accused of illegal trading after the Peach War. For another example, see Hans de Vos, underprosecutor in Beverwijk, who supposedly sold "brandy and spirits" to Native customers in 1657 (Minutes, Mar. 8, 1657, in *Fort Orange Records*, I, 95 [quotation]).

72. Petition and Ordinance, Jan. 22–24, 1657, NYCM, VIII, 427–434, NYSA.

sterdam eventually overrode this law as detrimental to overseas trade, efforts to tax or exclude traveling traders and boslopers show that colony officials in Manhattan, like other settlers, wanted to continue to be able to form individual trading relationships with Native Americans in their own towns and homes.[73]

New Netherlanders rose up in protest once again when professional traders threatened to dominate the trade in the 1660s, demanding equal access to their Native American neighbors. Ordinances in 1661 and 1662 forbade settlers from traveling themselves to meet and trade with Natives "in the woods" and even from hiring "Christian or wilt" agents to do so on their behalf. The ordinances demanded that "no one may take away any beavers from the wilden, be it in the woods, outside or inside the villages, houses, or places, in order to carry them for the wilden, be it by horse, cart, or on their persons." Instead, Mohawk and Mahican traders would be required to visit settler towns in person, where every resident had an equal chance of getting to know them. Settlers, officials, and Mohawks in the upriver Fort Orange area all argued over the best way to conduct the trade. Wealthier settlers seemingly preferred to hire boslopers or Mohawk agents to direct visiting Mohawks to their own houses, whereas poorer settlers feared such rules would subvert fair market practices in the town of Beverwijk. Mohawk diplomats simply wanted their people to be able to trade wherever they wanted without abuse. Whatever the competing interests on the ground, such anti-bosloper actions show that face-to-face interactions by men and women up and down the social scale had become both the norm and the ideal for how people understood the way the regional economy should work, just as these interpersonal networks undergirded the Dutch and transatlantic economies.[74]

73. Ibid. (quotations). See also Petition, Jan. 22, 1657, CMNA, II, 137–138, NYCMA (microfilm). The word given here as "natives" is "naturellen."

74. Ordinance, Aug. 5, 1662, NYCM, X, pt. 1, 185–188, NYSA (quotations); see also Ordinance, Apr. 25, 1661, NYCM, IX, 591–592, NYSA. For partial translations, see O'Callaghan, *Laws and Ordinances*, 394–395, 425–427. For a discussion of the social divisions fueling the controversy, see Dennis, *Cultivating*, 156–163. Donna Merwick sees the controversy as a step toward the greater independence of the town of Beverwijk from company governance, since settlers were tacitly allowed to flaunt the regulations and carry on trade through whatever chaotic means they liked; see Merwick, *Possessing Albany*, 88–99. However, this view tends to conflate the council with the WIC. Often, the council, composed of wealthy colonists, found themselves at odds with WIC officials in Amsterdam as they voiced interests shared with other New Amsterdam residents of their own class. Nor were Beverwijkers unified in their attitudes toward the regulation, as Dennis has shown, making a dichotomy of residents versus the WIC problematic.

Similar laws against traveling traders surfaced repeatedly in the later years of the colony, as settlers and leaders sought to protect their own extensive networks of face-to-face trading relationships. Colonial and municipal authorities recognized that broad intercultural contact played an essential role in New Netherland's society and economy. When monopolization of the food trade by itinerant traders threatened the New Amsterdam marketplace, for instance, the governor and council passed a new ordinance in 1661. The council decided to allow new regulation because

> all the corn, fish, and venison, which is brought to market by the wilden, is bought up by some self-interested people, who make a profession of trading with the wilden, and then is sold again to the community, to the great inconvenience and harm of the many residents here; [therefore] the aforementioned *Burgermeesteren* are authorized to draw up and determine such orders about it, as are to the greatest profit and the best of this city and of the residents of the same, [as they] shall find most advantageous.

The council's conviction that the interests of the community were best served if Native Americans continued to participate in the town market testifies to the extent to which Manhattanites had come to expect a participatory multiracial marketplace. They rejected a model in which male itinerant traders alone set the tone of the regional economy and held a monopoly on commercial and personal relationships with Algonquian and Iroquoian neighbors.[75]

Whatever its problems, New Netherlanders and the local authorities alike agreed that the system of regional trade that had developed over the Dutch period merited protection. Though people found the relationships they formed with neighboring villagers uncomfortable at best and too often dangerous, they preferred the broad-based exchange system it allowed. It was through these difficult, face-to-face relationships that people created, negotiated, and tried to profit from regional exchange. Just as Dutch people built and related to overseas empire through the medium of their personal relationships, residents of the Dutch colony created empire on the local level through the relationships they formed across lines of culture and community. Putting these relationships to work, they built webs based on face-to-face interactions that together constituted the regional economy. The relationships settlers, slaves, and Native Americans formed as they bartered,

75. Order, Oct. 13, 1661, NYCM, IX, 835, NYSA.

bickered, and bargained their way across the barriers of language and culture underpinned an inclusive network of trade running throughout the mid-Atlantic region.

Keeping One's Distance, 1659–1664

At the same time as New Netherlanders expressed their commitment to a widespread network of face-to-face exchange relationships through the creation of anti-bosloper laws, the Hudson Valley region entered a new, violent phase. This bloodshed did not stem from any move away from the intervillage trade network. To the contrary, people continued to travel among the mid-Atlantic's various villages and engage in the same sorts of trading relationships as they had since the early days of settlement. Yet, as people increasingly lived nearby one another, the weaknesses in the relationships joining them together proved too great to ensure tranquillity. Although people had come closer to one another economically, geographically, and physically, their failure to form strong personal, intimate, or kinship ties meant that they remained distant in all other ways. The explosion of violence highlighted these long-term dualities and reflected limitations in the personal networks reaching among immigrant and indigenous villages.

The fighting from 1658 to 1664 centered geographically on Esopus country, midway along the western shore of the Hudson River. The Esopus people, Munsee speakers like their immediate neighbors, had already experienced repeated settlements of individual European families who had moved in their midst since at least 1653. Traders, both local and sailing down from Fort Orange, purchased food and fur from Esopus villagers, but anger about Dutch trading practices, rather than friendships, resulted. In 1658, the disputes escalated, leaving one trader dead at the water's edge and settlers pointing the finger at Esopus men. Shortly thereafter, several outlying settler farmhouses were burned to the ground and settlers' cattle lay slaughtered in the fields. Stuyvesant sent soldiers and engaged in bullying diplomacy, quieting things down temporarily, but, in September 1659, after settlers fired on some Esopus men, the Dutch village of Wiltwijck found itself besieged. Once again, the arrival of forces led to a brief respite, but the burgeoning conflict grew increasingly bitter.[76]

76. For an instance of shipboard brandy trading in the Catskill / Esopus region, see Court minutes, July 15, 1653, in Gehring, ed. and trans., *Fort Orange Court Minutes*, 62. For Esopus complaints, see Journal, June 30, 1658, NYCM, XII, 85, NYSA. On events in 1658–1659, see Merwick, *Shame and the Sorrow*, 240–244, 248, 250, 257.

By March 1660, Stuyvesant began preparing for an all-out assault by concluding a treaty with downriver Munsee headmen, thereby cutting off the Esopus from their most likely allies, and declaring full-scale war. Rapacious attacks on Esopus fields and villages accompanied brutal killings and captures before a shaky peace was hammered out in June 1660. But sporadic, violent episodes continued and resentments built. Open war returned in June 1663. Once again, Stuyvesant succeeded in isolating the Esopus from their Munsee neighbors and ordered a brutal destruction of towns and fields. Amid hunger and disease, Esopus sachems finally negotiated a truce in May 1664, only a few short months before the Dutch themselves would be displaced.

Though the repeated conflagrations at Esopus necessarily disrupted trade there, the wars did not reflect a general move away from the trading system by colonists as a whole. Judging from the records, even the most illicit and volatile aspects of regional exchange, such as alcohol sales, continued unabated during the entire period of conflict. For instance, two men visiting New Amsterdam from the southern colony of Nieuwer Amstel along the Delaware River testified in 1660 that they had been sent by Jacob Aldrichs, the director and highest authority in the south, "with the sloop and some barrels of brandy and Spanish wine to the wilden in order to trade the same for maize or wampum," adding that they did indeed "sell and trade it," receiving "maize, wampum, and peltries" in exchange. Trading doubtless offered the director the simplest way to get corn to feed his soldiers or wampum to pay them. When settler Jan Juriaens Becker appealed his conviction for selling alcohol to indigenous customers, he sought out these men's testimony and explained that alcohol traded hands so openly that he could hardly understand how one could survive economically without it. He had never really thought of it as a crime to sell "strong drink to the wilden" because it "was done so publicly" in the southern regions of New Netherland "by people of high and low estate," and, after all, he himself had only done it "now and then for maize and venison to be used as necessary provisions." Unlike many others whom he named, including the leaders of the city government, Becker claimed he only "exchanged a little, without having made a profession of it." Even at the height of the Esopus conflicts, then, face-to-face trading, including that of illegal items, remained pervasive from the lowest to the highest levels of colonial society.[77]

77. Testimony, [Apr. 8, 1660], NYCM, IX, 191, NYSA ("with the sloop"); Petition, May 3, 1660, NYCM, IX, 190, NYSA ("so publicly"). For a translated version of these documents,

Despite the heavy fighting at Esopus, people throughout the region continued to depend on shared travel and trade networks. In 1660, indigenous canoeists remained essential to the colony's communication system. When Willem Beeckman wanted to send letters or representatives from the Delaware River settlement of Nieuwer Amstel to New Amsterdam, he had to find a local guide and paddler. Without Munsee or Lenape help, communication between the Delaware and Hudson River regions threatened to cease. At one point, Beeckman apologized to Stuyvesant for failing to write, saying he had been unable to find any Native American traveler willing to make the trip. In turn, indigenous paddlers continued to depend on Dutch sail craft throughout the Esopus wars, a fact that authorities hoped to turn to Dutch advantage. Canoeists so frequently climbed aboard Dutch ships midstream in 1663 that the colony council decided to exploit this practice. The council noted that "during these present disturbances and war with the Esopus wilden (just as in times of peace) sometimes some canoes, with Wilden, come on board the Yachts sailing up and down." They therefore ordered captains of river sloops to bring in as captives any Native American coming on board in the vicinity of Catskill "since the wilden can not be well distinguished" from one another and captured Esopus could be forced to work as guides. Though the war inspired Dutch authorities to try to exploit regional trade networks for strategic purposes, the law makes clear that no shift in daily practices of travel and trade occurred for those outside Esopus.[78]

Indeed, treaties negotiated with Munsee headmen sought to ensure the continuation of daily trade in the face of the explosions at Esopus. In March 1660, when the Esopus War was just beginning in earnest, Stuyvesant and Hudson Valley village leaders attempted to renew their peace. One of the most powerful of these groups, the Wappingers, were particularly close cultural and political cousins of the Esopus, and thus fighting could have very easily spread. To prevent any danger or troubles between "some Dutch [and] the wilden who come to market here with peltries fish, and other wares," Stuyvesant and his Wappinger counterparts agreed that, when Native

---

see E. B. O'Callaghan, ed., *Documents Relative to the Colonial History of the State of New-York; Procured in Holland, England, and France, by John Romeyn Brodhead, Esq.*, 15 vols. (Albany, N.Y., 1856–1887), XII, 342.

78. Ordinance, July 12, 1663, NYCM, X, pt. 2, 215–216, NYSA (quotations). For a translated version of this last document, see O'Callaghan, *Laws and Ordinances*, 444–445. On the lack of indigenous couriers, see Willem Beeckman to Peter Stuyvesant, Sept. 20, 1659, William Beekman Letterbook, 1659–1663 (translated by E. G. Squiers, 1842), BV Beekman, NYHS, Beeckman to Stuyvesant, June 17, 1660, Beeckman to Stuyvesant, Jan. 14, 1660.

American people came into New Amsterdam, the village leaders would try to encourage them to use a single road, "the former Beaver's Path." Anyone approaching the town by another path, then, must be coming with hostile intent. However, even in such explosive times, limiting Munsee people's movements along the streets of Manhattan made little sense. The treaty explained that those bringing firewood into town for sale "shall be able to go with it where they will." The agreement further stated that the many goods brought to New Amsterdam by Wappinger, Hackensack, and other traders should be sold at a designated place in front of the town scales, "on which . . . place fit housing for them shall be made." By promising to create a home, an intimate space of sorts, for visitors at the core of this Dutch town, officials recognized the centrality of face-to-face networks to the life of the community, uniting Munsees and colonists even as the colony's most bitter war shifted into high gear.[79]

The promises negotiated that day prevented outright warfare from spreading beyond Esopus country but did nothing to abate the tensions that proximity entailed. Resentments over trading, frustrations brought about by uneasy propinquity, and open hostility remained pervasive. When Native visitors traded inside colonists' homes, settlers' antipathies toward their guests were thinly concealed. In 1661, for instance, "Tytje Gommers, huys-vrouw of Davidt Wessels" faced a twenty-five-guilder fine for stealing from a Native trader who came to her house. The colony council found that she had taken "some Wampum from the wilt who had left it lying in her house" and then hidden it and lied about it, "once to the wilt, again once to a Boy, [and] afterwards to the under-sheriff." Such mistreatment was not uncommon. The prosecutor stressed the need for severe punishment precisely because she was not alone in her abuses and dishonesty. The prosecutor sought a serious penalty to respond to the many complaints by "various wilden" that "wampum and peltries are stolen from them first here and then there," accusations that settlers always angrily denied, often threatening "to want to beat the wilt" in response. The Esopus conflicts raised the stakes of such be-

<hr />

79. Treaty, Mar. 6, 1660, NYCM, IX, 118–122, NYSA (quotations). On Dutch-Esopus relations, see Merwick, *Shame and the Sorrow*, 237–258. Both the Wappinger and the Esopus spoke Munsee and they lived almost directly across the Hudson from one another. The exact political relationship among the many Munsee-speaking groups and villages in the greater Hudson Valley at any one point in time can be difficult to determine, but visiting, intermarriage, and political cooperation were common. By isolating the Esopus from the Wappinger, Stuyvesant scored a major strategic victory. In these years, Beverwijk similarly sought to control access to the town by building a palisade, although records make clear that Native visitors continued to move freely through town and stayed in residents' homes inside the palisade thereafter; see Venema, *Beverwijck*, 93–97.

havior, when the colony could ill afford to alienate Munsee allies and trading partners. In Tytje's sentencing, the council emphasized that stealing from the wilden "is a matter with bad consequences" that "could bring great unease between our Nation, and the Indians." In the council's view, the trading system as a whole was a fragile structure as weak as the tie between Tytje and her guest. Though settlers continued to invite Native men and women into their towns and homes, everyone seemed to recognize that it would not take much to bring down the entire house of cards.[80]

Years of contact and the Esopus conflicts perhaps only furthered many colonists' ideas that the visitors they had to accommodate were savages. Their harsh opinions had a way of breaking through their own economic and strategic interests. In late 1660, Nicolaes de Meyer found himself subject to a large one-hundred-guilder fine for injuring a Native trader at his house. He defended himself by claiming that "the wilt had previously thrown his child down such that he fell underfoot." However, the prosecutor countered that the child merely fell by accident when the man jumped back to get away from De Meyer's vicious dog. Even though De Meyer persisted that "he as a father could not bear that his child should be thrown down by a wilt, and that the wilt had first badgered the dog himself," the colony council saw the incident as too significant to ignore. By wounding the man "in the head such that the blood ran along his shoulder," the council concluded that De Meyer had risked causing "many calamities, especially for the country people who live separately." As a member of the colonial elite and sometime office holder, De Meyer knew as well as the council judging him the potential danger that could arise if more Munsee villagers joined with the Esopus, but, evidently, the sight of his own son under the feet of a wilt, or "savage" man, overwhelmed such considerations, as well as the trading interests that had drawn the victim to De Meyer's house in the first place.[81]

High-handed, dishonest, and inhospitable treatment such as this understandably drove colonists' Native neighbors to protest and challenge such behavior. To say the least, people like Gommers and De Meyer offended visitors by failing to treat guests in ways consistent with key Iroquois and Algonquian values of graciousness. One indignant indigenous female trader

80. Court minutes, Aug. 18, 1661, NYCM, IX, 729, NYSA (quotations). Jochem (or Jochim) the Baker in Beverwijk beat the Native man who complained about his missing notas full of wampum after he had bought a cake, even though the man had taken the precaution of returning in the company of the court messenger; see Court minutes, Feb. 8, 1658, in Gehring, ed. and trans., *Fort Orange Court Minutes*, 352.

81. Court minutes, Sept. 9, 1660, NYCM, IX, 413, NYSA.

had had enough contact with the Dutch to know who to turn to when she experienced poor treatment in the town of Beverwijk during the height of the fur-trading season in 1660. Marijke Rijverdinx van Dansick tried to force the woman to trade with her, and not with Volckert Jansen, as the woman trader preferred, locking her out of the house and forcibly keeping the woman's beaver skins. This unnamed Native woman rejected such treatment and immediately sought out the prosecutor Johannes La Montagne. She clearly recognized that such behavior violated not only her own ideas of hospitality but also Dutch laws. The prosecutor, however, could not prevent Marijke and her husband, tavernkeeper Adriaen Jansen van Leyden, from "forc[ing] the Indian woman to trade her beavers at their house." Mohawk diplomats in the late 1650s and 1660s repeatedly made complaints about the "viciousness" of the Dutch toward visiting traders, but colony records show just as clearly the continuation of such behavior, even at diplomatically critical moments.[82]

Local inhabitants' continuing criticisms suggest they never did come to see the Dutch as living up to their basic standards of appropriate behavior. Mohawk comments show that they did not view colonists' poor conduct as occasional aberrations but rather as part of a consistent pattern of moral failings among Europeans. Megapolensis noted that, when he tried to explain to Mohawk observers that he "instructed the Christians, that they must not steal, go Whoring, get drunk, kill, and that they must not do so either," they responded "that it is good that I teach the Christians," but asked "why then so many Christians do so." Megapolensis used the incident for his own purposes, to censure the behavior of his Dutch congregants, but the Mohawk criticism he paraphrased fit with concerns consistently expressed by Native speakers. Though these men were getting to know Megapolensis well enough to have theological conversations with him, their words point out that, in their overall view, colonists were morally lacking and poorly behaved at the best of times.[83]

With mutual opinions like these, it is not surprising that even the most personal of all face-to-face relationships failed to bring people any "closer" to one another. Mutual negative opinions and stark cultural divisions ensured that sex between Native women and colonial men divided people

82. Court minutes, Aug. 13, 1660, in Gehring, ed. and trans., *Fort Orange Court Minutes*, 523 ("forc[ing]"), 11, Propositions of the Maquas, Sept. 6, 1659, 454 ("viciousness").

83. Megapolensis, "Kort ontwerp," in *Beschrijvinghe van Virginia*, 48 (quotations). For examples of such criticism, see Propositions made by the Mohawks, Nov. 19, 1655, in *Fort Orange Records*, I, 83–85; Propositions of the Maquas, Sept. 6, 1659, in Gehring, ed. and trans., *Fort Orange Court Minutes*, 454; Venema, *Beverwijck*, 161–162.

more than it brought them together. Even in these interactions, colonists continued to show more concern with commerce than with individuals. Indigenous people viewed these relationships as just one more example of settlers' failures to behave decently.

From the earliest interactions between Hollanders and local women, colonists and traders expressed an interest in Native American women's bodies that at once pointed to their accessibility while also suggesting that those interactions need not result in abiding kinship ties. Writers repeatedly described Native American sexual behavior by using the word "hoer," or "whore," and its variants. In 1626, De Rasière wrote that "the womenfolk are beautiful . . . [with] black eyes set with beautiful eyebrows . . . they are very whorish." In the 1650s, Van der Donck concurred, claiming that "both men and women are beyond measure unchaste and whorish, without any shame." In 1661, another author alleged that the very name given a part of the southern Delaware colony, the *Hoeren Kill* (or "Whores Creek"), reflected the sexual availability of Native women. "The name of Hoeren Kill," he claimed, was said to have arisen "from the Indians' generosity . . . by generously giving our Netherlanders there their young women, or daughters." Such language depicted Native women as offering sexual opportunities for Dutch men while denigrating indigenous sexual practices.[84]

In part, these kinds of dubious pronouncements about Native sexuality reflected an inability to understand local marriage customs. "They generally live without marriage," Megapolensis asserted regarding the Mohawks, although he immediately contradicted himself by explaining that Mohawk marriages "last no longer than it pleases the both of them, and then they leave one another." Because marriages were dissoluble, he did not acknowledge them as marriages at all. "And even when they have wives," Megapolensis related, "they nonetheless do not stop whoring." Of course, plenty of seventeenth-century Dutch husbands did not leave off whoring when they married either. Indeed, these sorts of comments about indigenous women only make sense in the context of the development of commercial sexuality in Golden Age Holland. Soldiers and sailors, like those so common in New Netherland, often appeared in Dutch art and culture as ushering in commercialized sexual behavior at odds with the domestic ideal of burgher womanhood. New Netherland men tended to describe all sexuality that differed from the domestic

---

84. De Rasière to Blommaert, [1628], in Eekhof, "De 'memorie,'" *Nederlandsch archief voor kerkgeschiedenis*, n.s., XV (1919), 269 ("womenfolk"); Adriaen van der Donck, *Vertoogh van Nieu-Neder-Land* (The Hague, 1650), 10 ("both men"); *Kort verhael van Nieuw-Nederlants gelegentheit, deughden, natuerlijke voorrechten. . . .* (1662), 11 ("name").

burgher ideal as prostitution. "Hoer" in Dutch culture during this period had unmistakable connections to prostitution that show that these New Netherlanders viewed Native sexuality through a very particular prism. By choosing to explain indigenous sexual mores in terms of whoredom, authors thus made a familiar association between sexual activity and sex for pay.[85]

New Netherland men even imposed specific ideas about sexual markets onto their interactions with local women. Not only did they criticize Mohawk and Algonquian sexual mores in terms of commercialized sex, they interpreted and understood cross-cultural sexual contact to be, quite literally, prostitution. "The females are also extraordinarily prone to whoredom," Megapolensis claimed, "they will sleep with someone for the value of 1, 2, [or] 3 *schellingen,* and our Dutch very often have illicit intercourse with the whores." This figure tallies quite closely with amounts paid for sex in Amsterdam in the seventeenth century, where typical prices varied between one and five schelling. That Dutch men attached that particular price to sex shows that they used their preexisting notion of the sexual marketplace to make sense of their relations with indigenous sexual partners and to place sex in a separate category from the intimate family ties that surrounded sex in the burgher marital ideal.[86]

It is difficult to know how Native women interpreted sex with colonial men, but they certainly did not understand these relationships as a commercialized form of sex bringing a given amount on the market. They did

85. Megapolensis, "Kort ontwerp," in *Beschrijvinghe van Virginia,* 46 (quotations). On the thriving and widely acknowledged sex trade in seventeenth-century Holland, see Lotte Constance van de Pol, *Het Amsterdams hoerdom: Prostitutie in de zeventiende en achttiende eeuw (Prostitution in Amsterdam in the seventeenth and eighteenth centuries)* (Amsterdam, 1996); Van de Pol, *The Burgher and the Whore: Prostitution in Early Modern Amsterdam,* trans. Liz Waters (New York, 2011). On the entrance of the marketplace into depictions of sexuality as the number of soldiers in the Republic doubled between the 1630s and 1670s, see Ann Jensen Adams, "Money and the Regulation of Desire: The Prostitute and the Marketplace in Seventeenth-Century Holland," in Patricia Fumerton and Simon Hunt, eds., *Renaissance Culture and the Everyday* (Philadelphia, 1999), 229–253; see also Richard Helgerson, "Soldiers and Enigmatic Girls: The Politics of Dutch Domestic Realism, 1650–1672," *Representations,* LVIII (Spring 1997), 49–87.

86. Megapolensis, "Kort ontwerp," in *Beschrijvinghe van Virginia,* 46 (quotations). The commonly used translated edition gives the last phrase, "en onse Duytsen verloopen sich seer veel met de Hoeren," as "our Dutchmen run after them very much." However, the phrase "zich verloopen met" is better translated as "to have illicit sex with." See the reprint of this translation in Megapolensis, "A Short Account," in Snow, Gehring, and Starna, eds., *In Mohawk Country,* 43. A schelling equaled six stivers. One schelling represented the lowest price paid to street walkers, while women in more upscale bordellos could command many times that price; see Van de Pol, *Amsterdams hoerdom,* 323–325. It is important to remember that Dutch observers, not Native women, coded these relationships as commercial prostitution. The women and

not live in a monetized economy, and the ideas of sexuality that underlay such a view were entirely foreign. Yet, an openness toward sexual relations before marriage and children probably made such relationships acceptable to Algonquians and Iroquoians alike. A cultural connection between sex and commerce that differed greatly from Dutch notions of prostitution gave a familial and political cast to indigenous interpretations of cross-cultural liaisons. Sometimes Native women had sex with traveling traders as a way of giving a trader standing in, and perhaps a sense of obligation to, the local community. In these kinds of sexual encounters, Dutch ideas of commercialized sex conflicted with Native ideas about intimacy and intercommunity ties. Adriaen van der Donck explained that, among the Munsee, "some, like chiefs and prominent persons, having two or more wives, will readily accommodate a visiting friend with one of their own wives for a night." Sex in these circumstances might have represented Munsee women's attempt to incorporate foreign traders into the intimate networks of kin and community that defined village life.[87]

Some, but not all, Dutch traders might have known that local women saw these unions differently from their imported notions of prostitution. Van der Donck, for one, distinguished these kinds of relationships from outright harlotry. He observed that, according to Dutch ideas of sexuality, "both Women and Men are tremendously liberal about such things, not having any shame." Nonetheless, he differentiated such sexual freedom from "prostitution and adultery" during marriage, which he claimed Native men and women alike disapproved of as scandalous and shameful. Thus, sex with traders likely represented attempts to build bridges between communities and boslopers by local women and their villages, as distinct from Dutch interpretations of prostitution.[88]

---

their communities undoubtedly saw these relationships very differently. For an intriguing glimpse into why Pacific Island women, at their own or their male kin's instigation, engaged in sexual interactions that Euroamerican men increasingly interpreted as prostitution, see David A. Chappell, "Shipboard Relations between Pacific Island Women and Euroamerican Men 1767–1887," *Journal of Pacific History*, XXVII, no. 2 (December 1992), 131–149. For an example of a onetime sexual encounter in the 1650s that involved gift giving, not payment, see Venema, *Beverwijck*, 168–169.

87. Van der Donck, *Beschryvinge*, 63. For a translation, see Adriaen Cornelissen van der Donck, "Description of New Netherland," trans. Diederik Goedhuys, in Snow, Gehring, and Starna, eds., *In Mohawk Country*, 115.

88. Van der Donck, *Beschryvinge*, 63 ("both"), 61 ("prostitution"). For a translation, see Van der Donck, "Description of New Netherland," trans. Goedhuys, in Snow, Gehring, and Starna, eds., *In Mohawk Country*, 114–115.

In spite of the negative attitudes and legal prohibitions, longer-lasting relationships between traders and local women were occasionally acknowledged in New Netherland. Most notably, Cornelis Teunisz van Slijck and Arent van Curler, later credited as one of the founders of Schenectady and an important intermediary to the Mohawk community, were both widely understood to have had children with Mohawk women. One of Van Slijck's daughters, Hilletie, or Illetie, went on, after the Dutch period, to act as a translator, clearly living with a foot in both worlds. Cornelis Jansen established a lasting relationship on Long Island and fathered at least one child with a woman named Catoneras, later said to have been a sunksquaw among local Munsee villagers. The Mohawk and Munsee women who entered into these few recognized, permanent relationships and their male kinsmen might have sought to access the power inherent in the other-than-human quality of their odd neighbors. Like women of the Great Lakes region who married European men, these relationships placed women in unusual but important roles as cultural mediators within the beaver-skin trading system. They doubtless sought to extend kin networks into the Dutch community in parallel ways to the role of kinship in their natal communities. Mohawk and Algonquian communities alike thought marriage and the kinship ties it created a key way to solidify diplomatic bonds. Van Curler benefited from such ideas of kinship when he received land that lay between Fort Orange "and the Mohawk country" from Mohawk leaders Cantuquo, Sonareetse, Aiadane, and Sodacherasse, who doubtless thought that having a Dutch kinsman located nearby could help smooth relations. For the colonial men and indigenous women who formed such long-lasting bonds, sexual behavior and the world of commerce intertwined in complicated ways that better resembled Mohawk or Algonquian than Dutch expectations of what cross-cultural sex meant.[89]

89. Land grant, July 27, 1661, in *Fort Orange Records*, I, 197–198 (quotation, 198). For Hilletie, see Jacobs, *New Netherland*, 396; Venema, *Beverwijck*, 169–172. See also Thomas E. Burke, Jr., *Mohawk Frontier: The Dutch Community of Schenectady, New York, 1661–1710* (Ithaca, N.Y., 1991), 23, 203; Daniel K. Richter, "Cultural Brokers and Intercultural Politics: New York-Iroquois Relations, 1664–1701," *Journal of American History*, LXXV (1988), 40–67. Dutch attitudes toward intermarriage with locals could be strikingly different in other colonial locales. On the importance of interracial marriage in what is today Indonesia, see Eric Jones, *Wives, Slaves, and Concubines: A History of the Female Underclass in Dutch Asia* (DeKalb, Ill., 2010); Niemeijer, *Batavia;* Jean Gelman Taylor, *The Social World of Batavia: European and Eurasian in Dutch Asia* (Madison, Wis., 1983). On Catoneras, see John A. Strong, James van Tassel, and Rick van Tassel, "In Search of Catoneras: Long Island's Pocahontas," *Long Island History Journal*, XXI, no. 2 (Spring 2010), accessed Nov. 11, 2012, http://www.stonybrook.edu/lihj/IssueFiles/V21_2/Articles/Strong/strong.html#14a. For the cultural motivations of Great

Yet, not all men who had sexual relationships with Native women lived up to indigenous expectations about the obligations such relationships entailed. Instead, they offended their neighbors by regarding such interactions as temporary arrangements rather than kin-based commitments. In other words, they treated such relationships as prostitution, even though the women and their communities understood them differently. Kinship ties, including those created through marriage and reproduction, frequently served to reinforce intercommunity relations and diplomatic ties in the indigenous northeast. But Dutch interpretations of these sexual relationships as prostitution and, thus, a simple market exchange meant that once again the Dutch failed to act appropriately.

Mohawk diplomats repeatedly complained that Dutch men did not live up to their duties as kin. Mohawk representatives, for instance, pressed Dutch authorities to give presents to the family members of women who had relationships with traders when those women died. In other words, Mohawk leaders were trying to insist that men who had sex with Mohawk women needed to fulfill their duties as kin to the women's families. The Beverwijk court secretary noted that Mohawk representatives in 1659 said "that when any one of their people dies and one of the Dutch is her mate, he ought to give to the relatives of the deceased one or two suits of cloth." Their demand came as a part of a lament in which they pointed out numerous ways in which the Dutch failed to act as kin should. It is clear that these Mohawk men saw these relationships very differently from a commercialized "Amsterdam Whoredom," which lay entirely outside their experience, culture, and economy. For them, Dutch behavior in sexual relationships was consistent with their general vision of Dutch failures to be generous, hospitable, moral, and giving.[90]

Lakes women who married European traders and the argument that the attraction lay in these men's other-than-human qualities, see Jacqueline Peterson, "Women Dreaming: The Religio-psychology of Indian White Marriages and the Rise of Metis Culture," in Lillian Schlissel, Vicki L. Ruiz, and Janice Monk, eds., *Western Women: Their Land, Their Lives* (Albuquerque, N.Mex., 1988), 49–68. For the idea that Great Lakes women married French fur traders to extend kin networks, see Susan Sleeper-Smith, "Women, Kin, and Catholicism: New Perspectives on the Fur Trade," *Ethnohistory*, XLVII (2000), 423–452. In 1645, when Kiotsaeton, a Mohawk leader, sought to solidify ties with the French, Wendat, and Algonquins, he suggested that they could find wives among the Iroquois, and his Algonquin counterpart responded that from then on they would be "but one people, but one village, [and] one house"; see Parmenter, *Edge of the Woods*, 65 (quotation).

90. Propositions of the Maquas, Sept. 6, 1659, in Gehring, ed. and trans., *Fort Orange Court Minutes*, 454 ("when any one"). On differing ideas of kinship obligations, see Matthew Den-

The Mohawk diplomats went on to complain, "we have been here before and made a covenant. The Dutch say we are brothers and that we are joined together with chains, but that lasts only as long as we have beavers. After that we are no longer thought of." Clearly, these Mohawk men took the diplomatic language of brotherhood and kinship seriously and sought to use such metaphors to influence the behavior of their colonial neighbors. Indeed, the language of brotherhood was a common metaphor throughout the region as Munsee, Mohawk, and other leaders tried to encourage the Dutch to act as they felt neighbors and allies should during the dangerous and rancorous years of the Esopus conflicts. When Sauwenaare, a Munsee-speaking sachem from the lower Hudson region, wished to emphasize his commitment to peaceful trade despite New Netherland's conflict with the Esopus, he invoked the affective ties of family. He told Governor Stuyvesant and his council "that the peace was (^renewed), that his heart from now on should be as a Dutchman's and [he would] live with them as brothers." Sauwenaare's language implied a promise of a change "from now on" from brotherhood with the Esopus to brotherhood with Manhattan authorities. The vicious treatment of the Esopus by Stuyvesant's forces was anything but brotherly, and Sauwenaare, by performing this symbolic diplomatic language, hoped to secure something very different for his people.[91]

Similarly, when eight Mohawks passed through New Amsterdam on their way home from a diplomatic mission to the Susquehannocks in the Delaware River region in 1661, they greeted the colony council with the assurance that they "were happy that they had now come here among their brothers," the Dutch, to whom they felt "locked together as with a chain." Brotherhood entailed mutual obligations, and, based on this mutuality, the travelers "now asked to be brought by their brothers with a Yacht to Fort Orange," giving a

---

nis, "Family Business: Kinship and Commerce on the Borderlands of New Netherland and New France," in Jeremy Adelman and Stephen Aron, eds., *Trading Cultures: The Worlds of Western Merchants: Essays on Authority, Objectivity, and Evidence* (Turnhout, Belgium, 2001), 111–134, esp. 119–120. See also Venema, *Beverwijck*, 164.

91. Propositions of the Maquas, Sept. 6, 1659, in Gehring, ed. and trans., *Fort Orange Court Minutes*, 453 ("we have been here before"); Treaty, Mar. 6, 1660, NYCM, IX, 118–122, NYSA ("that the peace"). On the use of "brother" as a metaphor in diplomatic speeches between the Dutch and Mohawk, see Dennis, "Family Business," in Adelman and Aron, eds., *Trading Cultures*. On the persistence of the word "friend" in Iroquois-English diplomacy, see Nancy L. Hagedorn, "'A Friend To Go between Them': The Interpreter as Cultural Broker during Anglo-Iroquois Councils, 1740–70," *Ethnohistory*, XXXV (1988), 60–80. Variants of Sauwenaare's name include Sauwenar, Sauwenaroque, Showan Orockett, and Janorocket; see Grumet, *Munsee Indians*.

valuable belt of wampum as a ritual gift. The council agreed not only to send the visitors north on a yacht but also to give them "bread and peas for the journey." In this instance, the Mohawk diplomats succeeded in reminding Dutch authorities of the obligations "brothers" had to one another.[92]

For the Mohawk, the language of brotherhood reflected the key concept of *kaswentha,* or two-row diplomacy, by which they signified their belief that mutually beneficial relationships ought to reign between Haudenosaunee communities and the Dutch. But the Mohawk complaint that the Dutch only acted as brothers when Native people had beavers was not far from the truth. In treaty making, speeches, and formal interactions, Dutch men and New Netherland diplomats used the language of kinship and brotherhood freely. Seventeen colonial men and officials, for instance, spoke in intimate familial terms in 1659 when they visited the Mohawk town of Kaghnuwage, just a few weeks after the Mohawks' complaints. "Brothers, we have come here only to renew our old friendship and brotherhood and you must tell it to your children; our children will always be able to know and remember it through the writings which we leave behind us; we die but they remain forever. From them they will always be able to see how we have lived in friendship with our brothers."[93]

Other documents recorded when no Mohawks were present painted a very different picture. In 1660, the council noted with skepticism reports from Fort Orange that Mohawk and Mahican traders there were behaving peacefully, unlike Esopus villagers. Reports claimed that "the wilden in general keep very quiet, and behave well, without showing any insolence." The council concluded that "nothing else can be deduced but that the Wilden, through a pretty appearance and feigned countenance, seek to rock us to sleep, and then as opportunity permits to attack unexpectedly those of us in the outlying places." They reiterated their warnings for Beverwijk colonists to be on their guard, ordering them to bring in the grain from the outlying farms while sending along an extra dozen soldiers for good measure. In

92. Minutes, Apr. 7, 1661, NYCM, IX, 579, NYSA (quotations). For an analysis of the imagery of the chain and a discussion of diplomatic metaphors, see Richter, *Ordeal of the Longhouse.* The word "brother" had particular meaning among the Haudenosaunee, who explained the relationship among the five tribes, and often between themselves and subsidiary groups, in terms of brotherhood. The Mohawk repeatedly and successfully pushed Dutch officials to behave in more appropriately "brotherly" ways through the distribution of gifts and the acknowledgment of mutual obligations. For an excellent analysis of the use of the word "brother," see Dennis, "Family Business," in Adelman and Aron, eds., *Trading Cultures.*

93. Propositions to the Maquas, Sept. 24, 1659, in Gehring, ed. and trans., *Fort Orange Court Minutes,* 456–457 (quotation); Parmenter, *Edge of the Woods,* 24.

this case, however, the Dutch were the ones with the feigned countenances. They called Mohawks "brothers" to their faces and "savages" behind their backs.[94]

Since diplomatic arguments about brotherhood, attempted intimate alliances, and direct challenges to bad behavior all failed to move Dutch colonists to change their ways, proximity and conflict went hand in hand. These conflicts were remarkably similar to those that led to brutal violence at Esopus. The Marsepingh peoples of Long Island, for instance, had particular trouble with their English and Dutch near neighbors at Heemstede, troubles that mirrored those cited as the sparks for warfare at Esopus. Adriaen van der Donck described this settler town as "very rich with Cattle," which of course wandered into the fields of the Marsepingh. The Marsepingh became so frustrated with the situation that, in the 1660s, they killed some stock. They explained to the council that they had done so because "the pigs have done them great damage, and have destroyed various plantations." They also blamed the settlers for killing their village dogs, which the women relied on to help protect their crops and keep the pigs away. The Heemstede colonists responded curtly that "the wilden should make their fences tight" if the stock got into their cropland. The colony council ordered the Heemstede townspeople to provide for the fencing of Marsepingh fields, but it seems doubtful that such action would have solved the simmering tension. From the Marsepingh point of view, it was the settlers who needed to fence their animals. What was worse, the council stipulated that the fencing be paid for out of moneys the colony owed the Marsepingh for helping fight the Esopus. So, not only were colonists bad neighbors, they were also ungrateful allies who would find any excuse not to pay what they owed, even at the moment when the importance of an alliance with the Marsepingh should have been most obvious. Colonial officials justified the brutal attacks against the Esopus in 1660 because of the destruction of stock. Although the Marsepingh escaped full-fledged attacks like those launched against the Esopus, the tensions that underlay the Esopus Wars were all too familiar and all too likely to escalate further.[95]

All sides seemed to understand that only closer, more meaningful personal interactions had the power to stem such a vicious spiral of proximity and tension. Yet, in the years before 1664, the mid-Atlantic region lacked

94. Order, Jan. 23, 1660, NYCM, IX, 40, NYSA.
95. Van der Donck, *Vertoogh*, 13 ("very rich"); Minutes, June 23, 1663, NYCM, X, pt. 2, 152, NYSA ("the pigs"); Ordinance and Proposals, Feb. 9, 1660, NYCM, IX, 53–54, 55–63, NYSA; Merwick, *The Shame and the Sorrow*, 240, 253–254.

a strong community that straddled the borders among cultures. No métis community comparable to those of New France in the later seventeenth century ever developed during the Dutch period. With the exception of a few people, such as Hilletie van Slijck, who in later years lived with a foot in both societies, mixed-race children who resulted from the intimate exchanges between Dutch men and local women by and large seem to have been absorbed into their mothers' communities and did not come to act as a bridge between the two worlds. In 1653, Frenchman Pierre Esprit Radisson, captive among the Mohawks, encountered one such Mohawk woman of mixed parentage. Radisson's adopted Mohawk brother "was courting of a young woman, who by the report of many was a bastard to a flemish. I had no difficulty to believe, seeing that the colour of her hayre was much more whiter than that of the Iroquoits. Neverthelesse, shee was of a great familie." Her father's identity seemed to matter little, either to her standing in matrilineal Mohawk kinship structures or to her role in this area of intercultural contact. Though Radisson himself was on the point of departure to Fort Orange, he knew better than to rely on her as an intermediary, instead keeping his planned escape a secret from both her and her suitor.[96]

Another man known to the French as a "Flemish Bastard" and to the Mohawks as Canaquese did act as a negotiator with the French, English, and Dutch beginning around 1654. The Dutch referred to him as Smits Jan, and he evidently had a Dutch father, although who that was remains a matter of speculation. He might have been living among the Dutch in the Fort Orange area around 1647. Canaquese went on to become an important military leader and diplomat who played a key role in maintaining a strong position for the Mohawk within and beyond the Iroquois League. Yet, as a member of a matrilineal society whose mother was Mohawk, Canaquese's actions and leadership might have had little to do with having a Dutch father. And Canaquese remains an exceptional figure. In the web of villages

96. Radisson, *Voyages,* ed. Scull, 82 (quotation). On the bicultural and mixed-race families that characterized much of the fur-trading areas in the trans-Mississippi west from 1750 to 1850, see Anne F. Hyde, *Empires, Nations, and Families: A History of the North American West, 1800–1860* (Lincoln, Neb., 2011). After Dutch rule ended, more references to bicultural children appear in the documentary record, but references before 1664 are much harder to find. This difference should serve as a reminder not to project later patterns, even by ethnically Dutch colonists, back into the Dutch period. Janny Venema shows that Hilletie/Illetie, her brother, and her nephew, whose stories were recorded after the Dutch period, even then "were not accepted by the Indians when they showed sympathy to the Dutch; and the Dutch, for their part, ridiculed Illetie when she criticized their way of life"; see Venema, *Beverwijck,* 171.

that populated the mid-Atlantic region before 1664, bonds of kinship, caring, and family seem rarely to have reached from indigenous to colonial communities.[97]

The paucity of kinship bonds, and the relative absence of bicultural children who could symbolize and sustain those bonds, seemed to people at the time to make relationships unstable. This vacuum caused colonial leaders on one occasion to try to actively create bicultural knowledge in Native American children. Seeking to reaffirm peace and solidify the lower-Hudson cross-cultural economy in the face of fighting between the colony and the Esopus villagers to the north, a March 1660 peace treaty with lower Hudson Valley headmen put an emphasis on building individual connections with particular Munsee-speaking children. The council suggested to the gathered leaders, "So our descendants for many years shall be able to see, and to know that which we now speak and agree with them, which their descendants will not be able to do unless they can read and write, it is good and also needful that they allow some of their children to be raised by us." The sachems did not look askance at such a request, answering that they had already left one child at New Amsterdam "and should bring yet more when convenient." Giving children at once symbolized the commitment to the regional political and economic system by establishing a familial dimension while also ensuring the trade's continuation through shared linguistic and cultural understanding.[98]

Little evidence remains about the experience of such Munsee children raised among the settlers, but perhaps even for them, a truly bicultural identity remained elusive. Adriaen van der Donck explained that some young children had "indeed been taken home by some of us in order to make them servants" and that these children were "as well as time allowed" taught the Christian religion. However, he suggested that their cultural introduction to Dutch Reformed ways did not take: "When they begin to be Young women or Young men and again begin to associate with the Wilden, they forget easily . . . and return to the wilde ways and manners." Few young people seemed

97. On Canaquese, see Parmenter, *Edge of the Woods*, 117–124, 333–334 n. 34; Mark Meuwese, "From Intercolonial Messenger to 'Christian Indian': The Flemish Bastard and the Mohawk Struggle for Independence from New France and Colonial New York in the Eastern Great Lakes Borderland, 1647–1687," in Karl S. Hele, ed., *Lines Drawn upon the Water: First Nations and the Great Lakes Borders and Borderlands* (Waterloo, Ontario, 2008), 43–63; Tom Arne Midtrød, "The Flemish Bastard and the Former Indians: Métis and Identity in Seventeenth-Century New York," *American Indian Quarterly*, XXXIV (2010), 83–108; Venema, *Beverwijck*, 171.

98. Treaty, Mar. 6, 1660, NYCM, IX, 118–122, NYSA.

ready to mediate the distance between the two cultures, even when forced to experience life among their new neighbors.[99]

When it came time to form intimate bonds and families of their own, young people who had grown up in the midst of New Netherland's extensive cultural contact chose to keep their ties within their natal communities. Accordingly, the bonds between Natives and newcomers became no less friable. The fragility of intervillage relationships and the potential for these relationships to break down make clear that people remained divided and their "friendship" contingent, even when they came together extensively. Despite economic networks based on immediate relationships, colonists and Indians stayed distant from one another. Natives and newcomers did not always like each other very much, and they often struggled to accept one another in their homes and villages to trade. Their mutual ties stemmed from a desire for the other's goods, rather than from affection or respect. Even when they came together for sexual relationships, they never got much "closer" to one another. They mistrusted one another's motives and morality, and people on both sides of the cultural divide seemed to know that their friendship and brotherhood was but a semblance. Economic networks, but not intimate ones, reached among the region's villages. Given the duality of impulses driving people alternately together and apart, the networks that connected them, while essential to life in the Hudson Valley, remained weak. Even as people met one another in villages and countryside, the possibility seemed always to loom that people might have decided that the time had come at last to stop dissembling and start killing.

Conclusion

During the period of Dutch colonization in the mid-Atlantic, ordinary people—farmers, soldiers, hunters, and traders—from colonial and indigenous communities met one another again and again in the course of their daily lives. They struggled to get to know one another individually—not because they necessarily liked one another but because they all desired things the other had. Men and women from different cultures saw each other daily. They ate each others' food, they drank together, and they sat side by side in canoes and yachts. They traveled over wooded hillsides and up half-frozen streams to reach one another's towns, and they invited one another into the intimate spaces of hearth and home. Professional traders or backcountry

99. Van der Donck, *Beschryvinge,* 77.

travelers did not monopolize cross-cultural exchanges in the mid-Atlantic region; instead, men and women from all communities met every day and traded everything from beer to furs to firewood to food. They built an economy based on their web of relationships that allowed the exchange not just of beaver skins and wampum beads but also of food, drink, and daily necessities. Trade joined everyone in the region in a single network.

Yet, no matter how much people relied on one another, too much proximity brought conflict, not intimacy. Despite—or, often, because of—the perpetual contact among peoples, vast personal and cultural distances continued to divide them. Although Natives and newcomers often spoke to one another using terms of intimacy and endearment, such language reflected the importance of intimate networks and the desire to strengthen intervillage ties rather than existing deep interpersonal connections. The proximity that people experienced as a part of daily life in the greater Hudson Valley coincided with continuing, even growing, distances and divisions. The disgust and distrust people harbored for one another kept interpersonal networks fragile and defined the boundary between peoples even as they sought out trading relationships.[100]

So long as colonists and their indigenous neighbors needed one another, or at least needed one another's beaver skins, maize, or trade goods, they often found a way to get along. So long as colonists feared Mohawks, Munsees, and others, they hesitated to act out their dislike. But when the distance between villages narrowed too much, tensions erupted. And when Native

---

100. At times, New Netherland scholarship has stressed distance, not proximity. Scholars have painted the Dutch-Mohawk frontier as a no-man's-land between separate communities that people crossed but did not inhabit, see Dennis, "Family Business," in Adelman and Aron, eds., *Trading Cultures*, 118. For the argument that the Dutch and the Mohawk always maintained significant spatial distance between their communities, see Nan A. Rothschild, *Colonial Encounters in a Native American Landscape: The Spanish and Dutch in North America* (Washington, D.C., 2003), 23. William Starna argues that the distance between Mohawk and Dutch lands lessened the primary source of conflict; see Starna, "Native-Dutch Experience," in Shattuck, ed., *Explorers, Fortunes, and Love Letters*, 27–38. These approaches all make a crucial point about the placement of Dutch and Mohawk villages, yet, it is important not to overlook just how frequently people crossed the ground that separated them in pursuit of their shared trade networks (see Parmenter, *Edge of the Woods*, on the mobility of Mohawk traders over vast distances). Contact was frequent and took place in the heart of people's homes and communities, for Mohawks and Munsees alike. And the distinct separation of colonial and Native villages throughout the region owing to the continued disjuncture between people's intimate networks was striking, whether those villages lay side by side or miles apart. So alongside the physical distances, we must also see the distances people maintained within their closest relationships and most critical social networks.

people stood in the way of what settlers wanted for themselves, there was little affection to lessen the fury of the attack.

Looking closely at the kinds of personal relationships that underlay New Netherland's patterns of proximity and distance provides a key to understanding the shape of colonies on the ground. In the mid-Atlantic region, people built a widespread interpersonal network, but their relationships with one another stopped short of intimacy and kinship. In all of the early modern cultures that met along the shores of the Hudson River, intimate networks provided the strongest basis for the building of economic and social ties. Coming together and forming face-to-face connections enabled New Netherland to take root and allowed all the people of the region to participate in trade systems that reached deep into the continent and across the Atlantic Ocean. Yet, coming so close together without the bonds of intimacy that made networks strong created an environment ripe for bloodshed.

Interpersonal, yet not truly intimate, economic networks developed throughout the mid-Atlantic in the Dutch period, but they did not keep people from trying to kill one another. In 1643, 1655, 1660, and 1663, colonists demonstrated their increasing penchant for escalating conflict from daily indignities and small-scale violence to full-fledged war, and the scale of fighting only grew as economic connections brought people ever closer together. Networks that existed before, during, and after these episodes did not change how people thought about one another. How *intimate* networks really were determined the ways Natives and newcomers related to one another.

The complicated interplay between economic connection and cultural division explains the endlessly alternating rounds of coexistence and violence characteristic of seventeenth-century colonies like New Netherland. Personal, social, and cultural distance remained even in the face of daily contact and mutual dependency. Indeed, it is only with extensive interaction that people learned enough about their neighbors to dislike them so much. This sad truth explains why this seeming middle ground, or area of accommodation, dissolved so quickly and thoroughly into a zone of killing. With each meeting and each parting, powerful yet inconstant human relationships determined whether the people of the mid-Atlantic region would continue to live together or die at one another's hands.[101]

101. Pekka Hämäläinen has argued that varying moments of coexistence and attempts at domination formed one of the principal patterns of frontier relationships in North America; see Hämäläinen, "The Shapes of Power: Towards a Comparative History of North American Frontiers, Borderlands, and Empires" (paper presented at the "Borderlands Seminar," USC-Huntington Early Modern Studies Institute, Huntington Library, May 8, 2010).

CHAPTER FOUR

"To Be Together with One Another"

Creating an African Community

Just as human relationships shaped transatlantic and regional networks, they also shaped networks within the colony. These networks created community, determined people's economic position, and undergirded social hierarchies and inequalities. For one particularly vulnerable population, enslaved Africans in the service of the WIC, those human relationships and social networks proved especially crucial, determining the boundary between suffering, survival, and success.

On February 25, 1644, the African population of New Amsterdam celebrated a rare and crucial victory. That morning, the director of the colony of New Netherland, Willem Kieft, issued an extraordinary decision. "Having considered the petition of the Negroes named Paulo Angolo, Big Manuel, Little Manuel, Manuel de Gerrit de Reus, Simon Congo, Antony Portuguese, Gracia, Piter Santomee, Jan Francisco, Little Antony and Jan Fort Orange," he granted these long-serving slaves of the WIC, along with their unnamed wives, their freedom. However, this freedom was not absolute; these men were explicitly "permitted to earn their livelihood by agriculture," and they were bound to pay an annual tax of thirty schepel of grain and "one fat hog," on pain of returning to slavery. Thus, these men and their wives were granted what has become known as "half freedom," a remarkable if conditional success in the history of African resistance to the growing slave system in colonial North America. The experience of privately owned slaves in the colony, who formed the majority of the African population, remains opaque, since they appear very little in the colonial records, but this group of Africans in New Amsterdam, many of whom began their lives in the colony as property of the WIC, can be traced more clearly. Their exceptional experience reveals the interplay between personal relationships and racial order. The lives of these Africans show how intimate networks provided the framework both for survival and for the creation of social hierarchy.[1]

This grant forms an important passage in the history of slavery in North America. The success of these eleven African petitioners seems to support the idea that racial slavery in North America developed gradually. Given that slavery was not allowed in the Dutch Republic, it is not clear how much Kieft knew about practices elsewhere or on what legal or religious texts he might have based his decision; perhaps he was simply unaware of how slavery worked. Historians have taken the experience of this particular group as characteristic of the "elasticity" of slavery in the Dutch colony as a whole, where racialization supposedly occurred only "haltingly." Following the work of Edgar McManus, some historians have cited the half-freedom grants as proof that slavery in the early years was less rigidly defined than it later became, allowing Africans more room to maneuver.[2]

Although it is certainly possible that some colonists and officials in New Netherland had malleable ideas of slavery, slavery and forced labor

1. For a translation of the petition and decision, see Council Minutes, Feb. 25, 1644, in *Council Minutes*, I, 212–213 ("Having considered," 212, "permitted," 213). Using the term "African" to describe this group can in some ways be problematic. The men and women who made up the black population of New Netherland were quite diverse, with African- and New Netherland–born individuals living side by side with Brazilian and Caribbean creoles. It is not always possible to know everyone's origins, and people formed families and groups together that contained members from many backgrounds. The modern term "African American" seems inappropriate in this very early setting because many, especially but not exclusively those born in Africa, would have rejected an identification with an America they were forced to inhabit. When possible and necessary, I try to make clear where individuals came from and how they identified themselves, but, when discussing the group as a whole, I use the term "African" to refer to both African-born forced migrants and American creoles of African parents. Ira Berlin applies the term "Atlantic Creole" to this population to point out that all, regardless of birthplace, can in some sense be considered native to the Atlantic world; see Berlin, "From Creole to African: Atlantic Creoles and the Origins of African-American Society in Mainland North America," *WMQ*, 3d Ser., LIII (1996), 251–288. However, I avoid this term here to alleviate confusion between New Netherlanders of African descent and the equally mobile and Atlantic ethnically European New Netherlanders.

2. Vivienne L. Kruger, "Born to Run: The Slave Family in Early New York, 1626 to 1827" (Ph.D. diss., Columbia University, 1985), 43 ("elasticity"), 49–50; Leslie M. Harris, *In the Shadow of Slavery: African Americans in New York City, 1626–1863* (Chicago, 2003), 12 ("haltingly"); Graham Russell Hodges, *Root and Branch: African Americans in New York and East Jersey, 1613–1863* (Chapel Hill, N.C., 1999), 6–33; Christopher Moore, "A World of Possibilities: Slavery and Freedom in Dutch New Amsterdam," in Ira Berlin and Harris, eds., *Slavery in New York* (New York, 2005), 47–49; Edgar J. McManus, *A History of Negro Slavery in New York* (Syracuse, N.Y., 1966). These arguments about the early fluidity of slavery in New Netherland build on arguments about the development of slavery in the Chesapeake, where scholars agree that slaves in the earliest years seem to have faced looser interpretations of the meaning of en-

had already taken root in the broader Dutch empire during the years of the half-freedom grants, with legal and commercial apparatus to support their growth. In some ways, the development of slavery in Dutch overseas colonies was similar to the process in English colonies. Slavery had largely disappeared in both Amsterdam and London following the Middle Ages. Consequently, unlike Spain and Portugal, where the persistence of some slavery throughout the Renaissance meant that a body of laws regarding slaves already existed when overseas colonization began, the Netherlands, like England, had no legal system in place when it started sending ships across the Atlantic and Indian Oceans at the end of the sixteenth century. Despite the absence of a cultural and legal background at home, slavery quickly became established in Dutch colonies and trading posts around the world. By the time of Kieft's grant in 1644, the Caribbean colony of Curaçao, acquired by the Dutch in 1634, had become a collection point for slaves to be sold throughout the Americas and a major entrepôt for the slave trade with Spanish America. Likewise the Dutch colony of Batavia functioned as the seat of a trade system moving thousands of slaves from Arakan, Bengal, and Coromandel throughout Southeast Asia. Just a few years later, in the 1650s, the Cape colony would begin to expand from a small refreshment station to a settler colony, using both slave and unfree exile and convict labor to build infrastructure and to work on farms.[3]

slavement than their children and grandchildren would experience; see Edmund S. Morgan, *American Slavery, American Freedom: The Ordeal of Colonial Virginia* (New York, 1975); A. Leon Higginbotham, Jr., *In the Matter of Color: Race and the American Legal Process: The Colonial Period* (New York, 1980); Anthony S. Parent, Jr., *Foul Means: The Formation of a Slave Society in Virginia, 1660–1740* (Chapel Hill, N.C., 2003), 107. On Kieft, see Jaap Jacobs, *New Netherland: A Dutch Colony in Seventeenth-Century America* (Leiden, 2005), 383–385.

3. On the establishment of a legal structure for slavery in the East Indies, see J. Fox, "'For Good and Sufficient Reasons': An Examination of Early Dutch East India Company Ordinances on Slaves and Slavery," in Anthony Reid, ed., with Jennifer Brewster, *Slavery, Bondage, and Dependency in Southeast Asia* (New York, 1983), 246–262. Although directors had objected to the slave trade (as distinct from slavery) on moral grounds during the WIC's first year, by 1626 the company was moving into the trade rapidly. By the time of the capture of Brazil in 1630, the WIC had wholly abandoned its initial opposition; see Joh[annes] Postma, "A Monopoly Relinquished: The West India Company and the Atlantic Slave Trade," in Elisabeth Paling Funk and Martha Dickinson Shattuck, eds., *A Beautiful and Fruitful Place: Selected Rensselaerwijck Papers,* II (Albany, N.Y., 2011), 217–222. On Dutch involvement with slavery and the slave trade outside the Atlantic, see Markus Vink, "'The World's Oldest Trade': Dutch Slavery and Slave Trade in the Indian Ocean in the Seventeenth Century," *Journal of World History,* XIV (2003), 131–177; Nigel Worden, *Slavery in Dutch South Africa* (New York, 1985); Kerry Ward, *Networks of Empire: Forced Migration in the Dutch East India Company* (Cambridge, 2009). Robert C.-H. Shell argues that the Cape must be considered a slave society from its inception,

Few voices in the Netherlands protested the rising importance of slave trading to the Dutch economy during these years. Though court records and literature provide some examples of hostility to slavery in the Netherlands at the end of the sixteenth and the earliest decades of the seventeenth century, most notably by the projector and investor Willem Usselincx, by the 1640s legal and religious justifications for the slave trade circulated in widely read texts. The idea that the half-freedom grants of the 1640s through the 1660s reflected a flexible attitude toward slavery sits uneasily with the growing commitment to slavery in other colonies in the same decades.[4]

The timing of the 1644 freedom grant is also difficult to square with the increasing commercialization of slave labor and the growing importance of the slave trade in New Netherland. Dutch authorities made similar grants to company and private slaves in 1659, 1663, and 1664 just as the slave trade was becoming more and more significant to the Dutch Atlantic economy. As P. C. Emmer points out, Dutch involvement in the transatlantic slave trade exploded around 1636, with more than twenty-five thousand slaves being shipped to Brazil alone between 1636 and 1645. With the capture of the Portuguese trading outpost Elmina in 1637, the Dutch established a continuous presence in Africa and became consistent players in the Atlantic slave system, eventually transporting more than half a million slaves to the Americas.[5]

Slaves were particularly in demand in New Netherland, where residents and officials frequently called for more WIC slave ships to make the jour-

"since the Dutch East India Company had supported slave societies in their possessions in the East from at least 1609. When the Dutch landed at the Cape, they introduced a legal system partly based on slave holding"; see Shell, *Children of Bondage: A Social History of the Slave Society at the Cape of Good Hope, 1652–1838* (Hanover, N.H., 1994), xxx. For Curaçao, see Johannes Menne Postma, *The Dutch in the Atlantic Slave Trade, 1600–1815* (New York, 1990), 27; Ernst van den Boogaart and Pieter C. Emmer, "The Dutch Participation in the Atlantic Slave Trade, 1596–1650," in Henry A. Gemery and Jan S. Hogendorn, eds., *The Uncommon Market: Essays in the Economic History of the Atlantic Slave Trade* (New York, 1979), 353–375.

4. P. C. Emmer, *The Dutch Slave Trade, 1500–1850*, V, *European Expansion and Global Interaction*, trans. Chris Emery (New York, 2006), 13–16; Martijn van Lieshout, "Het morele spagaat van de Nederlandse slavenhandel: Interview met Piet Emmer," *Spiegel historiael*, XXXV, no. 6 (June 2000), 240–243. The few clergymen who criticized slavery tended to emphasize only the need for better treatment and Christianization; see Gerald Francis De Jong, "The Dutch Reformed Church and Negro Slavery in Colonial America," *Church History*, XL (1971), 423–436.

5. Emmer, *Dutch Slave Trade*, 18; Postma, *Dutch in the Atlantic Slave Trade*, 13; Johannes Postma, "A Reassessment of the Dutch Atlantic Slave Trade," in Postma and Victor Enthoven, eds., *Riches from Atlantic Commerce: Dutch Transatlantic Trade and Shipping, 1585–1817* (Leiden, 2003), 137.

ney north from the Caribbean. Slaves, owned by both the WIC and settler families, had been present in the colony from the early 1620s, and Africans, slave and free, had worked aboard trading ships sailing to the mid-Atlantic coast since the 1610s. Because of the growing demand for slaves, the price of slaves in the colony rose during the 1650s and 1660s, the very years when the half-freedom grants were made. New Netherland officials also showed increasing interest in making the colony a center for the sale of slaves to nearby English settlements. Slavery became entrenched in the last decades of Dutch colonization in the Hudson Valley, such that "on the eve of the English conquest, New Amsterdam had already been transformed into a slave society." The commercialization of African labor in New Netherland and the Dutch Atlantic during the same years as the half-freedom grants raises questions about why half freedom was devised when it was, rather than earlier. After all, the petitioners, by 1644, had served "the Company for 18 or 19 years," Kieft's grant noted, and they had "long since . . . been promised their freedom." The men and women covered by the grant also represented only a small number of the slaves working in the colony for the WIC and private owners. Why them, and not others? Given the solidification of the Atlantic slave system as a whole and the rising commodification of African labor in New Netherland from the 1640s through the 1660s, the petitioners' success seems even more extraordinary.[6]

Perhaps the answer to the riddle of the freedom petition and its half approval does not lie outside the African community, that is, with Dutch attitudes or the development of colonial society as a whole. Perhaps, instead, it lies inward, in the heart of the African population itself. Ira Berlin has argued that the success of this first generation of African slaves in North America, especially the success of the half-free population of New Amsterdam, reflected the particular diverse, cosmopolitan, and coastal origins of the Africans brought to North America as slaves during these early years. The familiarity of New Amsterdam as a multiethnic Atlantic port city and the ability to see slavery as another form of clientage enabled these "Atlantic Creoles," as Berlin calls them, to integrate themselves into the local economy and society, just as their counterparts to the south were able to do in the Chesapeake. The opacity of the past cultural experiences of this particular group of Africans makes Berlin's point hard to prove, but the social cohe-

6. Joyce D. Goodfriend, "Burghers and Blacks: The Evolution of a Slave Society at New Amsterdam," *New York History*, LIX (1978), 127 ("on the eve"), 133–136; Council Minutes, Feb. 25, 1644, in *Council Minutes*, I, 212–213 ("the Company," 212); Jacobs, *New Netherland*, 381.

sion of these slaves after they arrived in New Netherland stands out clearly. This group of people responded collectively to challenges from the outside. They also worked together to develop and enforce notions of appropriate behavior among themselves. Their ability to work together made them able to work with and resist colonial court authority in the 1640s. How they managed to form such a strong community under adverse circumstances helps explain how they achieved half freedom in the 1640s through the 1660s.[7]

The fate of the petitioners of 1644 and those of subsequent years ultimately rested on their intimate networks. Looking again at the petition and grant, familial relationships afforded both the justification and the necessary context for half freedom and explain why these particular individuals achieved this status while others did not. The eleven petitioners for freedom in 1644 noted their need to support their families and children in calling for an end to their enslavement to the WIC. Kieft's grant, in turn, allowed partial freedom not only to the men but also to their wives. He justified the grant by referring to the burden of the couples' many children, who nonetheless remained the property of the WIC. Both petitioners and officials couched half freedom in terms of intimate ties. The answer to the riddle of New Amsterdam's half-freedom grants lies there.

These Africans' lives reveal how deeply personal connections, formed among a core group of New Amsterdam slaves, overlapped to link Africans not only to one another but also to the wider colonial society in which they lived. By joining together, they succeeded in transforming themselves into something even more valuable to their white neighbors than their individual worth as commodities within the local and international slave economy. This triumph did not come at once; it did not come in the 1620s when Dutch attitudes toward slave trading might still have been inchoate. Instead it came

7. Ira Berlin, *Many Thousands Gone: The First Two Centuries of Slavery in North America* (Cambridge, Mass., 1998), 50; see also Berlin, "From Creole to African," *WMQ*, 3d Ser., LIII (1996), 251–288. John K. Thornton and Linda A. Heywood elaborate on Berlin's generational theory and stress the Central African origins of the New Amsterdam Africans and their continuing cultural influence in Thornton and Heywood, *Central Africans, Atlantic Creoles, and the Foundation of the Americas, 1585–1660* (New York, 2007), 263. Not all scholars are convinced that Berlin is accurate in his assessment of the extent of cultural mixture on the coast of Africa in the seventeenth century; see Robin Law and Kristin Mann, "West Africa in the Atlantic Community: The Case of the Slave Coast," *WMQ*, 3d Ser., LVI (1999), 310. Hodges suggests their patterns of self-government were like African confraternities in Brazil; see Hodges, *Root and Branch*, 17–18. On this community as a bastion for runaways, see Moore, "A World of Possibilities," in Berlin and Harris, eds., *Slavery in New York*, 46. On their cohesion, see Cynthia J. van Zandt, *Brothers among Nations: The Pursuit of Intercultural Alliances in Early America, 1580–1660* (New York, 2008), 137–138.

over time, as decades of social connections solidified. Banding together enabled these Africans to participate in the local economy as a group, and their success at carving out an economic niche for their community ensured their survival and, eventually, their freedom. By forming families and a community woven into the wider social and economic fabric of the Hudson Valley, the Africans of New Amsterdam made themselves free.

Or, rather, half free. The intimate network Africans in New Amsterdam fashioned allowed them to remake themselves but not to subvert the colonial hierarchies in which they lived. They made themselves indispensable to white society by occupying a particular social position, a position that entailed negotiating the persistent demands and desires of their white neighbors. Kieft's grant tied them forever to that local social and economic nexus and rooted them to the land, ensuring their continued participation in the food exchange system of New Amsterdam. The support of the white community for the presence and partial freedom of this group arose from the economic benefit that white settlers felt they derived from the work that this group did together, and that support hinged on the continued ability of whites to extract labor on unequal terms. Tracing intimacies among New Amsterdam's black population, charting the shape of the webs that resulted, and mapping the place of their network within colonial society elucidate the context and meaning of the half-freedom grants. Intimate networks formed the strength and shaped the realities of the African population of New Amsterdam.

Tracing Intimate Ties

When the eleven petitioners presented their bid for freedom in 1644, they had already strived to overcome isolation and alienation through the creation of personal relationships. Family and kinship groups, built on a core group of WIC-owned slaves who lived together in New Amsterdam, gradually encompassed the first migrants, new arrivals, and creole children alike, stretching across boundaries of culture. Despite the large-scale forces threatening to pull people apart, these unions and small-scale connections helped draw Africans in New Netherland together.

Although we know little about how the first slaves arrived in New Netherland, the nature of Dutch transatlantic expansion in the colony's early years ensured that slaves came from many places and cultures. Because of New Netherland's particular position in the regional and international slave economy, African individuals remained in constant danger of being sold, traded, or leased. Appreciating the significance of the eventual growth of family, friendships, and community requires acknowledging the force of those pressures threatening the formation of durable relationships.[8]

New Netherland never developed a mass system for the importation of large numbers of culturally similar Africans to the colony. Whereas in some other Atlantic slave colonies, groups of slaves from particular regions were able to preserve cultural identities and use them as the basis for organizing communities in the Americas, New Netherland's slaves came in small numbers from widely dispersed cultural backgrounds. The Dutch established a number of trading posts in Africa in the seventeenth century, eventually obtaining slaves from throughout central West Africa. A lasting Dutch presence in Africa began as early as 1612, with a trading post called Mori on the Gold Coast, in present-day Ghana. However, the earliest Dutch traders there wanted gold at least as much as they wanted slaves. Dutch interests in Angola also increased during the seventeenth century, but, even there, the slave trade formed just one aspect of the economic relationship Dutch traders sought in Africa. Although Jan Huyghen van Linschoten, perhaps Holland's most important travel writer of the late sixteenth century, acknowledged Angola's human resources, he repeatedly stressed the country's mineral wealth. Angola, he wrote, "is populous beyond all credibility; it also overflows with Silver, Copper, and other metals, [and is] rich with all sorts of victuals and stock, especially cattle." Thus, even as he remarked on the size of Angola's human population, he also pointed to Angola's potential both for trade in metals and as a way station for ships bound to the East Indies. Diverse Dutch trading interests along a broad region of West Africa put a wide array of cultures within reach of Dutch slave buyers.[9]

8. There is an increasing tendency in the secondary literature to conflate the eleven petitioners in 1644 with the first eleven slaves in the colony. Though the petition mentioned that all of them had been there for nearly twenty years, they might or might not have represented the very first arrivals, and there is no reason to suppose that all of the earliest slaves joined in the petition. Certainly, in the intervening years, some slaves had died or been exported, and men without children would not have qualified. Furthermore, colony records from the 1620s have not survived, making it difficult to be certain about the experiences and identities of the first New Netherland slaves.

9. Jan Huyghen van Linschoten, *Itinerario, Voyage ofte schipvaert, van Jan Huygen van Linschoten naer Oost ofte Portugaels Indien. . . .* , III, *Beschryvinghe van de gantsche custe van Guinea, Manicongo, Angola, Monomotapa, ende tegen over Cabo de S. Augustijn in Brasilen* (Amsterdam, 1596), 12 (quotation). For the way that diverse ethnic backgrounds shaped community on one English plantation, see Lorena S. Walsh, *From Calabar to Carter's Grove: The History of a Virginia Slave Community* (Charlottesville, Va., 2001). On the role that cultural and ethnic ties played in resistance, see Douglas B. Chambers, *Murder at Montpelier: Igbo Africans in Virginia*

Not only did trade expose the Dutch to numerous coastal cultures, the people exported as slaves also likely came from diverse inland communities outside the immediate vicinity of Dutch trading posts. As one WIC employee explained regarding the slave trade in the Kongo, most slaves were not a part of local families and lineages but were instead people "who were born into slavery, and who were captured in war." Africans, he observed, followed "the law of nature and friendship among their kin as much, even in some things better than, we Christians" and so took great care not to sell their own kin into slavery, assuring that those exported came from a variety of backgrounds.[10]

Not all slaves in New Netherland even left Africa through Dutch ports. Piracy accounted for the majority of slaves sold from Dutch ships during the early period. Johannes de Laet, a contemporary chronicler of the WIC, estimated that Dutch raiders captured and sold 2,356 slaves between 1623 and 1636 from Spanish and Portuguese ships. In 1656, the Spaniard Juan Gallardo Ferrara appeared in New Netherland, seeking restitution for "forty-four Blacks and female blacks" hijacked from him and later sold in the Dutch colony. Ferrara explained that in April 1652 he was attacked "by one Geert Tÿsen near Morant Point" in Jamaica. "Because he . . . [had] found some of his blacks here" in New Netherland, Ferrara demanded their return. Despite a letter on his behalf from the States General and instructions from the directors of the WIC ordering Governor Peter Stuyvesant to do justice by the claimant, New Netherland officials resisted granting Ferrara's request.[11]

(Jackson, Miss., 2009). On Kongolese identity and resistance, see John K. Thornton, "'I Am the Subject of the King of Congo': African Political Ideology and the Haitian Revolution," *Journal of World History,* IV (1993), 181–214; Thornton, "African Dimensions of the Stono Rebellion," *American Historical Review,* XCVI (1991), 1101–1113. On African ethnic identities in the shaping of a maroon community in Dutch Suriname, see Richard Price, *Alabi's World* (Baltimore, 1990). On African trade, see Postma, *Dutch in the Atlantic Slave Trade,* 13; Van den Boogaart and Emmer, "Dutch Participation," in Gemery and Hogendorn, eds., *Uncommon Market,* 354. See also John Thornton, *Africa and Africans in the Making of the Atlantic World, 1400–1680* (New York, 1992). For more on the Dutch in Africa, see the works of Pieter Emmer, whose many English essays are collected in Emmer, *The Dutch in the Atlantic Economy, 1580–1880: Trade, Slavery and Emancipation* (Brookfield, Vt., 1998).

10. F. Capelle, Beschrijving van Angola, no date, Oude West-Indische Compagnie (OWIC), access number 1.05.01.01, inventory number 46, Nationaal Archief, The Hague (quotations). See also Van den Boogaart and Emmer, "Dutch Participation," in Gemery and Hogendorn, eds., *Uncommon Market,* 356.

11. Petition, Sept. 6, 1656, NYCM, VIII, 166–167, NYSA (quotations). On the numbers of slaves seized by pirates, see "Kort Verhael wt de voorgaende Boecken getrocken," in Johannes de Laet, *Historie ofte Iaerlijck verhael van de verrichtinghen der Geoctroyeerde West-Indische Com-*

Colony officials admitted that Captain Tÿsen had arrived on the Delaware River in late summer 1652 but claimed he displayed a license "in appropriate form from the Lord France governor of Christoffel Poinci." Based on this dubious pass, the New Netherlanders welcomed the pirates "as ministers of the French Crown, and thus as allies and good friends." The council evidently allowed the pirates to "repair and revictual their ship" without asking many questions. When Tÿsen "exchanged" slaves for "foodstuffs," colonists bought the slaves, they insisted, in good faith as "purchased chattel servants." The council referred Ferrara back to the directors of the WIC in the Netherlands. Ferrara's unusually persistent quest to recover his property brought to light the presence of these Spanish-owned slaves, whose existence might otherwise have remained hidden. It is impossible to say whether they had originally come from Africa or the Caribbean, or how many other slaves similarly followed such complicated paths to the colony.[12]

In addition to being seized and sold by pirates, some slaves in New Netherland seem to have entered the colony through the black market, ensuring that they came from varied ports of origin in Africa and arrived in the colony in small numbers through the back door. Twelve petitioners requesting permission from the WIC in 1660 to trade for slaves in Africa based their appeal on the promise that the WIC would benefit from New Netherland's existing healthy slave trade if slave trading by non-WIC ships became legal. Currently, the petitioners alleged, Dutch colonists bought their slaves from "our neighbors, French, English, Swedes, Danes, and Courlanders." Other Netherlanders simply sailed slaving vessels under other flags. They gave as examples "Arent de Groot," who traded for slaves in "Cormantyn in the year 1638 for the English, and . . . Hendrick Caerloff (former *fiscael* [or, the colony's chief prosecutor])" who built a rival slave post in West Africa at "Cabo Cors in the year 1650 for the Swedes." Such smuggling kept New Netherland slaves' origins dispersed.[13]

Even the men and women on board the few dedicated slave ships to arrive in New Netherland came from many places and cultures. For instance, the

pagnie (Leiden, 1644), 21. See also, Van den Boogaart and Emmer, "Dutch Participation," in Gemery and Hogendorn, eds., *Uncommon Market*, 355.

12. Answer to petition, Sept. 6, 1656, NYCM, VIII, 168–171, NYSA (quotations); Petition, Sept. 6, 1656, NYCM, VIII, 166–167, NYSA; Decision, Oct. 31, 1656, NYCM, VIII, 258–259, NYSA.

13. Petition, May 3, 1660, NYCM, IX, 193–195, NYSA (quotations). For more on Caerloff, see Postma, *Dutch in the Atlantic Slave Trade*, 75–76. Kormantine sits on the coast of present-day Ghana, just east of the original Dutch trading post Mori.

skipper of the *Gideon,* a slave ship that arrived in New Amsterdam in 1664, agreed to stop both at Elmina, in today's Ghana, and at Angola, taking on board "as many slaves as he can conveniently transport," ideally more than 275 individuals. After taking the slaves, copper, and ivory to Suriname and Curaçao, the skipper agreed to transport 300 to 350 slaves from Curaçao to New Netherland. Curaçao acted as a slaving depot, where people from many ships and origins awaited sale. The contract that the *Gideon's* skipper signed specified that the slaves he had taken aboard in Africa could be exchanged for others at Curaçao, presumably because many would be too ill to make the journey north. The shipment of slaves that arrived in Manhattan in 1664 represented a collection of people who had been exported from different ports at different times, very few of whom were likely to have been kinsmen or former neighbors.[14]

Many of New Netherland's legally imported slaves came in small groups of five, ten, or forty a year. For instance, the ship *New Netherland's Indian* delivered some forty "pieces" of slaves from Curaçao in 1660. Although most Dutch slave ships sold nearly all of their slaves in the Caribbean or Brazil, many of those ships scheduled stops in New Netherland for repairs and supplies before crossing the Atlantic back to Holland. Retaining a few slaves for sale in New Netherland would offset the cost of food and stores. Slaves who did arrive in New Netherland somewhat resembled the "'refuse' slaves" who arrived in eighteenth-century Pennsylvania after remaining unsold in several more profitable ports before reaching the mid-Atlantic coast. Slaves sold in such small groups would have experienced even more social isolation and alienation than those sold in larger "lots" directly from the ship to a single plantation owner.[15]

14. For an English translation of the *Gideon's* contract and a discussion of the few dedicated slave ships, see Emmer, "Slavenhandel," *Economisch- en sociaal-historisch jaarboek,* XXXV (1972), 114–115, 144–147 (quotation, 145). For several more ships whose cargo was at least in part slaves, see Goodfriend, "Burghers and Blacks," *New York History,* LIX (1978), 125–144. On illness during the journey north, see Testimony, Nov. 4, 1647, Not. Arch. 1294, 183v, Not. H. Schaef, SA. Slave testimony from 1664 suggests that two shipments of slaves arrived in 1664. Thus, the *Gideon* might not have been the only slave ship to arrive that year; see Petition, Sept. 4, 1664, NYCM, X, pt. 3, 317–318, NYSA. On the disruption of social ties during disembarkation and sale in the Caribbean, see Stephanie E. Smallwood, *Saltwater Slavery: A Middle Passage from Africa to American Diaspora* (Cambridge, Mass., 2007), 160–181.

15. Resolution, [Sept. 2, 1660], NYCM, IX, 760–761, NYSA ("pieces"); for an early translation of this document, see E. B. O'Callaghan, ed. and trans., *Voyages of the Slavers St. John and Arms of Amsterdam, 1659, 1663; Together with Additional Papers Illustrative of the Slave Trade under the Dutch* (Albany, N.Y., 1867), 189–193, esp. 190. On refuse slaves, see Darold D. Wax, "Preferences for Slaves in Colonial America," *Journal of Negro History,* LVIII (1973), 371–401 ("'re-

If the slaves reaching the colony traveled routes as complicated as those of the sailors who worked the ships, then those who eventually ended up in New Netherland likely came from diverse backgrounds indeed. For instance, Gerrit Broersz van Amsteldam sailed as a mate aboard the *Swarten Arent* "to Guine" in the WIC's service in 1658. Once in Guinea, he transferred to the yacht *Rob*, which sank, causing him to move first to the *Graef Enno* and later to the Portuguese ship the *Prinse*. Seven weeks later, he transferred again to the *Noortsche Leeuw* before finally landing aboard the *Eyckenboom*, sailing "to Ardre [in Ghana] to [take] slaves with it to Curaçao, from there to New Netherland and from there to here." The *Eyckenboom*'s charter for this voyage commissioned the ship to trade "from Cape Verd down . . . unto the Castle St. George d'el Mina . . . [a]nd sail towards the Bight of Guinea . . . [and] proceed . . . to the islands of Curacao, Bonaire and Aruba in the West Indies, and also to New Netherland." Thus, slaves aboard the *Eyckenboom* could have come from anywhere along a long stretch of coastline in West Africa or even from several islands in the Caribbean, possibly having seen the holds of several ships before reaching the Hudson Valley. Some of New Netherland's slaves, then, arrived literally alone, having traveled from ship to ship and port to port before ending up in New Amsterdam.[16]

Large shipments of slaves from a single African port rarely came to New Amsterdam in the early seventeenth century because the extra distance from Africa to the mid-Atlantic coast, as compared to Brazil or the Caribbean, remained fraught with risks. These additional hazards made skippers and investors prefer to seek quicker profits by selling their slaves farther south. Those slaves forced to make the longer, more treacherous journey north necessarily experienced greater danger and trauma as a result. For example, one joint slaving voyage from Ghana to New Netherland in 1659 went disas-

fuse,'" 375). On the difficulties of those sold in such small groups, see Smallwood, *Saltwater Slavery*, 169, 171 ("lots"), 174, 181. For an example of slave ships' planned stops in New Netherland for resupplying, see Contract, Nov. 23, 1656, Not. Arch. 2117, 161–165, Not. J. Thielmans, SA. Marcus Rediker also explores the pain of separation endured by slaves at the end of the Atlantic crossing; possibly New Netherland's more isolated arrivals would have lacked the "new sense of community" that some captives formed on board; see Rediker, *The Slave Ship: A Human History* (New York, 2007), 265 (quotation), 306–307.

16. Empowerment, Apr. 16, 1661, Not. Arch. 1364, 51v, Not. H. Schaef, SA ("to Guine"); Emmer, "Slavenhandel," *Economisch- en sociaal-historisch jaarboek*, XXXV (1972), 143–144 ("from Cape Verd," 144). The charter left the cargo unspecified, binding the captain to follow the orders of the WIC's ministers in each port; nothing either bound or prevented the transportation of slaves to New Netherland in particular. Emmer says that the slaves aboard were taken off the ship at Curaçao and smuggled into surrounding areas (124).

trously awry in the face of hostile Spanish authorities. When the *Geboorte Christij* and the *St. Jan* left Holland together headed "to the Guinea Coast, in order to load Negroes there and transport them to New Netherland," both ships encountered trouble during the middle passage. While the ships struggled against hostile winds, the skipper of the *Geboorte Christij* died and the skipper of the *St. Jan* was almost always "drunken."[17]

By the time the two ships neared "the coast of the Spanish West Indies," the vessels were "ravaged by contrary wind and weather." In addition, supplies had dwindled to the point of desperation for both crew and cargo until, finally, the ships "were necessitated, by lack of water and victuals, to seek refreshment" in the Spanish Caribbean. On their eventual return to Amsterdam, the sailors reported that they had been "forced by need" to enter the harbor at Cartagena "in order that they not all perish from misery." There, their troubles only multiplied, as Spanish authorities arrested, convicted, and condemned their surviving drunken skipper to hang. The sailors left the fates of their human cargo unmentioned. Presumably, those who had survived the long crossing, thirst, and starvation aboard the ill-fated ships found themselves slaves in South America rather than New Netherland. Their disastrous passage, however, illustrates the risks inherent in the voyage from Africa to New Netherland and serves as a reminder of the hardships faced by the survivors.[18]

The particular trauma experienced by slaves bound for New Netherland should not be underestimated. In 1647, the *Tamandaree* took on several groups of slaves in Brazil and Curaçao before picking up more slaves from the "warehouse" in Mauritsstadt and then proceeding from there to New Netherland. As several sailors reported on their return to Amsterdam, "the majority [of the slaves] were sick and infirm and very miserable" before they

17. Testimony, Dec. 14, 1661, Not. Arch. 3015, 1407, Not. H. Venkel, SA (quotations). On the nature of the Caribbean–North American passage, see Gregory E. O'Malley, "Beyond the Middle Passage: Slave Migration from the Caribbean to North America, 1619–1807," *WMQ*, 3d Ser., LXVI (2009), 125–172.

18. Testimony, Dec. 14, 1661, Not. Arch. 3015, 1407, Not. H. Venkel, SA. Although the sailors insisted that the ships had neither smuggled in the West Indies nor committed piracy, their story leaves a great deal in question. No doubt the skipper realized that delivering slaves to the Spanish colonies was quicker, easier, and more lucrative than taking them on to New Netherland. Given their supposed misery, why did they not stop at the friendly island of Curaçao, which they must have passed under way? What conceivable contrary wind could push a ship bound for New Netherland into port at Cartagena? In any case, the misadventure of the two ships illustrates the many physical and economic barriers to the mass importation of slaves to New Netherland.

ever headed north, many near starvation already. During the voyage, the *Tamandaree* beat against unfavorable winds, and, before long, people began to die. "And so the journey from the West Indies passed, with fair numbers dying miserably, the one day more, the next day fewer, at times three, four, five, six, eight, ten and more, up to fourteen in one day . . . without the witnesses really remembering, much less making note of, how many negroes died, [just] that it was a great number." Such visible deaths renewed the trauma of the Atlantic crossing and compounded the horror of the second round of social disconnection these reexports suffered. Those who survived to be auctioned off had been uprooted several times before being forced onto that death ship, and, if they had boarded alongside any kinsmen or countrymen, most likely they had seen them thrown overboard long before reaching New Amsterdam.[19]

In addition to the pressures of social isolation and cultural distance caused by their alienating journeys to the colony, the African population of New Netherland had to endure the pressures of the marketplace, which threatened to keep people mobile and uprooted, making it difficult to form stable social connections even after arrival. Many slaves entered the colony as property of the WIC. Some remained in the company's service for years, but many others faced sale into private hands. In cash-poor New Netherland, where people relied on commodities such as beaver skins, wampum beads, and grain crops to take the place of currency in regional exchanges, Africans' growing prices within the Atlantic economy exceeded the cash reserves of many locals. This disparity destabilized slaves' lives, placing them at risk of resale. For example, Dirck Jansen van Oldenburgh purchased one African slave in Curaçao on the account of New Netherlander Cornelis Pluvier in 1661, but, when the unnamed woman arrived in the colony, Pluvier lacked the "150 pieces of eight" he had contracted to pay. Although Pluvier acknowledged the debt, he claimed "for the present to have no ability to pay with pieces of eight, or beavers" and offered instead "to pay with grain or peas." Not satisfied, Dirck Jansen insisted on payment in currency, and the governing council of the colony ordered that Pluvier find a way to pay with pieces of eight or see the woman sold at public auction at his expense. The rising value of slaves as commodities threatened to keep New Netherland's black population at constant risk of relocation.[20]

19. Testimony, Nov. 4, 1647, Not. Arch. 1294, 183v, Not. H. Schaef, SA (quotations); Smallwood, *Saltwater Slavery*, 135–147, 152, 178.
20. Court case, [Sept. 29], 1661, NYCM, IX, 811, NYSA.

The disjuncture between the value of slaves in the Atlantic economy and the cash reserves of colonists made resale abroad appealing and raised the risk of multiple sales or leases within New Netherland. Taxes and legislation intended to enlarge the population of New Netherland likely prevented many men and women from being sold outside the colony, but not always. When the governor and council sought to sell thirty-six company slaves in 1660, they agreed to accept as payment "beavers, or foodstuffs such as meat, bacon, wheat, or peas at beavers' price" because demanding payment strictly in beavers or tobacco would permit "neither Burgher nor Farmer" to purchase slaves. Since the populace had "no tobacco, much less beavers" at the time, insisting on currency was out of the question.[21]

Yet, at other times, the WIC needed cash more than supplies, and the company reexported slaves for sale in the Chesapeake. Many of the slaves aboard the *Witte Paert,* a WIC slave ship that arrived in New Amsterdam in 1654, seem to have been shipped out again for sale shortly after their arrival, even though the company had cited the need to increase the population of New Netherland in the ship's charter. The WIC had allowed the slaving expedition because importing slaves "tends toward the advancement of the population and the bettering of the place." Since the WIC seems to have sold the slaves abroad anyway, such anti-export statements should not be taken at face value. In November 1661, the company decided to "sell publicly to the highest bidder" an unnamed group of "four of the seven negroes which were held over last year." By paying a two-beaver tax (equal to sixteen guilders) the buyers had permission to export the slaves for resale. When the company coffers ran low, the council sometimes paid its debts in kind through the bodies of its slaves. For example, in 1660, the company owed Captain Thomas Willet some eight thousand guilders for provisions he had delivered, yet they could not pay because of "the scarcity of the *cassa* [cash funds]." In payment, the council elected to give him three or four company slaves, with permission to export them. Given the strong financial advantages of sales abroad, private owners and colony officials always had incentives to ignore, elide, or flout the official anti-export stance of the WIC's Amsterdam directors.[22]

21. Resolution, [Sept. 2, 1660], NYCM, IX, 760–761, NYSA. A small part of the original is illegible due to fire damage; for a prefire translation of this document, see O'Callaghan, *Voyages of the Slavers,* 189–193, esp. 190.

22. Resolution, Nov. 19, 1654, NYCM, XII, 11, NYSA ("tends"); Order, Nov. 12, 1661, NYCM, IX, 882, NYSA ("sell publicly"). For an alternative translation, see O'Callaghan, *Voyages of the Slavers,* 193. For tax, see Order, Nov. 7, 1661, NYCM, IX, 882–883, NYSA. For

The fates of the forty-four slaves sought by the hapless Spaniard Ferrara illustrate just how vulnerable slaves in New Netherland remained to export and continual resale. Listing the difficulties inherent in returning Ferrara's former slaves, the colony council pointed out that "some already are dead, some are fugitives, some are still nearby here with various residents as purchased and paid-for chattel servants, but mostly sold and changed masters two, three, or more times." Only four years had elapsed since the slaves' arrival, yet not all could be located, and the majority had been sold more than once.[23]

Slaves' high value also led to complicated ownership arrangements. For instance, Ide van Vorst said he owned "half of the Negro that was given to [his brother-in-law Jacob Stoffelsen] by Capt. Geurt Tysen," although he was unable to prove his case to the satisfaction of the New Amsterdam court. Other private owners hired out their slaves to fellow colonists who needed slave labor yet lacked the cash to purchase slaves, such as when Jan Cornelis Cleyn rented out the services of his slave to Breuckelen resident Joris Rappelje. Colony officials regularly leased or half-leased wic-owned slaves to the city of New Amsterdam or to private settlers, blurring any strict distinction between privately owned and company slaves. Such arrangements kept slaves geographically mobile and imperiled intimate bonds. In 1644, "Big Pieter" saw his young daughter Maria, a wic slave, leased for four years to Nicolaes Coorn, who lived far upriver in the *colonie* of Rensselaerswijk. Pieter doubtless worried about his daughter's fate at Coorn's hands; in 1638, Coorn had been demoted from his post as a sergeant of wic troops for insubordination, theft, illegal trade with Native Americans, and adultery. The fiscael accused Coorn of having "at divers times had Indian women and Negresses sleep entire nights with him in his bed, in the presence of all the soldiers." Separated from her father and family, young Maria had few defenses against her new master if he attempted to repeat his earlier cross-racial sexual activity. Patterns of half ownership and leasing, tied to the high price of slaves in a cash-poor economy, kept slave lives disrupted and threatened.[24]

Willet, see Order, Sept. 30, 1660, NYCM, IX, 427, NYSA ("scarcity"). For an alternative translation, see O'Callaghan, *Voyages of the Slavers,* 225–226, esp. 225. See also, Agreement, May 31, 1664, NYCM, X, pt. 3, 232, NYSA; Letter, June 14, 1656, NYCM, XII, doc. 39, 4, NYSA. For the *Witte Paert,* see Emmer, "Slavenhandel," *Economisch- en sociaal-historisch jaarboek,* XXXV (1972), 114–115.

23. Answer, Sept. 6, 1656, NYCM, VIII, 168–171, NYSA.

24. Court Minutes, Sept. 14, 1654, CMNA, I, 270, NYCMA (microfilm) ("half of the Negro") (for the published translation, which contains several errors, see *RNA,* I, 242); In-

Powerful forces worked to keep Africans in New Netherland distant from one another and set apart from the communities in which they lived. Forced mobility, the marketplace, and cultural isolation posed real barriers to the creation and nourishment of social connections. Despite these impediments, however, Africans in New Netherland formed intimate bonds with one another and began carving out an African space within the colony. This endeavor started among a group of WIC-owned slaves who shared a common living space in New Amsterdam. Colony officials relied on these slaves to do the critical heavy labor, harbor work, and construction needed to build a new colony. Company slaves erected the defenses and maintained the fort of New Amsterdam. Jacob Stoffelsen van Ziericksee, overseer of the company slaves during the administration of Director Wouter van Twiller, testified to the essential work done by company-owned slaves in the 1630s. Stoffelsen explained that he "was as overseer of the Negroes belonging to the Company constantly employed with said Negroes in the building of Fort Amsterdam, which was completed in the year 1635; also, in cutting timber and firewood, as well for the large house as for the guard house, splitting rails, clearing land, burning lime and helping to gather the Company's grain in the harvest and considerable other such work." Indeed, the "other" work done by the slaves during the 1630s must have been "considerable"; additional company employees testified that unnamed hands built at least twenty-five structures and eight ships and repaired or modified many more during Van Twiller's brief administration.[25]

The company slaves' labor was not limited to WIC business. The mayors of New Amsterdam also rented or borrowed them for "City use," promising to provide them with "appropriate Food and Clothing" at city expense. In 1661, the mayors relied on company slaves to build a boat and to transport stones for the repair and strengthening of the city's "defenses in times of need." Without slave labor, the mayors warned, the city would have to "pay

---

denture, May 25, 1644, in *Provincial Secretary*, II, 223–224 ("Big Pieter," 223); Minutes, Dec. 2, 1638, in *Council Minutes*, I, 33–34 ("at divers," 33). Coorn's sexual contact across racial lines had only been illegal, strictly speaking, for a very short time. The director general and council had explicitly outlawed "adulterous intercourse with heathens, blacks, or other persons" just eight months earlier; see Ordinance, Apr. 8, 1638, ibid., 4 ("adulterous"). For mention of this regulation, see Jacobs, *New Netherland*, 388. For Rappalje, see Court Minutes, Aug. 16, 1655, CMNA, I, 370–371, NYCMA (microfilm); overexposure makes it necessary to supplement the microfilm with the translation found in *RNA*, I, 338. The term "colonie" indicated a semi-independent settlement within the colony of New Netherland, sometimes translated as "patroonship."

25. Deposition, Mar. 22, 1639, in *Provincial Secretary*, I, 108–112 (quotation, 112).

and give out a remarkable sum of money annually to the working man." Female WIC slaves also did personal housework for the families of colony officials. Drawing in part on the example of the enslaved and unfree workers who helped build colonies for the VOC, settlers and officials alike saw the presence of company-owned slaves as vital to building colonial infrastructure affordably, ensuring their continued presence in New Amsterdam throughout the Dutch period.[26]

These essential WIC slaves lived together in a shared house on Slijksteeg in New Amsterdam rather than being dispersed on the outlying farms or plantations. Since New Amsterdam acted as the port of entry for a great many of New Netherland's incoming slaves, this circumstance allowed newcomers to come into contact with this core group, facilitating connections between company and privately owned slaves. As the site of the principal downriver market, port, and court, New Amsterdam likewise served as a regional center that many rural slaves had occasion to visit, and private ownership of slaves was concentrated among New Amsterdam's burghers, further enabling social connections to form between WIC slaves and many privately held ones. New Amsterdam acted as a central meeting point for Africans throughout the greater Hudson Valley.[27]

From the colony's earliest years, these New Amsterdam Africans formed intimate connections through the institution of marriage. Though the marriage registry for the years before 1640 has been lost, the first recorded marriages do refer to earlier unions. For instance, the first unmistakably African couple listed in the marriage book in May 1641 mentioned former spouses on each side. The marriage of "Anthony van Angola, Widower of Catalina van Angola, and Lucie D'Angola, Widow of Laurens van Angola" indicates that marriages recognized as valid by the white minister existed in New Amsterdam before the surviving record begins. Anthony and Lucie were not alone; for each of the first five African couples included in the record in the 1640s, one or both spouses identified themselves as widows or widowers. Africans clearly embraced formal marriage from their earliest days in New Netherland.[28]

26. Order, [Dec. 8, 1661], NYCM, IX, 917–918, NYSA ("City use"); Petition, Nov. 7, 1661, NYCM, IX, 915–916, NYSA ("defenses").

27. On the slave house, see Jacobs, *New Netherland,* 383.

28. Samuel S. Purple, ed., *Records of the Reformed Dutch Church in New Amsterdam and New York: Marriages from 11 December, 1639, to 26 August, 1801,* Collections of the New-York Genealogical and Biographical Society, I (New York, 1890), 10–12 (quotation, 10).

The New Amsterdam church marriage register, although not a complete record of local marriages, offers evidence that, by the 1640s, Africans were building bridges across the cultural distances and forced divides among them. The names of couples included reveal that black New Netherlanders asserted a variety of cultural identities and that broad regional identifications united rather than split them apart. Many men and women in the registry identified themselves as coming from Angola. But, "Angola," in Dutch parlance at the time, could refer to anywhere along the entire coast spanning present-day southern Nigeria, Congo, and northern Angola, so New Netherland's many Angolans did not necessarily all share a common language, ethnicity, or cultural heritage. Palesa van Angola, for instance, retained her Bantu first name. On the other hand, the prevalence of Latinate Christian first names like "Francisco" and "Domingo" point to Portuguese cultural influence, suggesting that some Angolans had been exposed to the Luso-African Catholic culture developing in the Kongo Kingdom. Not everyone, however, referenced Angola to invoke Kongolese heritage. Anthonÿ de Chongo, already named for the patron saint of the Kongo Kingdom, chose a still more specific place-name to make his background clear. Although the Kongo formed a part of that region the Dutch called Angola, Anthonÿ managed to assert a sense of origin that met his definitions, not those merely of Dutch New Netherlanders.[29]

Despite the cultural differences among them, those who identified themselves as Angolan formed families with one another and with other Africans in New Netherland. Anna van Angola, for instance, was married to "Francisco Van Capo Verde," whose origins and identity lay far to the north. In 1642, Anthony Ferdinand married Maria van Angola. However, he did not share his wife's African birthplace but identified himself as a "bachelor from Cascalis, in Portugal." Philip Curtin has estimated that, by the early seventeenth century, when African trade remained dominated by Portuguese ships, slavers had shipped some fifty thousand African slaves to Europe. Iberian Africans in the colony included "Pieter Portugies, *Neger*"

---

29. People from the African coast where the Dutch traded in the seventeenth century did not have a clear identity or "country" based on geography or polity. Matriclan and matrilineal affiliations that did not necessarily follow regional, political, or linguistic boundaries remained far more important; see Smallwood, *Saltwater Slavery,* 110–120. On Feb. 26, 1642, Palesa van Angola, the widow of Francisco d'Angola, married the bachelor Francisco van Angola; see Purple, ed., *Marriages,* 11. On the involvement of the king of Kongo with Dutch slave traders beginning in the late 1630s, see Van den Boogaart and Emmer, "Dutch Participation," in Gemery and Hogendorn, eds., *Uncommon Market,* 361–364.

and Manuel the Spaniard. Still others of New Netherland's early African population came from ports and colonies spread throughout the Americas and Caribbean. Sebastiaen de Britto, for instance, came from "St Domingo." This Caribbean creole man married an Angolan woman, Isabel Kisana van Angola.[30]

By the 1640s, the first complete decade covered by the marriage register, the first generation of American-born slaves started to marry. These creoles, from both Latin America and, over time, New Netherland itself, wed across lines of culture and birthplace. "Jan Augustinus, bachelor from Cartagena" published banns with "Susanna Van Nieuw Nederlt" in April 1647. Susanna was a popular name among New Netherland's Africans. Church registry books include Susannas who asserted a variety of ethnic and regional identities, including Susanna van Angola, Susanna D'Angola (who retained the Portuguese *de* rather than adopting the Dutch *van*), Susanna Simons van Angola (who asserted both African origins and descent from a man with a Christian name), Susanna Pieters, *Negrinne* (whose use of a patronymic and lack of a notation on her origins suggests creole identity), Susanna Congoy, *negrinne,* Susanna *Negrinne,* and a "Susanna, 17 years old." The last, sponsored by African godparents and baptized on April 14, 1647, thirteen days before Susanna and Jan's appearance in the marriage record, seems likely to have been the Susanna betrothed to Jan Augustinus. At seventeen, she would have been one of New Netherland's earliest creole Africans, making her part of the first generation of African-American children to reach the age of marriage in the colony. Jan Augustinus's origins in South America connect him with one of the primary destinations of Dutch slavers and pirates. After the 1634 WIC conquest of Curaçao, Dutch slavers and smugglers used the island, only forty miles from the Venezuelan coast, as a slave depot and naval supplies station. The young couple serves as a reminder that American

---

30. Purple, ed., *Marriages,* 11–12 ("Francisco," 11, "bachelor," 12), 14 ("St Domingo"); Philip D. Curtin, *The Atlantic Slave Trade: A Census* (Madison, Wis., 1969), 17–28, 268. Baptismal records point to Anthony Ferdinand's African heritage, despite his European birthplace. In the 1640s, an "Anthony Portugies, *Neger*" baptized children in New Amsterdam. There might have been at least two men with that name in New Amsterdam in the 1640s. See the entries for "Anthony Ferdinandus" and "Anthony Fernando, Portugees" in Thomas Grier Evans, ed., *Records of the Reformed Dutch Church in New Amsterdam and New York: Baptisms from 25 December, 1639, to 27 December, 1730,* Collections of the New York Genealogical and Biographical Society, II (New York, 1901), 10 ("Anthony Fernando"), 12 ("Anthony Portugies"), 13–15 ("Pieter Portugies," 15), 17, 20, 26 ("Anthony Ferdinandus"); Manumission, Feb. 17, 1649, in *Provincial Secretary,* II, 82–83.

creoles endured forced mobility, just as their parents had. Yet this enforced movement did not disrupt people's ability to come together within the black population of New Amsterdam.[31]

Many creole Africans incorporated their diverse origins in their names. Elara (or Hilary or Larie) Criolyo, for instance, asserted her creole identity in place of the patronymics or surnames commonly used by Dutch speakers in the colony. The Latinate roots she chose serve as a reminder that "creoles" did not necessarily hail from New Netherland. Elara had come north from Brazil with masters fleeing the gradual Portuguese reconquest of New Holland, thus Elara was both an American creole and a first-generation New Netherlander. Christoffel Crioell made clear that he was a creole but not a New Netherlander by birth when he kept the place-name "Van St. Thomas." Creoles born in New Netherland, on the other hand, often disappear, chameleon-like, against the backdrop of Dutch names in the surviving records. The Lucas Pieterszen and Anna Jans who wed in 1657 would, at first glance, appear as Dutch as the names that surround theirs in the registry were it not for the word *"Negros"* inscribed after their names. Creoles created families together, despite differences of culture and generation.[32]

By intermarrying, creoles and immigrants helped unite African- and American-born black residents. In February 1664, for instance, "Swan Van Loange" married the New Netherland–born Christina Emanuels. The bridegroom's invocation of Loango reflected his connection with the seventeenth-century African state by that name north of the Congo River. Though Loango fell within the broad region of West Africa known by the Dutch as "Angola," Swan's sense of place and culture made him assert a more specific identity. In spite of his continuing African allegiance, by marrying the daughter of some of New Netherland's earlier African immigrants Swan made himself a part of the increasingly close-knit group of immigrants and creoles. Swan was also not a WIC-owned slave but belonged instead to the private merchant Govert Loockermans, showing that family connections reached between company and private slaves. Shortly after Swan and Christina's marriage, Francisco de Angola married the creole Elisabeth Pieters in April 1664, continuing the pattern of strong attachments between first- and second-generation African New Netherlanders. These marriages dem-

31. Purple, ed., *Marriages*, 14 ("Jan Augustinus"); Evans, ed., *Baptisms*, 10–13, 15, 18, 22 ("Susanna"); Postma, *Dutch in the Atlantic Slave Trade*, 27.

32. Purple, ed., *Marriages*, 21–22 ("Van St. Thomas," 21, "Negros," 22), 26; Minutes, Aug. 2, 1646, in *Council Minutes*, I, 333–334.

onstrate that creole and immigrant Africans created one diverse interconnected group, not several groups divided by ethnicity or birth.[33]

Regardless of the powerful forces working against the creation of family and kinship, by the 1640s Africans joined together across lines of culture, language, and origin. The particularly traumatic and isolating nature of New Netherland's slave trade and the continuing threat of forced mobility did not prevent people from starting new families through marriage. Through these relationships, people united across the many divides that separated them. By establishing these connections, this particular group of slaves took the first step toward resisting their enslavement. The eleven petitioners for freedom in 1644 mentioned their wives and families, and Kieft's half-freedom grant extended beyond the petitioners to include their unnamed wives. Understanding how family formation intertwined with half-free status requires seeing how families overlapped to structure an intimate network.

Charting Intimate Networks

Relationships among Africans in New Netherland crisscrossed and overlapped, forming a complicated pattern. Familial and fictive kin relationships helped relocate people within a social web, even when far removed from the kin, clans, and villages that had ordered life in Africa. Based on a core group of WIC-owned slaves but reaching throughout and beyond the New Amsterdam black population, social networks turned individuals into a community, with established lines of authority and connections to outsiders. This African fellowship was able to work together to meet the challenges and dangers that faced them. In this sense, a flexible and growing intimate network formed the necessary precursor to the development of half freedom beginning in the 1640s.

Formalizing interfamily alliances in church helped Africans build community. African New Amsterdammers actively embraced baptism within the Dutch Reformed congregation. By turning to the colony's established religion in this formal way, they provided widely recognized fictive kin for their children by electing baptismal "witnesses" from among the faithful.

33. Purple, ed., *Marriages*, 29 (quotation); Postma, *Dutch in the Atlantic Slave Trade*, 57. Elisabeth Pieters was baptized on Mar. 1, 1643, making her as young as twenty at her marriage. Christina Emanuels was baptized on Feb. 12, 1645, making her at least nineteen at marriage. The fathers of both girls offered children for baptism at regular intervals throughout the 1640s, suggesting that the girls were probably infants when baptized. See Evans, ed., *Baptisms*, 15, 18. On Swan and Christina's ownership, see Jacobs, *New Netherland*, 385.

Although having godparents, called merely witnesses in the Reformed tradition, had become optional under the Synod of Dordt (1618–1619), most New Netherlanders, black and white alike, opted to have them present at a child's baptism. By selecting witnesses, Africans began to respin the web of family and lineage.[34]

Most often, parents asked an African man and an African woman to stand as witnesses for their children. To act as witnesses, the adults had to have been previously baptized themselves, yet only one African woman received baptism as an adult in the period covered by the registry. Therefore, before 1640, when the first surviving register begins, the church must have already taken root among the African population. For instance, Mayken van Angola originally came to the colony in 1628, though her name first appears in the registry in 1645, when she acted as godmother to young Christina Emanuels. Similarly, "Simon Congoy" and Isabel D'Angola acted as witnesses for little Maria Jansz, offered for baptism by her father Jan van Fort Orangien in July 1640. These witnesses, despite their foreign birth and active identification with Africa, must have already been accepted as baptized Christians to be allowed to become fictive kin in this formal way. Sometimes, married couples acted as witnesses for African creole children, although witnesses were not always spouses. In 1641, the newlyweds Anthony and Lucie were among the four Angolan witnesses to the baptism of Anthony Portugees's twins. Although lateral kinship, which had played such a large role in family life in Africa, had been destroyed by the dislocations of forced migration, godparentage allowed fictive kinship to connect newborns into a larger web of community. Literal uncles and aunts might have been missing, but, through witnessing, a child acquired a quasi-familial relationship to a married couple willing to stand in their stead.[35]

34. Given the continued use and importance of baptismal witnesses among the white Dutch Reformed population, it is not possible to characterize the African embrace of baptism and witnessing as necessarily reflecting a Catholic tradition. Clearly, some Kongolese New Netherlanders would have been exposed to Catholic godparentage practices in Africa, whereas African-desecended New Netherlanders from Brazil could have been introduced to Portuguese Catholic practices there. Yet, there was nothing in Africans' use of the institution in New Netherland that would have been unfamiliar or uncomfortable to their Dutch fellow congregants, and I can find no document by a Dutch writer expressing the idea that Africans' behavior in this instance seemed more Catholic than Reformed. Therefore, the use of baptism by this population appears broadly consistent with both Catholic and Dutch Reformed traditions and evidently functioned to draw slaves—and to some extent whites—from various religious backgrounds together, rather than dividing them along Catholic or Protestant lines.

35. Evans, ed., *Baptisms,* 10 (quotation), 11, 12, 18; Petition, [Apr. 19, 1663], NYCM, X, pt. 2, 71, NYSA. Mayken's name also appears as Mayken d'Angola. On baptism as a protective strat-

Overlapping patterns of witnessing reaffirmed and reflected a growing social web uniting the African population of New Amsterdam. Between the beginning of the registry in September 1639 and February 1655, children of the African community received baptism in New Amsterdam's church with some regularity. Africans put up at least fifty-five children for baptism in just over fifteen years. These children had as few as two or as many as six witnesses. Baptism created a complicated pattern of fictive kinship. The interweaving of relationships that witnessing enabled and revealed shows up especially clearly in the records for July 1641. On the seventh of that month, Jacom Anthony van Angola brought in his daughter Catharina for baptism with two African witnesses, Cleyn Anthony van Angola and Susanna van Angola, in attendance. Just one week later, "Anthony portugies, *neger*" brought in his twins, Anthony and Maria, for baptism. Once again, Cleyn Anthony stood by, joined by the other new father, Jacom Anthony, in addition to the newly married Angolan couple Lucie and Anthony. As a result, multiple and overlapping fictive kin relationships linked the three children to one another. Not only did Catharina's father witness the twins' baptisms, the three babies also shared the care and oversight of Cleyn Anthony. From their very first days, these children lived within a web of relationships that joined them not only to the adults in the black population but also to one another.[36]

Parents turned to one another and to prominent members of the black population again and again, making it possible to trace a network of wit-

---

egy by African parents, see Joyce D. Goodfriend, "The Souls of African American Children: New Amsterdam," *Common-Place*, III, no. 4 (July 2003), accessed Dec. 20, 2012, http://www .common-place.org/vol-03/no-04/new-york/.

36. Evans, ed., *Baptisms*, 10–38 (quotation, 12). Partial records exist for 1639, when one African-American child was baptized. There are other children whose names or parents' names suggest possible African origin, but it is impossible to be certain in every case. Thus, tallies of African baptisms may vary. In addition, Jaap Jacobs has noted references in other documents to baptisms of African children that were not included in the official registry book; see Jacobs, *New Netherland*, 314–318. The number given here represents the minimum number of African children baptized, not the total. This number excludes the 1647 baptism of six-year-old Eva, the daughter of Anthony Jansz van Salee, who was half Moroccan and half Dutch and married to the Dutch woman Grietje Reyniers, thus occupying an anomalous racial category. Considered a "Turk" by his neighbors, he does not seem to have truly belonged either to New Amsterdam's African community or to its Dutch population; see Leo Hershkowitz, "The Troublesome Turk: An Illustration of Judicial Process in New Amsterdam," *New York History*, XLVI (1965), 299–310. I also exclude the incomplete entry by his brother Abraham and the entry for Dominco Dies's daughter, since I am unsure of her parents' background. This number does take account of the baptism of Captain Jan de Vries's mixed race child; adds one child to the count for February 2, 1646, though the infant's name was not recorded; includes all children offered by men with variants of the names Anthony Portugees

nesses that shows just how tightly baptism helped unite Africans in New Amsterdam. In 1645, for example, Pieter St. Thome offered his son Mathias for baptism, choosing as witnesses "Groot Emanuel, *neger*, [and] Susanna Congoy, *negrinne*." Groot, or Big, Emanuel himself put a son named Philip up for baptism just five months later, having "Sebastiaen, Capt. of the negroes" and Palesa van Angola serve as witnesses. Groot Emanuel again witnessed for the child of a fellow African when he stood by as Paulo D'Angola had his son Dominicus baptized in June 1646. Among the three witnesses at the baptism of Paulo's next son, Jacob, in 1653 were Mayken van Angola, who had also witnessed in 1645 for the daughter of Emanuel Trompetter, alongside, once again, Sebastiaen, or "Bastayen," Captain of the Negroes. Through the repeated ritual of baptism, Africans in New Amsterdam linked the entire community together and formalized the bonds among them. As Africans stood by the baptisms of one another's children, they performed the intimate connections between themselves anew, fashioning a common fellowship by becoming godparents.[37]

The complicated chain of witnessing that began with Pieter St. Thome's son also hints at the emergence of authority within the developing African community. By choosing witnesses for their children, Africans affirmed nascent leaders who could help transform a group of individuals into a community. Some witnesses appear again and again, suggesting the respect they commanded within the black population. Palesa van Angola, for example, appeared as godmother four times. The African drummer Pieter van Camp similarly witnessed at least four children. Likewise, Cleyn Anthony witnessed five children. Perhaps the most intriguing name to appear regularly as a witness was a man known variously as Sebastiaen, Bastrÿn, or Bastiaen, often called the "Captain of the Negroes." In him, the African population might have found a leader with crucial access to the wider Atlantic world.[38]

Although it is impossible to be certain of his exact identity, this nascent leader seems likely to have been a free black sailor whom the colony council

---

or Anthony Fernando; and assumes that Anthony Matthyszen offered twins for baptism in May 1651. One seventeen-year-old girl offered herself for baptism, which would increase the total number to fifty-six.

37. Evans, ed., *Baptisms*, 18 ("Groot"), 13 ("Sebastiaen"), 18 ("Bastayen"), 19, 21, 34. There were several African men named Emanuel, including one often called Groot, or Big, Emanuel and one called Cleyn, or Little, Emanuel. Paulo's name also appears here as Paulus van Angola and elsewhere as Paulo Angolo. Palesa van Angola's name also appears as Pallas.

38. Other names, such as Susanna, Anthony, and Emanuel also appear frequently but were so common among the black population that it is difficult to be certain how many times a single Susanna, for example, acted as a witness.

first recognized as an employee of the company in 1640. Their acknowledgment of his emancipation testifies to the relatively democratic structure aboard privateer ships that allowed black sailors to earn their freedom based on their skills as seamen, whether or not they had been free before their work at sea. The council clarified his free status in a declaration:

> Whereas Bastiaen from Pariba, Portuguese, taken on the 15th of November anno 1638 with a prize, entered the service of the honorable directors of the Chartered West India Company on the ship *Neptunes* and until now has together with other sailors done his work on said ship, for which he was allowed fl. 8 a month by the ship's council of the said ship, therefore we, the director and council of New Netherland, accept and approve the resolution passed by the said skipper and ship's council that he, Bastiaen, is to earn fl. 8 a month from the time that he came on the ship *Neptunes*.[39]

In effect, the colony council simply gave legal imprimatur to a decision already made by the "ship's council." Bastiaen's access to the wider Atlantic world might explain his popularity as a godparent. Other black sailors from the colony had traveled to Amsterdam, even delivering a petition for payment to WIC directors in 1635; doubtless, New Amsterdammers remembered the alternative possibilities sailing allowed. Yet, another African Sebastiaen, from Santo Domingo, lived in New Amsterdam during those years, making it uncertain which man was identified as the "Captain." Other scholars have supposed that the title indicated that Bastiaen served as a work boss among company slaves. Whatever Bastiaen's origins, he frequently acted as a godparent to African children, including, for example, young Jochem, the son of "Larie *Swartinne*." There, Bastiaen's name was given as "Bastrÿn, Capt. van de *Swarten*," that is, "Captain of the Blacks." Twice in 1645, the church secretary identified him in baptismal records as Bastayen and Sebastiaen, "Captÿn van de *Negers*." Bastiaen's repeated presence at baptisms in the 1640s indicates the gradations of status and authority developing in the

39. Minutes, Nov. 23, 1640, in *Council Minutes*, I, 96 (quotation). The document does not explicitly state Bastiaen's race. However, his lack of a last name, his Brazilian origins, his designation as a prize, and his identification as "Portuguese" all indicate African heritage. On the importance of skills over race onboard pirate ships, see Peter Linebaugh and Marcus Rediker, *The Many-Headed Hydra: Sailors, Slaves, Commoners, and the Hidden History of the Revolutionary Atlantic* (Boston, 2000). In 1654, a Bastiaen d'Angola was similarly manumitted after being taken with a prize; see Peter R. Christoph, "The Freedmen of New Amsterdam," in Charles T. Gehring and Nancy Anne McClure Zeller, eds., *A Beautiful and Fruitful Place: Selected Rensselaerswijck Seminar Papers* (Albany, N.Y., 1991), 159.

African population. The intimate network among Africans functioned not simply as a haphazard collection of relationships; instead, it had a particular shape, with nodes of authority and overlapping lines of respect.[40]

Bastiaen, the frequent witness, had connections to the multiracial group of maritime workers. These links give further credibility to the idea that Sebastiaen, the Captain of the Negroes, was the man taken as a prize in 1638. Bastiaen joined several white settlers to serve as the witness for the mixed-race son of "Capt. Jan de Vries" and a woman identified only as "Swartinne" or "black woman." De Vries, a sea captain with multiple friends and acquaintances among Africans in New Netherland, proved a key ally until his death at sea in 1647, leasing land, for instance, to African farmers. Bastiaen, then, not only sailed the ocean himself, he also knew white seamen like De Vries who could ship goods or take messages even while he stayed ashore.[41]

Based on Bastiaen's exceptional connections, at least five Africans chose to incorporate him into their growing web of kin by selecting him as a child's godparent. In addition, Jan van Angola, while preferring Emanuel Congoy as his son's godfather, nonetheless opted to name him Sebastiaen, and the familiar forms "Bas" and "Basje" persisted in the African community for generations. That he frequently served as godfather reflected West African ideas of the relationship between kin or lineage and status. Having the "Captain of the Negroes" as fictive kin for one's child substituted for powerful lineage relationships American-born children lacked.[42]

40. Evans, ed., *Baptisms*, 17–19 ("Larie," 17, "Captÿn," 18–19). For black sailors in Amsterdam, see Nov. 19, 1635, Notulen, Amsterdam Chamber for 1635–1636, Oude West-Indische Compagnie (OWIC), access number 1.05.01.01, inventory number 14, Nationaal Archief. Sebastiaen de Britto van St. Domingo married Isabel Kisana van Angola in 1646; see Purple, ed., *Marriages*, 14. Whereas the majority of children, black and white, were put up for baptism by their fathers, Jochem was brought in by his mother. It seems likely that Larie Swartinne was another name for Elara / Hilary Criolyo. On Bastiaen as a slave work boss, see Christoph, "The Freedmen of New Amsterdam," in Gehring and Zeller, eds., *A Beautiful and Fruitful Place*, 159.

41. Evans, ed., *Baptisms*, 23 (quotations). His name is given there only as Bastiaen. Other witnesses included Simon Joosten, Michiel Janszen van den Berg, and a "Susanne Simons," whose race was not mentioned, although a Susanna Simons van Angola appears in another baptismal record (13). Just three weeks before, De Vries had empowered the same two men to "have supervision over [his] free Negroes and Brasilian woman during his absence"; see Empowerment, Aug. 3, 1647, in *Provincial Secretary*, II, 463–464 (quotation, 464). For an excellent discussion of De Vries and his ties to the African community, see Moore, "A World of Possibilities," in Berlin and Harris, eds., *Slavery in New York*, 47–48.

42. Evans, ed., *Baptisms*, 15, 17, 18, 19, 22–23. Two of the five times Bastiaen appears as a witness, his title of captain is not mentioned. The name Basje Pietersz, or Pietersen, appears in African petitions from 1663 and 1664; see Certificate, Dec. 11/21, 1664, NYCM, X, pt. 3, 327,

Because witnessing provided children links to people with status and power, parents did not always restrict their children's fictive kin to the African community. Parents recognized that giving local whites a sense of obligation to their children provided them with important potential sources of aid. Such was the case for little Anna, baptized in 1644, when New Amsterdam's minister Everardus Bogardus joined three Africans as witness to her baptism. Perhaps the inclusion of such a prominent white witness reflected a need for special protection for this child. Though fathers sponsored the overwhelming majority of children, both black and white, baptized in the 1640s, a woman, Philippe Swartinne, brought in Anna. Anna might well have lacked a father willing to be part of her life. Whatever made Anna special, she was the only child of African parents whose baptism Bogardus witnessed, and, in total, he witnessed just six other baptisms. No matter what motivated his decision, he would have been a powerful friend for a young African-American girl to have had, had he lived. In 1647, Bogardus drowned in the sinking of the ship *Prinses,* alongside Director Kieft and Captain Jan de Vries. In any case, being godchildren of powerful whites allowed liminal children in need of special protections to form important patron-client relations within New Amsterdam society.[43]

No doubt parents who appealed to white witnesses hoped that godparents would act as benefactors. For example, Emanuel Trompetter's daughter, Christina, not only had Mayken van Angola and Bastiaen as godparents, she also had white New Amsterdammers Geertruÿd Roelofs and Claes van Elslandt. Christina thus had a tie to a wealthy settler and former member of the colony council, a man able to act as a powerful patron for the girl, if he so chose. Emanuel Trompetter clearly sought to build a powerful social network for his daughter not only within the African community but also beyond it.[44]

NYSA. With the handover to the English, the colony switched from the New Style calendar to the Old Style still used by the English, causing the dates to shift back ten days. Most documents from the colony in the days after the surrender carry double dates, as above. However, the dating system used in this work is the Dutch New Style calendar system.

43. Evans, ed., *Baptisms,* 17. Beginning in mid-1655, the mother's name began to be listed alongside the father's. Throughout the keeping of the register, bastard children form the majority of children sponsored for baptism by a mother alone. On Bogardus, see Willem Frijhoff, *Wegen van Evert Willemsz: Een Hollands weeskind op zoek naar zichzelf, 1607–1647* (The Hague, 1995).

44. Evans, ed., *Baptisms,* 18. For Claes van Elslandt's council membership, see Jacobs, *New Netherland,* 484.

Parents clearly longed to give their child an important resource by having a powerful white settler as a witness. When Mattheus de Angola chose to name his son after his white witness, Augustyn Hermans, he no doubt wanted the wealthy and prominent man to provide young Augustyn Mattheussen with some real help in the future. By choosing Hermans's wife, Janneken Varleth, as the godmother, Mattheus also allied the boy with one of New Amsterdam's most powerful merchant families. Perhaps Mattheus or his wife was the Hermans's slave. The parents might have desired that the baptism would create feelings of reciprocity between the owners and this vulnerable boy. Similarly, Anthony Ferdinandus chose to have his son's baptism witnessed by Paulus Heymans, a settler who worked as the overseer of the company slaves between 1647 and 1654. He might have thought that having Heymans act as a witness would change his relationship with the boy from one solely based on authority to one mediated by shared faith.[45]

Sometimes baptism did motivate white godparents to at least attempt to protect children, although the extent of that protection should not be exaggerated. When the wife of Governor Stuyvesant realized that some children she had sponsored for baptism had been sold abroad in Curaçao, she managed to get her husband to try to have the children returned to New Netherland. Though Stuyvesant and the director of Curaçao regretted the sales as a dreadful mistake, records do not make clear if the children ever returned home. This kind of action on behalf of African children, though not always as effective as parents must have wished, nonetheless testifies to the sense of obligation parents sought to create for children when they chose baptismal witnesses.[46]

Although witness records demonstrate the growth of connections among and beyond New Amsterdam Africans, immense challenges faced this poor and enslaved population, almost guaranteeing conflict and dissension. In 1641, the WIC slaves in New Amsterdam faced an unprecedented threat, one that originated in a dispute among the slaves themselves. A bitter fight among company-owned slaves led to the death of African Jan Premero. The records do not reveal what caused the altercation or what Premero did to enrage his companions, but the fight suggests the intense pressures the WIC slaves lived under and the potential for the nascent African community to fracture under those pressures. Living together within the close confines

45. Evans, ed., *Baptisms*, 26, 38; for Heyman's position as overseer, see Jacobs, *New Netherland*, 383.

46. Jacobs, *New Netherland*, 316.

of the WIC slave quarters, disputes had the potential to spiral out of control. With Premero's death, Africans in New Amsterdam had to overcome two enormous challenges. Would his death cause a rift in their community? And could the accused survive the Dutch legal process? For, with Premero's death, the prosecutor and colony council turned their attention to discovering and punishing his killer.

The Dutch authorities' investigation focused, not on the cause of the brawl, which took place "in the woods near their houses" on January 6, 1641, but on discovering the person responsible for the killing. Eight defendants—Antonio Paulo d'Angola, Gracia D'Angola, Jan van Fort Orangien, Manuel de Gerrit de Reus, Anthony Portugees, Manuel Minuit, Simon Congo, and Big Manuel—admitted to fighting with Premero as a group but refused to name one among them as the killer. Not satisfied without the name of the killer, the governing council "examined the defendants, asking them who was the leader . . . and who gave . . . the death blow." Even under interrogation, a process that could include torture in the Dutch system, "the defendants said that . . . they committed the deed together." Despite repeated questioning, the group persisted in their assertion that "they jointly committed the murder and that one is as guilty as another." This refusal to name one among the group as the killer suggests that regardless of the pressures that had led to the fight and the new pressures put on them in its aftermath, the WIC slaves continued to stand by one another. Yet, the Dutch legal system demanded that someone be punished for the killing. Although eight men together had committed the crime, the law only insisted on a single execution. Dutch authorities, therefore, needed to select one man to pay the price. Forcing the eight defendants to draw lots, Manuel de Gerrit de Reus came up the loser, and the council condemned him to hang. Even then, none of the defendants spoke up to name a leader or killer, not even Manuel. Again, the cohesion among the men testifies to the strength of their ties to one another.[47]

The events of the following day, when Manuel faced execution, emphasize the importance of those relationships and those they had with others. The morning after lots had been drawn, Manuel was hanged. "Standing on

47. Minutes, Jan. 17, 1641, in *Council Minutes,* I, 97–100 ("in the woods," 99, "examined," 98). For a similar use of lots to determine punishment for a crime committed by three men together in the Cape Colony in Africa, see Ward, *Networks of Empire,* 256. It is important to note that the authorities were not appealing to God or chance to determine guilt, but, rather, to determine who among the guilty would bear the burden of punishment. For comments on the use of ordeal to ascertain guilt in central Africa, see Hodges, *Root and Branch.*

the ladder, [Manuel] was pushed off by the executioner, being a Negro, having around his neck two good ropes." Yet, as the knots pulled taut with Manuel's weight, both ropes broke, and he fell to the ground still alive, "whereupon the inhabitants and bystanders called for mercy." At this critical moment, then, Manuel's white neighbors, gathered to watch the spectacle of his death, called out on his behalf. Confronted with the crowd's pleas for mercy, the council "graciously granted him his life and pardoned him and all the other Negroes, on promise of good behavior and willing service." Although the stakes had been very high, the group of slaves held fast, and, by the narrowest of margins, their resistance paid off for all.[48]

A published translation of this extraordinary court case has been available for some time, and many scholars of New Netherland have noted the tenacious way the defendants stood by one another. The men's bravery in the face of questioning is undoubtedly remarkable. Yet, relationships reaching beyond the African population also had a hand in saving Manuel de Gerrit de Reus's life that day. Had the largely white population of New Amsterdam cried out for blood instead of mercy, the outcome of the tale would have been very different. And the care with which the secretary recorded the race of the executioner (who, though unnamed, was another WIC-owned slave) suggests that the secretary might have had the same suspicion that jumps almost immediately to mind today: that someone within the African community had got ahold of those ropes and found a clever way to sabotage the execution of one of their own. But local whites and company officials tacitly supported this sabotage by asking for mercy and pardoning all defendants without investigating the ropes. Perhaps the extraordinary performance of solidarity enacted by the slaves motivated the crowd's unified response. The dramatic events on the day Manuel de Gerrit de Reus was hanged demonstrate the strength of the social network that the WIC-owned slaves had managed to build both among themselves and within the wider community. Before they ever submitted a petition for their freedom, the men and women of the WIC slave house had created relationships that enabled them to work together and to draw on limited yet crucial support from their neighbors.[49]

Intimacies connected the participants in the drama even before the start

48. Minutes, Jan. 17, 1641, in *Council Minutes,* I, 97–100 (quotations, 100).

49. See Cynthia Jean van Zandt, "Negotiating Settlement: Colonialism, Cultural Exchange, and Conflict in Early Colonial Atlantic North America, 1580–1660" (Ph.D. diss., University of Connecticut, 1998), 142–186. Van Zandt has noted how the "intracolonial alliance of Africans" enabled them to "create cultural spaces within their community that New Netherland colonial officials could not penetrate"; see Van Zandt, *Brothers,* 158.

of the trial. Less than six months preceding their arrest, Simon Congo acted as godfather to Jan van Fort Orangien's daughter Maria. Because most of the baptismal records before Premero's death have not survived, other potential fictive kin connections remain invisible today, and the fluidity of naming practices in the records makes it difficult to trace all the associations among the accused and their families. Even in the years after the trial, the defendants continued to form an African community through marriage and fictive kinship. As early as July 1641, just six months after the trial, Anthony Portugees called on four fellow "Angolans" to witness the baptism of his twins, despite his confessed role in Premero's death. A little more than a year after his hanging, Manuel de Gerrit de Reus baptized his son Michiel, making Domingo Theunis and Susanna Simons van Angola kin to his son and showing that his ordeal had not marked him as an outcast. Others of the accused were fictive kin through baptism with such prominent members of the African community as Bastiaen, Captain of the Negroes, and Palesa van Angola. Nor did whites shy away from acting as godparents to the children of Premero's killers; Sara Cornelis witnessed for Anthony Portugees's son Jochem in 1643. Fathers' involvement in Premero's killing did not mean social ostracism for their children.[50]

Other Africans continued to choose the accused as witnesses for their children, such as when Groot Emanuel, or Big Manuel, witnessed little Mathias Pietersz's baptism in 1645. New family unions even helped to smooth the loss of Jan Premero. Less than one year after his death, his widow, Marie Grande, married one of his confessed killers, Jan van Fort Orangien. Four years later, she witnessed for the child of a man who was probably another of her husband's killers. Community connections brought the accused through the trial, and new intimacies rebuilt and solidified the community in the wake of the attempted execution.[51]

50. Only a year and a half of baptismal records survive prior to 1641, containing six clearly African children, and only a year of marital records survive, containing no clearly African couples; see Purple, ed., *Marriages*; Evans, ed., *Baptisms*, 10–11. One defendant, Manuel Minuit, cannot definitely be identified in the church records; however, African men named Manuel and Emanuel abound in the surviving documents, and it seems safe to assume that the unusual surname simply went unrecorded most of the time. Another defendant, Gracia, or Gerasÿ, D'Angola, died sometime after the trial and does not appear in the baptismal record, though the exact date of his death is not clear. His widow, Maria Angola, remarried in 1656; see Purple, ed., *Marriages*, 21. For baptisms after the hanging, see Evans, ed., *Baptisms*, 12, 13, 15, 19.

51. Purple, ed., *Marriages*, 11; Evans, ed., *Baptisms*, 18, 19. Marie (Mary) Grande witnessed the baptism of Michiel, son of a man identified as Emanuel van Angola, who was very likely one of the three men named Emanuel/Manuel who confessed to participating in her late husband's death.

The petition for freedom in 1644 rested on the strength of these alliances. The colony council explicitly cited family responsibilities as one of the reasons for granting the petitioners' requests. Because "they are burdened with many children, so that it will be impossible for them to support their wives and children as they have been accustomed to in the past," the council decided to look favorably on their plea. No single men could thus have achieved their freedom in this way. The very ties of family that helped create a community also helped rescue part of that community from the deepest abuses of slavery. The joint petitions for freedom, furthermore, reflected the growth of an intimate network among WIC slaves. Big Manuel, Manuel de Gerrit de Reus, Simon Congo, Anthony Portugees, Gracia D'Angola, and Jan van Fort Orangien were among those named in Kieft's grant, and all of them had endured the trauma of the Premero trial together.[52]

Surely everyone in New Amsterdam knew they had been involved in a murder, including the men who deliberated on their freedom petition. But they succeeded in their request anyway. Not only did they have extensive ties to one another, they were also fictive and real kin of Paulo Angolo, Little Manuel, Pieter St. Thome, Jan Francisco, and Little/Cleyn Anthony, the other WIC slaves named in Kieft's grant. The complicated web among them allowed them to work together not only to overcome traumas like Premero's death but also to jointly make a plea for freedom. Their appeal, grounded in their invocation of their families and supported by the network uniting them, led Kieft to declare them "free and at liberty on the same footing as other free people here in New Netherland," noting that from then on they must be paid "fair wages." Through the creation of fictive kinship, parents helped to change New Amsterdam's disparate black population into a community capable of cooperatively escaping the perils of slavery.[53]

A clear victory for the twenty-two people given freedom and for the larger community of which they were a part, the half-freedom grant rested on their shared pattern of multiple and overlapping personal relationships. New social networks had allowed people to triumph over the forces pushing them toward social distance and isolation. In addition, these relationships reveal patterns of authority and respect that demonstrate how the African population had begun to evolve into a community. By acting together, they

52. Minutes, Feb. 25, 1644, in *Council Minutes*, I, 212–213.
53. Minutes, Feb. 25, 1644, ibid., 212–213 (quotations, 213). The Paulo Angolo named in Kieft's grant might certainly have been the same man called Antonio Paulo d'Angola in the trial records. Although a Paulo Angola (or Paulus van Angola) appears in the baptismal record more than once, an Antonio Paulo does not appear there.

overcame obstacles, and, when challenges threatened to tear them apart, their new intimacies helped repair the damage. Continuing to survive and to thrive, however, would depend not only on the ties reaching within the African population but also on those reaching outside it. Both before and after Kieft's grant, the place of New Amsterdam's Africans within larger colonial society shaped their experience in crucial ways.

Mapping African Networks within Colonial Society

Although Kieft's grant gave Africans much to celebrate, the language he used limited the petitioners to a particular place within colonial society. Kieft was not anomalous in his apparent ambivalence. Africans did find aid among whites at critical moments, such as when the crowd spoke out at Manuel de Gerrit de Reus's hanging or when the colony council responded to the 1644 petition. But their continuing success depended on their ability to fulfill a specific economic and social role within colonial society. Whites' seeming support of half freedom for these Africans flowed from a desire to keep them in that role. Understanding what Africans' intimate network enabled them to achieve, then, requires understanding how that network was situated within the larger society and economy. The accomplishments of these Africans came, not from subverting colonial hierarchies, but from carving out a foothold within them.

Colonists and Africans developed an oxymoronic term for the petitioners' new status reflective of the dual nature of Kieft's grant: "halve vrydom," or "half freedom." Few dichotomies seem so stark in colonial America than that between slavery and freedom, yet Kieft defined a category that blended elements of both. Though the grant included words that must have been received joyously by the participants, "releas[ing] the aforesaid Negroes and their wives from their bondage for the term of their natural lives, hereby setting them free," the grant also contained restrictions. Though Kieft claimed to put them "at liberty on the same footing as other free people" he bound them to a particular economic activity: farming. The grant tied them forever to the colony of "New Netherland, where they shall be permitted to earn their livelihood by agriculture on the land shown and granted to them." The allocation of land undoubtedly helped the African families, but Kieft's grant demanded, not suggested, that they become farmers by his "condition" that "in return for their granted freedom, [they] shall, each man for himself, be bound to pay annually, as long as he lives, to the West India Company or their agent here, 30 schepels of maize, or wheat, pease, or beans, and one fat hog valued at 20 guilders." Should anyone fail to pay this annual tithe, he would forfeit his freedom and return to being a WIC slave.[54]

With the 1644 grant, Kieft established a pattern. In December 1663, the governor and council very carefully spelled out the terms by which another eight WIC slaves would become "half free." When the half-free slaves "have done one w[eek] of labor for the Honorable Company, then they may work one week for themselves, or if they shall have worked one month for the Company, then in return [they will] have one month of freedom for it. When they work for the Honorable Company, they shall have one bread per week without more, furthermore they shall have to take care of their food and clothing themselves." Some privately owned slaves received somewhat similar grants from their masters, suggesting that Kieft's initial grant served as a broader model. In 1647, Captain Jan de Vries, before leaving on a voyage, empowered two men to "have supervision over [his] free Negroes and Brasilian woman during his absence," who evidently lived on his land and, though free, remained under his oversight. Philip Jansz Ringo freed his slave Manuel the Spaniard on condition of payment of one hundred guilders annually for three years, payable in wampum or grain.[55]

Such partial manumissions prevented former slaves from seeking their fortunes elsewhere. The 1644 grant tightened this tether to the local area by stipulating that the "children, at present born or yet to be born, shall remain bound and obligated to serve the honorable West India Company as slaves." Later, some Africans disputed this stipulation, insisting that Kieft verbally promised otherwise, and, in at least one case, official freedom was allowed to an African child on the basis of Kieft's grant. But, by leaving the children at best in jeopardy and at worst enslaved, he chained the parents to New Amsterdam for the rest of their lives, using their own families to bind them to the regional economy.[56]

54. Minutes, Feb. 25, 1644, in *Council Minutes*, I, 213 (quotations). Although Kieft's 1644 order only speaks of granting the petitioners freedom, Africans and locals understood that a new status had been created and over the next two decades developed the term "half freedom," which has since become common among historians; see Certificate, Dec. 11/21, 1664, NYCM, X, pt. 3, 327, NYSA.

55. Certificate, Dec. 8, 1663, NYCM, X, pt. 2, 429, NYSA ("half free"); Empowerment, Aug. 3, 1647, in *Provincial Secretary*, II, 463–464 ("have supervision," 464); Manumission, Feb. 17, 1649, in *Provincial Secretary*, III, 82–83.

56. Minutes, Feb. 25, 1644, in *Council Minutes*, I, 213 (quotation). Some members of the second generation also seem to have acted and been regarded as free people, although no surviving document grants them that status, suggesting that Kieft's stipulation might not have been applied to every child. The fluidity of naming practices and the repetition of a few common given names make it difficult to be certain, however.

Kieft's grant placed the former slaves in a very particular social position in the colony. Survival and freedom depended on their economic success. Africans had long grown garden produce for their own consumption and in surplus quantities. Even during their years as slaves in the company's New Amsterdam slave house, Africans had found the space to grow garden crops. The land and its produce, however, remained in danger of being taken away from slaves who worked it informally. In 1638, for example, WIC-owned land cultivated by slaves along Broadway was rented out to a settler family. Again, in 1642, white settler Adam Roelants similarly sold a New Amsterdam house to Uldrick Klein described as "the small house in which the honorable Company's Negroes are now lodging, with the garden adjoining thereto." Although Klein purchased only the house, not the land, the two men took care to divide the produce, the contract stipulating that the buyer receive "half the vegetables which are growing at present in the aforesaid garden." Nothing indicates that the slave gardeners received anything for their crops. Africans' cleared land and gardens mattered enough for whites to expropriate them even before the first freedom grants.[57]

Around the time of the half-freedom grant, some members of the African community moved out of the WIC slave house and began working larger plots of land further north on Manhattan Island. Their relationships with white colonists proved critical to their success. Some of the WIC slaves who had not been a part of Kieft's grant joined the half-free families in their new houses. Taking advantage of their access to land, Africans, slave and half free, expanded from the garden crops they had grown outside the slave house to grain and livestock production. African families worked together to raise the corn and hogs needed to maintain their status and to survive economically. Anthony Fernando and his family, for instance, harvested grain and hogs on land hired from Jacob Corlear. White settlers appreciated and sought to benefit from their skills as farmers, as evidenced when Paulo D'Angola oversaw the livestock and managed the farm of Captain De Vries when he left on his fatal voyage to Holland in 1647. The two men already had

---

57. Contract, Aug. 8, 1642, in *Provincial Secretary,* II, 59–60 (quotations, 59). Roelants's name appears here as Roelantsen. For the Broadway parcel, see Lease, Apr. 19, 1638, in *Provincial Secretary,* I, 2–4. Although the documents provide no suggestion of who, among the African slaves, grew and sold these garden crops, the importance of women in garden crop exchange in the vicinity of Portuguese African ports drew notice from Lusophone observers; see Philip J. Havik, "Women and Trade in the Guinea Bissau Region: The Role of African and Luso-African Women in Trade Networks from the Early 16th to the Mid 19th Century," *Studia,* LII (1994), 83–120.

a deep personal relationship, De Vries having acted as godfather to Paulo's son, Dominicus, in 1646. In addition to renting and working the land of whites, a number of African farmers acquired land near company-owned farms that Governor Stuyvesant later purchased. These farms included desirable arable fields and rich salt hay meadows.[58]

Baptismal records suggest that these African agriculturalists did not stand apart from their white neighbors. Cosyn Gerritsen, a colonist from Putten in the Netherlands, had land adjoining a number of African farmers. He acted as a witness to the birth of at least one African child, little Pernante Emanuels, as did his wife, Vrouwtie, who witnessed for Anthony Ferdinando's daughter Marye. Such neighborliness aided African farmers' struggles to hold on to land and to profit from their labor. After Governor Stuyvesant became a major landowner in the neighborhood, for instance, he sued "Anthony de *Neger*" and Gerrit Hendrickszen over road access, pasturage, and use of fenced land. Anthony, however, does not seem to have spoken in court on the matter, perhaps fearing retribution from the man who determined the fate of his enslaved kin. Instead, Anthony's white neighbor and codefendant protested the governor's actions, leading to the appointment of arbiters to investigate the land titles and observe the area. The arbiters, in turn, brought to light neighborhood complaints about Stuyvesant's enclosure of a former shared avenue, which left residents without access to town and the marketplace for their goods in the wintertime. Based on the actions of Anthony's white neighbors, Stuyvesant promised he would see to it, thus rectifying a situation that potentially imperiled African farmers' attempts to participate in the food marketplace. Cooperation with white neighbors underlay this victory.[59]

58. Court Minutes, Oct. 26, 1654, CMNA, I, 285, NYCMA (microfilm); *RNA*, I, 255–258. See note 30, above, on the identities of Anthony Fernando / Anthony Portugees. On De Vries and Dominicus, see Moore, "A World of Possibilities," in Berlin and Harris, eds., *Slavery in New York,* 47–48; Evans, ed., *Baptisms,* 21. For a neighbor dispute between Stuyvesant and "Anthonij de *Neger*," see Court minutes, May 6, 1664, CMNA, IV, 365, NYCMA (microfilm); for a translation, see *RNA,* V, 51.

59. Court minutes, May 6, 1664, CMNA, IV, 365, NYCMA (microfilm) (quotation) (for a translation, see *RNA,* V, 51); Certificate, Apr. 20/30, 1665, NYCM, X, pt. 3, 329–332, NYSA. For a map of the area that misidentifies the race of some residents, see Hodges, *Root and Branch,* 14. On Cosyn Gerritsen as a witness, see Evans, ed., *Baptisms,* 10, 13. African men did sue and testify in New Amsterdam courts on occasion, showing that no blanket prohibition on black testimony existed. Yet, care should be taken not to see such testimony as a "right" accorded to Africans, as some scholars have asserted. The language of rights as a whole speaks more to our culture than New Netherland's, and there is no way of knowing whether Africans were always permitted court standing when they sought it.

Slave and half-free workers' engagement with the regional firewood and fur trades also helped give this African community standing within wider colonial society. Just as with farming, these activities depended on Africans' relationships to others. Production of firewood, a bulky consumable greatly in demand among settlers year-round, provided slave and half-free African men with an entry point into the local economy, but they had to rely on whites if they were to profit from it. Cutting the wood and transporting it formed separate tasks. Although African men, slave and free, did the brutal labor of felling the trees in the forest, they sometimes lacked the resources (beasts or boats) required to move cords of wood into town for sale. Instead, they had to cooperate with local whites to profit from their labor or sell the lumber while it still lay in the forest, offering a discount if buyers found someone to haul it to town on their own.

The cooperative patterns of firewood production sometimes led to confusion. In 1662, Matthys, a slave belonging to Anneke Jaartvelt, found himself blamed for the disappearance of a large load of firewood. The complicated case that resulted reveals the intertwined personal relationships that lay behind the wood trade. Matthys himself had cut more than five hundred pieces of firewood in the forest, seeking to ship it to Fort Amsterdam. He negotiated with colonist Andries Andriesen to move the wood in Andries's two canoes, giving him half the logs as payment. He also cut other wood that Jan, a WIC slave who lodged in the African neighborhood with a woman named Catryn, claimed had been transported to town by the white colonist Focke Jans. Both Thomas Hall, an elite white colonist, and "Domingo de *Neger*" had wood go astray at that time, and Hall blamed Matthys, noting in court that "other negroes say that Matthys is the reason that the wood was stolen." Both Matthys and Hall, then, relied on the words of other members of the African community for their knowledge about the ownership of the various caches of cut logs lying in the forest. Matthys faced serious trouble in the dispute, finding his goods arrested and spending time in jail before the court condemned his owner to pay Hall for the wood. Although the court did not find him guilty of theft, by ordering his owner to pay for Hall's wood the court suggested that Matthys had failed to keep careful track of whose wood was whose when he had Focke Jans take his logs to market. Matthys's difficulties show that African lumberjacks had to do more than just the heavy work of woodcutting. They also needed to negotiate with their fellow African woodcutters, white consumers, and potential transporters to make good on their efforts. Failing to manage these complicated situations correctly could cause their attempts to participate in colonial exchange to backfire.[60]

Yet, African men's firewood production filled an important niche in colonial life and gave their white neighbors reason to desire their continued labor. White settler Cors Jansen, for instance, was willing to host a party thrown by Domingo Angola one Saturday night in 1661 for his fellow "Negroes and Negresses" of New Amsterdam, perhaps in part because the social connections he formed through such hosting would give him access to firewood cut by African men. When several of the partygoers awoke Sunday morning and asked Cors Jansen "if they owed anything" for having stayed the night at his house, he answered, "No not at all, for you have not drunk my drink nor eaten my food and the place I have made you a present of, but if you will do me a friendship and deliver me a hundred sticks of firewood, I shall pay you for them." Even though Cors later tried to duck payment, the incident shows that the cooperative work of firewood production helped weave the African population into the social and economic networks of New Amsterdam's settlers.[61]

That some Africans remained enslaved while others were free or half free complicated questions of ownership and payment. The woodcutters' ambiguous status made it unclear, in settlers' minds at least, who owned the wood they cut, leading some colonists to simply appropriate Africans' wood. In 1657, Jan Rutgersen found himself in court because he had purchased firewood from someone else's slaves. Colombie, who oversaw or leased Jacob Haey's slaves, considered Rutgersen's actions to be theft. By buying wood from slaves, Rutgersen "stole the service that the negroes owed their masters." Colombie requested not only restitution but also that Rutgersen be punished as a receiver of stolen goods, and the New Amsterdam court agreed, even though Rutgersen argued that he had not paid the slaves for the wood. Conflicts such as these demonstrate that colonists valued African labor precisely because the social position of the African community in New Netherland made them subject to colonists' whims and demands. Africans did important and necessary work, but, rather than allow them to

60. Court minutes, Feb. 14, 21, Mar. 7, 21, Apr. 25, 1662, CMNA, III, 435, 445–446, 459, 465, 482, NYCMA (microfilm) (quotations, Feb. 21, 1662, III, 445–466). See also RNA, IV, 31, 39, 48, 53–54, 66.

61. Testimony, Jan. 14, 1662, in Kenneth Scott and Kenn Stryker-Rodda, eds., Register of Salomon Lachaire: Notary Public of New Amsterdam, 1661–1662, trans. E. B. O'Callaghan, NYHMD (Baltimore, 1978), 99–100 (quotations, 100).

profit from it, settlers fought over who had the right to appropriate it for free. The products they produced faced competing claims among colonists, but whites sought their labor precisely because they could extract it on their own terms. Firewood production, like farming, connected Africans to the larger economy and to their white neighbors, even as it subordinated their own interests and desires to those of their owners and neighbors.[62]

Participation in the regional fur economy had a similar effect. When trading operations crossed too far into the grey economy, the vulnerability of slave and half-free Africans put them at greater risk than their white partners. In 1657, the governor and council closely examined the baker Jochem Wesselsz and Pieter Pietersen, a "Company Negro," about their activities at the trading post near Fort Orange. The council asked Jochem, "What was he doing with the negro, when he stood at the post and spoke with him in a strange language?" The prisoner denied that he and Pieter Pietersen had plotted anything nefarious, answering that he "simply asked what are you doing here." However, the governor and council clearly worried that the use of a "strange language" functioned as a code between criminals, and their wariness paid off when they questioned the other suspect. Pieter Pietersen admitted to having stolen gunpowder, presumably from WIC stockpiles, at the behest of Jochem Wesselsz, giving the gunpowder once to Jochem himself and once "to his wife," Geertruyt Jeronimus, among other offences.[63]

Pieter Pietersen's admission made the matter more serious, and the officials had Wessels held "in detention" and Pietersen "secured in the *Corps du Garde*." Jochem Wessels realized that imprisonment in New Amsterdam would force him to miss the rest of the Fort Orange trading season, and he begged for release, claiming that his family would be "ruined" if he stayed in prison. "Because the principal trade has arrived now at Fort Orange," Wessels lamented, staying downriver "would be to the total destruction and ruin of his wife and children." Although the governor and council decided that Pieter Pietersen would be "beaten with rods" and banished from Fort

62. Court minutes, Jan. 8, 1657, CMNA, II, 109, and Jan. 22, 1657, II, 121, NYCMA (microfilm) (quotation). The ethnic identity of Colombie is a bit of a puzzle; Rutgersen called him a "france bougre," or "French bugger." Unusually, the city prosecutor acted as his "gevoechde," or guardian, in the case, and he was only referred to by a single name. Clearly, he was not Dutch, and might have even been of African heritage, but ultimately his origins remain uncertain. For the ethnic slur, see Feb. 11, 1658, CMNA, II, 177, NYCMA (microfilm); thanks to Kenn Cobb for sending a copy of this court date. The published translation is an essential help to navigating the faint microfilm images; see *RNA*, II, 268–269, esp. II, 268.

63. Examination and proceedings, May 8, 1657, NYCM, VIII, 571–576, NYSA.

Orange, they soon took pity on his white accomplice and let him return to Beverwijk in time to finish the trading season. Pieter Pietersen's experience with the face-to-face regional exchange economy hinged on his ability to talk to and work with white as well as Native American neighbors. Yet Africans and settlers shared the risks unevenly. With many of the items traded to Native Americans—such as alcohol, armaments, and even baked goods— subject to legal regulation, participation in the exchange economy posed risks. Jochem Wessels essentially got off with a good scare, and his wife never seems to have entered the courtroom at all, whereas Pieter Pietersen endured banishment and a beating. Even though social interactions with whites, strengthened by a shared language, had facilitated Pieter Pietersen's attempt at a little black market dealing, he played a much more dangerous game than white traders.[64]

The uneven footing that members of the African community stood on also shaped African women's work as paid servants or unpaid domestic laborers in the homes of white Manhattanites. Such work gave them access to the intimate spaces of elite New Amsterdammers. Palesa van Angola, the woman chosen as godmother to so many of the African community's children, worked in the house of the Manhattan minister, Johannes Megapolensis, in the 1650s and felt comfortable enough with her status there to upbraid a white domestic servant for theft and dishonesty. Other members of New Amsterdam's upper crust also depended on the labor of African women and girls. These women found their labor sought after, but they occupied a vulnerable position. The *huysgezin,* or household, of another minister, Samuel Drisius, similarly included African women, employing the ill-fated child worker Lysbeth Anthonijszen in the 1660s. Faced with multiple beatings while in service in several homes, she eventually barely escaped execution when convicted of arson. The daughter of Maria Portugees was bound as a domestic servant to colonist Maria Becker, who sued the young woman for the price of the clothes she had received when she chose to return to her mother before her term of service was up. Thus, even with the move toward participation in New Amsterdam's exchange economy in food, firewood, and furs, free and half-free Africans continued to work in the intimate yet perilous spaces of their white neighbors' hearths and homes.[65]

64. Ibid. ("in detention"); Decision, May 15, 1657, NYCM, VIII, 582, NYSA ("beaten"); Petition, May 15, 1657, NYCM, VIII, 583–584, NYSA.

65. Court minutes, Feb. 28, 1656, CMNA, I, 517, NYCMA (microfilm). See also *RNA,* II, 46. On Lysbeth Anthonijszen, see Romney, "Intimate Networks and Children's Survival," *Early American Studies,* VII (2009), 270–279. Maria Portugees's daughter went unnamed, but

The governor and members of the colony council, on whom the success of freedom petitions turned, themselves depended on the domestic labor of African women, and this dependence might explain why they supported requests for half freedom. In 1662, three company-owned women petitioned Stuyvesant and the council for their freedom, hoping to join those among their friends and family who had achieved half freedom in earlier years. Lucretia Albiecke van Angola, Mayken van Angola, and the wife of Pieter Tamboer (whose name has been lost) asked to be fully manumitted after decades of service as WIC slaves. Citing their old age and ill health, they asked that the council "grant them freedom in order that they may support themselves by their labor along with the other free negroes and female negroes." They pointed to their desire, "in their old age, just to be together with one another" as well as their failing strength as reasons for their request for freedom after years of service to the company. By mentioning their wish to be with other freed Africans, the trio made clear that they intended to live out their lives in the farming neighborhood near Stuyvesant's own land. The governor and council granted their request with one caveat: "One of the three of them, by turns, shall come and do [Governor Stuyvesant's] housework one day each week." Clearly, the women's appeal did not fall on deaf ears, in part because Stuyvesant realized the attraction of having three unpaid skilled domestic laborers so close to home. It would be too easy to dismiss these grants as given only after slaves lost their ability to labor because of old age. But, the insistence in the grant that these women had to continue to do housework points out that it was precisely because the white council members wanted to exploit their labor themselves that their petition was granted. The backing of whites like Stuyvesant and the council for half freedom is explained by Africans' success, in the decades following their arrival, in integrating themselves within the local society and economy. Instead of relying on loose or flexible ideas of enslavement, half freedom for these women reflected the value local whites placed on the work they did within the intimate spaces of settlers' homes.[66]

In the case of these three African women, partial freedom came late indeed. Less than four months later, in April 1663, Lucretia and the wife of Pieter Tamboer had already passed away from old age. Faced with the entire

---

she could well have been Lysbeth Anthonijszen, who later worked for Reverend Drisius, since Maria Portugees's husband was named Anthony; see Court Minutes, Nov. 30, 1660, *RNA,* III, 242.

66. Petition, Dec. 28, 1662, NYCM, X, pt. 1, 296, NYSA.

burden of Stuyvesant's housework, Mayken petitioned for full freedom, finding one day a week of labor beyond her strength. She appealed for unconditional freedom, since she was "an old, weak woman, sick most of the time because of an accident . . . also having been used as a slave since the year 1628." This time, the governor and council granted without condition her request to "live out her short lifetime in freedom." Mayken van Angola's manumission illustrates well the way New Netherland's half freedoms rested on a foundation built from overlapping social and economic relationships. Mayken desperately wanted freedom, seeking to become a member of the free community to which her husband had belonged since 1659. She, like the women who joined her first petition, wanted to finish her life in the company of her friends and family, many of whom had been partially freed in the 1640s and 1650s. The presence of a group of Africans who "labored with their hands" as free people gave strength to her request and provided her a community to turn to for support when old age prevented her from working any longer. The work that group did also gave whites reason to tolerate the presence and freedom of their African neighbors and to desire them to continue as a part of the local economy, albeit in a deliberately disadvantaged position.[67]

Although white colonists and officials clearly sought to benefit from the work done by members of the African intimate network, it seems that they did not wish that intimate network to grow. Rather than having their own slaves become a part of the nascent African community that had developed around the core group of WIC slaves in the 1640s, elite colonists and officials preferred to open up the labor of WIC slaves to the wider community through the creation of half freedom while raising new barriers to entry into that community for newly arrived, privately owned slaves. These new barriers, together with those increasingly imposed by civil and religious authorities, restricted Africans' ability to formalize family and kinship. In the 1650s and 1660s, decreasing access to formal marriage and baptism threatened the basis for communal acknowledgement of the very relationships that had allowed the early WIC slaves to begin to climb as a group out of slavery.

Over time, fewer Africans managed to obtain church recognition of their marriages. Between 1640 and 1664, the New Amsterdam marriage book recorded twenty-six marriages involving at least one clearly African partner.

---

67. Petition, [Apr. 19, 1663], NYCM, X, pt. 2, 71, NYSA ("an old, weak woman"); Certificate, Apr. 17, 1664, NYCM, X, pt. 3, 170, NYSA ("labored").

Because of the difficulty of determining race from the records, almost certainly more Africans married than the twenty-six couples identified here, and Dutch tradition allowed for marriages outside the church. However, even allowing for more marriages in later years, the New Amsterdam marriage book shows a clear trend. Fewer Africans married in the church in the second half of the twenty-four years that the registry covers than married during the first twelve years. For the five years after the first African marriage, 1641 to 1646, New Amsterdam's minister preformed twelve weddings for Africans; in the final five years of the registry, from 1659 to 1664, only five such unions occurred. The decline flies in the face of the increase in the African population during the 1650s. Joyce Goodfriend, Pieter Emmer, and others have clearly delineated an increase in importations of Africans from 1650 to 1664. Direct shipments of slaves, often sold at auction to New Amsterdam residents, expanded the overall population of Africans of marriageable age during the exact years when the number of marriages in the registry declined.[68]

The inability to have their marriages formally sanctioned by the European population would have made it more difficult for privately held new arrivals to follow the same path out of slavery as that traveled by the WIC-owned slaves. For the original unnamed eleven women granted half freedom by Kieft in 1644, recognition of marriages by whites had played an essential role. Since their names were not even listed in the grant, their ability to achieve half freedom depended on Kieft and his successors' acceptance of the validity of their marriages to the male petitioners. Trying to secure the free status of children also depended on being able to identify them as a part of a family. If marriages remained unofficial, such proof would be difficult to provide. White officials might not acknowledge the children of informal marriages as legitimate and thus able to inherit their fathers' farms. Restricting the access of Africans, slave and free, to formal marriage weakened the potential benefits of strong families.

68. Again, counts of marriages by Africans may vary, given the difficulty in positively identifying individuals and the fluidity of racial categories; for an alternative number, see Hodges, *Root and Branch*. The dramatic decline in African weddings recorded in the registry began in 1647, the year that New Netherland's minister, Everardus Bogardus, died in a shipwreck. Bogardus had worked in Dutch outposts in West Africa before his journey to New Netherland, where marriages between European men and African women were not uncommon. Perhaps his experiences there made him more accepting of African marriages than his successors as minister of New Amsterdam; see Frijhoff, *Wegen van Evert Willemsz*, 538, 603. On the rising slave population, see Goodfriend, "Burghers and Blacks," *New York History*, LIX (1978), 125-144; Emmer, "Slavenhandel," *Economisch- en social-historisch jaarboek*, XXXV (1972), 94-147.

Formal baptism of African children also declined over time, just as the rate of African marriages did. After the second month of 1655, no clearly African baptisms appear in the New Amsterdam baptismal registry until after the English takeover of New Netherland in 1664, despite the increase in the black population of the colony. Some African children received baptism without being listed in the registry, but without the formal acknowledgment of a child by the congregation and without the sponsorship of godparents sanctioned by a minister, children lost important protections. By forbidding these baptisms, the white ministers excluded Africans from the means by which family became official and received public respect. Ministers knew that denying baptism would limit Africans' ability to free their children. As the minister of Breuckelen in the 1660s, Henricus Selijns, explained to his superiors in Amsterdam, "We were sometimes asked by the negroes to baptize their children, but we refused, partly because of their lack of knowledge and faith, and partly because of the material and wrong aim on the part of the aforementioned negroes who sought nothing else by it than the freeing of their children from material slavery." Denying baptism thus explicitly reflected a desire to deny Africans' hopes for their children's freedom. Africans arriving in the colony in the 1650s and later lacked the means to build widely recognized fictive kin and form useful alliances between their children and white society.[69]

The hostility of Reverend Selijns and others toward African families

69. A. P. G. Jos van der Linde, *Old First Dutch Reformed Church of Brooklyn, New York: First Book of Records, 1660–1752*, NYHMD (Baltimore, 1983), 232–233 (quotation, 231). Between January 1640 and the end of 1647, thirty-nine recorded baptisms can be identified among the African community, averaging just under five per year. For the next eight years, between 1648 and 1655, only seventeen such baptisms took place, or an average of barely more than two per year; see Evans, ed., *Baptisms*, 10–41. No doubt Selijns's concerns stemmed from the legacy from ancient times that Christians could not be held as slaves. Willem Frijhoff has speculated that Selijns's fears might not have been without basis; several of the parents of baptized children and witnesses were freed in the same period in which their names appear in the registry. No manumission cites religion as a reason, however; see Frijhoff, *Wegen van Evert Willemsz*, 774. On the issue of slavery and baptism in the Dutch Reformed tradition, see Hodges, *Root and Branch*, 18–23. Slaves with Angolan backgrounds might have brought their own ideas about a link between conversion and manumission to America. In later years, Luandan slaves gained freedom "through the baptismal font"; see José C. Curto, "'As If From a Free Womb': Baptismal Manumissions in the Conceição Parish, Luanda, 1778–1807," *Portuguese Studies Review*, n.s., X, no. 1 (2002), 26–57 (quotation, 27). That practice should not simply be ascribed to Portuguese, rather than Angolan, approaches to baptism and emancipation, as baptismal manumissions in Brazil in the same period seem mostly limited to offspring of the owner; see James Patrick Kiernan, "Baptism and Manumission in Brazil: Paraty, 1789–1822," *Social Science History*, III (1978), 69.

even as authorities continued to grant half freedom in the 1650s and 1660s suggests the specificity of colonial attitudes regarding African residents. In relation to WIC-owned slaves and half slaves who were part of the African intimate network that took root in New Amsterdam in earlier decades and whose social ties extended into the white community, attitudes sometimes supported requests for at least limited forms of freedom. White attitudes toward privately owned slaves who stood outside that network, however, were often harsher.

The fates of two African children illustrate the difference. When a free African couple tried to adopt an infant slave owned by Egbert van Borsum, their efforts came to naught. Antony Matys's wife, Maria Anthony, had agreed, "in the presence of other negroes," to take the child in and breast-feed it herself, presumably after the death of its mother. When Van Borsum failed to pay the couple anything for the care they were providing the infant, Antony Matys sued him, "seeking that the child shall be declared free, in which case he promises to raise the same at his own expense." Antony Matys and his wife had tried to strengthen their bid by integrating their adopted infant into the web of intimate connections with which they had enveloped their own children through baptism. Less than a month before his court petition, Matys offered a baby girl named Cecilia for baptism, choosing Simon Congo and Christina d'Angola as witnesses. Cecilia's baptism came less than a year after that of Matys's youngest son, Cosmus. Given that a space of around two years between births was more the norm in New Netherland, Cecilia was most likely his foster, not biological, child. Maria Anthony and Antony Matys sought to make this little girl their own, to create a web of kin for her, and to endow her with their own freedom.[70]

Just a few weeks later, the couple's attempt to secure Cecilia's freedom backfired. Van Borsum's wife, Anna Hendricks, defended her family's financial stake in Cecilia's ownership, denying that she had refused payment for

70. Court minutes, Mar. 15, 1655, CMNA, I, 323, NYCMA (microfilm) (quotations). See also *RNA*, I, 298. Antony had baptized twins in 1651, just over two and a half years before Cosmus; however, his marriage to Maria Anthony was solemnized only a few weeks before Cosmus's birth, in February 1654; see Purple, *Marriages*, 18. Thus, it is uncertain if the twins were from his current or a former relationship. His court case also mentions that the child he sought to adopt was still nursing and had been with the couple for less than a year. It would make more sense to suppose that Cecilia was the child given to the couple by the Van Borsums than to suppose that Maria could have nursed both Cosmus and the Van Borsum child in 1654 while also becoming pregnant and giving birth to Cecilia by February 1655; see Evans, ed., *Baptisms*, 29, 36, 38. Variants of Antony's name include Anthony Matteuszen, Mattÿs, and Matysz. Simon Congo also appears as Simon Conck.

her care and demanding, "if they do not want to keep the child any longer, that it should be handed over to her again." The court agreed with this solution, ordering that Matys should give the *"negers* kint" back in return for payment, pro rato, for the time they had kept the child. After this, no more definitively African names appear in the baptismal record. With the failed attempt to include little Cecilia in the African intimate network, a door closed for African children.[71]

Officials came to quite a different decision, however, when faced with a child who belonged to the WIC rather than a private settler. In 1661, Reytory Angola successfully petitioned for the recognition of free status for her adopted child, Anthony Anthonysz, who had been born and left motherless in the early 1640s. As the biological and adopted child of former WIC slaves, Anthony was deeply embedded within the African intimate network and had no private owner. Perhaps because Reytory's petition threatened no one's personal finances, her request was granted. Furthermore, by the time of the petition, Reytory's adopted child was a young man who had lived his life as a member of the half-free population. Since his age allowed him to contribute to the local economy, Anthony's white neighbors likely wanted him to be a free yet exploitable worker rather than a slave whose labor would serve public and company, not private and individual, interests.[72]

The very different outcomes of these two adoptions represented what was in the best interests of local whites in each case. Although settlers allowed company slaves to become partially free, they did not wish to give their own slaves a path out of slavery, and they did not want to encourage the family ties that underlay the freedom of the former WIC slaves. Thus, freedom and half-freedom grants, like that of young Anthony Anthonysz, reflected very specific interests in a particular group of intimately connected Africans. Whites' desire to have the intimate network of former slaves contribute to the welfare of the local economy, rather than to the profits of the company, explains why settlers and officials made half-freedom grants even as racial hierarchies tightened in the colony generally.

71. Court minutes, Mar. 15, 1655, CMNA, I, 323, NYCMA (microfilm) (quotations); see also *RNA*, I, 298. For other discussions of this incident, see Goodfriend, "The Souls of African American Children," *Common-Place*, III, no. 4 (July 2003); Joyce D. Goodfriend, "Black Families in New Netherland," in Nancy Anne McClure Zeller, ed., *A Beautiful and Fruitful Place: Selected Rensselaerswijck Seminar Papers* (Albany, N.Y., 1991), 147–155.

72. Petition of Reytory Angola, Mar. 21, 1661, NYCM, IX, 557–558, NYSA. A different version of this document appears in translation in Scott and Stryker-Rodda, eds., *Register of Salomon Lachaire*, 22. For a fuller discussion of this petition, see Romney, "Intimate Networks and Children's Survival," *Early American Studies*, VII (2009), 293–299.

In the right circumstances, officials even backed African petitions for full freedom and landownership. With the takeover of the colony by the English looming in 1664, New Netherland's half-free residents began to fear for their fates if the WIC pulled out or handed its assets over to a new regime. No one could be sure whether an English government would recognize them as free or enslaved. The destiny of WIC property—including human property—remained unclear, and they might end up in English hands. Or would WIC slaves, and possibly half slaves, be exported for sale abroad as the company sought to repair its losses? With the arrival of the English ships in New Amsterdam harbor in September 1664, eight of the community's half-free Africans, Ascento Angola, Christoffel Santome, Pieter Pietersen Criolie, Antony Antony Criolie, Louwies Guinea, Jan Guinea, Salomon Pietersen Criolie, and Basje Pietersen, "request[ed] and pray[ed], with folded hands and bended knees, that upon the handover of this province to the English they may not be handed over, but rather released from their slavery and be granted freedom." The council had allowed them partial freedom in December 1663, but the men expressed concern that their ambiguous status would place them in danger of re-enslavement, and they asked to be "granted whole freedom."[73]

Claiming that they had received a promise, when given their partial freedom, that the council would grant them full freedom "when the Fortress should be completed, or [when] new Negroes should arrive here for the company," the petitioners pointed out that both conditions had already been met. Vowing that, should the council free them, they would be "continually prepared [to give] your High Honors particular service from thankfulness," they effectively reminded the members of the council of the important role half-free African men and women had come to play in local homes and the local economy. Should half-free men and women find themselves in the hands of the English, there was no guarantee that they would continue to do the "particular service" New Netherlanders had become accustomed to having them do.[74]

With the half-free men's allusion to the important place they filled within New Amsterdam society, the governor and council approved their request,

---

73. Certificate, Dec. 11/21, 1664, NYCM, X, pt. 3, 327, NYSA. Fire damage has partially destroyed some of the men's names, although correlation with other documents and a prefire index by E. B. O'Callaghan make the petitioners' identities clear; see O'Callaghan, *Calendar of Historical Manuscripts in the Office of the Secretary of State, Albany, N.Y.*, part 1, *Dutch Manuscripts: 1630–1664* (Albany, N.Y., 1865).

74. Petition, Sept. 4/Aug. 25, 1664, NYCM, X, pt. 3, 317–318, NYSA.

even as they fought among themselves over a response to the ominous English ships in the harbor. They took time, in other words, to ensure the continued presence of the whole of this particular African community, even as they faced the surrender of the colony. Several months later, after the English takeover, the council and governor met on Stuyvesant's farm to draw up the final WIC books and to take care of administrative matters involving the evacuation of company soldiers. As the penultimate act of the now-moot Dutch colonial government, they drew up an official certificate of manumission for the eight former company slaves. In doing so, they demonstrated their continuing interest in ensuring that the African intimate network would stay ensconced within the wider colonial economy and society.[75]

The final document of the governing council illustrates that their interest in these men's manumission arose from the work that the free and half-free Africans had long done together within the regional food economy. The manumission reveals that the council saw these men as part of a productive community, not simply as individuals. In April 1665, eight months after New Netherland became New York, the council confirmed land grants made to free Africans in 1659 and 1660. The certificate noted that the land had been "cleared, worked, possessed, and settled by them since that time, unmolested, [with] our foreknowledge and order." Indeed, African families had been in the vicinity considerably longer, at least since the early 1640s. In total, the council confirmed Africans as the rightful proprietors of landed property, including fourteen numbered house and garden lots near Stuyvesant's farm, giving them title "in a True and Free ownership with such Privileges as all Lands are given to the Inhabitants [of this] Province." Although fire has destroyed some of the names on the grants, the remaining names reveal that the land belonged to men who were married, fathers, and, among the older generation, those who had been active as godparents within the African community. In 1660, Reverend Selijns had estimated that some forty Africans lived near the governor's *bouwerij*, or farm, without noting whether they were enslaved or free. Thus, the fourteen house and garden lots were worked by couples and families, not single men.[76]

The council further stated that they wanted the freed Africans to form a community together instead of living scattered and separated. The council noted that the land had been granted to encourage the freed slaves to

75. Certificate, Dec. 11/21, 1664, NYCM, X, pt. 3, 327, NYSA.
76. Certificate, Apr. 20/30, 1665, NYCM, X, pt. 3, 329–332, NYSA (quotations); Van der Linde, *Old First Dutch Reformed Church of Brooklyn*, 227. Unfortunately, council records from 1659 have been missing since before O'Callaghan's prefire index.

"move into a village" together and "tear down their separate dwellings." The council, then, gave full title to individual African men, but they explicitly intended to allow the entire intimate network of Africans who had worked the land and formed a community together to continue living and working as a group. By working as farmers and living in a village, Manhattan's African residents had played a crucial role in fulfilling the colonial authorities' vision of the ideal form of colonial settlement and had also made themselves into something more valuable to local whites than their individual worth as commodities. African families had used that land to contribute to the regional and local food, firewood, and household economies, playing an economic role within wider society that the council did not want to see extinguished, even as government passed into English hands. Colony officials thus recognized the crucial role these African farmers and workers played and prevented their dispersal during the confusion of the 1664 transfer of power.[77]

As the final acts of the governing council, then, the former Dutch government of New Netherland sought to ensure the continued working of the familiar multiracial exchange economy by protecting the continuity and stability of a particular set of African kin groups. Despite the perils they had faced as slaves and conditionally freed people, by forming a productive social web, a core group within the African population managed to pull itself finally into full freedom and titled landownership at the end of the Dutch era. The connections of kin and community that had united them with one another had also integrated them within wider settler society and, in the end, saved them from the grave threat of re-enslavement and exportation. That threat was real; some of the Africans who remained slaves of the WIC at the time of the English takeover found themselves appropriated by the new governor, Richard Nicholls, as personal property, while others were used to pay at least one Dutch official's back salary, who sent them to Saint Christopher for sale as plantation laborers. Being WIC property was dangerous in 1664.[78]

By building familial and personal ties, a particular group of Africans had succeeded in avoiding a desperate fate by redefining their status from enslaved to free. Yet, only the Africans in this interconnected group enjoyed this freedom. The council's grants did not reflect a flexibility of racial hi-

77. Certificate, Apr. 20/30, 1665, NYCM, X, pt. 3, 329–332, NYSA.
78. Decision in the case of Johannes de Decker in Victor Hugo Paltsits, ed., *Minutes of the Executive Council of the Province of New York: Administration of Francis Lovelace, 1668–1673*, II (Albany, N.Y., 1909–1910), 447–449.

erarchies in the colony. Whites had made it increasingly difficult for privately owned slaves and newcomers to join that intimate network, and, at the handover of the colony to the English in 1664, negotiators made sure to protect the private property of settlers, ensuring that the majority of Africans and their descendants in the colony remained enslaved. The more common experience of Africans in the colony was to be treated as property, but social and economic networks made it possible for this group to achieve something different. Mapping the place of Africans within wider society shows that Africans' personal and economic ties with one another and with whites formed the key to their survival. They were able to achieve what they did only because of their position as exploitable and desirable workers and farmers within the local economy. Africans depended on their intimate network, yet that network offered limited equality for a limited number of people.

Conclusion

Africans navigated the long-distance systems and forces of the early modern Atlantic through relationships that existed at the smallest and most personal level. The close spaces shared by Africans in New Netherland—first the WIC slave quarters and later the half-free neighborhood—formed the beginnings of social connections. Although these relationships existed in the face of great stress, threats of sale and challenges by authorities, they nonetheless provided the basis for negotiation of the worst excesses of colonized life. For those Africans sold into private hands in the isolated corners of the colony, the ability to form such sustaining relationships was probably more limited. But the Africans who became connected to the population in and outside New Amsterdam had a source of strength. The power to resist and the power to escape slavery came from personal relationships that Africans in New Amsterdam struggled to create and protect.

By relying on intimate relationships to overcome the isolation and distance of the first years of enslavement, Africans initiated the beginnings of a community, one that was woven into wider society. Marriage and family united people across culture, language, and generation, allowing immediacy to triumph over distance and isolation. These intimacies overlapped and reinforced one another, forming a system of connections that allowed for cohesion and strength in the face of challenges and oppressions. The members of this group worked together in slavery and half freedom to construct a niche for themselves economically, becoming important participants in the regional food, fur, firewood, and household economies. The support that this particular group of Africans found with Director Kieft and with other white New Amsterdammers reflected the specific place that they occupied within the colony's social and economic webs. Because white elites and settlers alike depended on the work this group did, whites supported their transformation into free laborers, farmers, and traders. Ultimately, the success of their various bids for freedom hinged on their ability to maintain this place within colonial hierarchies.

The African intimate network in New Amsterdam, then, explains the context and significance of the half-freedom grants. Specific relationships, not general Dutch attitudes toward slavery, underlay New Netherland colonists' creation of the category of half freedom. Very particular desires, interests, and relationships structured the white response to African petitions. These specific feelings grew from actions and interactions initiated by a core group of intimately connected slaves, who succeeded by tying themselves not only to one another but also to their white neighbors, customers, and fellow congregants. Africans, in other words, gave rise to the conditions that allowed them to become free.

Intimate relationships among Africans made possible the situation in which half freedom appealed to the whites who had the power to grant it. But, the relationships among Africans only grew into a network strong enough to support a community over time, not all at once. It is testimony to the power of that intimate network that Africans in New Amsterdam were able to begin the ascent from slavery to freedom even as racial hierarchies within the Atlantic world increasingly solidified and the colony became more intertwined with international slave trading.

Through the alliances that Africans in New Amsterdam formed with one another and with their white neighbors, they were able to remake themselves. White New Netherlanders came to value this group of Africans for the role they performed within the colony and economy together, rather than for their worth as individuals on the slave market. Thus, even as their connections to one another allowed key members of this community to become fully free and to gain title to land by the time the English took over the colony in 1664, their intimate network should not be understood as subversive of the fundamental hierarchies of New Netherland society. The creation of a social web allowed Africans to define a different place for themselves within that hierarchy, but it did not permit them to fundamentally alter it. Whites continued to expect that newly freed Africans would clean their houses and cut their firewood, perhaps without being paid. Whites also demanded that Africans would contribute to local food exchange through their farming, gardening, and trading. And white officials and ministers took steps to try to prevent this group from growing too large. New Amsterdam's Africans managed to integrate their families within colonial hierarchies through immediate interpersonal ties, although those hierarchies not only remained intact but even became more rigid over time.

The African experience in New Amsterdam demonstrates the centrality of face-to-face relationships and social networks to any understanding of African lives in the colonial Atlantic world. Though the large-scale forces of market, mobility, and cultural distance threatened to cut off Africans transported to the Americas from all social connections and kin, the immediate interactions of those brought forcibly together provided a means to subvert that threat. By forming families, fictive kinship, and friendships, this group of Africans became a community shaped by its place within larger colonial hierarchies. Confronted with the potential extinction of their every social tie, these Africans formed unions that helped them cope with the most immediate dangers they faced individually and collectively.[79]

To survive, newly arrived Africans throughout the Americas needed to overcome their threatened social death, resist devastating power imbalances, and fight against economic forces alienating them from their own bodies. New Netherland's Africans reveal how slaves in one particular part of the Americas responded. By using immediate relationships as the basis for a web reaching throughout and beyond the black population, New Amsterdam's slaves built kin and community, claimed ownership over themselves, and carved out a place within black-white colonial hierarchies. The ability to form intimate and interpersonal attachments, always endangered by the intervention of white authorities, needs to be seen as central to the survival of Africans as individuals and as communities. Deep, personal relationships served as slaves' primary weapons as they tried to combat social distance and alienation.[80]

Face-to-face relationships and immediate personal ties shaped the fates even of people subject to the developing large-scale systems moving thousands of forced African migrants across the ocean. Mapping the place of African intimate networks shows that, while immediate social connections allowed colonial subjects to redefine themselves, they also located people

79. Vincent Brown, "Social Death and Political Life in the Study of Slavery," *American Historical Review,* CXIV (2009), 1239.

80. Smallwood, *Saltwater Slavery,* 190.

firmly within colonial realities. How much power people had to remake the situations in which they found themselves hinged on the interplay between individual relationships and surrounding hierarchies. As the WIC's colonial power itself began to unwind in the late 1650s and 1660s, that intricate dance became even more complicated for all the region's residents.

* * *

CHAPTER FIVE

"The Almost-Sinking Ship of New Netherland"
Personal Networks and Regional Power

 In late summer 1664, rumors began to swirl throughout the greater Hudson Valley. They spread from neighbor to neighbor, among Native villagers, English townspeople, black farmers, and Dutch burghers: dramatic change, perhaps violent change, was at hand for everyone. Gathering at City Hall one Saturday morning near the end of August, New Amsterdam's *burgermeesteren en schepenen,* or municipal council leaders, decided these persistent whispers and murmurs could no longer be ignored. "The rumors say," the secretary recorded, "that the Frigates that have arrived in Baston will come here." How much these English ships would threaten, the schepenen did not know, but, suddenly, they looked on the city's defenses with new eyes. What they saw—crumbling earthworks, fences pilfered for firewood, walls undercut by hogs—alarmed them. In a flurry of concern, they "thought it good . . . to request" from the governor and council "five and twenty *negers* for the period of eight days in order to make a beginning of the work on the city works next week." The tide of voices continued to rise, however, and, by the following Monday, the labor of slaves alone seemed woefully inadequate, given the "present circumstances and the current rumors." They ordered the town as a whole, rich and poor, to join the company slaves in a last-ditch effort to save their way of life from English domination. They stipulated "that every third day one third of the residents and burghers alike shall labor on the city works, no one excepted" and that everyone should "appear in person or supply another in his place, supplied with a shovel, spade, or wheelbarrow." Desperate to shore up their quickly eroding colony, New Amsterdam leaders looked to each and every resident to make a tangible contribution to restoring the strength of Dutch authority.[1]

1. Court Minutes, Aug. 23, 25, 1664, CMNA, IV, 439–440, NYCMA (microfilm) (quotations). For a translation, see *RNA*, V, 104–105. They did not detail the condition of the

Such efforts, tardy and too small, would not be enough to avert the coming crisis. This eleventh-hour flutter of fortification was perhaps intended to mislead any censorious WIC officials at home, drawing their gaze away from the slower processes of change and delicate shifts of power that had been occurring for several years. Although the international skirmishes that would lead to the Second Anglo-Dutch War (1665–1667) provided the immediate context for the sailing of the English warships, the way had been paved for their successful invasion long before. In the 1650s, the growing power of the English empire, supported by a burgeoning population the Dutch could not counter, had forced the WIC and Governor Peter Stuyvesant to cede claims to the Connecticut Valley and eastern Long Island. That English-allied population had also established towns inside New Netherland itself that had occasionally tried "to erect the standard of Parliament," much to the recurrent concern of New Netherland leaders. But it would be wrong to imagine power in the Hudson Valley as a seesaw, with Dutch power declining as English power rose; nothing about the greater Hudson Valley worked quite as linearly as that. The 1650s also witnessed the expansion of WIC power and territorial control. In the mid-1650s, Dutch forces recaptured the Delaware Valley from Swedish administration, and, in the late 1650s and early 1660s, colony fighters moved aggressively and successfully into the lands of the Esopus people on the shores of the Hudson River. The Mohawk, too, exerted widening influence in the region. As trade at Fort Orange expanded, settlers relied increasingly on Mohawk political intermediaries, eager to expand their own brotherhood of peace. These and other shifts changed the power relations among villages—Native American, Dutch, and English—throughout the greater Hudson Valley and Long Island in the years preceding the rumors that so unsettled New Amsterdam leaders in 1664 (Figure 6).[2]

Facing the moment of truth, the leaders of the Dutch administration turned to everyday residents for support. Their call for all hands on deck points to the reality that existing patterns of colonial governance rested on the associations and actions of many individuals. The multiple and

---

defenses here, but both the municipal and colony councils had lamented firewood and hog damage many times before.

2. WIC Directors to Peter Stuyvesant, Nov. 4, 1654, NYCM, XII, doc. 10, fol. 3, NYSA (quotation); Cynthia J. van Zandt, *Brothers among Nations: The Pursuit of Intercultural Alliances in Early America, 1580–1660* (New York, 2008), 179–184; Donna Merwick, *The Shame and the Sorrow: Dutch-Amerindian Encounters in New Netherland* (Philadelphia, 2006), 237–259; Matthew Dennis, *Cultivating a Landscape of Peace: Iroquois-European Encounters in Seventeenth-Century America* (Ithaca, N.Y., 1993).

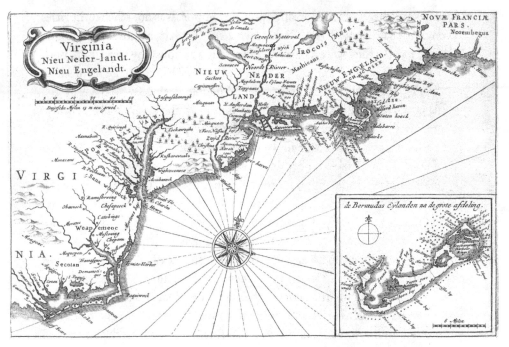

FIGURE 6 ✦ Virginia, Nieu-Nederlandt, Nieu Engelandt. From *Beschrijvinghe van Virginia, Nieuw Nederlandt, Nieuw Engelandt, en d'Eylanden Bermudes, Berbados, en S. Christoffel* (Amsterdam, 1651). This item is reproduced by permission of The Huntington Library, San Marino, Calif.

New Netherlanders recognized that they lived in a crowded political context by the 1650s, nestled among multiple indigenous and imperial polities.

overlapping social and economic networks of the greater Hudson Valley ultimately depended on face-to-face relationships and family ties among women and men throughout the region. Just as intimate networks had built the colony, so now they seemed the best bulwark for its defense. Thus, the plea for everyone—burgher, resident, and slave—to join together in giving the colony a hand in desperate times reflects an important truth about politics in this particular colony. People and the connections they maintained with one another undergirded polities' claims to power. People's intimate networks intertwined with imperial politics and, in doing so, formed the basis for the colony's very existence.

In New Netherland, as in many other colonial regimes, colonial officials occasionally sought to regulate the personal lives and relationships of the region's residents. The attention paid to sex and family shows that those in positions of authority understood that the intimate had political significance. Yet, what gave relationships political import was not what authorities thought or said about them. Rather, what made relationships, and the intimate networks they were a part of, important was how they were used, both by the people involved and by political authorities. Embedded within social networks, personal connections provided people with ways to navigate the shifting currents coursing through the region in the seventeenth century. People used social networks to achieve their own goals as competing political influences waxed or waned. But political actors also sought to employ people's social webs to support their own pretensions to power.

In the mid-Atlantic region at the end of the 1650s and the beginning of the 1660s, the shifting influence of the region's multiple polities tugged at different threads in overlapping intimate networks. Particular knots and nodes developed in those networks as a result, creating new patterns of power and influence within intimate and social relationships. Women's crucial roles as creators of personal ties situated them in the center of these nodes at key moments. Tracing the actions of a few individuals reveals that women and men used their social and intimate connections to help them survive or succeed in these changing times, much like the initial Dutch settlers and African slaves in New Netherland had done to either navigate the nascent Atlantic economy or attain a modicum of freedom.

At the same time, colonial authorities themselves turned to influential intimate networks to stake claims on the colony's behalf, relying on well-situated women and men to do so. An investigation of the interaction between power and intimacy in the latter years of Dutch rule shows that webs of relationships gave people access to subtle and flexible forms of authority that conformed to changing realities and sometimes proved more durable than formal polities.

In this colonized context, however, the influence of intimate connections depended in part on the willingness of political forces to recognize and employ them. The interplay between the intimate and the imperial explains the actions of five people from both colonial and Native communities: Oratam of Hackensacky, Sara Roeloffs Kierstede, Quashawam, Lydia / Luda van Dyck de Meyer, and Hillegond Megapolensis van Ruyven. These people—four women and one man, three settlers and two Native Americans—became important actors within regional networks because of their personal and immediate ties. Each of these five had particular sway at critical moments in the last years and hours of Dutch rule, and the leverage they exercised made them unusual. Yet, a closer look reveals that the sources of their influence lay in the intimate networks that shaped the lives of everyone in the region. The colonial authorities who turned to these five individuals both drew on and reinforced the strength of their intimate networks. Their actions uncover the composite nature of power in this early modern colony. Together, these five helped determine the complex ebb and flow of power among Native peoples and competing colonial polities in the last years of Dutch rule in North America.

Oratam of Hackensacky and Sara Roeloffs Kierstede

As the rumors of the impending English attack wended their way from mouth to ear, from village to village throughout the region in 1664, they traveled a well-worn course. Voices had spoken and hearers had listened to words washing back and forth between indigenous and settler villages for years. The flow of chatter had even carved regular channels reaching among the various communities in the region. Words streamed along established waterways, traveling between recognized speakers and designated listeners. The face-to-face interactions of those people as they alternately talked and heard one another represented not just the meeting of two individuals but also the point where two separate intimate networks intersected.

Two key talkers and listeners in the politically charged latter years of Dutch colonization were the Munsee-speaking man Oratam of Hackensacky and the Dutch-speaking woman Sara Roeloffs Kierstede. One or both of them took part in many of the most important diplomatic meetings in Manhattan and the lower Hudson area during the last years of Dutch administration. Together, they cemented a bond between lower-Hudson-area Munsees and New Netherlanders that endured even as vicious warfare engulfed nearby villages between 1659 and 1664. The intricate shifts in power during those final years, which saw the Dutch increase their ability to project military might throughout the Hudson Valley (and perhaps led to the overconfidence that allowed New Amsterdam's defenses to crumble), depended in part on the connections these two maintained.[3]

Oratam and Sara emerged from radically different backgrounds, cultures,

3. Dutch residents described Oratam as "van Hackensacky." The term "Hackensacky" and its variants could indicate either a people or a place, depending on context. For clarity, I will call the people "the Hackensack" and reserve "Hackensacky" for geographical references. The Hackensack occupied today's Hackensack and Passaic Valleys on the western shore of the Hudson, and, over time, Dutch residents came to know a number of places within that area by Munsee names. Sometimes, they used Hackensacky to indicate the whole of the Hackensack homeland, and at other times they clearly used it to refer to a specific village within that

and positions. The first, an older man, came from a local village and had long held authority; the other, still in the prime of her life, lived a comfortable domestic existence in New Amsterdam as a burgher's wife. Yet, similar forces brought them together and allowed them to speak one another's thoughts in their own words. For both of them, their moments of political engagement arose out of their positions within two strong social networks. Family ties and face-to-face connections made each of them matter and gave each of them voices that could be heard. During the weightiest and most difficult hours in establishing the balance of polities in the Hudson Valley, intimate networks shaped who would speak and who would listen.[4]

The career of Oratam of Hackensacky reveals the complicated give-and-take between colonial authority and kinship that enabled one Munsee voice to be heard. The politics of the Munsee-speaking people of the lower Hudson Valley area relied on immediate familial and extended kin networks

---

area. Similarly, the Dutch designated other Munsee and Algonquian groups within an area by employing the name of the principal village within the district as both a regional and ethnic designation. For specific place-names within Hackensacky, see Robert S. Grumet, *The Munsee Indians: A History* (Norman, Okla., 2009), 316–317 n. 16.

4. In some ways, Sara Kierstede and Oratam meet historians' definition of "go-betweens," since they acted as diplomatic mediators. Yet, for some scholars of English America, the term "go-between" connotes a quasi-official position, a "unique social status"; see Laura E. Johnson, "'Goods to Clothe Themselves': Native Consumers and Native Images on the Pennsylvania Trading Frontier, 1712–1760," *Winterthur Portfolio*, XLIII (2009), 115–139 (quotation, 139). Many eighteenth-century go-betweens held formal positions; see Nancy L. Hagedorn, "'A Friend to Go between Them': The Interpreter as Cultural Broker during Anglo-Iroquois Councils, 1740–70," *Ethnohistory*, XXXV (1988), 60–80. The term is even applied to some colonial leaders, such as John Smith; see Rachel B. Herrmann, "The 'Tragicall Historie': Cannibalism and Abundance in Colonial Jamestown," *WMQ*, 3d Ser., LXVIII (2011), 47–74, esp., 52. Sara Kierstede, on the other hand, was acceptable as an interpreter because of her unofficial status, as argued below. The term could also deflect attention from the region's broad-based pattern of contact; many people "went between" Munsee, Mohawk, and Dutch villages. Contrast New Netherland with eighteenth-century Pennsylvania, where professional traders and mediators predominated; see James H. Merrell, *Into the American Woods: Negotiators on the Pennsylvania Frontier* (New York, 2000). Other uses of "go-between" emphasize indigenous women's roles in bridging cultures. La Malinche, Pocahontas, and Sacajawea all experienced alienation from local indigenous groups and acquired considerable cultural knowledge as captives or slaves among the colonizers; see Frances Karttunen, *Between Worlds: Interpreters, Guides, and Survivors* (New Brunswick, N.J., 1994); Stephen Greenblatt, *Marvelous Possessions: The Wonder of the New World* (Chicago, 1992), 119–150. Building on this analysis, Alida C. Metcalf formulates go-betweens as those who broke down the dyadic encounter of Native American–European culture by acting as "third parties"; see Metcalf, *Go-Betweens and the Colonization of Brazil, 1500–1600* (Austin, Tex., 2006), 2. None of the individuals discussed here fit this definition, remaining instead immersed and embedded in intimate networks within their own communities.

reaching throughout and between villages. As the number and importance of personal economic and political associations with settlers increased, Oratam used his intimate network to help his people, the Hackensack, maintain their position in the convoluted, dangerous world of competing polities. Oratam's role as a designated speaker-hearer reflected the strength of his particular set of connections emanating from Hackensacky. Yet, the interplay of imperial politics and intimate networks goes deeper than that. Munsee speaker-hearers like Oratam approached diplomatic interactions with the Dutch in much the same way as they did intervillage politics—through a series of face-to-face relationships. And colonial officials were forced, despite military attempts to establish more hierarchical arrangements, to operate through these same means. Those who served as intermediaries accrued power for themselves and their village and kin groups. Thus, Oratam's life demonstrates that Native American intimate networks not only shaped who would emerge as speaker-hearers, they also channeled and limited colonial power.

The Hackensack lived in the lower Hudson region as one of the many peoples scholars increasingly call Munsee. People from villages on both sides of the lower Hudson River spoke some variation of the Munsee language, and all maintained similar subsistence and cultural strategies. However, it would be wrong to see these various villages as part of a single polity. Instead, the village, organized around family groups and matrilineal clan allegiances, remained the primary site of political organization and personal identification. Indeed, neither the term "Munsee" nor any substitute for it appear in the records from the time. Dutch writers and the secretaries who recorded treaty negotiations in which local people identified themselves consistently named people's affiliations according to their village. Although villages often worked together in war and peace, Dutch leaders and scribes did not draw a clear distinction, for example, between Munsee-speakers as a group and non–Munsee-speaking villages on eastern Long Island. Whereas Dutch writers used collective terms for the Mohawk, Mahican, Susquehannock, and other peoples, neither they nor the Munsee-speakers they negotiated with seem to have understood lower Hudson Valley towns as a single polity, and no sharp boundary separated the lower Hudson Munsees from indigenous Long Islanders.[5]

Neither should the Munsee villages be conceived as atomized or separate,

5. For an example of how scholars have come to use the term "Munsee," see Paul Otto, *The Dutch-Munsee Encounter in America: The Struggle for Sovereignty in the Hudson Valley* (New York, 2006), 3–6.

however. Instead, kinship, fictive and real, united the people of these villages. Marriage practices, which forbade unions within clan or matrilineage, ensured that family bonds always reached among towns. Overlapping ties of family and clan bound these villages to one another and gave people rights in different areas that descended from both parents. Exogamy also ensured that families had ties to people living farther afield, giving villages connections to Long Island and to Lenape and Susquehannock villages in the Delaware Valley. One contemporary Dutch observer was surprised to find a woman and man he knew from the mid-Hudson area when he visited a Native village on Long Island. When the Dutch traveler asked, "How came they to be so far from their home," the man answered that the groups hunted together and they had friends and kin in the Long Island village. A web of kinship, friendship, and clan connections tied Munsee-speaking villages to one another and to their neighbors.[6]

These kin networks proved an adaptable form of political organization, allowing Munsees to create changing social and political groups as needed. Leadership, though not directly inherited, flowed from the strength of one's kinship ties within and beyond one's village. In one 1664 negotiation, for instance, Dutch officials met with Quemacheme, son of an Esopus sachem, and "the Sachem from the Haverstroo [who] is the brother of Semackese the Sachem of the Esopus." For Munsee villagers, both leadership and intervillage relations followed the contours of family. Oratam and the Hackensack lived and worked within a flexible political and personal network that reached throughout the region.[7]

With the arrival of Dutch settlement in the 1620s, these Munsee villages and their sachems faced the expansive pressures of the region's competing imperial and local polities. Beginning around 1641, these pressures erupted into violence, with Munsee villages on both sides of the lower Hudson River and on Long Island enduring repeated attacks from Dutch-commissioned forces (sometimes comprised partly or primarily of English and Native American fighters) as well as occasional attacks by Mahicans and Mohawks from farther North. In addition, not only Dutch and English authorities

6. David Pietersz. de Vries, *Korte historiael, ende journaels aenteyckeninge, van verscheyden voyagiens in de vier deelen des wereldts-ronde. . . .* (Hoorn, 1655), 180–181 (quotation, 181). De Vries used the Dutch word "vrienden," which could mean either kin or friends depending on context, throughout this passage, so his choice of the word in transcribing the Munsee man's explanation could suggest either bonds of affection or kinship, or most likely both (181).

7. Treaty minutes, March 15–23, 1663, NYCM, X, pt. 3, 21–24, NYSA (quotation); Grumet, *Munsee Indians*, 19, 51.

but also Mohawks and Mahicans attempted to extort protection payments from Munsee towns in the form of grain, pelts, and wampum. Between 1641 and 1645, Munsee villagers sent representatives time and again in the midst of continuing violence to negotiate treaties with New Netherland officials. However, whereas many downriver Munsee groups formed multiple broad coalitions to take part in these negotiations, other Munsees such as the Raritan, Esopus, and Minisinks did not participate. No united polity, in other words, emerged among the Munsee from this crucible of violence and political pressure. Instead, these coalitions reveal a strengthening of existing cross-village networks. Groups of villages turned to influential local sachems with whom they had kin ties to represent them at these negotiations. The Munsee answered the political challenges of the 1640s with networks, not polities.[8]

Designated speakers from Hackensacky, the leading village in one of the main Munsee coalitions, not only drew their authority from their kin and clan connections but also viewed cross-border diplomacy as another network of personal relationships. Hackensacky's leaders held a complicated position within regional politics, as a tragic murder in 1642 reveals. When a young Hackensack man, not quite sober and infuriated that he had been treated inhospitably and robbed by a Dutch trading partner who had plied him with drink, killed the unwise settler with an arrow, some sachems "from Ackinsack and from Reckawanck" immediately sought to restore peaceful relations with their Dutch neighbors. Though the sachems went unnamed, Oratam was almost certainly among them. The sachems responded to the crisis by employing interpersonal connections, in effect, trying to extend Munsee political traditions to diplomatic relations with the Dutch.[9]

First, they turned to a friend in the Dutch community for help. They went initially to the house of David Pietersz de Vries, a prominent settler and the brother of a WIC director in Amsterdam. De Vries lived close by Reckawanck and only an hour's walk from Hackensacky. The Munsee leaders chose De Vries carefully; in addition to his powerful family connections, De Vries and the Hackensack killer had previously treated one another with signs of "friendship." De Vries reported that the accused man even described

8. Grumet, *Munsee Indians*, 56, 58, 62.

9. De Vries, *Korte historiael,* 165–166 (quotation, 166). Given the timing of the event in 1642, nearly the exact moment when Oratam first appears as the main representative of the Hackensack, he seems likely to have been one of the unnamed sachems; see Grumet, *Munsee Indians,* 58. Discrepancies exist between the sequence of events given by Grumet and that offered by De Vries in his 1655 text.

him as "a good Chief, [because when] they came to my House I gave them Milk and every thing for nothing." Generosity to neighbors and personal relationships made De Vries someone the Hackensack would likely choose to speak for them, and they considered him to be an *overste,* that is a chief or leader, among the Dutch. Under De Vries's personal protection, the sachems agreed to go to the fort to speak to Director Willem Kieft. There, the sachems presented the tragedy as one of emotion and family relationships; they spoke of their desire to condole the widow's grief on behalf of their people through a gift of wampum. Kieft, though, insisted that the killer be handed over to Dutch officials, presenting the matter as an issue of authority and sovereignty rather than of personal ties. In contrast to the Hackensack and Reckawanck speakers, Kieft tried to force Dutch-Munsee diplomacy into a hierarchical form that would de-emphasize kinship and political relationships among the Munsee.[10]

Kieft's goal of favoring hierarchies over intimate networks ultimately failed, though his attempts to enforce his new vision cost the Munsees dearly. Although the Hackensack speakers blamed the killing on the pernicious influence of Dutch alcohol sales, they did not sway Kieft. Taking their leave, they promised to do what they could to bring the young killer in. However, the local sachems admitted to De Vries afterward that "they could not deliver" the young man. The personal and familial nature of Munsee politics made it impossible; the man had drawn on the mobility enabled by intervillage Munsee ties to run away to Tankitekes, a town on the eastern edge of Munsee country. He had strong family ties protecting him, and Munsee politics did not give these sachems the power to force his kin to give him up. The killer was "a Sachem's Son," and he had connections just as strong as the men who spoke for him. No hierarchical authority could force the young man to sacrifice himself on Kieft's demand.[11]

Over the next three years, Kieft attempted to impose a more hierarchical model of Dutch-Munsee relations. Backed by the strong arm of military might, he sought to compel Munsee villages to recognize Dutch sovereignty through the payment of taxes in maize and submission to the Dutch legal system. The attacks he commissioned and the bounties he paid did tremendous damage and resulted in many Munsee deaths. In the end, Kieft was forced to negotiate with sachems who spoke on behalf of a malleable

10. De Vries, *Korte historiael,* 165.
11. De Vries, *Korte historiael,* 166 (quotations); Grumet, *Munsee Indians,* 5, 58. On the location of Tankitekes, see ibid., 320 n. 9.

network of power. If anything, the strength of the Hackensacks' regional networks grew in the face of Kieft's violence. By 1643, Oratam, now named individually in the records, negotiated treaties with Kieft as a sachem "living at Achkinkes hacky" who also represented the people of "Tappaen, Rechgawawanc, Kichtawanc and Sintsinck." These lines of authority remained fluid and voluntary, however, and did not indicate political submission to a regional power. Rather, Oratam and other sachems represented Munsee villages because of the strength of their connections to fellow villagers and one another. In August 1645, Oratam, sachem of "Achkinckeshacky," negotiated alongside "Sesekemu and Willem, chiefs of Tappaens and Rechgawawanck," towns that Oratam himself had spoken for two years before. These sachems acted, not as rulers of all these towns, but as designated speakers, "Pacham [and] Pennekeck having been here yesterday and empowered them to act for them, and answering further for those of Onany and their neighbors." Joined by two other regional leaders, the sachems managed to bring an end to the worst of the violence that had wracked the lower Hudson Valley for the first half of the 1640s. In the face of military aggression and political pressure, the Hackensack and their Munsee neighbors expanded the reach and strength of their intervillage networks, and Kieft died in 1647 without achieving the authoritative, hierarchical model of diplomacy that he desired.[12]

Whereas other lower Hudson Munsee towns lay abandoned by the mid-1640s and several local sachems disappeared from the records during those years, Hackensacky and Oratam emerged from the period intact and continued to act as conduits for the flow of words between Munsee villages and New Netherland authorities. Warfare would again explode in the vicinity of Manhattan between 1655 and 1657, but, once more, the village managed to survive the worst of the violence. Staten Island, where Hackensacky kin groups had extensive interests and for which Oratam and other Hackensack leaders often spoke, saw the worst of the fighting, ensuring that these diplomats would be at the center of negotiations. A treaty signed in early 1656 by a prominent Long Island sachem, Tapausagh / Tackapousha, and Oratam's intermediary, Pennekeck of Hackensacky, gradually put an end to the violence as leaders distributed gifts and returned captives over the following year. Hackensacky's strong and established record as the representative for a wide patchwork

12. Treaty, Apr. 22, 1643, *Council Minutes*, I, 192 ("living at Achkinkes hacky"), Treaty, Aug. 30, 1645, 279 ("Achkinckeshacky"). On the conflict usually called Kieft's War, see Otto, *Dutch-Munsee Encounter*, 116–126.

of villages would make Oratam and his village increasingly indispensable diplomatically to a growing number of people throughout the region.[13]

Oratam continued to represent multiple villages, giving voice to concerns shared by indigenous inhabitants throughout the area. In 1660, he signed a treaty as "Oratam leader of Hackinkasacky for himself and the leader of Hoogelant." Later, the Dutch also called him the leader of Staten Island. Among the issues Oratam spoke about were Native anxieties regarding the alcohol trade and the poverty, violence, and debt that accompanied it. A rapid rise in settlement in the 1650s, which brought settler and Native dwellings ever closer together, made the alcohol trade an even more pressing problem. As early as 1642, in the negotiations with Kieft over the Hackensack murderer, Hackensack and Reckawanck sachems had asked "why we sold their young *Wilden* Brandy or Wine, since it made them crazy and rebellious to drink, even saying that indeed our people, who were used to drinking strong drink, often drank themselves drunk and fought with Knives, therefore they wanted people to sell no drink to the Wilden in order to prevent all accidents." Such worries only grew over time. In 1663, two Munsee sachems complained that the sale of spirits left Munsees "completely penniless . . . because once they had the taste, they always wanted more."[14]

Munsee villagers looked on the behaviors associated with drinking as a dangerous innovation. As Adriaen van der Donck explained, "Beer, Brandy or strong waters are not known among them, except by some who traffic much with us and have learned, that Beer and Wine taste better than Water." He observed that alcohol offended most Munsee people, who were unaccustomed to its use and disapproved of its effects. "The Indian languages are diverse and all very rich, but nonetheless there is none among them all that has a word which they can use for drunk," he wrote. "They call drunkenness *Craziness* and they say drunk people are Crazy, when they traffic much

---

13. On Hackensacky kin groups' rights to Staten Island land, see Deed, July 10, 1657, NYCM, XII, 61, NYSA, where at least seven men from Hackensacky were among those present at an attempted purchase of land on Staten Island by Lubbert van Dinklagen. On the 1656 treaty, see Grumet, *Munsee Indians*, 63, 71–72. Elsewhere, Tapausagh was called "Tapusagh sakima of Marsepeack"; see Letter, Apr. 3, 1660, NYCM, IX, 136, NYSA. Tapausagh was also known as Meautinnemin, leader of "Marsepingh and Rechkawyck"; see Treaty, Mar. 6, 1600, NYCM, IX, 118–122, NYSA. Grumet gives his name as Tackapousha. I have chosen the spelling that appears most frequently in the records used here.

14. Treaty, Mar. 6, 1660, NYCM, IX, 118–122, NYSA ("Oratam leader"); De Vries, *Korte historiael*, 166 ("why we sold"); Treaty, July 10, 1663, NYCM, X, pt. 2, 203, NYSA ("completely penniless"). For a translation of this last heavily damaged document, see *DRCHNY*, XIII, 276–277, esp. 277.

with us or some can acquire drink, because the majority do not want to taste any drink at all." Most disapproved of drinking as aberrant and divisive; it threatened not only a community's economic well-being but also its social fabric.[15]

The alcohol, food, and firewood exchange system on which colonists depended thus could disrupt the intimate networks of kin and authority that were at the heart of Munsee life. In 1658, during a diplomatic meeting along the Hudson River between Governor Stuyvesant and around fifty Munsee men "and some though few women and children," one Esopus sachem complained that "the Dutch" had sold whiskey to the young men such that the "leaders could not curb the young Wilden who then wanted to fight." Any leader who lessened the volume of the alcohol trade, then, would be protecting the very ties of authority on which his own status depended, voicing concerns shared by villagers throughout Munsee country, and helping to preserve peace between Munsees and settlers.[16]

Oratam used his voice with the governor and council to express Native peoples' complaints about the abusive sale of liquor by New Amsterdammers. In 1662, Oratam, along with other Hudson area sachems, "complained several times, that many selfish people dare not only to sell brandy to the wilden in [New Amsterdam], but also carry whole barrels of it into their country and peddle it out there." The leaders feared that the behavior associated with drinking caused conflicts between settlers and Munsees; "if it is not prevented in time," the colony council worried in response to Oratam's complaints, "many troubles will arise." Yet, extensive networks of individual trading relationships reaching between Munsees and settlers made it difficult for the hierarchically organized colonial administration to police settlers' trading behavior. Since the council had to admit that antialcohol laws passed by New Netherland officials had utterly failed to stop the liquor dealers, they authorized Oratam and the sachem Mattano to seize the sellers and the brandy "brought into their country." In doing so, Governor Stuyvesant and his council tacitly admitted the sovereignty of Munsee sachems and the village-based networks they represented. The lower Hudson remained "their country," where Native sachems alone had the ability to exercise authority and police settlers.[17]

15. Adriaen van der Donck, *Beschryvinge van Nieuw-Nederlant....* (Amsterdam, 1656), 54–55.

16. Journal, June 30, 1658, NYCM, XII, 85, NYSA.

17. Order, Mar. 30, 1662, NYCM, X, pt. 1, 95, NYSA. Because of fire damage to the original, portions of this translation come from *DRCHNY*, XIII, 218–219. Mattano is also called Mattenonck. This last quotation comes from the original document.

Even though colonial leaders had acknowledged the status of Oratam and Mattano, Oratam continued to use his role as a respected speaker to push for wider recognition of other actors within Munsee networks instead of seeking to enhance his own personal power. When two other Hudson area sachems, "Sauwenaare, leader of Wiechquaeskeck," and "Metsewackos, leader of Kichtawangh alias Sleeper's Haven," complained the following year about alcohol sales, "Oratam of Hackinsacky" accompanied them. Colony officials lamented that they had done everything possible to stop the trade, reiterating that Oratam had permission to arrest the liquor peddlers. Rather than extend permission to arrest settlers to a broader range of village sachems, however, colonial functionaries preferred to reaffirm Oratam's special position. Only when the sachems pushed colonial representatives further by naming names and suggesting official connivance did the governor and council agree to set up a bounty system giving cloth as payment to anyone bringing in a whiskey trader. In his role as speaker-hearer, Oratam not only spoke the concerns of a wide number of Munsee villagers, he also forced colonial authorities to accept Munsee power networks.[18]

In the last years of Dutch rule, a strong voice like Oratam's would become an even more critical resource for the people of Hackensacky and surrounding communities. As rising migration, voluntary and forced, brought more Europeans and Africans into New Amsterdam, expanding settlement brought more settler homes closer to Munsee towns. The daily trade in consumables, including alcohol, increased, along with the frustrations and problems such close contact brought. In addition, by 1659, violence would again explode, this time in nearby Esopus towns. To mediate these growing pressures in the final years of Dutch administration, indigenous residents would look once more to Oratam.

For Oratam's words to have any power at all, however, they had to reach people who had the capacity to understand and the ability to present them to colonial officials in a form they would trust. Since Oratam and his fellow Munsee speaker-hearers seem to have spoken primarily in their own language, they depended on translators to render their words into Dutch. Although the New Netherland government turned to more than one *tolk*, or interpreter, in the course of their many negotiations with local people, one name stands out among the rest: Sara Kierstede. She was almost always either the only woman present or the only woman recognized and named in the record. Her life and abilities and the important place that she, though

18. Treaty, July 10, 1663, NYCM, X, pt. 2, 203, NYSA; see also *DRCHNY*, XIII, 276.

female, came to occupy again reveal the intermingling of colonial influence and personal relationships. Just as colonial officials needed to work through Munsee kin and clan ties, so, too, they had to make use of settlers' intimate networks.

In some ways, Sara seems the very antithesis of the man whose words she channeled. Though Oratam's ties to people and places in the Hudson Valley reached back for generations, Sara's were new, representative of her family's extreme mobility within the expanding Atlantic world. Born in Amsterdam in 1627, she was the child of Scandinavian immigrants who had come to the Netherlands from the island of Marstrand (Maesterland). Her father, Roeloff Jansz van Maesterland, a simple sailor, doubtless relocated to the thriving Dutch port city in hopes of finding better work. When he and his bride, Anneke Jans, married in 1623, they both belonged to the Lutheran church in Amsterdam. By the time they left for New Netherland, the couple had two living children. Arriving in 1630, they were one of the earliest settler families of Rensselaerswijk. For a few years, the family worked together there as tenant farmers. Eventually, Roeloff Jansz rose to become a member of the patroonship's governing council. The family then moved to Manhattan, where they worked first as tenant farmers for the WIC and then as free, landowning farmers.[19]

A look at Sara's growing web of connections shows that, despite, or maybe because of, her family's mobility, she developed an extensive and powerful network within colonial society; the continuing mobility of her kin merely increased the reach of her intimate ties. After her father's death in 1636, her mother married New Amsterdam minister Everardus Bogardus. Although the family continued to work the farm, their new affiliation with the minister allowed them to join the upper levels of Manhattan society. The marriages of Sara and her female relations further extended the family's reach, allying them with many merchant households. Sara herself married Mr. Hans Kierstede, a New Amsterdam surgeon originally from the German

19. In the early seventeenth century, Marstrand, called Maesterland by the Dutch, was part of Norway, although it changed hands a number of times in succeeding centuries. Kierstede's parents were part of a substantial immigrant community in Amsterdam. Simon Hart has estimated that during the seventeenth century some 7,784 Norwegian men and women married for the first time in Amsterdam. Fully 13.7 percent of the 183,033 foreigners who married for the first time in Amsterdam between 1601 and 1800 came from Scandinavia; see Hart, *Geschrift en getal* (Dordrecht, 1976), as quoted in Sölvi Sogner, "Young in Europe around 1700: Norwegian Sailors and Servant-Girls Seeking Employment in Amsterdam," in Jean-Pierre Bardet, François Lebrun, and René Le Mée, eds., *Mesurer et comprendre: Mélanges offerts a Jacques Dupaquier* (Paris, 1993), 515–532.

city of Magdeburg, who was employed in the service of the WIC. Her sister, Trijntjen Roeloffs, married three times—first to New Amsterdam merchant Willem de Key; second to Lucas Rodenburg, who served at one time as a member of New Netherland's governing council and later as the vice director of Curaçao; and finally to Johannes Pietersz Verbrugge, a powerful fur trader and sometime municipal leader of New Amsterdam. Her younger sister, Sijtgen Roeloffs, married the brewer, fur trader, tobacco planter, and frequent officeholder Pieter Hartgers van Wee. In 1649, Sara's aunt, Marritgen Jans, married the widower Govert Loockermans, agent of the Verbrugge merchant house and frequent member of the municipal government, and her cousin, Elsie Tymens, married Jacob Leisler in 1663. Thus, Sara lived enmeshed in a growing network of family in New Netherland with ties to some of the most powerful households in the colony.[20]

Sara had begun building her own household in 1642 when she was just fifteen years old. Her husband, fifteen years her senior, already occupied an important place in New Amsterdam society when they married. The couple further expanded the family's network through the institution of godparentage. They baptized their first son, Jan/Hans, in 1644, choosing godparents from among their family (Sara's stepfather, Reverend Bogardus, and Sara's aunt, the midwife Tryn Jonas) and from prominent members of New Amsterdam society, including Director Kieft. In total, the couple baptized ten children between 1644 and 1665, despite Hans Kierstede's overseas travel in the late 1640s. In turn, Sara and Hans acted as godparents themselves, strengthening bonds of blood and creating fictive kinship ties throughout the colonial elite. For instance, both acted as witnesses to the baptism of Sara's young half-brother, Pieter Bogardus, in 1645, and Sara joined several other prominent New Amsterdammers as witness to the baptism of fur trader Harmen Meyndertsz van den Bogaert's son, Meyndert, in 1643. Although Sara was an immigrant daughter whose parents had migrated themselves, who lost a father young, who lost her stepfather when she was

20. Much of Sara Roeloff Kierstede's family background has been painstakingly reconstructed in Willem Frijhoff, *Wegen van Evert Willemsz: Een Hollands weeskind op zoek naar zichzelf, 1607–1647* (The Hague, 1995). See, especially, the appended genealogies of the Roeloff and Bogardus families (881–888). Surgeons, like Hans Kierstede, in one seventeenth-century North Holland town "were classed as dignitaries"; see A. Th. van Deursen, "The Trades in the Village of Graft," in Elisabeth Paling Funk and Martha Dickinson Shattuck, eds., *A Beautiful and Fruitful Place: Selected Rensselaerwijck Papers,* trans. Charles Forceville, II (Albany, N.Y., 2011), 17–25, esp. 22–24 (quotation, 23). On the familial connections to Leisler, see David William Voorhees, "Leisler's Pre-1689 Biography and Family Background," ibid., II, 47–54.

only twenty, and who had a husband, siblings, and in-laws who crossed the Atlantic in all directions, she would have been constantly surrounded by people with whom she had intimate ties.[21]

The narrative of Sara's life, up to 1663, would seem to be one of developing burgher respectability and settler stability. Suddenly, though, comes her curious meeting with Oratam. The answer to the riddle of why Sara was selected to hear and speak the words of these sachems at this delicate political moment lies in her network of immediate relationships. Two factors led colonial administrators to choose her as tolk: trust and fluency. She came by both through her position within her social and intimate networks.

Sara's broad family and intimate ties to the elite of New Amsterdam made her eminently trustworthy in the eyes of the men who acted as colonial authorities. Captain Marten Cregier, for example, who led military operations against the Esopus and headed diplomatic missions to other Munsee towns in the 1660s, shared bonds of faith with Sara through his wife, Lysbeth Cregiers, who witnessed the baptism of Sara and Hans's daughter, Blandina, in 1653. Sara's connections through her aunt to the Loockermans family also made her a "cousin" to several leaders of the city and colony, including Oloff Stevensz van Courtlandt, a key municipal leader in 1663 and 1664, and Govert Loockermans, who accompanied Captain Cregier on his mission to the Navesink in 1663. As a high-status woman from New Amsterdam society, her interests mirrored those of the high-status New Amsterdam men who made up the governing body. But she also stood at one remove from political factions in ways that most men of her status did not. Because of her sex, she had never been a member of civil or colony government, nor had she ever been an employee of the WIC or one of the Amsterdam merchant houses.[22]

21. Thomas Grier Evans, ed., *Records of the Reformed Dutch Church in New Amsterdam and New York: Baptisms from 25 December, 1639, to 27 December, 1730*, Collections of the New York Genealogical and Biographical Society, II (New York, 1901), 15–80, esp. 15, 19. One son, baptized Jacob in June 1662, was followed with unusual rapidity by a brother in November 1663 named Jacobus, suggesting that the first Jacob had died in infancy. The rest of the ten children had unique names and were born at regular intervals, indicating that the couple could have had as many as nine living children by Hans Kierstede's death in 1666.

22. Evans, ed., *Baptisms*, 15, 34. On Cregier's mission, see Journal, Dec. 6–11, 1663, NYCM, X, pt. 2, 431–434, NYSA. Sara was particularly close to her cousin Marritje Loockermans, who witnessed the baptism of Jacob Kierstede in 1662 and who went on to marry Governor Stuyvesant's nephew; see Evans, *Baptisms*, 65. Van Cortlandt was married to Anna, or Annetje, Loockermans, Govert Loockerman's sister and Marritje's aunt. On the role of genealogies and reliance on lateral kin among the burgher classes in the Netherlands and the use of the term "cousin" for relatives up to eight degrees removed, see Julia Adams, *The Familial State: Ruling Families and Merchant Capitalism in Early Modern Europe* (Ithaca, N.Y., 2005), 76–77.

Her gender might have similarly made her an attractive translator in the eyes of Oratam and other Munsees. Munsee ideas of gender "complementarity" probably made sachems like Oratam willing to accept women's participation in decision making. Furthermore, Sara had not taken part in warfare or negotiations in the 1640s and 1650s and had never stood in for the colony government in an official capacity. At least one male translator, Pieter van Couwenhoven, sparked distrust among Oratam and other Munsee sachems because he had justified whiskey dealing by showing a piece of paper he claimed was a legal license. Munsee sachems did not know whether to doubt that he was presenting the written words honestly or whether to suspect him of political maneuvering and connivance to obtain a license in violation of treaty obligations. Van Couwenhoven served in New Amsterdam's municipal government in 1663 and also headed a troop of "natives and volunteers" at the height of the Esopus War that same year, making him hardly a neutral force in Munsee eyes. Sara, on the other hand, remained untainted by any claims to political influence or authority in her own right because her sex had prevented her from holding office. Since she stood outside of the formal lines of power and authority, she remained transparent in negotiations, suspect from neither side.[23]

Yet, Sara also needed proficiency in Native languages to act as she did. The significance of her linguistic achievement should not be belittled. Clearly, she was confident and comfortable in the Munsee dialect spoken by Oratam. But when she translated for the Wappingers, who lived farther north on the opposite shore of the Hudson from Hackensacky, the words she heard might have differed in meaningful ways from the Munsee spoken

23. Margaret M. Caffrey, "Complementary Power: Men and Women of the Lenni Lenape," *American Indian Quarterly*, XXIV (2000), 44–63; Appointment, July 6, 1663, NYCM, X, pt. 2, 199, NYSA ("natives and volunteers"); Treaty, July 10, 1663, NYCM, X, pt. 2, 203, NYSA; see also *DRCHNY*, XIII, 276. For a list of municipal office holders, see Jaap Jacobs, *New Netherland: A Dutch Colony in Seventeenth-Century America* (Leiden, 2005), 490–492. For a similar discussion of Mistress Margaret Brent in seventeenth-century Maryland, who also had family-based influence but stood outside faction because of her sex, see Mary Beth Norton, *Founding Mothers and Fathers: Gendered Power and the Forming of American Society* (New York, 1996), 281–287. Women also acted as "squaw sachems" and spiritual leaders among the Munsee and "stood ready to help guide people in Munsee country in making decisions," thus laying the groundwork for the acceptance of Sara Kierstede at diplomatic meetings with the Dutch; see Grumet, *Munsee Indians*, 20. Sara claimed in 1669 that Oratam had granted her a 2,260 acre tract by the Hackensack River. If true, the gift suggests that Oratam particularly valued her services; see William Nelson, ed., *Documents Relating to the Colonial History of the State of New Jersey*, XXI, *Calendar of Records in the Office of the Secretary of State, 1664–1703* (Paterson, N.J., 1899), 8; Grumet, *Munsee Indians*, 122.

closer to Manhattan. Furthermore, Tapausagh and Rompsicka came from Long Island, where Munsee speakers lived close by Shinnecock, Montauk, and others who spoke different Algonquian languages, and it is possible that Munsee was not the only local language spoken when Sara served as a translator. It is impossible to gauge the accuracy of her translations today, but that she was selected repeatedly shows that people perceived her as fluent at the time. Perhaps when she lived upriver at Rensselaerswijk between ages four and seven she had played with Mahican children. Given her Scandinavian parents and German husband, Sara was very likely multilingual in European languages from her childhood and teens, potentially easing the acquisition of more languages as an adult.[24]

Other New Amsterdam women did not find Munsee easy to learn. The steadfastly monolingual Aeltie Sybrants provides an example. On April 26, 1664, Sara and Oratam negotiated the return of Aeltie Sybrants from a group of Wappinger women who had given her protection after her husband, Mattys Roeloffsen, had been killed in a disagreement with a Wappinger man named Eihtaworis. When Aeltie was asked to comment on the accuracy of Sara's translation of the Wappinger representative's story about her husband's death and her rescue, Aeltie had to confess that she had little understanding of the Munsee tongue. Although she said the story seemed to be accurate in the main, there had been "many more words [said] about it in their children's prattle" that she did not understand. To Sara, somehow, that speech meant more than mere *kinterhaye*, or prattle.[25]

No dramatic rupture or unusual experience explains her talents. Whereas translators along colonial frontiers sometimes endured captivity or resided in Native American villages for purposes of trade, Sara seems to have undergone nothing like that (and, in any case, captivity had done little to improve Aeltie Sybrants's linguistic abilities). The documentary traces of Sara's life instead testify to domestic stability. The baptisms of babies in New Amster-

24. Linguistic boundaries on Long Island are difficult to reconstruct. Ives Goddard notes that "it may be, for example, that the Massapequa and Matinecock were not Munsee speakers at all, but the linguistic ancestors of the eighteenth-century Unquachog"; see Goddard, "Delaware," in William C. Sturtevant, ed., *Handbook of North American Indians*, XV, *Northeast*, ed. Bruce G. Trigger (Washington, D.C., 1978), 214–215 (quotation, 215). On the possibility that young Sara could have played with Mahican children, see Janny Venema, *Beverwijck: A Dutch Village on the American Frontier, 1652–1664* (Hilversum, Netherlands, 2003), 166–167; and Willem Frijhoff, *Wegen van Evert Willemsz: Een Hollands weeskind op zoek naar zichzelf, 1607–1647* (The Hague, 1995), 627.

25. Minutes, Apr. 26, 1664, NYCM, X, pt. 3, 211–212, NYSA. Thanks to Janny Venema for help with *kinterhaye*. Aeltie could also have meant "council" in Munsee; either way, she lacked fluency.

dam in 1644, 1647, 1651, 1653, 1655, 1657, 1660, 1662, 1663, and 1665 speak to a certain regularity of habits and suggest at least that she was never absent for very long. Indeed, her life of colonial domesticity seems to have continued despite her newfound role in Dutch-Munsee politics in the 1660s. During the whole of the time she worked as a translator, Sara still lived the ordinary life of a New Amsterdam *huysvrouw,* or housewife, probably even taking her newborn son along to the 1664 negotiations, since he would still have been nursing. At the time of her first duties as translator, in the summer of 1663, Sara was pregnant with Jacobus and perhaps still mourning the baby who had died the previous year. Given Sara's growing family and uninterrupted presence in New Amsterdam, it is unlikely that the secret to her linguistic talents lies far from her home.[26]

Indeed, the reason Sara had the skills she needed can be found by looking at the face-to-face relationships that shaped her daily work. Although nothing suggests that Sara had ever traveled to Munsee villages before her work as a translator, the Munsee presence in New Amsterdam cannot be denied. As participants in the Hudson Valley's regional exchange economy, Hackensacks and other Munsee-speakers appeared regularly in New Amsterdam's households and marketplace, hawking everything from furs to food to firewood. As the young mother of a growing family and as the manager of a vital burgher *huysgezin,* or household, Sara would have often had occasion to buy many of the goods local villagers brought to town for sale. In addition, her particular household placed her literally at the center of the New Amsterdam exchange system. Since Sara's childhood in New Amsterdam, visitors had brought goods, often by canoe, to the shore for sale, and the Kierstede home lay at the heart of that part of town. By 1656, with the organization of municipal governance for the town, officials formalized the time and place of these face-to-face transactions. The colony council called for the establishment of Saturday as the official market day, "as now and then, various wares, such as meat, bacon, butter, cheese, rape, roots and cabbage, and other produce, too, are sent to this City by the country people for sale, and having arrived here on the shore with them they often must wait for a long time with their wares, to their great detriment, because the people

---

26. Evans, *Baptisms,* 65, 71. On the possible loss of a child in 1662, see note 20, above. Dutch women generally nursed children until around age one and a half; see Lily E. Clerkx, "Kinderen in het gezin," in G. A. Kooy, *Gezinsgeschiedenis: Vier eeuwen gezin in Nederland* (Assen, Netherlands, 1985), 117. Grumet calls Sara Kierstede a "former captive" but leaves the basis for this description unstated; see Grumet, *Munsee Indians,* 122.

or at least the majority of those that live away from the shore do not know that such goods have been brought for sale." They chose as the market site the area "on the shore by or near the house of Master Hans Kierstede" and directed "anyone who has something to buy or to sell" to gather there. Beginning at age twenty-nine, then, Sara had weekly instruction just outside her door in to-and-fro bartering and face-to-face conversation with Munsee and other traders, in addition to the daily encounters that came her way as a shoreside resident and ordinary huysvrouw. The personal interactions of New Amsterdam's exchange economy acted as Sara's language lab, providing her with the skills she needed to become a designated speaker-hearer during the politically complicated final years of Dutch governance.[27]

When Sara spoke for Oratam in 1663 and 1664, she did so based on the strength of her personal and economic relationships, just as personal and immediate relationships also underlay Oratam's role as a conduit for the flow of words among the villages of the Hudson Valley. Dutch officials' reliance on Sara and Oratam belied the hierarchical, authoritative model of Dutch-Munsee relations Kieft had sought to establish as early as the 1640s. Colonial authorities admitted as much when the council searched desperately for translators as escalating fighting with the Esopus in 1660 made negotiations with other Munsee villages critically important. The council voted to appoint Claes Jansen Ruyter as a translator at the considerable salary of four hundred guilders a year because the WIC "had no one in service who can understand the *Wiltse* language readily, much less speak it." The formal, hierarchical structure of colonial government simply did not provide the knowledge and interpersonal communication skills that the council recognized were needed "in weighty dealings to do with peace or war and otherwise."[28]

Sara and Oratam, on the other hand, possessed the skills and positions of trust necessary to handle exactly such weighty dealings, as Hackensacky and New Amsterdam struggled to remain at peace with one another during the period when violence engulfed nearby Esopus from 1659 to 1664. Beginning in July 1663, Sara acted as a translator in crucial treaty negotiations. She interpreted for Sauwenaare, sachem of Wiechquaeskeck, and Metsewackos,

27. Court Minutes, Sept. 18, 1656, CMNA, II, 12, NYCMA (microfilm) (quotations). See also Jacobs, *New Netherland*, 460–461. On the centrality of the "groot markt," or main marketplace, as a central business area in plans for Dutch colonial towns, see Ron van Oers, *Dutch Town Planning Overseas during VOC and WIC Rule, 1600–1800* (Zutphen, Netherlands, 2000).

28. Appointment, Mar. 1, 1660, NYCM, IX, 112, NYSA.

sachem of Kichtawangh, when they agreed to remain neutral during the fighting at Esopus. She also aided these sachems in forwarding their complaints about the abusive sale of liquor by settlers. The treaty represented a key diplomatic victory for the Dutch, who most feared a general alliance of Native peoples living along the Hudson. Oratam likewise played a part in the negotiations throughout the Esopus conflicts that assured that other Munsees would not join in on the Esopus side. In one July 1663 appearance, he informed Governor Stuyvesant and the council that the best efforts of the Esopus to induce the "menissinghse" villagers to join them had failed. Sara acted as the middlewoman for the middleman that day, translating for Oratam when he recounted that he had successfully convinced these Munsee villagers to remain at peace with New Amsterdam. During the conflicts, Hackensacks acted as runners, passing on news of battles north at Esopus before the Dutch could send word themselves. For example, one Munsee villager "named by the Dutch Pieter van Hackensackij" reported on September 10, 1663, that the Dutch had led a successful raid on the Esopus. Together, Oratam and Sara helped ensure that WIC soldiers could isolate the Esopus peoples from their neighbors.[29]

Oratam also proved instrumental in helping to end the Esopus conflict, often with Sara by his side. In attempting to halt the killings, Oratam continued to speak, not on his own behalf, but as a mouthpiece for the wider Munsee network. In November 1663, this "leader of hackingsacky and Staten Island" appeared at a colony council meeting, bringing with him "one of the principle matrons of this place" who, speaking through Oratam, explained "that she was besought and bidden by both [the Esopus and Wappinger] nations" to seek peace with the New Netherland authorities. In response, the council instructed representatives to begin mediation. Though the council resisted dealing directly with a woman, Oratam's presence forced the colonial authorities to listen to her words. In July 1664, Sara served as the lone translator for the final peace negotiation between the council and Seweckenamo, one of the principal Esopus sachems. She forwarded his report of famine among his people and his unsuccessful plea for a shipment of food. The Esopus conflicts brought Oratam and Sara to the peak of their joint influence, as they drew on the skills and power given to them through their

29. Minutes, July 10, 1663, NYCM, X, pt. 2, 203, NYSA (see also *DRCHNY*, XIII, 276); Minutes, July 20, 1663, NYCM, X, pt. 2, 228–229, NYSA ("menissinghse") (see also *DRCHNY*, XIII, 280); Minutes, Sept. 10, 1663, NYCM, X, pt. 2, 294, NYSA ("named"); Minutes, July 8, 1664, NYCM, X, pt. 3, 261, NYSA. For Oratam in other negotiations, see Feb. 23, 1664, NYCM, X, pt. 3, 88, NYSA; Otto, *Dutch-Munsee Encounter*, 153.

participation in their personal networks to form the channel through which words streamed at this critical time.[30]

Yet the influence that flowed through and from intimate networks was different from personal power. During the Esopus negotiations, when Oratam's importance was at its height, he deliberately shifted the focus away from himself. At a February 1664 meeting held to negotiate peace between the Esopus and the Dutch, he sought Dutch recognition of a successor to his role as designated speaker-hearer. He requested that, in the event of his death, the Dutch regard his kinsman, named Pieweherenoes but frequently called "Hans de Wilt," as his people's representative. In Hans's presence, Oratam presented the Dutch with an otter pelt as a symbolic gift and "said that Hans shall be Sackima over the Hackinghkesackse and Staten Island Wilden after him; when they had something to say to the Wilden, they should call upon Hans (when he, Oratamy, was dead)." By endeavoring to secure the flow of words through Hackensacky, Oratam hoped to guarantee the continued influence of the Hackensacky intimate networks that he had relied on so long and so successfully to protect and expand the interests of his people.[31]

Just a few weeks after Oratam recommended him as speaker-hearer to the New Amsterdam authorities, Hans acted alongside Oratam and others in a meeting between colonial authorities and sachems from Minisink, a Munsee community farther north and thus much closer to the brutal fighting taking place at Esopus. At this meeting, the Minisinks spoke of their new alliance with the Susquehannocks and their fear of attack by western Iroquois groups. Oratam, Hans, and the Minisink sachems stressed the deeply personal nature of their relationship with the Dutch. "As a sign of their good heart," they brought in the child of Jan Lootman, who had been taken captive at Esopus. These and other negotiations gave Hans experience at forming immediate relationships with the Dutch and insight into the region's competing polities and his people's place as an intermediary among them.[32]

Oratam's choice to honor Hans before the Dutch government shows that Oratam saw himself as representative of the Hackensack intimate network.

30. Instructions, Nov. 21, 1663, NYCM, X, pt. 2, 393–395, NYSA (quotations); Minutes, July 8, 1664, NYCM, X, pt. 3, 261–262, NYSA.

31. Minutes, Feb. 23, 1664, NYCM, X, pt. 3, 88, NYSA (quotations). Other names for Hans / Pieweherenoes include Pierwim, Sewahheronos, and Pearawe; see Grumet, *Munsee Indians*, 342 n. 27.

32. Minutes, Mar. 6, 1664, NYCM, X, pt. 3, 89–91, NYSA. The Minisink feared attack by the Seneca, a term often used in this period to refer to all western Iroquois groups.

As he worked to do his best for the Munsee as a whole, Oratam, in effect, tried to secure for Hackensacky kin groups the personal relationships with the colony council that underlay Hudson Valley diplomacy. Thus, Oratam used his moment of greatest visibility as he sought to end the devastating Esopus War to push colonial administrators to recognize a particular set of kin and clan relationships. In naming Hans to New Netherland officials, Oratam also acknowledged the interweaving of local and imperial sources of power. Oratam clearly felt Hans needed this recognition to operate successfully as an intermediary between Hackensacky and the Dutch colony, suggesting that respect within the village and within local intimate networks was not enough to give Hans the power he needed to help protect Hackensacky in an increasingly complicated environment. Intimate networks and colonial authority had begun to mold each other through the process of speaking and hearing, talking and listening that had taken place in the repeated face-to-face meetings between the Munsee and the Dutch.

Oratam's and Sara's experiences reveal the true nature of power in the greater Hudson Valley. In this early modern zone of encounter, intimate networks and imperial authority intermingled through the words of those chosen to speak and to listen. Together, the pair connected New Amsterdam and Hackensacky intimate networks in a way that sealed the alliance between the Dutch and the lower Munsee at a critical time in the late 1650s and early 1660s. Even as hostilities exploded at Esopus, Manhattan and the lower Hudson region remained at peace. As Dutch authorities extended Dutch claims in the mid-Atlantic region through military means, they nonetheless relied on these two individuals and their complicated webs of connections to create the right political context. Their dependence on them illustrates that the influence of colonial authorities flowed both from and through intimate networks. However much colonial officials sought to use hierarchical structures to impose their will throughout the region, in the end networks of face-to-face relationships determined who had the capacity to speak and the ability to understand. As Dutch power in the region grew in the early 1660s, it did so in ways informed and shaped by a pattern of relationships between New Amsterdam and lower Munsee villages, relationships sustained by Oratam and Sara. And even as Dutch officials celebrated the extension of Dutch military might in the middle of the Hudson Valley, Oratam and Sara both began issuing warnings about the weakening of Dutch power elsewhere, relaying words reaching Manhattan from Long Island.

Just as the Esopus War was nearing an end, Dutch authorities faced a growing threat to their east. In December 1663, Oratam's emissary and chosen successor, Hans, acted as the main runner for Captain Cregier on his diplomatic voyage to the Munsee village of Navesink. On reaching Navesink, Cregier found a group of twenty English settlers from Long Island that the villagers reported had come to buy land under "the King's patent," even though these Englishmen had placed themselves under the Manhattan government. The words Oratam's network reported, then, warned that Dutch control over Long Island settler villages was evaporating. Settlers were openly encroaching on Munsee land while flouting Dutch authority. And in 1664, Sara joined Pieter van Couwenhoven as a translator during a diplomatic mission by two key regional leaders, Tapausagh and Rompsicka of Long Island. She relayed not only their complaints about land-hungry English Long Islanders but also their warnings that the English intended to send ships to conquer New Netherland. Ultimately, their words pointed to an area where Dutch alliances with powerful intimate networks remained weak and where Dutch authority would be undercut even as it reached new heights elsewhere.[33]

Quashawam

As the conflict among the competing expansive polities of the mid-Atlantic coast intensified in the 1650s, Long Island became hotly contested ground. With its fertile farmland, fish-filled streams, and bountiful wetlands and shorelines, Long Island presented tempting territory for settlers from both New Netherland and New England. It was also home to a rich tapestry of Native villages, including both Munsee-speakers and other Algonquians. The coming of the Dutch and English newcomers presented many opportunities for these indigenous residents to enter into the new fur, wampum, and food economies. Yet, as the number of settlers increased and as the various regional polities came into conflict, these Native inhabitants faced new dangers and difficult choices. One of the primary tools Long Islanders used to meet these challenges were the immediate relationships that bound them in a single intimate network. The evaporation of Dutch influence on Long Island in 1663 and 1664 would in part reflect colonial authorities' inability to build strong relationships within that network.

The experiences of a woman named Quashawam illustrate how politics and relationships interacted. Because she inherited a place at the heart of Montauk and Shinnecock kin and village connections, this powerful woman

33. Journal of Marten Cregier, Dec. 6–11, 1663, NYCM, X, pt. 2, 431–434, NYSA (quotation), partially translated in *DRCHNY*, XIII, 314–316; Minutes, Jan. 7, 1664, NYCM, X, pt. 3, 7–8, NYSA (see also *DRCHNY*, XIV, 540).

stood at the center of the negotiations among Native and settler villages and between competing imperial polities at the very moment when Dutch influence on Long Island began to slip away. Investigating her response to the changing situation reveals the adaptability and strength of the relationships she employed. Yet she was not the only political actor who recognized that kin and village ties had the potential to solidify claims to Long Island ground. Just as Quashawam used personal relationships to legitimate her power among Algonquian communities and to craft a coordinated response to expanding polities, actors within those polities variously tried to gain access to Long Island territory through Quashawam or to deny the validity of others' encroachments by refusing to recognize her position. The varied responses of colonial authorities shaped at once the strength of imperial and territorial claims and the strength of her political power. Quashawam exemplifies the complicated interface between personal ties and empire in the 1660s. Her actions demonstrate the composite nature of power in this region of early modern colonial activity and suggest that, in the seventeenth century, territorial and political ambitions alike often rested on a combination of intimate and imperial relationships.

Personal relationships and kinship networks had guided the response of Montauk residents to the region's expansive polities for decades before Quashawam's name first appears in the written record. From the 1630s through the 1650s, Quashawam's father, Wyandanch, acted as a key village leader, and the diplomatic strategies he and his fellow local sachems employed focused on building networks of relationships among villages—both settler and Native. In 1637, Montauk sachems faced the threat of political subjugation by the Rhode Island–allied sachem Ninigret, who attempted to expand the power of his town Niantic by making Montauk and other Long Island towns pay tribute. On an unsolicited visit to Long Island, he threatened and shamed the sachems, saying, "Plant your corne and weede it well and I will come att harvest and eate it." Wyandanch responded by appealing to Connecticut colonial leaders in person for help. Long Island sachems clearly saw the English through the lens of their own political network and thought of the separate settlements at Connecticut and Rhode Island as individual actors capable of forming independent alliances cemented by personal relationships.[34]

34. Roger Ludlow to John Winthrop, July 3, 1638, *Winthrop Papers*, IV (Boston, 1929–), 43–45 (quotation, 44); John A. Strong, *The Montaukett Indians of Eastern Long Island* (Syracuse, N.Y., 2001), 12–13.

Wyandanch's analysis was correct. Connecticut representatives Thomas Stanton and John Mason succeeded in pushing Ninigret to return the tribute wampum, no doubt in part because of their own desire to limit the influence of Rhode Island. Montauk leaders solidified these relationships soon after by inviting or allowing Lion Gardiner to establish his island settlement near Montauk. Having a neighboring settler village gave Montauk leaders the chance to form close relationships with a potentially powerful ally in the way that would have been most familiar to them—that is, through daily local associations among neighbors. Although interactions did not always go smoothly, Gardiner and Montauk villagers cooperated in some day-to-day activities. The Montauks carried goods and messages across the sound by canoe, and Gardiner forwarded various requests to colonial authorities in writing.[35]

By 1644, four Montauk sachems including Wyandanch "p[ro]fesse[d] themselves frends both to the English and the Dutch." Balancing these two friendships remained tricky. In 1647, Poggatacut from Manhasset, Momoweta from Corchaug, Nowedonah from Shinnecock, and Wyandanch moved to counter Dutch attempts to expand New Netherland's land claims in eastern Long Island by allowing English settlers to establish another village. Together, these sachems designated the land for what was to become the new English community of Easthampton. Clauses in the contract allowed Native inhabitants to selectively use these lands, showing that the sachems interacted with Easthampton settlers as just one more Long Island village among many. The sachems stipulated that local Algonquians would still "have Libertie, freely to fish in any or all the cricks and ponds, and hunt up and downe in the woods without Molestation. . . . Likewise, they are to have the fynns and tails of allsuch whales as shall be cast upp. . . . Allsoe, they reserve libertie to fish in all convenient places, for Shells to make wampum." The sachems added one more condition that according to local practice signified that the Montauk retained authority over Easthampton land. They insisted that "if the Indyans, hunting of any deare, they should chase them into the water, and the English should kill them, the English shall have the body, and the Sachem the skin." In return for being allowed to use the land, these new neighbors aided Wyandanch and Montauk villagers several

<hr>

35. Roger Williams to John Winthrop, circa Aug. 1, 1638, *Winthrop Papers,* IV, 48. For the identification of the Long Island sachem who visited Connecticut as Wyandanch, see Strong, *Montaukett,* 13. For cooperation over messages and letters, see Lion Gardiner to John Winthrop, Jr., Apr. 14, 1649, in "Letters of Lion Gardiner," *Collections of the Massachusetts Historical Society,* Ser. 4, VII (Boston, 1865), 58.

times in the succeeding decades in their struggle against Niantic expansion. Montauk and other Long Island leaders responded to neighboring expansive polities by establishing new relationships with English settlements that would parallel the kind of networks already joining the diverse Algonquian villages on the island.[36]

Wyandanch coupled this strategy of forming relationships with English towns with that of strengthening his ties to other Algonquian communities on Long Island. He did so by drawing on the kinship and marriage bonds that united these peoples to act as a regional designated speaker in relations with the English. Indigenous island villages had long been linked together through kinship and clan ties formed through intervillage marriages, and Wyandanch sought to reinforce these connections. In 1649, after a diplomatic incident, Wyandanch represented the Shinnecock in multiparty negotiations, when "Mandush with many other of the cheifee of Shinecock Indians as ancient men, did manifest their consent and that they were contented, by their ordinary signe of stroaking Wyandanch on the back." Both Assawkin, sachem of Oyster Bay, and Nassetteconsett, sachem of Nesaquauke, were kinsmen of Wyandanch and his wife and evidently allowed (or were forced to allow) Wyandanch to treat with English settlers on their behalf in the 1650s. Wyandanch's regional influence reached the point that English settlers sometimes referred to him as the Chief Sachem of all of Long Island. Though English perspectives and interests doubtless led them to state Wyandanch's power in inappropriately strong terms, by the time of his death in 1659 he had succeeded in bringing Long Island Native villages closer together at the same time as he forged tight relationships with his new settler neighbors. Personal and social networks guided the Montauk response to expansive polities from the 1630s onward.[37]

36. Acts of the Commissioners of the United Colonies, Sept. 6, 1644, in David Pulsifer, ed., *Records of the Colony of New Plymouth in New England*, IX (Boston, 1859), 18–19 ("p[ro]fesse[d]," 19). The Montauks' names are given as Youghcoe, Wiantause, Moughmaitow, and Weenagaminin. On Easthampton, see Deed, Apr. 29, 1648, in Jonathan T. Gardiner, Jonathan Baker, and Joseph S. Osborne, eds., *Records of the Town of East-Hampton, Long Island, Suffolk Co., N.Y., with other Ancient Documents of Historic Value*, I (Sag Harbor, N.Y., 1887), 2–4 ("have Libertie," 3). For English aid against Niantic, see Minutes, Aug. 23, 1654, in Charles J. Hoadly, ed., *Records of the Colony or Jurisdiction of New Haven, From May, 1653, to the Union, Together with the New Haven Code of 1656* (Hartford, Conn., 1858), 117–118; Agreement, September 1660, in J. Wickham Case, ed., *Southold Town Records*, I (Southold, N.Y., 1882), 363.

37. Deposition, Sept. 19, 1666, in Henry P. Hedges, Wm. S. Pelletreau, and Edward H. Foster, eds., *The First Book of Records of the Town of Southampton, with Other Ancient Documents of Historic Value* (Sag Harbor, N.Y., 1874), 158 (quotation). Long Islanders were "linked in an intricate web of kinship relationships which was continuously reinforced through exogamous

Quashawam rose to regional influence because of her place within these webs of personal political relationships. Wyandanch died just as smallpox repeatedly wracked the region. Deeds and negotiations between the Montauk and Hamptons villagers in the immediate aftermath of his death mention his young son, Wyancombone, and his unnamed widow as sachem and sunksquaw of Montauk and Shinnecock. They remained part of a broader regional web of sachems related by kin and marriage, however, including Cockenoe, a designated speaker and translator who married Wyandanch's sister. Quashawam extended this network of political and kin relationships through her own marriage to a Pequot sachem. She also had preexisting ties to English settlers, having been ransomed from Ninigret as a young girl with the help of English intermediaries. Thus, when her brother and mother succumbed to the smallpox outbreaks that would claim the lives of what Lion Gardiner estimated to be some two-thirds of the Algonquian villagers on Long Island, Quashawam inherited a widespread and complicated network of connections reaching out in all directions from Montauk.[38]

Quashawam occupied a particularly crucial place by virtue of her sex. As a woman, she stood at the center of the kin and social webs linking people to land in a way perhaps not entirely shared by her late father and brother. Gendered divisions of labor in villages throughout Long Island and the Hudson Valley placed land in women's hands. Adriaen van der Donck explained these gendered work patterns among the Hudson-area Algonquians, writing that "the Men-folk are generally lazy, and do not want to do

---

marriage customs"; see John A. Strong, "Wyandanch: Sachem of the Montauks," in Robert S. Grumet, ed., *Northeastern Indian Lives, 1632–1816* (Amherst, Mass., 1996), 48. For an analysis of politics among sachems in this period, see ibid., 50–61; Strong, *Montaukett*, 10–34. On Assawkin and Nassetteconsett (Nasaskonsuk), see Statement and deed, May 4, 1665, in William S. Pelletreau, ed., *Records of the Town of Smithtown, Long Island, N.Y., with Other Ancient Documents of Historic Value* (Smithtown, N.Y., 1898), 8–9, Deposition, June 22, 1666, 16–17. On the ability of sachems to alienate land, see Kathleen J. Bragdon, *Native People of Southern New England, 1500–1650* (Norman, Okla., 1996), 137–139. For Wyandanch as chief sachem, see Statement / Deed, Jan. 15, 1661, in Case, ed., *Southold Town Records*, 168–170; Deed, [Apr. 10, 1665], in Thomas W. Cooper, ed., *The Records of the Court of Sessions of Suffolk County in the Province of New York, 1670–1688* (Bowie, Md., 1993), 174.

38. On the "hot pestilents [and un]heard of feavors" afflicting Long Island and the Hudson Valley in 1662, see Proclamation, Jan. 26, 1662, NYCM, X, pt. 1, 27–29, 31–32, NYSA. For Quashawam's marriage, see Thomas James to the governor and assistants of Connecticut, [June 1664], in Massachusetts Historical Society, *Collections*, Ser. 4, VII (1865), 483–484, and Thomas James to John Winthrop, Jr., Sept. 6, [1654], 482–483. On the death of Wyancombone in 1662, see Declaration, Dec. 1, 1662, in Gardiner, Baker, and Osborne, eds., *Records of the Town of East-Hampton*, I, 198; on smallpox at Montauk, see Order, Mar. 2, 1663/4, ibid., I, 201.

anything, before they are old and unregarded, and then they make Spoons, wooden Bins, hemp Bags, Nets, and more other suchlike Trifles, otherwise they do nothing but Fishing, Hunting, and going to War, women must do the rest of the work, such as planting grain, cutting and hauling fire wood, cooking, and watching the Children, and everything further that there is to do." Though Van der Donck disparaged men's fishing and hunting as lazy pastimes rather than work, he nonetheless did not miss the close connection between women's work and the land.[39]

Shifts in labor as a result of new interactions with Europeans did not weaken women's intimate relationship with the land. Long Island women harvested the region's estuaries for both plants and shellfish. With the coming of European traders and settlers, coastal Algonquian women likely spent even more time preparing wampum for sale. The development of the Hudson Valley wampum economy thus made access to shoreline lands and their rich shell beds particularly important. Long Island women also seem to have begun farming corn more, perhaps owing to the advent of the regional food economy or perhaps because of the need to use land more intensively. Villages at the eastern end of Long Island began herding cattle sometime during this period as well. Similarly, men might have begun spending more time in the woods, hunting, trading, or fighting for more beavers as the role of colonial trade increased. Both men's and women's work patterns underwent a series of subtle and overt changes as villages became woven into the wider networks of trade, but gendered patterns continued to tie women's work closely to the land.[40]

Extensive networks of authority reflecting the close bond between women's work and the land frequently placed Algonquian women at the heart of regional political life. At the smallest level, an individual's ties to

39. Adriaen van der Donck, *Vertoogh van Nieu-Neder-Land* (The Hague, 1650), 10 (quotation). Weaving nets tended to be a woman's task in the seventeenth-century Netherlands; see Annette de Wit, "Zeemansvrouwen aan het werk: De arbeidsmarktpositie van vrouwen in Maassluis, Schiedam, en Ter Heijde (1600–1700)," *Tijdschrift voor sociale en economische geschiedenis*, II, no. 3 (2005), 72.

40. Though Lynn Ceci's archaeological work suggests little dependence on farming by Long Islanders before European settlement, the historical records make clear that farming was critically important by the time Quashawam rose to her position of authority; see Ceci, *The Effect of European Contact and Trade on the Settlement Pattern of Indians in Coastal New York, 1524–1665* (New York, 1990). This emphasis on farming showed up in Native Long Islanders' complaints about damage to their crops caused by settlers' stock and insistence in land deeds that local villages retain the right to plant on land sold; see Deed, July 30, 1656, in Charles R. Street, ed., *Huntington Town Records, Including Babylon, Long Island, N.Y.*, I (Huntington, N.Y., 1887–1889), 6–7.

a particular clan, usually matrilineal, determined residence in Algonquian villages. Villagers and clan members decided subsistence strategies, including the extent to which farming, gathering, or wampum production would be emphasized. Women's roles as the determinants of clan identity and the producers of both corn and wampum put them at the forefront of critical questions for Long Island groups. Women also played important parts in regional diplomacy. Throughout Algonquian society, women served as sachems, often given the title of sunksquaw, sometimes called "Queenes" by the English on the mainland. This leadership was commonly a function of their kinship ties, marital bonds, inherited territories, and personal influence. Montauk villagers acknowledged Quashawam's authority in land sales as descending originally from Wyandanch's "granmother" who "lived on that land formerly." Intersecting patterns of land distribution, authority, and kin-based leadership endowed Quashawam with a particularly strong position within Long Island Algonquian networks.[41]

The multiple and layered use of territory—for gathering, fishing, farming, and living—gave the women of Long Island's interrelated Algonquian villages varied and overlapping interests. Deeds to the English villages show that Montauks and Shinnecocks regarded landownership in terms of shared use, including the ground that they permitted settlers to inhabit. Sunksquaws like Quashawam oversaw the distribution of farming plots and the use of other resources within and among villages. As the growing regional food trade with colonists sparked competition for the best croplands, women's tasks in this regard became more complex. Competing needs by different villages and regional groups led to complicated and tangled claims to key resources.[42]

In 1667, the English town of Southampton tried to determine a seemingly simple question: What were the boundaries of Shinnecock lands?

41. Deposition, June 22, 1666, in Pelletreau, ed., *Records of the Town of Smithtown*, 16–17 ("granmother," 16). For a good brief overview of Algonquian social-political structures and women's place within them, see Robert Steven Grumet, "Sunksquaws, Shamans, and Tradeswomen: Middle Atlantic Coastal Algonkian Women during the 17th and 18th Centuries," in Mona Etienne and Eleanor Leacock, ed., *Women and Colonization: Anthropological Perspectives* (New York, 1980), 43–62 ("Queenes," 49). Grumet classifies the levels of Algonquian political organization, in ascending order, as the clan, village, district, tribe, and confederacy. For many Long Island and Hudson groups before 1664, however, organization above the district level was minimal. For an analysis of women leaders and kinship, see Bragdon, *Native People*, 156–168, 177–178.

42. For more on women's roles in land distribution, farming, and economic life among the Algonquian peoples, see Bragdon, *Native People*.

Finding the answer required appealing to the right women, women who knew about the land in question. The Southampton representatives asked "two old women livinge at Mantaukut who formerly were of the Acabuck Indians who could give further information concerning the matter." The women affirmed that "they formerly were of your Ackobuck Indians and that they knew the bounds the severrall Plantations in those parts: one of them an Ancient woman: called by the Indians Akkobauk Homes Squaw: to which the other also assented called wompquaine squaw a middle aged woman." The women explained "that formerly many years since there was A small Plantation of Indians att akkobauk: and that these Indians being few were driven of their land being Conquered by other Indians," namely, the Shinnecock. These conflicts led to an intricate hierarchy of ties to the land. The two speakers stated that

> in those tymes the bounds of these akakkobauk Indians came East-
> ward of the river Pehikkonuk [Peconic] to a creeke which she named.
> And they gathered flags for matts with in that tract of Land; But since
> those Indians were conquered that lived att Akkobauk the Shinocut
> bounds went to the river Pehikkonuk where the Indians catched
> Alewives: And the shinokuk Indians had the drowned Deere as theirs
> one this side the sayd River and one beare ssome years since: And
> the old Squaw Said by the token shee eat some of it Poyinting to her
> teeth: And that the skin and flesh was brought to Shinnocut as ak-
> knowledging their right to it to a saunk squaw then living there who
> was the old Mantaukut Sachems sister: And first wife to chekkanow.

The testimony identified political authority over land in terms of women, and women had the knowledge to best explain claims to specific tracts of land.[43]

These women also distinguished tracts of land based on women's work and leadership, naming Quashawam's aunt as the former authority over it. The gathering of reeds to make mats for wigwams, traditionally women's work, defined both the use and the boundaries of Aquebogue lands in earlier times. Villagers signified their "conquest" through honorary gifts to a woman, a sunksquaw in her own right and a leader tied to important

43. Deposition, Oct. 18, 1667, in Gardiner, Baker, and Osborne, eds., *Records of the Town of East-Hampton*, I, 260–261 ("two old," 260, "that formerly," 260–261, "in those tymes," 261). For a similar document dated the day before and signed by women named Aquabacack and Impeagwam, see Hedges, Pelletreau, and Foster, eds., *First Book of Records of the Town of South-ampton*, 159–160.

regional sachems by blood and marriage. Through tribute in the form of products of the hunt, such as deer caught by being driven into the water or the occasional bear, Aquebogue villagers affirmed new ties of authority to Quashawam's father's sister and through her, the Shinnecock. The village signified its political and military subjugation by symbolically acknowledging the rights, within recognized geographical bounds, of a female outsider. Thus, the new context of increasing conflict among expansive polities over territory influenced not only women's use of the land as farmers and gatherers but also women's authority over land as regional leaders. The network of relationships that gave women rights to land concentrated authority in the hands of specific sunksquaws.[44]

When these women testified about Aquebogue lands, they spoke about matters at once deeply personal and tied to wider colonial realities. The elder woman took the occasion to reaffirm her own authority to her English questioners by indicating that she, too, had eaten of these ritual gifts. For her, the questions had an immediacy that stemmed from her own status within village and regional politics. In addition, the authority of the unnamed sunksquaw remained connected, in the deponents' minds, to her intimate ties to kin as a sister and a wife. Yet, the larger context of the interview, indeed the very reason why Southampton had any interest in the question at all, was the validity of various land purchases by settlers, Dutch and English alike, across Long Island. Competing purchasers, both towns and individuals, contested the legality of opponents' claims by questioning the rights of different Native American sellers. Southampton had a vested interest in finding that the Shinnecock held the right to sell particular tracts, even if the people living there were Aquebogue. Increasing pressure for resources with the coming of colonization made women leaders' ties to land of both immediate and imperial concern.

With the death of her parents and brother in the early 1660s, Quashawam inherited this especially broad web of intervillage associations, and her role as sunksquaw gave her intimate ties to land throughout the region. During her brief years of influence before her own death around 1666, Quashawam attempted to use her intervillage connections to maintain her peoples' precarious position among competing polities. Local English residents looked

44. Tails or fins of beached whales or eagle hatchlings found in the nest played a similar tribute role in other instances on Long Island. Such gifts had a ritual political function, but their economic value should not be underestimated, especially from the 1670s onward as whale oil became a major export product; see Hedges, Pelletreau, and Foster, eds., *First Book of Records of the Town of Southampton*, 157.

to Quashawam to act as the primary liaison and cultural broker between the Montauk and the settlers, just as her father had before her. Indeed, the English so valued what they understood as the pro-English faction her father represented that they tried to secure her authority within the region by a written contract designating her as the primary leader of both the Montauk and Shinnecock. In contrast, Dutch authorities at New Amsterdam hesitated to even name Quashawam as a leader, preferring to do their business with other kinship networks. The divergent responses to Quashawam's leadership reveal the complicated interplay between cultural expectations and the political necessities of settlement at the meeting point of European empires and indigenous polities. The complex ties of clan, community, and authority that placed women in influential positions became inseparable from the larger international context, as Native American people and villages redefined themselves within a new economic and political system.[45]

The increasing imbrication of local Algonquian networks and the new colonial context is starkly illustrated in a February 1664 contract signed by the "great Sunk squa Quashawam" in agreement with four representatives of the Shinnecock, witnessed by four "English of Southampton." The contract makes clear that Quashawam already acted as a recognized leader among the Montauk people. In return for the Shinnecock's recognition of her as "their supreme" and their willingness to "pay her all honour according to the custom of the Indians," Quashawam promised to protect them from attack by her people. The "chiefe English namely the authority" had the power to oversee any violations of the agreement. In addition, should her own people fail to "pay tribute to Quashawam, true heyre of their master Wyandanch," the Shinnecock and English promised to use force on her behalf to "cause them . . . to pay their obedience in every respect." The notion that leaders had the right to force obedience from their people was wholly alien to local Algonquian concepts of governance, along with the very idea of a written

45. John A. Strong has argued that Quashawam was "appointed" by the English, with the threat of military intervention to back up their choice, but it is important to keep in mind that Quashawam would have been an influential voice in Montauk affairs, based on her own kin and marital relationships, even without English support. Her agreement with the English followed from, rather than caused, her increasing importance as other members of leading kin groups died in the smallpox epidemics; see Strong, "The Imposition of Colonial Jurisdiction over the Montauk Indians of Long Island," *Ethnohistory*, XLI (1994), 565. For another argument that the English "appointed" Quashawam that also takes account of her "diplomatic skill" thereafter, see Lara M. Strong and Selcuk Karabag, "Quashawam: Sunksquaw of the Montauk," *Long Island Historical Journal*, III (1991), 189–204 ("appointed," 195, "diplomatic," 197).

contract as the basis for power. Although Wyandanch had been an influential sachem, the statement that he was the "master" of the Montauk drew on English ideas of leadership, not Native ones. These and other elements of the agreement suggest that Quashawam's leadership reflected the realities of colonization as much as her place within the intimate networks of the Montauk and Shinnecock.[46]

Quashawam was not simply a tool in the hands of English land purchasers, however. She also made use of colonial authority for her own purposes. Like Oratam of Hackensacky, she worked to secure the continuing role of her own intervillage kin as the primary political intermediaries on Long Island. Her agreement with the English in Southampton also stipulated "that after the death of Quashawam, Awansamawge her unchles son have the sole power, and after his decease hee not having an heyre male, to the son of Corchaug Sachem. And after his death to Ponoqt son of Sasagatacco whoe is the meantime to bee looked upon as a Sachem. And for want of heyres male from him, to the children of Quashawam, and for want of ishue from them to the nearest of blood to Wyandank then to bee found." The wording and notions of power expressed in the agreement mixed English concepts of inheritance descending to "heirs male" with Algonquian notions of kinship and leadership. Despite the presence of such English norms as entailed estates and inherited authority, the Algonquian recognition of matrilineages, lateral kin, and the intertwined families of those in leadership attest to the continuity of Montauk practices. Quashawam's agreement shows that ties of authority, based on gender and family, had become thoroughly interwoven with the networks of power that crisscrossed among indigenous and immigrant villages of multiple cultures, and, through this contract, she got English negotiators to name and recognize the authority of her kin.[47]

Quashawam's agreement also represents a clever attempt to employ English legal systems to preserve her people's power within the context of colonization by English and Dutch settlers. She took the opportunity that day to empower "her ancient and great friend John Scott to examine and demand and sue" for payment "for all lands on Long Island bought and not paid for and on the Islands adjacent possessed by English or Dutch." Scott, then, had the legal authority to take Native complaints of squatting into court. Quashawam's empowerment certainly exemplifies one of the earliest

46. Treaty, Feb. 11, 1663, in Henry P. Hedges, Wm. S. Pelletreau, and Edward H. Foster, eds., *The Second Book of Records of the Town of Southampton. . . .* (Sag-Harbor, N.Y., 1877), 36–37 (this would have been Feb. 21, 1664, following Dutch dating).

47. Ibid., 36–37.

attempts by Native Americans to turn the colonizers' court systems to the advantage of Native inhabitants. However, John Scott also had the power "to sell all lands not already sold." Presumably that referred only to the lands on which the colonists had already encroached. Yet, did Quashawam really intend that Scott would have the power to settle her people's land disputes "for ever"? The English actors that day had their own agendas; Quashawam, like her father, proved willing to sell land—particularly ground inhabited by tributary villages—to settlers in exchange for military alliance. Establishing a "legal" basis for Quashawam to sell acreage that lay far beyond her hometown of Montauk fit with English plans for expansion and personal enrichment. Both Quashawam and colonial authorities used one another to pursue their own ends by mixing colonial authority and local intimate networks.[48]

The New Netherland government lacked the Hamptons settlers' strong incentive to recognize Quashawam's authority over land. In part, their refusal to do so might help explain why Quashawam made the contract with Scott. In January 1664, less than one month before Quashawam's written agreement with the Shinnecock and the English, Dutch officials met with two Long Island sachems who complained of bullying at the hands of the settlers at Vlissing (Flushing), a largely ethnically English town under the government at Manhattan. The written record carefully included the names of the two male Native leaders present that day, Tapausagh and Rompsicka. Perhaps the most important person involved, however, was a "wildin" who went unnamed and did not appear before the colony officials. Tapausagh reported that he and "the woman" had been summoned before three English leaders from Vlissing who attempted to coerce them into selling lands that had been in dispute between settlers and local villagers for the past six years. According to Tapausagh, "the woman" claimed that "she indeed . . . wanted to sell a part of the Land that the English possessed" but that she never intended to sell it "altogether." The English insisted that they wanted the land "altogether." By coming before the New Amsterdam officials, Tapausagh and Rompsicka acted as her envoys, suggesting that the woman was

48. Empowerment, Feb. 11, 1663, in Hedges, Pelletreau, and Foster, eds., *Second Book of Records of the Town of Southampton*, 37–38 (quotations) (this would have been Feb. 21, 1664, following Dutch dating). Quashawam's role here parallels, in some aspects, the indigenous women studied by Clara Sue Kidwell, who acted as mediators in ways that "led finally to the loss of Indian land" but did so for motives that were determined by their own cultures; see Kidwell, "Indian Women as Cultural Mediators," *Ethnohistory*, XXXIX (1992), 97–107 (quotation, 97). Quashawam's actions could also be interpreted as protecting the land around Montauk while sacrificing the land of other, subsidiary, villages.

an important sunksquaw. Stuyvesant, however, simply reminded Tapausagh that the land had already been sold by his father in 1639 and again by himself in 1656. The unnamed woman, then, saw her entire role in the conflict dismissed by the New Netherland authorities, who instead chose to recognize a different kinship network, one that validated previous Dutch purchases.[49]

Ironically, the dismissal came despite the Long Island Algonquians' attempt to use the negotiation as an opportunity to cement their relationship with New Amsterdam. With Sara Kierstede helping to translate, Tapausagh and Rompsicka informed the Dutch that the residents of Vlissing had purported that three English ships were on their way to New Netherland with the intent to "chase the Dutch altogether from the land, and Stuyvesant, too." The two envoys added that the English asserted "that all the land was theirs." They cautioned that the English threatened to kill Stuyvesant unless he kept quiet, in which case he would be allowed to remain in his home and live "like any other man." Tapausagh and Rompsicka's words, offered partly as the woman's intermediaries, were intended to serve as a dire warning.[50]

Although the ships would not sail for several more months, Tapausagh and Rompsicka reported very accurate information about the stance of English Long Islanders. Just three days after Tapausagh and Rompsicka spoke in New Amsterdam, ethnically English towns under Dutch rule, such as Middleburgh (now Newton, N.Y.), declared allegiance to Charles II and promised to back their words with action, saying they hated to see "his magistys rights usurped by the Hollanders: to the great scandall of government and discoragment of his magistys hopfull plantation which we will for the futter defend as Englishe men just propryetours and loyall subyects with our lives and fortunes." The overtures of the two Algonquian envoys came at a desperate time for Dutch rule in the mid-Atlantic region, as authority on Long Island began to disintegrate. Their information, linked with the unnamed sunksquaw's complaint about encroachment by English settlers

---

49. Minutes, Jan. 7, 1664, NYCM, X, pt. 3, 7–8, NYSA (quotations). For a translation of the record that precedes the 1911 fire (which has obscured the names of Tapausagh and Rompsicka), see *DRCHNY*, XIV, 540. O'Callaghan gives their names as "*Tapausagh,* Sachem or Chief of the *Long Island* Indians and *Rompsicka,* alias Capt. *Lambert.*" For an analysis of the life of Rompsicka / Suscaneman, see Robert S. Grumet, "Suscaneman and the Matinecock Lands, 1653–1703," in Grumet, *Northeastern Indian Lives,* 116–139. For earlier evidence of the dispute between Marsepingh and English villagers, see Letter, Apr. 3, 1660, NYCM, IX, 136, NYSA (owing to damage, see *DRCHNY,* XIV, 460); Letter, May 13, 1660, NYCM, IX, 250, NYSA; Petition, Apr. 13, 1662, NYCM, X, pt. 1, 117, NYSA; Minutes, June 23, 1663, NYCM, X, pt. 2, 152, NYSA.

50. Minutes, Jan. 7, 1664, NYCM, X, pt. 3, 7–8, NYSA.

at Vlissing, shows that Long Island Algonquian leaders sought to convince Stuyvesant that New Amsterdam villagers and Native Long Island villagers shared a common interest in blocking the expansion of the English villagers among them.[51]

By tying their information to their report of the unnamed woman's struggles to hold on to Long Island ground, Tapausagh and Rompsicka cleverly sought to link Algonquian problems with land-hungry English villagers to Stuyvesant's own. These Long Island leaders continued to treat settler villages as distinct political actors, just as Wyandanch had in the 1630s, but Stuyvesant saw the matter differently. In his hierarchical idea of colonial authority, Vlissing was a Dutch town regardless of its English inhabitants. The oversight of New Netherland's government made the town Dutch, and he was loath to negate the validity of the land purchases that delineated Dutch territory. In doing so, he would have recognized a female sunksquaw's power, legitimating any sales she had made to other settlers affiliated with Connecticut. In the end, Tapausagh, Rompsicka, and the sunksquaw they spoke for understood the politics of Long Island's ethnically diverse villages better than Stuyvesant did. Despite New Netherland's official jurisdiction over Vlissing, Quaker residents allied with the Rhode Island general meeting had a history of personal conflict with the religiously intolerant Stuyvesant, making their allegiance to Dutch hierarchy weak. In spite of the clear danger posed by English settlers, Stuyvesant did nothing to mitigate the claims of the Vlissing residents to the Algonquians' land "altogether." The two Long Island envoys failed to form an anti-English alliance with Dutch authorities, and, within days, the settlements on western Long Island began to drift from Stuyvesant's grasp forever.[52]

The woman who stood behind this attempt to form a Dutch-Algonquian alliance was almost certainly Quashawam. Although she was only one of many Algonquian women leaders on Long Island—women called Pamet-

51. Declaration, Feb. 4, 1663, *Town Minutes of Newtown, 1656–1688*, Transcriptions of Early Town Records of New York, I (New York, 1940), 53 (quotation) (this would be Feb. 14, 1664, following Dutch dating). On previous attempts by ethnically English Long Island villages to defy Dutch authority, see Martha Dickinson Shattuck, "An Uneasy Alliance: The Dutch and English on Long Island," in Funk and Shattuck, eds., *Beautiful and Fruitful Place*, II, 167–172.

52. John Bowne, Diary, 1649–1677, B. V. Sec. B., NYHS; Account Book, John Bowne, 1649–1703, Bowne Family Papers, Rare Books and Mss. Div., NYPL. For conflicts with Long Island towns dating from the 1650s, see Simon Middleton, "Order and Authority in New Netherland: The 1653 Remonstrance and Early Settlement Politics," *WMQ*, 3d Ser., LXVII (2010), 31–68. On Stuyvesant, Vlissing, and religious intolerance, see Evan Haefeli, *New Netherland and the Dutch Origins of American Religious Liberty* (Philadelphia, 2012).

sechs, Weany, Goabes, "Mandush his daughter," and Impeagwam all took part in Montauk and Shinnecock land negotiations with the Hamptons in the 1660s—Quashawam held a particularly important position, given the deaths of so many leaders and high-status villagers from smallpox and other diseases in the first four years of the 1660s. In addition, she cited ties of kin with many of Long Island's important sachems, including Tapausagh, explaining that "those Sachems . . . were kindred to [Tapausagh] and to her father and mother, and they had an interest in the land above said but passed it over to her father for him to dispose of and to give them . . . part of the pay he received of the English." Tapausagh had been forced to recognize Wyandanch's authority in some negotiations and land sales. Rompsicka, the other representative to meet with the Dutch that day, had kinship ties to Tapausagh and, therefore, lateral connections to Quashawam. Quashawam, in other words, had ties of kinship to Tapausagh, a special relationship with the English that might have given her access to key intelligence, and exceptional status as Wyandanch's daughter. Thus, Quashawam is the most likely candidate to have been the unnamed "wildin" dismissed by the New Netherland government in 1664. The rebuff offered her by New Netherland leaders, followed by the daily erosion of Dutch authority, explains why she was driven to consolidate her ties to the English shortly thereafter in the contact witnessed by the Hamptons settlers.[53]

Assuming that Quashawam was the woman Tapausagh and Rompsicka spoke for that day puts her leadership in a new light. Overtures to the Dutch government at Manhattan represented an attempt to settle land claims without having to empower Scott or to rely so heavily on the patronage of the Hamptons settlers. If Quashawam was the unnamed woman under discussion, it would suggest that she had legitimacy as a regional leader and that her power did not depend on English contracts or English threats of force. Vlissing lay far to the west of Montauk. As a leader at the western end of Long Island, Tapausagh had strong cultural and political allegiances with Munsee villages in the Hudson Valley in addition to his ties reaching east-

53. Hedges, Pelletreau, and Foster, eds., *First Book of Records of the Town of Southampton*, 167–169 ("Mandush," 169); Hedges, Pelletreau, and Foster, eds., *Second Book of Records of the Town of Southampton*, 27; Pelletreau, ed., *Records of the Town of Smithtown*, 16–17 ("those Sachems," 17); Gardiner, Baker, and Osborne, eds., *Records of the Town of East-Hampton*, I, 172–174. For Tapausagh's family tree, see Grumet, *Munsee Indians*, 21. For Wyandanch in land transactions, see Deed, Aug. 17, 1658, in Street, ed., *Huntington Town Records*, 16–18, Testimony, Nov. 2, 1667, 90–91. For a brief analysis of the power struggles between Tapausagh and Wyandanch, see Grumet, *Munsee Indians*, 98–100. On Rompsicka's ties, see Grumet, "Suscaneman," in Grumet, *Northeastern Indian Lives*, 121–122.

ward, and he was recognized by the Dutch as sachem of "Marsepingh and Rechkawyck." The willingness of Tapausagh and Rompsicka to defer to the authority of a woman from the other end of Long Island supports the image of Quashawam as a sunksquaw rising to regional importance, even before the Shinnecock signed a document to that effect.[54]

However, the refusal of the Dutch government to accept Quashawam as a potential ally made her course of action clear. Her people's future would depend on the ties of power she formed, and Scott was a rising influence willing not only to recognize but confirm and support her own kin and village. Indeed, it would be Scott who would be credited with the English takeover of Long Island in the summer of 1664. In September, a Dutch diplomat in England reported hearing from a captain of a tobacco ship that Long Island "was taken by the English through one Capt. Scott, from the Hollanders with a good number of people pressed upon the Island." In the wake of her failed overtures to New Netherland authorities, Quashawam picked a powerful ally in John Scott. Viewing her as the female leader mentioned by Tapausagh and Rompsicka shows the complicated web of diplomacy she negotiated.[55]

Dutch officials' refusal to deal with Quashawam might have reflected European cultural attitudes that deemed politics as the province of men. After all, the Esopus matrons Oratam accompanied to the council chamber to make peace found their status largely ignored when the council chose instead to send envoys to treat with male sachems upriver. That the Esopus and Wappinger women, like the woman on Long Island, went unnamed by the recording secretary signals a changing context for sunksquaws and matrons in the seventeenth-century mid-Atlantic. The failure of colonial representatives to recognize a woman's name or influence placed her in a bind. Women leaders had important roles to play in their own communities, but surviving in the new colonial context required forming diplomatic, political, and personal ties with the newcomers. Quashawam and the Esopus women found themselves forced back on their own resources because of their inability to forge such bonds with Dutch functionaries. Their sex made it difficult for them to extend their networks of power across the cultural divide.

54. Treaty, Mar. 6, 1660, NYCM, IX, 118–122, NYSA (quotation). Grumet describes Tapausagh as "one of the most widely known Indian culture brokers of his time"; see Grumet, *Munsee Indians*, 20. For Tapausagh's earlier diplomatic ties to New Netherland, see Otto, *Dutch-Munsee Encounter*, 147.

55. Ambassador van Gogh to States General, Sept. 12, 1664, State Papers, Foreign, Holland, Sept.–Oct. 1664, SP84/172, fol. 193, National Archives, Kew, England (quotation). For payment of those pressed on Long Island, see Minutes, Dec. 13, 1664, in Hoadly, ed., *Records of the Colony or Jurisdiction of New Haven*, 550.

Such exclusion, in turn, privileged the status of male leaders who stepped into the void. Esopus sachems who finally treated for peace and men like Tapausagh and Rompsicka who spoke before the colony council gained the power that came from face-to-face interactions and personal connections, power that was reinforced in their own villages as they became the ones who told of successful treaties or distributed the wampum and other gifts received from colonial officials. Cross-cultural ties thus influenced the ties of authority within Native villages to the detriment of women's political power. English settlers, too, favored treating with men and tended to conceive of political authority as a predominantly male domain. Such attitudes affected English interactions with female sachems just across the sound in the wake of King Philip's War. Despite these cultural views, English settlers on Long Island acknowledged the political importance of individual women when doing so benefited their aspirations to acquire land. Quashawam's predicament might say more about competing colonial authorities' interests in solidifying their colony's power and property by recognizing or rejecting specific Native intimate networks than about abstract European gender norms.[56]

Colonial authorities' varied responses to Quashawam shaped at once the strength of colonial land claims and the strength of her political networks. Her life demonstrates the complicated interface between intimate ties and imperial influence in the 1660s. Uncovering the relationships behind her actions reveals the nature of power at this early modern cultural meeting point and suggests that in the seventeenth century territorial and political ambitions alike often rested on a combination of intimate and imperial connections. Long Island's indigenous villagers sought to balance competing expansive polities by relying on their immediate network of intervillage bonds. The desire to form close associations directly between village leaders guided the diplomacy both of Quashawam and of her predecessors and fellow sachems and sunksquaws. In turn, competing colonial claims to Long Island territory in the 1660s rested in part on the recognition of specific Algonquian intimate networks and the ties to land these networks gave sachems and sunksquaws. An investigation of Quashawam's role in Algonquian-Dutch-English Long Island land disputes in the 1660s shows that networks of relationships offered access to subtle and flexible forms

56. Ann Marie Plane, "Putting a Face on Colonization: Factionalism and Gender Politics in the Life History of Awashunkes, the 'Squaw Sachem' of Saconet," in Grumet, *Northeastern Indian Lives*, 140–165. Awashunkes, another sunksquaw like Quashawam, eventually used her relationship with the English to uphold her authority among her people in factional disputes.

of power that individuals and colonial authorities both strove to employ. The willingness or refusal of imperial forces to recognize these networks and powerful actors within them influenced the options available to local villagers. Quashawam's actions, and English and Dutch authorities' use or rejection of the power inherent in her intimate networks, created a climate on Long Island in the 1660s where English influence grew while Dutch influence quickly drained away. By refusing to link the fate of the colony with that of Quashawam's network of power, Dutch officials lost a potential ally just as the English ships finally sailed into view.

Lydia van Dyck de Meyer and Hillegond Megapolensis van Ruyven

With Quashawam's contract and the defection of the Long Island settler towns, the days of Dutch administration in the greater Hudson Valley were rapidly coming to a close. When the much-rumored frigates arrived at Manhattan in August, the handover of the colony likely seemed inevitable to many. One final episode, however brief, speaks still further to the importance of intimate networks in shaping imperial power on the ground, even as the colony transitioned from Dutch to English rule. The incident has not only been forgotten, it was barely even acknowledged at the time. Indeed, "unacknowledgement," as it were, was a central part of the incident. In the tense final days of WIC administration, as questions of imperial authority hung in the balance, the ability to act without attracting attention represented a key asset. Intimate networks offered individual actors and even colonial officials access to forms of influence that operated subtly and almost invisibly as people sought to negotiate the gaps in imperial power. At the moment of greatest danger, political figures turned to their intimate networks to stake claims on settlers' behalf. The actions of two women from within New Netherland's most powerful social webs reveal how intimate networks proved ultimately more durable than colonial regimes. Lydia van Dyck de Meyer and Hillegond Megapolensis van Ruyven took matters into their own hands at a critical juncture in New Netherland's final hours, drawing on their powerful connections as they sought to guide settler society smoothly from Dutch to English administration.

Lydia de Meyer and Hillegond van Ruyven both occupied important places at the intersection of influential familial and local connections. Just like Sara Kierstede, these two women had ties linking them in multiple ways to powerful members of New Netherland's social, religious, and political worlds. Both women were the daughters of crucial members of the founding generation of New Netherland's elite, and both married men who were influential colonial leaders in their own right. To understand who they were and how they came to be actors within their social networks requires grasping the nature of their personal connections.

Both women were born in the Netherlands—Lydia in Utrecht and Hillegond in the North Holland town of Pancras. Lydia's father, Hendrick van Dyck, migrated to the colony by 1641, where he served as an ensign of the WIC. From the beginning, Van Dyck established powerful alliances with colony leaders, asking Director Kieft and the *fiscael,* or colony prosecutor, Cornelis Teroyken to serve as two of the witnesses for the baptism of his son, Cornelis, in March 1642. Van Dyck played a critical role in Kieft's brutal military action against Munsee villages in the lower Hudson Valley in 1643. After going back to Holland for a time in the mid-1640s, he returned to the Hudson Valley in 1646 as part of the entourage of the newly appointed governor, Peter Stuyvesant. He went on to act as a member of the colony council and as the colony prosecutor in the 1640s and 1650s. Though Lydia's father had a tempestuous relationship with both Kieft and Stuyvesant, he undoubtedly remained a member of the colony elite. Hillegond grew up in a similarly prominent household. As a young child, Hillegond joined her parents and at least three siblings when the family migrated to the Hudson Valley in 1642. Her father, Johannes Megapolensis, became the minister of the upriver community of Rensselaerswijk and lived on the front lines of cultural contact with Mohawk traders, eventually publishing an important account of his ethnographic observations. After heading the upriver congregation for six years, Megapolensis moved his family south to New Amsterdam, where he acted as the leading religious official in the capital town for the rest of the Dutch period. Thus, from their earliest days as child migrants in the colony, both Lydia van Dyck and Hillegond Megapolensis had connections to the New Amsterdam elite.[57]

As they became young women, Lydia and Hillegond expanded their networks of intimate connections further through marriage with high-status settler men. Hillegond married Cornelis van Ruyven in 1654. Her husband,

57. Samuel S. Purple, ed., *Records of the Reformed Dutch Church in New Amsterdam and New York: Marriages from 11 December 1639, to 26 August 1801,* Collections of the New-York Genealogical and Biographical Society, I (New York, 1890), 19; Johannes Megapolensis, "Kort ontwerp, vande Mahakuase Indianen. . . . ," in *Beschrijvinghe van Virginia, Nieuw Nederlandt, Nieuw Engelandt, en d' Eylanden Bermudes, Berbados, en S. Christoffel. . . .* (Amsterdam, 1651); Minutes, Nov. 18, 1642, in *Council Minutes,* I, 174; Evans, *Baptisms,* 13; Jacobs, *New Netherland,* 486.

as secretary of the colony council from 1653 to 1664 and council member from 1659 to 1664, was privy to every major discussion and decision of the colony government during the last decade of Dutch rule. Less than a year after Hillegond, Lydia van Dyck also married. Her husband, Nicolaes de Meyer, originally came from Germany but, by the time of their marriage in 1655, lived as a well-established trader, merchant, brewer, and member of the settler society in New Amsterdam. After his marriage, De Meyer continued to rise socially, serving as a member of the New Amsterdam municipal council in 1664. Marriage for both Hillegond and Lydia placed them even more securely at the heart of New Amsterdam society.[58]

Not only were Lydia and Hillegond connected to several influential families by birth and by marriage, the baptismal registry shows that they had fictive kin ties to many more. Between their marriage and the end of Dutch rule in 1664, Lydia and Nicolaes de Meyer baptized four children in New Amsterdam. In addition to strengthening their familial bonds by asking the children's maternal grandparents and aunt to act as witnesses, the couple chose several prominent men to act as godfathers. Willem Beeckman, a member of municipal government and an orphanmaster during the 1650s, witnessed for little Johannes, the couple's firstborn son, in 1656. Johannes Nevius, the secretary for and former member of the city council, witnessed their daughter Deborah's baptism in the summer of 1664, as did Skipper Pieter Reyersen. Both Lydia and Nicolaes stood as witnesses for the children of their friends, relations, and neighbors in the New Amsterdam congregation. By 1664, one or the other of them had witnessed for nine children listed in the baptismal registry, showing the extent to which they were trusted by fellow New Amsterdammers.[59]

Hillegond and Cornelis acted as godparents even more frequently, together and separately witnessing for sixteen children between 1650 and 1664. Although Hillegond's father, Reverend Johannes Megapolensis, served as the sole witness at the baptism of their only son, Johannes, in 1655, their network of godchildren tied them to numerous burgher households, including those belonging to leaders of the military (ensign Dirk Smith and lieutenant Daniel Litscho), municipality (city councilmen Jacobus Backer and Jeronimus Ebbing), merchant class (Maria Varleth and Margriet Hardenbroeck), and colony (councillor Johannes de Decker and Margrietje Stuyvesant).

58. "Nicolaes van Holstyn" was taxed thirty guilders in 1655, establishing him in the upper-middling ranks of New Amsterdam's economic pecking order; see Tax list, Oct. 12, 1655, CMNA, I, 405, NYCMA (microfilm); Jacobs, *New Netherland*, 332, 338.

59. Evans, *Baptisms*, 22–80, esp. 73.

That numerous influential families asked them to witness for their children testifies to the trust placed in them. In both cases, the women of the family did the most to form these intimate fictive kin ties. Hillegond witnessed eleven times, whereas her husband only witnessed seven, and Lydia witnessed eight children to her husband Nicolaes's one. Intimate networks that Lydia and Hillegond inherited, married into, and actively created located them squarely in the colony's elite.[60]

As formal avenues of political authority became paralyzed in the face of the English ships' arrival, the indirect and latent political power inherent in social networks like Lydia's and Hillegond's suddenly seemed very attractive. When the frigates anchored off of Manhattan in late August 1664, New Netherland's future as a Dutch colony looked grim. Both officials and settlers had long realized that the colony's towns lacked defenses against any sustained attack, and New Netherland's English towns on Long Island had been refractory to symbols of Dutch authority for some time. With the appearance of an English show of force, their defection was immediate and complete. The population of the neighboring English colonies had long ago far surpassed New Netherland, and no New Netherland settlers voiced any illusions about their ability to fight off invading English troops. Finally and most critically, there was little if any hope of military support from the United Provinces or the WIC. The company had grown increasingly frustrated with the passing years over the colony's inability to yield it a profit. WIC officials regarded New Netherland as a low priority compared to sugar plantation colonies in the Caribbean. If any possibility remained for New Netherland to survive as a Dutch colony, it existed only at the bargaining table at the close of hostilities. New Netherland's settler community by and large recognized that an English offer of surrender on terms constituted the best chance for life—and the economy they relied on—to continue as they knew it.[61]

However, Governor Stuyvesant did not immediately voice that opinion. On the contrary, he first promised to fight at any cost and refused to discuss conditions of surrender with Richard Nicholls, commander of the English ships and future governor of New York. In his letters to Nicholls, Stuyvesant insisted on the legitimacy of Dutch claims and asked for time to hear directly from England. Whether he thought his position tenable or

60. Evans, *Baptisms*, 22–80. All four would go on to witness more children after the English takeover. Dirk Smith's name appears as Dirck Smidt or Smit in the baptismal records.

61. The individual English burghers of New Amsterdam were not eager to support the Dutch cause either; see the Petition for neutrality by John Lawrence, Aug. 18, 1664, NYCM, X, pt. 3, 297, NYSA.

whether he simply felt that as a WIC employee he had no other choice but to publicly oppose capitulation is open to question. Some soldiers later maintained that his belligerence had been all show and no substance. Nicholls, for his part, let Stuyvesant's letter go unanswered and insisted that he would only agree to talk if Stuyvesant made his intention to surrender explicit. With Stuyvesant uttering brave speeches and the council members trapped inside Fort Amsterdam working hard to bring him to his senses, someone had to negotiate with Nicholls.[62]

Lydia and Hillegond evidently decided that they were the ones best suited to solve the diplomatic paralysis. Their involvement in the handover negotiations went wholly unmentioned in official accounts and has been largely overlooked since. No doubt, that very invisibility provided them with the cover they needed to go behind enemy lines in the first place. Their sex was their strongest asset. Just as Sara appeared neutral in diplomatic talks because her sex had excluded her from office, Lydia and Hillegond walked across the no-man's-land between the fort and the English forces without violating any oaths of office. Unlike the men of their status and families, these women had never held office or served in the military and could thus travel and act without being much observed.[63]

Their actions attracted notice only because not everyone supported their intentions. In 1667, two former WIC soldiers stationed in New Amsterdam during the English attack testified regarding their frustration at not being allowed to fight and about their anger toward the "cowardly" New Netherlanders who had "sold them" to the English. The soldiers relayed that they had seen Hillegond van Ruyven and Lydia de Meyer leave the fort together during the siege. They reported that "the wife of Nicolas Meijer, free merchant there, having gone out of the fort with the aforementioned *Juffrouw* Ruyven, said, after she saw that the soldiers wanted to resist, now these lousy dogs want to fight, now they have nothing to lose from it, but we have our goods here, which we would surely lose thereby." One soldier added that "he saw that the secretary and Councilman van Ruyven had sent his wife after agreement [?] to the English, [and he] asked the aforementioned secretary what they, that is the government, intended, [and] to what end had

62. Peter Stuyvesant to Richard Nicholls, Sept. 2, 4, 1664, Colonial Office, CO 1/18, fols. 214–219v, National Archives. For a nice yet brief discussion of Nicholls and the transition to English rule, see Jacobs, *New Netherland,* 178–185.

63. Stuyvesant to Nicholls, Sept. 2, 4, 1664, Colonial Office, CO 1/18, fols. 214–219v, National Archives. Stuyvesant's correspondence mentions several male deputies but no female ones.

he sent his wife among the English and the same answered, that they had no gunpowder and the English were their friends." Shortly after the women's visit across enemy lines, a council of residents and colonial leaders presented Stuyvesant with English terms, and he finally empowered a group of New Amsterdammers to negotiate the peaceful handover.[64]

Lydia's and Cornelis's statements about the irrationality of resistance likely typified the reaction of many New Netherlanders to the prospect of an English takeover. Hillegond accorded with the views of her family when she crossed enemy lines to meet with the English. As per the frustrated soldiers' testimony, "the Ministers Megapolensis, father and son," had previously convinced Stuyvesant not to order the gunners to fire on the English frigates. Her husband, as colony secretary and a council member, had penned several reports over the previous two years about the impossibility of long-term defense and the unlikelihood of serious military support from the WIC. Lydia de Meyer's scolding of the belligerent soldiers probably epitomized the feelings of most New Netherlanders toward those too proud to consider surrender.[65]

Surely Lydia represented the views of her husband, Nicolaes de Meyer. As a member of New Amsterdam's governing and judicial council that year, De Meyer participated in the trial and sentencing of one Adam Onckelbagh for daring to back up his allegiance to the WIC with violence. Just as the colony was transitioning from Dutch to English rule, at the last court meeting before "New Amsterdam" began calling itself "New York," De Meyer and his colleagues heard a complaint against Onckelbagh. The local prosecutor alleged that he "had taken away bread and drink from the negro of the Heer Cornelis van Ruyven, which he was bringing to the aforementioned Heer van Ruyven's huysvrouw in Midwout [Long Island]." Not everyone, then, supported the women's decision to negotiate behind enemy lines. The fiscael further complained that Onckelbagh had beaten the unnamed African servant such that he had "two wounds in the head," which, the prosecutor observed, "in the present circumstances smacks of riot." Onckelbagh replied that he was "bound by Oath to ensure that there were no victuals sent over to

64. Testimony, Mar. 4, 1667, Not. Arch. 3191, 101–102, Not. H. Outgers, SA (quotations); my translation of this document relies on a typescript done by the late archivist Simon Hart. On the local council's presentation of Richard Nicholls's terms, see Peter Stuyvesant to Nicholls, Sept. 5, 1664, Colonial Office, CO 1/18, fol. 220v–221, National Archives.

65. Testimony, Mar. 4, 1667, Not. Arch. 3191, 101–102, Not. H. Outgers, SA (quotation). The governor and council had referred to the colony as "the almost sinking ship of New Netherland" just a few months before; see Minutes, Apr. 12, 1664, NYCM, X, pt. 3, 157–161, NYSA.

the enemy" and that the African had spoken to him confrontationally in any case. Since Lydia and Hillegond had crossed lines to negotiate with the English, Onckelbagh evidently saw the women and the English invaders as one and the same. Equating the wife of one of his judges with the enemy perhaps did not benefit his case; the court decided to fine him fifty guilders, arguing that his bad example "could have caused further calamities." Onckelbagh was the only New Netherlander who seems to have tried to interfere with Hillegond and Lydia's strategy of backdoor diplomacy, and De Meyer and the rest of the judicial council voted to punish such displays of loyalty to the lost WIC cause.[66]

Lydia and Hillegond's sex enabled them to leave the fort to meet with the English, and their extensive intimate networks with people in power made them trustworthy representatives in the eyes of elite Dutch settlers. Had their husbands, as representatives of the Dutch government, undertaken the negotiations, they would have exposed themselves to charges of cowardice or even mutiny. The English also would have seen them as speaking for the governmental bodies of which they were a part, potentially weakening their bargaining position by making clear the Dutch intention to capitulate. But women were far less threatening, especially a woman with a baby at her breast. Just two months before, Lydia and Nicolaes had baptized little Deborah, named for her maternal grandmother and witnessed by three honorable residents. It seems very unlikely Lydia would have traveled to Long Island without her. Those who knew Hillegond and Lydia (and many people knew Hillegond and Lydia) could be confident that betrayal was out of the question for two such known and trusted huysvrouwen. Yet these women's loyalty lay not with the WIC or Dutch imperial authority, as the soldiers rightly observed. Rather, it lay with their network of intimate connections reaching throughout the Hudson Valley. Their ties of family, friendship, and trade held their loyalty, and the two women helped ensure that, despite Stuyvesant's recalcitrance, those ties would survive the transition from Dutch to English administration.[67]

Indeed, their own personal networks of influence would flourish unabated in the days and years following the colony's formal capitulation. After

66. Court Minutes, Sept. 16, 1664, CMNA, IV, 448, NYCMA (microfilm) (quotations). For a foiled plot to attack Nicolaes de Meyer's house by Dutch soldiers, see Donna Merwick, *Stuyvesant Bound: An Essay on Loss Across Time* (Philadelphia, 2013), 116.

67. Evans, *Baptisms*, 73. An interesting question is whether linguistic capacity could have also shaped their selection as representatives, just as ability to speak Munsee led to Sara Kierstede's role. The documents do not indicate if either or both of these women spoke English.

penning a letter to the WIC that was half apology and half complaint, the New Amsterdam city council of which De Meyer was a member simply began writing "Jork" instead of "Amsterdam" at the top of the page, dated the entry twice to reflect the new calendar, and carried on as before. Lydia's husband went on to serve as an alderman in 1668. Hillegond's husband would serve multiple times as an alderman and also as deputy mayor to the new English city. Her father and brother kept baptizing the community's babies, and both women continued to act as witnesses for new settler children. This is not to say that things stayed the same; of course, change came in multiple forms in rapid succession as the Hudson Valley became quickly integrated into English overseas networks and ever-more English immigrants flooded into the region.[68]

Yet, in the late summer of 1664, intimate networks proved stronger than imperial polities. The strength of those networks came from their flexibility and their subtlety. Women like Lydia and Hillegond did not hold positions of political authority in New Netherland, but they had political capital nonetheless. The extensive personal, familial, and economic connections female and male settlers alike relied on to create colonial society channeled political power into networks of relationships. When the hour came that political authorities found themselves unable to act, hamstrung by hierarchical relationships of obedience to the governor and the company, political power flowed through intimate networks to empower these two settler women. Lydia van Dyck de Meyer and Hillegond Megapolensis van Ruyven became actors within their intimate networks, helping ensure that settler society glided smoothly from Dutch to English rule. In doing so, they demonstrated the importance of immediate relationships and social connections to the politics of empire in the early modern period.

Conclusion

Declaring themselves "your Honors' dutiful, distressed, and abandoned servants," the New Amsterdam municipal council undertook the painful task, in September 1664, of bringing their former employers at the WIC up to

---

They might well have, but, even if they did, many men in positions of power in the colony did, too. Thus it seems that they traveled to the English side, not because of any particular unique skill, but rather because of who they were.

68. For an exploration of the difficulties posed to ethnically Dutch settlers by the transition, see Donna Merwick, *Death of a Notary: Conquest and Change in Colonial New York* (Ithaca, N.Y., 1999).

date. Pointing to the bloodthirsty nature and overwhelming number of their English besiegers, the city councilmen bemoaned the lack of powder, soldiers, and promised reinforcements from Holland. They also had to admit that even while the New Netherland government stood firm, the people of the colony did not. "Because the farmers, of whom every third man was summoned, refused, we, along with the majority of the residents judged it necessary to remonstrate with our Lord Director General and Council" and urge them to capitulate. Evidently, the last-minute call for all hands on deck yielded few takers. The majority had watched the events of the politically complicated latter years of Dutch rule and realized that the final flutter of fortification sought by the city council meant little. In the face of the community's collective shrug, the councillors declared New Amsterdammers to be a "poor, dejected, and abandoned community" and signed off on the end of the Dutch era.[69]

Investigating the years and months preceding the handover reveals a series of interesting and perhaps unexpected names. Oratam, Sara, Quashawam, Lydia, and Hillegond all played a role in the myriad face-to-face negotiations and personal interactions that constituted politics in this complicated and contested region; and all of them became influential on the basis of their intimate networks—the series of overlapping immediate, familial, and personal relationships that gave them access to a particular kind of power. All of them, also, served as conduits through which politics coursed. These five people became important participants within their social networks, drawing on the trust and influence latent in their nexus of relationships to negotiate the changing realities of the 1650s and 1660s. Yet they also became critical actors within the politics of early modern empire, which in acknowledged and unacknowledged ways depended on the relationships and actions of many individuals.

As expansive polities competed for control on the ground in the Hudson Valley in the middle of the seventeenth century, individuals, villages, and colonial authorities turned to peoples' familial and social connections. To respond to the challenges of Dutch expansion in the 1650s and 1660s, Native leaders like Oratam and Quashawam relied on the dense web of kin and family that knit together the villages of the greater Hudson Valley. Oratam used immediate relationships among Munsee leaders and towns to achieve recognition in the eyes of the Dutch authorities with whom he sought to

69. New Amsterdam councillors to WIC Directors, Sept. 16, 1664, CMNA, IV, 452–454, NYCMA (microfilm).

form personal ties. Despite Director Kieft's hostility in the 1640s to this diffuse political system, by the 1660s, Dutch authorities worked with and through Oratam's sphere of influence. They refused to recognize Quashawam's intimate network, however, even though her kin and personal connections reaching out from Montauk allowed her to speak for a number of Long Island villages and even though her interpersonal ties with English villagers made her a force to be reckoned with. Dutch leaders' reluctance to support her January 1664 attempt to craft a united Dutch-Montauk response to expansive English claims left her with few options but to strengthen her ties with the English. The handover signaled the arrival of a new set of challenges. Quashawam's and Oratam's communities would face a novel onslaught of land pressure as nascent English colonies competed with one another and with established settlers for territory. Yet these two leaders ended the Dutch period with their homelands and kin networks intact, having successfully navigated the uncharted shoals that emerged during New Netherland's ebb tide. They both derived their power from similar sources and similarly negotiated the intertwining of the intimate and the imperial. The inclination or disinclination of colonial powers to acknowledge intimate networks affected the options available to women, men, and communities.

At the same time, the ability for power to remain unspoken when it operated through intimate networks was an important asset. Lydia de Meyer and Hillegond van Ruyven's journey across English-Dutch lines enabled Dutch settlers to try to preserve their social hierarchies even as the official hierarchies of Dutch colonial authorities froze and then shattered. They were able to speak because of the power and trust latent in their extensive webs of intimate connections among the elite of New Amsterdam society. Yet, they spoke safely because that power remained unofficial.

Sara Kierstede's extensive network of intimate and familial ties likewise rendered her trusted and familiar, even as her sex insulated her from the perception of arguing for or on behalf of colonial authorities. Her experience with the face-to-face interactions that were part of New Amsterdam's regional exchange networks gave her the skills she needed to hear and understand the concerns of sachems like Oratam. When power flowed through the latticework of personal connections, female sex offered a potential advantage. Women in this colony had the skills and experience needed to negotiate successfully; they cultivated extensive social and kinship relationships that gave them powerful connections; and they had the freedom to act independently from official structures that the men in their lives did not always possess. In this episode in the history of empires, women's place within gendered social circuits gave them key political positions. Intimate networks offered a subtle and flexible form of power that individuals and officials alike invoked to stake claims as expansive polities clashed.

The willingness of people and polities to recognize and employ those networks serves as a reminder of the complex interplay of the immediate and the imperial in this period. Intimacy and empire remained deeply intertwined in the last years of Dutch rule, just like they had been at the inception of Dutch colonial efforts in North America, and power traveled through intimate relationships in many directions. As multiple empires competed for power with one another and with Native peoples, intimate relationships played a crucial role. Studying official regulation of sexual interactions among subject people can only scratch the surface of the interaction of intimacies and empire. A wide range of intimate, familial, affective, and personal ties, including those within (not just between) communities, both created and reflected the influence of contending political entities along the early modern mid-Atlantic coast. Examining immediate relationships as a part of networks reveals the use and function of those individuals' personal associations. People's overlapping webs of ties channeled and shaped competing polities' claims to power; formal hierarchies of colonial governance were only part of the picture. At the same time, colonial powers' varying recognition of particular actors and networks molded the power and influence of those networks. In the context of contesting claims to power in the greater Hudson Valley, intimacy and empire blended inextricably through a complicated maze of personal ties.

Conclusion

The last months of 1664 were a dark time in the Netherlands. The country and the WIC faced the depredations of what would become the Second Anglo-Dutch War, including the capitulation of New Netherland. Plague ran rampant in the cities. Rising prices and hard times made life difficult for ordinary women and men on the streets and docks of Amsterdam, Rotterdam, and the other port towns. With their husbands' lives in danger, sailors' wives had little desire for a protracted fight. Finally, in December 1664, an English diplomat reported that in Rotterdam "the seamen fell into a great mutiny saying that they would not goe and ride this wintertime att Sea, but would stay where they were; Moreover yesterday the wives of the Seamen in Van Campen's Fleet, and others came in a very tumultuous way to the Admiralty house there demanding money in very high Termes and that otherwise they would pull downe their house." Because they felt its effects in personal terms, the men and women of the maritime community rated the price of continuing the colonial conflict with England very high.[1]

After decades of building and maintaining a transatlantic network that tied the Netherlands and the Hudson Valley together through both personal

1. George Downing to Henry Bennet, Dec. 13/23, 1664, State Papers, Foreign, Holland, Nov.–Dec. 1664, SP84/173, fol. 85, National Archives, Kew, England (quotation). On the early reverses and economic effects of this war, see Jonathan I. Israel, *Dutch Primacy in World Trade, 1585–1740* (Oxford, 1989), 270–279. For women's centrality to street protests and riots in the early modern Netherlands and for the importance of informal networks based on neighborhood and work, see Rudolf M. Dekker, "Women in Revolt: Popular Protest and Its Social Basis in Holland in the Seventeenth and Eighteenth Centuries," *Theory and Society,* XVI (1987), 337–362. On the plague epidemic that spread to London from Amsterdam and Rotterdam in the winter of 1663–1664, see Daniel Defoe, *A Journal of the Plague Year. . . . ,* ed. Louis Landa (Oxford, 1990), 1; *Hollandtze Mercurius, Vervatende de voornemste geschiedenissen, voor-gevallen in 't gantze Jaer 1664,* XV (Haarlem, 1665), 134, 193–194.

and economic connections, perhaps the maritime community decided, just like the settler community of New Amsterdam had three months before, that keeping the formal authority of the WIC alive through military means was not in their best interest. Though Dutch settlers would briefly retake the administration of the Hudson Valley colony from 1673 to 1674, by that time even the WIC had lost interest, signing the colony back over to the English at the close of hostilities in exchange for the more lucrative Suriname. With that, the sun set on the Dutch empire in North America.[2]

Although Dutch claims to the Hudson Valley did not endure, the surviving Dutch records reveal a great deal about the making of empire in the seventeenth-century Atlantic world. The English empire might have ultimately emerged as the stronger power, but Dutch sailors, traders, and settlers between 1609 and 1664 succeeded in building a web of connections to the Hudson Valley that proved both durable and expansive. They did so by using relationships to conquer the power of distance through intimacy. One of the central seeming tensions about early modern colonization—the conflict between the vast distances of cross-ocean or cross-cultural travel and the persistent centrality of face-to-face relationships in economic and social life—turns out not to be a tension at all. Rather, distance and intimacy were mutually constitutive, as mobility and the malleability of geographic and cultural distances supported the creation of widespread networks of immediate relationships.

Understanding how this colony worked starts with understanding these immediate relationships. People formed ties with one another, ties that

2. On changing Dutch depictions of the Atlantic from ones that encouraged the Dutch Republic to actively intervene in the West to ones that minimized the formal Dutch presence and "promoted a broadly internationalist view," see Benjamin Schmidt, "The Dutch Atlantic: From Provincialism to Globalism," in Jack P. Greene and Philip D. Morgan, eds., *Atlantic History: A Critical Appraisal* (Oxford, 2009), 166. In the East Indies, such changes reflected the growing ties individual merchants had outside the VOC. As merchants developed personal and economic networks with English principals, their interests lay less in promoting the formal monopolies of Dutch companies than in supporting an opening of trade, meaning that the demise of the VOC at the close of the eighteenth century stemmed from shifting patterns of networks; see Julia Adams, "Principals and Agents, Colonialists and Company Men: The Decay of Colonial Control in the Dutch East Indies," *American Sociological Review*, LXI (1996), 12–28. The merchants Adams studies functioned at a higher level than many of the small-scale traders, burghers, settlers, and sailors who participated in the Atlantic trade; yet, the growth of contact and trade with English settlers and merchants might have similarly shifted individual networks and interests away from the WIC in the Atlantic at a much earlier date. As Schmidt notes, the troubles of the WIC did not stop individual merchants in the later seventeenth century from participating in and profiting from Atlantic trade as the Dutch Atlantic was reconfigured along new lines.

could withstand separations for years. Moving around the ocean, whether voluntarily, like many Dutch travelers, or forcibly, like African migrants, threatened to break such ties irrevocably. Doubtless, sometimes ties were forever severed, especially for slaves who had no means to contact those left behind. Whatever new relationships a woman like Isabel Kisana van Angola made through marriage and her role as a godmother in New Amsterdam, family, kin, and clan ties from her life before her forced migration could never be resumed. But the human ability to form connections persisted, and for many people, even slaves, new relationships grew in place of those disrupted by travel. Through baptism, blacks and whites alike created fictive kin ties that, in day-to-day life, could help stand in for ties to kin and community back home. Mayken van Angola, for instance, spent her last days among friends and family, despite her decades of enslavement in a foreign land. People found, in their travels, partners in marriage, which gave them one of the primary tools they needed to function in their newly imperialized lives. Africans who married in New Amsterdam began building family and community once more and found a way to make their neighbors recognize the validity of their social ties. Young Amsterdammers who wed on the ships plying the Atlantic or on their arrival in Manhattan's harbor not only formed the beginnings of a *huysgezin,* or household, they also used travel to enhance their web of economic relationships. Though she had to fight for it with her brother-in-law in the courts, Maria Varleth looked to her marriage in the American colonies to build a place for herself in the Van Beeck family's international trade dynasty. Whatever the stress or damage done to people's relationships by the vast distances of Atlantic empire, the propensity to form attachments prevailed, and people once again came to find themselves surrounded by those with whom they had intimate ties. They put those ties to work to try to survive and to succeed as they negotiated the advent of transatlantic commerce.

Through these immediate relationships, people built webs that formed the basis for local life and the local economy in the colonial Hudson Valley. Out of the forced intimacy of the WIC slave house, African men and women forged intense connections with one another that persisted even as some began to carve out lives as farmers outside New Amsterdam. Ties of neighborliness and ties formed through work in the intimate spaces of whites' homes gave these Africans a foothold within wider settler society. These new local networks provided the structure for much of colonial society on the ground. Africans' webs of community afforded them with some means to resist and survive their precarious, colonized existence in New Amsterdam. For the men who managed to achieve half and then full freedom, their social and intimate ties offered them a place in settler society and made them valuable as an economically functional network, rather than simply as individuals worth a given amount on the international slave market. Yet, because they found a place in local society through their associations with others, they found themselves rooted to a particular social and economic position. And, as the African community discovered with the failed attempt to adopt little Cecilia, even that limited safety was not open to many. Social webs underpinned the colony's social hierarchies, rather than undermined them.

Social attachments also underlay developing lines of power within white society, as European settlers, too, wove their personal ties of marriage, family, kin, and neighborhood into ever-denser webs of community. Connections within and among families determined who was trusted and who remained an outsider. Women's centrality as cocreators of intimate ties of family, kin, and neighborhood meant that trusted women sometimes became influential players within local power structures. Elite women like Lydia van Dyck de Meyer and Hillegond Megapolensis van Ruyven discovered that their roles as mothers, godmothers, traders, and skillful face-to-face negotiators of tricky local economic networks gave them both the skills and the insider knowledge necessary to become actors in contested political realms. Though these privileged white women might at first glance seem to have little in common with the half-free women and men of the African community, all these people, in fact, shared a great deal. They all found their place in local society through webs of deeply personal ties. They also all helped define the structure of colonial society through the relationships that gave their daily experience meaning. Through the creation of networks, the most immediate of personal connections spread outward to form colonial life at the local level.

In ever-widening concentric circles, immediate ties reached out to shape connections throughout the region. Face-to-face and personal ties among settlers, between settlers and Native Americans, and within Native villages linked local networks together. These relationships, often formed through close contact in the intimate areas of the home or village, made it possible for a remarkably widespread exchange economy to develop. Local and personal webs also provided the basis for individuals on both sides of the cultural divide to become political actors. Ties of kin and clan, which anchored indigenous villages to the land, presented well-situated women and men, like Quashawam, with the standing and authority to participate in regional politics. These personal and local ties structured Native society in the mid-

Atlantic and came to structure relations with the colony as well, as power flowed within and among communities through these indigenous networks. Participation in the area's daily exchange networks could even give settler women like Sara Kierstede the skills to influence the complicated balance of power between the various peoples and polities in the mid-Atlantic region.

For all that personal webs shaped regional economics and politics, however, these local Native and settler webs did not meld in any fundamental way. Underneath it all, these webs consisted of people's individual connections to one another. True intimate relationships across cultural lines remained rare. Far more common, perhaps, were men like Nicolaes de Meyer, a man who invited indigenous traders into his home but instantly resorted to violence when he felt his huysgezin even unintentionally disrespected by his visitor. Families and communities stayed divided, even as face-to-face exchange brought people from immigrant and indigenous communities together daily.

Like a ripple spreading through water, the circle of personal ties reached yet farther, even across the Atlantic Ocean. Webs of immediate, local, and regional connections intertwined with associations stretching from the Hudson Valley to the Caribbean, Brazil, and Amsterdam. These transatlantic networks did a great deal of work, keeping finances moving, carrying furs to the Amsterdam market, and even giving rise to a maritime community that helped staff the ships of the WIC. Sustained through the constant movement of people, letters, and gossip, immediate interpersonal relationships formed chains that kept the Americas and Europe tightly joined. At the root of even these, the most far-reaching of New Netherland's social webs, were once again simply people, individual sailors, soldiers, shoemakers' wives, and maidservants who sailed the seas in crisscrossing patterns. The myriad names of travelers, rich and poor—the many Jans, Annas, Grietjes, and Johanneses—recorded repeatedly or fleetingly in Dutch records testify to the thousands of individuals who together sustained the small-scale and independent transatlantic economies that ran alongside the WIC. What they did on behalf of themselves and others built the transatlantic economy from the ground up. By looking after people's finances, providing credit, or conveying wages across the seas, they wove an intimate network that reached all the shores of the Atlantic.

All these ties sustained colonial efforts in North America throughout the era of Dutch rule. From the first years after Hudson's voyage in 1609, networks of face-to-face relationships made the infant fur trade possible and enabled European traders to survive (most of them, anyway). When settlers and slaves first arrived in Manhattan in 1624, they, too, would depend on a mesh of face-to-face interactions for everything from their food to their firewood to their currency. As intimate associations developed among this new immigrant population, the tiny settlement gradually became a colony dispersed throughout the Hudson and Delaware River valleys and along the mid-Atlantic coast. Immediate ties supported the development of communities and guided trade and diplomatic relations between indigenous and settler villages. As the region grew increasingly contested in the 1650s, the tangle of interpersonal relationships dictated where there was peace and where there was war. Even in 1664 as New Netherland transitioned to English rule, this tessellation of personal connections endured, continuing to shape life on the ground for Africans, Europeans, and Native Americans despite the change in administration.

Looking closely at the complicated mosaic formed by these ties and at the people who built them shows several things about the structure of society in the seventeenth-century Hudson Valley. The quality of the personal relationships that constituted these networks was important in constructing this early modern empire. Travelers and would-be traders in Amsterdam like Govert Loockermans and his "cousin" Seth Verbrugge appealed to family obligation and mutual dependencies in their contact with one another because they knew that intimate relationships held together the ties reaching across the ocean. Personal relationships, or the hope of forming them, motivated a portion of the journeys that served to keep cross-ocean connections alive. Hostility and friendship between Natives and newcomers shaped the nature of encounter in this region by maintaining distance even as trade brought people close to one another physically. Very specific interpersonal ties influenced the fates of the particular network of Africans at New Amsterdam, even when the destinies white authorities determined for them did not fit easily within larger Dutch racial politics and attitudes. Specific human interactions that defined deeply personal and individual relationships constituted empire in the greater Hudson Valley.

The Dutch colony also fundamentally depended on the extensive participation of women in several ways. Women not only engaged in the economic connections that made colony and empire possible, they helped build them at both the local and transatlantic levels. Whether they were poor servant women like Maddelena Michiels or Amsterdam women from the merchant class like Catharina Varleth, their important roles as builders of kin and community and their economic activities made them essential to the creation of this early modern Atlantic colony. And they used the connections they helped initiate to take advantage of new economic realities and opportunities. Women also participated in developing ties reaching deep into the North American continent. Both Native American and white women took part in key ways in the daily face-to-face exchange in furs and consumables taking place between indigenous and immigrant communities. Native women from Algonquian communities on Long Island and the Hudson River areas derived political power through their position within the weft of intimate, kin, clan, and village webs as well as through women's special ties to land. At the personal, local, regional, and transatlantic level, women played an essential role in shaping the Dutch colonial period on the mid-Atlantic coast.

In addition to women's activities in their own right, gendered relationships between women and men built a latticework of ties that made New Netherland function. The spousal tie, especially when one or both of the spouses set sail on the Atlantic Ocean, served as a crucial resource for families and others who fought to stay afloat personally and economically. Hollander Geertien Abrahamsz and her New Netherland husband Gerrit Jansz Klinckhamer built on their transatlantic marital relationship to move money across the ocean in ways neither of them could have done on their own, and in doing so provided a financial connection that other travelers could tap into. Cross-gender cooperation, then, and the gender roles and relationships that underlay such cooperation, provided an essential framework for the colony and the empire. Gendered family roles also functioned to strengthen and force recognition of social and economic interdependencies, such as when African men's appeal to gendered ideas about family responsibilities, based on their recognized marriages, helped force white New Amsterdammers to acknowledge their role in local economic networks. In multiple ways, gendered roles and ties sustained the intimate networks undergirding the Dutch colony in the Hudson Valley.

Understanding that women's relationships built this empire makes Johannes Vermeer's iconic painting *Officer and Laughing Girl* take on new layers of meaning. Although women's actions disappeared over the centuries from accounts of empire building, they were perfectly visible to men and women at the time; every time the WIC arranged free passage for impoverished soldiers' wives, every time travelers empowered women to act in their stead, every time colonial authorities negotiated with or through women and their intimate networks, and every time elite Dutch families relied on marriage to build commercial links, Vermeer's contemporaries made use of the obvious role of women in making early modern empire work. Seeing women's roles once again can complete the circle of references to empire that run through the painting. Just as the officer, the hat, the window, and the map all point to growing Dutch overseas connections, so, too, does the woman in a burgher house. The glow of light that Vermeer surrounds her with suggests the vital power of her possible union with the officer. His silhouetted face is bathed by the reflected light coming from her, animating an otherwise immobile figure. Her hand reaching toward him, with the promise of more suggested by her expression, is on the verge of making an essential final imperial connection by creating an intimate tie. Such relationships were the framework of the very empire the painting depicts.

The centrality of all these relationships to so many aspects of life in Dutch North America and the Dutch Atlantic forces us to jettison any distinction between the intimate and the imperial. The personal realm not only blended with, it wrought the economic, political, and social aspects of empire. Ignoring the personal and intimate realms in New Netherland would make any true economic, social, or political history of the colony incomplete. Thus, in this particular seventeenth-century colonial venture, empire was something lived through individual lives and choices. Many small-scale actors, through their participation, negotiation, resistance, cooperation, or rejection of what others around them did, made the connections that created this particular historical moment.

As people began traveling across vast distances, distances of geography, culture, and community, they continued to rely on the basic tool that structured daily life for early modern people in societies around the Atlantic basin and beyond. That tool was their network of immediate, familial, and face-to-face relationships. People as diverse as Oratam of Hackensacky, Annetgen Arents Hontoms, and Manuel de Gerrit de Reus all used this tool to shape, profit from, or survive the Dutch outpost in North America. Oratam sought to use his kin and clan connections to keep the peace and protect his Munsee village in the changing politics of the region. Annetgen Arents Hontoms endeavored to build on her relationships in maritime Amsterdam through her skipper husband to create a profitable trading business. Manuel de Gerrit de Reus counted on his ties within and beyond the African community to save him first from hanging and later from slavery. These and other networks grew and changed as a varied group of people became willing and unwilling participants in overseas expansion through the creation of the Dutch colony along the mid-Atlantic coast. Taking a closer look at networks like these reveals how people reconciled the challenges of distance posed by the new Atlantic world. Yet it also shows how empire took shape, through the actions of diverse collections of people pursuing their own differing goals and interests. Transoceanic empires were a novel form of political and economic organization in the sixteenth and seventeenth centuries, but, within this new system, people used familiar tools. Continuity, not rupture, characterized the early years of overseas empire. The deeply personal ties and connections that defined people's intimate lives also helped them define long-distance imperial connections. Only by taking seriously the intimate networks people created together can we understand the origins of empire in the early modern world.

Index

under the Synod of Dordt, 213; and African leadership, 214–217; of Africans, with white witnesses, 218–219, 227; barriers to increase of, among Africans, 233, 235–237; and Angola, 235n; and social connections among white New Amsterdammers, 260–261, 287–289, 293

Barents, Willem, xvii

Barentsz, Pieter, 134–135

Batavia, 11, 15–16, 123, 181n, 193

Beaver skins: hats made from, 3, 8, 63; as currency, 11, 17, 102, 150, 204–205, 302; and Mohawks, 11, 139, 148, 155–156, 165; sale of, in Amsterdam, 49–51, 93, 97, 100n; scarcity of, 114, 132; and Oneidas, 139–140; destruction of, by fire, 147; exchange of, for alcohol, 165; seizure of, by settlers, 177; Dutch greed for, 183–184; increased demand for, 274

—trade in: as basis for colonial prosperity, 12, 17, 19, 124, 189; and colonial elites, 13; face-to-face nature of, 19; and laws, 41, 48–49, 136, 170; as livelihood, 83, 89, 96, 168; and early trade voyages, 124, 130; and women as mediators, 181. See also Fur trade

Beeckman, Willem, 174, 288

Beer: exportation of, to New Netherland, 53–54, 95, 97–98; sale of, in New Netherland, 158–159, 164–167, 189; and Native Americans, 256. See also Alcohol

Beverwijck / Fort Orange, 10; fur trade at, 11, 96, 124, 129, 134–136, 170, 176–177, 230–231, 246; immigration to, 12, 83, 92; civic governance at, 13; and Mohawks, 14, 24, 141, 145–146, 155–156, 159, 164, 175n, 181, 182, 184, 186, 246; settler women in, 83, 90n, 96; travel to, 149, 183–184, 186; food trade in, 152–153, 155–157; alcohol trade in, 164–167, 169n; traders in, 169; and itinerant trade with Esopus, 172; palisade around, 175n

Bigamy and polygamy, 94, 138

Bills of exchange, 57n, 88–89

Bloemmaert, Adriaen, 60; wife of, see Jacobs, Helena (Bloemmaerts)

Bogardus, Everardus, 218, 234n, 259, 260

Bontekoe (ship), 55, 81

Boslopers, 138–141, 180; hostility toward, 169–170

Boston, 71, 94, 245

Bottomry, 58–59, 87

Brazil: and New Amsterdam's Africans, 14, 192n, 203, 211, 213n, 216; trade with, 17, 50n, 98–99, 106, 301; West India Company workers in, 37n, 72, 98–99; and Dutch slave trade, 70, 193n, 194, 201–203; as destination for single women, 78; and New Netherland colonists, 86–87, 98–99, 167; African communities in, compared to New Netherland, 196n, 235n

Bread, 44, 137, 151, 155–157, 166, 184, 225, 291. See also Bakers

Brotherhood: in cross-cultural discourse, 127, 140–141, 159, 183–185, 188, 252; meaning of, among Haudenosaunee, 128n, 184n, 246; among Munsee sachems, 252

Burghers, 1n, 3–6, 13, 46, 104, 261n, 298n; citizenship of, 5; as investors, 7, 63, 103; in New Netherland, 13, 24, 41, 76, 108, 119–120, 155–156, 162, 169, 245, 247, 250, 264, 288, 289n; domestic ideal of, 178–179, 261, 304; and slave-ownership, 205, 208

Canada. *See* New France

Canaquese, 186–187

Cape of Good Hope, 63n, 123, 194n, 220n

Captain Lambert. *See* Rompsicka

Children, 108–109, 112, 152, 176, 264n; place of, in the household, 5; support of, as reason for West India Company employment, 45; on transatlantic voyages, 74–75, 81, 113; in the

136, 140, 144, 146, 163–164, 166, 172, 180, 253–254, 263, 279, 302; among sailors, 77; and transatlantic trade connections, 110; definition of, 115n; as intimacy, 128n; in diplomatic speech, 140–141, 145, 159, 183n, 184, 271; as strategic necessity, 161, 188; feigned nature of, 162–163; among Africans, 198, 199, 217, 218, 229, 232–233, 243, 299; and pirates, 200; among Munsees, 252–253; among New Amsterdammers, 288, 291–292

Frontier: and exchange economy, 17, 125n; definition of, 17n–18n, 190n; and New Amsterdam, 169–170

Fur trade, 18–19, 59, 189, 301; in New France, 21; and transatlantic networks, 24, 48, 51, 55, 65, 69, 100–101; and laws, 41, 48, 50, 65, 136; and the black market, 48–50; women in, 51–52, 55, 100–101, 136, 303; in Beverwijk / Fort Orange area, 124, 134–136, 141, 145–148, 170, 177, 246; during wartime, 126, 173–175, 302; early years of, 128–134; and initial settlement, 135–137; and indigenous trade networks, 138–140, 150, 167, 274; and *boslopers*, 138–141, 169–170, 172; at trading posts, 146; in colonial communities, 147–148, 169–170, 174–175, 264, 301; at Esopus, 172–173; and Africans, 228, 230–231

Gender: and the household, 5–6, 303; in *Officer and Laughing Girl*, 8; and intimate networks, 19, 103, 118, 120; aboard ship, 40n, 80n, 85n; and economic alliances, 67, 69, 110, 112, 116, 303; and cultural contact, 126n, 137, 142, 152n, 262, 273–274, 279, 285, 295–296

Gillis, Agnieta, 112

Guardians: on slave ships, 39n, 79n; of orphans, 45–46, 95, 108–109; husbands as, 88, 119n; prosecutors as, 230n

Hackensacks, 14, 175, 248–258, 262, 264–269

Hackensacky, 10, 249n. *See also* Hackensacks

Half freedom: grants, 191–197, 212, 223–226, 232–234, 236–239, 242; definition of, 224–225

Hans (Pieweherenoes), 267–269

Harmans, Bielke, 72–73

Haudenosaunee: trade with, 14, 139–140, 148; and early knowledge of Europeans, 130; food production by, 151–152; values of, 176–177, 182; and diplomacy, 186, 267. *See also* Mohawks; Oneidas

Hermans, Augustyn, 105, 219

Hontom, Hans Jorisz, 134n, 141

Hontom, Willem Jorisz, 48, 49, 61, 131–134, 141; wife of, *see* Hontoms, Annetgen Arents

Hontoms, Annetgen Arents, 24–25, 47–49, 61–62, 304

Households: in Dutch society, 5–6, 8; in historiography, 18n; and women, 23, 43, 75; ties among, in New Netherland, 24–25, 259–260, 287–288; and the wider economy, 30, 34, 299; and maritime employment, 34, 40n; and African women's work, 76, 231; and Native Americans, 138, 169, 264; and itinerant traders, 156; and alcohol dealing, 163–166

Hudson, Henry, 11, 124, 128–131, 153

Huysgezin, definition of, 5. *See* Households

Huysvrouwen, definition of, 5

Illiteracy, 96–98

Innkeepers, 31, 34–40, 158–159

Intimacy: literature on, 21n; definition of, 128n

Jacobs, Helena (Bloemmaerts), 60

Jans, Adriaentje, 110–111

Jans, Janneken, van Leeuwarden, 17,
22–23, 25, 98–102, 119, 122
Java. *See* Batavia
Jews, 13, 15n, 86–87, 97
Juet, Robert, 128–131, 153

Kaswentha, 184
Kichtawangh, 255, 258, 266
Kieft, Willem, 113, 287; as empowered
agent, 52; and attempts to tax Munsees,
144–145; and half-freedom grants,
191–193, 223–225, 234, 242; death of,
218; and diplomacy, 254–256, 265, 295;
baptisms witnessed by, 260, 287
Kieft's War, 14, 15n, 144–146, 160,
253–255, 287
Kierstede, Hans, 259–261, 265
Kierstede, Sara Roeloffs, 248–250, 258–
269, 281, 286, 290, 292n, 294–295, 301
Kisana, Isabel, van Angola, 16–17,
22–25, 210, 213, 217n, 299
Klinckhamer, Gerrit Jansz, 93, 303

Lace, 55, 65
La Montagne, Johannes, 112–113, 161,
177
Lenapes, 14, 122, 162, 174, 252, 262
Letters: of introduction, 58n; and
courtship, 67n; conventions of, 88;
and news networks, 91, 92n, 301; and
illiteracy, 96–97; as legal evidence, 97,
199; conflicts over, 103–104, 106–110;
and merchant houses, 110–116; carried
by Native Americans, 174, 271; and
the English takeover, 289–290, 293
Liefde (ship), 94
Livestock, 91, 198, 226, 274; conflicts
over, 143–144, 159–161, 172, 174n, 185
Long Island: settlements on, 9, 11–12,
124, 145; Munsees on, 24, 122n, 125,
144, 251–252; minister of, 74n, 86;
ferries to, 149; food exported from,
152–153; claims to, 246; weakening
of Dutch influence on, 268–269, 289,
291–292

—Algonquians of: diversity of, 14,
122n, 263n; political complexities
of, 17, 246; trade with, 129–133, 138,
141, 150; wampum and, 131–133, 141;
food production by, 143n, 185; settler
dependence on, 159; conflicts with,
160, 185, 255; and diplomacy, 161, 255,
262–263, 268–286; intermarriage with,
181; Dutch perceptions of, 251 (*see also*
Montauks; Shinnecocks); women
leaders among, 303
Loockermans, Anna (Annetje), 115
Loockermans, Govert: as legal agent,
55, 57; letters of, 91, 110–116, 302; marriages of, 110–111, 260–261; kinship
ties of, 111–112, 261; slaves owned by,
211
Love, 67n, 90, 115, 129
Lutherans, 13

Maes, Grietje, 97–98
Mahicans, 122, 165; and connections
with upriver settlements, 14, 24, 124,
146, 155, 159, 184; trade with, 138, 155,
157n, 170; use of ferries by, 149; and
Peach War, 160; Dutch perceptions
of, 251; and conflicts with Munsees,
252–253
Maidservants, 96, 105; in *Officer and
Laughing Girl,* 1n; and their place
in the household, 5, 75; in inns, 36;
mobility of, 66, 76, 81, 94, 301–302;
and marriage, 75–77, 82, 87, 94; and
perceptions of sexuality, 77; and rape,
79–80; and food trade, 152; Native
American children as, 187; African
women as, 231–233
Maize: and the regional economy, 12;
settlers' dependence on, 136–137,
173, 189; and damage from livestock,
143; tax on, 144, 254; shipment of, by
canoe, 148; Native American production of, 151, 153–154, 157, 274, 275; sale
of, in New Amsterdam, 171; African
farming of, 224, 226

Manhattan, 10; settlement on, 12, 124, 149, 259; and economic links, 17, 50, 59, 82, 152; Africans on, 24, 201, 226, 231, 240, 302; travel to, 66, 78, 101, 299; trade at, 135, 171, 175; Native communities near, 144, 159, 249, 263, 283; violence near, 160, 255, 268; colony leaders at, 170, 183, 269, 280, 283 (*see also* Council, New Amsterdam); English takeover of, 286, 289

Marechkawick, 14

Marketplace: in New Amsterdam, 141, 171, 174–175, 208, 227, 264–265

Marriage: and prostitution, 4n; and overseas travel, 18, 66, 68, 75–80, 87, 119, 299; and empire building, 20, 85, 116–117, 120, 303; legal and social regulation of, 21, 93–94, 104n, 108; among Africans, 24, 208–212, 217n, 222, 233–234, 236n, 241, 299, 303; and transatlantic trade, 30, 45, 51, 67–69, 81–85, 89–91, 94–102; legal implications of, for women, 43, 61, 119n; and affect, 67n; as an economic strategy among merchants, 69, 103–110, 115–116, 120, 299; and women's ability to travel, 73–75, 119; as a basis for loans, 88–89; as an economic resource for others, 93; as a basis for kinship ties, 111, 115, 121; among Native Americans, 138, 175n, 178, 180–182, 252, 272–273, 277; and links among New Amsterdam burghers, 259–260, 287–288, 300

Marsepingh, 185, 256n, 281n, 284

Mattano, 257–258

Mayauwetinnemin, 144

Megapolensis, Johannes: on Native Americans, 146–148, 164, 177–179; on the food trade, 151–152, 155; African domestic servant of, 231; as New Amsterdam minister, 287; as a baptismal witness, 288; during the English takeover, 291

Menissingh, 266

Michiels, Maddelena, 76–77, 87, 302

Migration: to Amsterdam, 8, 15, 35, 39, 46, 259, 260; to New Netherland, 11, 23–24, 124, 145; diversity of, 13; and the establishment of transatlantic networks, 41, 52–55, 65, 302; by sailors and soldiers, 72; by maritime families, 73–75; and women's economic mobility, 81–87, 98–102; by elite families, 105, 287; and friction with Munsees, 258; to the Hudson Valley after 1664, 293

Minisinks, 10, 253, 267

Ministers. *See* Bogardus, Everardus; Drisius, Samuel; Megapolensis, Johannes; Polhemius, Johannes

Mohawks, 122; beaver-skin trade with, 3, 10–12, 83, 124, 126, 135, 145–146, 170; trade routes controlled by, 14; presence in documentary record of, 23; and proximity to Fort Orange, 24, 124, 189n; and diplomacy, 112, 182–185, 250n; violence against, 125–126, 134n, 141, 189; and interactions with the French, 130, 182n, 186; and hosting of *boslopers,* 138–141; in settler towns, 147–148, 159, 164, 170; canoes of, 148; and role in regional politics, 149, 182n, 246, 252–253; and food production, 151; and purchases of baked goods, 155–157; and criticism of Dutch, 159, 170, 177, 182–184; and alcohol, 165, 167; marriage among, 178, 182n; and perceived prostitution, 179, 182; and intermarriage, 181; mixed-race children among, 186-187; Dutch perceptions of, 251, 287. *See also* Haudenosaunee

Montauks, 10, 14, 17, 122, 124, 131, 159, 263, 269–286, 295. *See also* Long Island: Algonquians of; Quashawam

Munsees, 10, 23, 122, 165; beaver-skin trading and, 3, 12, 124, 135, 138, 146; and proximity to colonial settlements, 14, 24, 126–127, 135–136, 159, 189n, 258; wars against, 14–15, 17, 125–127, 144,

160–162, 172–173, 251, 253–255, 262, 265, 267–268, 287; politics among, 25, 175n, 251–258, 283; and colonial diplomacy, 112, 144–145, 147, 162, 174–176, 183, 187, 249–269, 294, 304; definition of, 122n, 251; and commodities trade, 124, 143–144, 150–152, 155–158, 166–167, 175, 264–265; women among, 141, 143, 150, 157, 180, 181, 262, 266; attitude of, toward Dutch, 143, 162–163; and transportation networks, 149, 174; children of, 187–188; kinship structures among, 250–252, 254, 267, 294, 304; and the alcohol trade, 254, 256–257, 266. *See also* Esopus; Hackensacks; Raritans; Wappingers

Naming practices, Dutch, xviii, 61n
Nanningsdochter, Geertge, 22–23, 25, 81–85, 119
Native Americans: terminology for, xvii, 122n; and reliance on intimate networks, 8, 16, 21, 25, 122, 138, 167, 269–270, 300–301; and food production, 11–12, 143, 151–154 (*see also* Bread; Food trade; Maize); diversity of, 14–15, 269; and violence with colonists, 15, 26, 125, 160–161, 172–173, 189–190; impact of distance on, 16–17, 23; and trade with settler women, 17, 136, 151–152, 155, 168, 175, 264–265, 303; use of face-to-face relationships by, to trade, 19, 24, 126, 146, 148, 300; and other colonies, 21, 23, 123–125, 263; and intimate networks, 25, 127, 189, 251, 301–302; and women, 126n, 131, 134, 137–138, 141–143, 147, 150, 152–153, 156–157, 160, 177–182, 185–186, 252, 278, 284–285, 303 (*see also* Quashawam); and early trade interactions, 128–145; diplomatic metaphors of, 128n, 141, 183–184; difficulties of trade with, 131, 146; use of wampum by, 133, 141, 183–184; settlers' dependence on, 136, 151–152, 157–158;

extensive contact of, with Dutch, 138, 145–172; antipathy of, toward Dutch, 141, 143, 162–163, 177; treatment of, in settler communities, 141–142, 175–177; canoes of, 148–149, 174, 188; use of colonial watercraft by, 149, 174; bread trade with, 155–157; restrictions on, in settler communities, 161–162, 174–175; and colonial towns, 169–171; and conflict with settlers, 172–188; and sexual contact with Dutch, 180–182 (*see also* Sex); as allied combatants, 185, 252, 262; children of, in Dutch communities, 187–188 (*see also* Children: bicultural; Children: of Native Americans); and trade with Africans, 230–231; and regional power balance, 245–286, 294, 296; and land sales, 277, 279–280; and alcohol trade, *see* Alcohol trade; and arms trade, *see* Arms trade, Smuggling; and firewood trade, *see* Firewood. See also *specific groups, regions, and individuals*
Navesinks, 10, 166–167, 261, 268–269
New France, 21–22, 116n, 123, 130, 134, 136, 182n, 186
New Netherland Company, 28
New Sweden, 11, 12, 158, 160, 200, 246
Nicholls, Richard, 240, 289–291
Notas (bags), 150–151, 155–156, 176n

Oneidas, 14, 139–140. *See also* Haudenosaunee
Onondagas, 139. *See also* Haudenosaunee
Openbare koopvrouwen. See Public businesswomen
Oratam of Hackensacky, 144, 248–269, 279, 284, 294–295, 304
Orphans' court, 13, 45–46, 108–109, 288

Pacham, 144, 255
Patroons, 29, 67, 81, 84, 87, 142n, 149, 155
Pawning, 32, 88n
Peach War, 14, 18n, 103, 125, 160–163, 190, 255; and illegal trading, 166, 167; New Amsterdam's role in, 169

slaves among, 208, 211; firewood production by, 228–229; and recognition of families, 233, 236–237; during the English takeover, 291–292
—of the West India Company: solidarity among, 191, 195–196, 220–223, 304; wives of, 191, 196, 212, 223–224, 234; children of, 196–197, 206, 212–219, 222, 225, 235 (see also Baptism: among Africans; Children: of Africans); sale of, 198, 204–205; leasing of, 198, 206, 207; work done by, 207–208, 226, 232; houses belonging to, 207–208, 226, 241; conflict among, 219–221; half freedom of, see Half freedom
Slave trade: sailors in, 39n; inheritance of interests in, 60; African ports involved in, 70; West India Company involvement in, 70n; growth of Dutch involvement in, 193–195, 209–210; and New Netherland, 197–206, 212, 234
Smith, Lieutenant Dirk, 168, 288–289
Smuggling: of beaver skins before 1638, 48–50; of slaves into Spanish America, 70, 203; to Native Americans in New Netherland, 157–158, 164–169, 173, 230–231 (see also Arms trade; Bread; Food trade); of slaves into New Netherland, 200, 206
Soldiers: in art, 4–5, 36n, 179n; military actions by, 11, 14, 125, 160, 172–173, 178–179, 266; outfitting and lodging of, 31–33, 35–36; rowdy behavior of, 36, 206; loans to, 39–40, 99; financial strategies of, 41–42, 44, 57, 65, 71; poverty of, 60n; wives of, 72, 75, 303; mobility of, 74–75, 82–84, 301; presence of, in the Hudson Valley, 124, 144, 184; transportation of, 149; during the English takeover, 239, 290–292, 294. See also Debt: and the maritime workforce; West India Company (WIC): workers of
Soul selling, 6, 38–40
Stam brothers, 49–50, 112n

Staten Island, 10, 17, 125, 160–161, 166–167, 255–256, 266, 267
Stuyvesant, Anna, 105
Stuyvesant, Peter: and call for day of thanksgiving, 9, 11; title of, 9n, 13; competence of, 12; arrival of, 12, 72, 83, 94–95, 287; religious intolerance of, 13, 86, 282n; kinship ties of, 105, 110, 261n, 288; fatherhood of, 112; wife of, 112, 113, 219; and Govert Loockermans, 113; and diplomacy with Munsees, 145–146, 161, 174–175, 183, 257–258, 266; and diplomacy with English, 157, 246; and campaign against New Sweden, 160; regulations passed by, 163, 169, 171; and actions against Esopus, 172–173, 175n, 183; West India Company orders to, 199; sale of West India Company slaves approved by, 205; and attempt to retrieve enslaved children, 219; proximity of, to African farmers, 227, 232, 239; judicial actions by, 230; and approval of half freedom, 232–233; freedom and landownership of Africans approved by, 238–239; and the English takeover, 238–239, 245–246, 281–282, 289–293; rejection of Quashawam by, 281–282
Suscaneman. See Rompsicka
Susquehannocks, 122; trade with, 14, 17, 124, 135, 162; and indigenous politics, 149, 183, 267; and competition between New Netherland and New Sweden, 158; and Peach War, 160; presence of, in settler homes, 162; Dutch terms for, 251; and ties to Munsees, 252
Swarte Beer (ship), 26–27, 42, 130–131

Tackapousha. See Tapausagh
Tamandaree (ship), 203–204
Tankitekes, 254
Tapausagh, 255–256, 263, 269, 280–285
Tappan, 14

Wappingers, 10, 174–175, 262–263, 266, 284

Wesselsz, Jochem (the baker), 155, 156, 167, 176n, 230–231

West India Company (WIC): kinship networks and, 7–8, 65, 102–104, 110, 116; structure of, 8n, 12–13, 170; struggles of, 11, 24, 246, 286, 297–298; expanding claims of, 11, 246; directors of, 12–13, 28–29, 48–49, 65, 68, 81, 104, 253; criticisms of, 13; and religious minorities, 13, 86; shareholders and investors in, 28, 117; reach of, 30; formal economy of, 30, 40, 49, 69, 116, 301; formation of, 41; policies of, 41, 48, 50, 65, 74n, 136; skippers of, 60; depiction of directors of, 63–64; officers of, 69, 105, 110, 258–259, 287, 290; factor for, 135–137; malfeasance of, 142, 168; and Native Americans, 157–158; and colony council, 169–170; and English takeover, 246, 287, 290, 292–294; and tenant farmers, 259; and translators, 265; and role in slave trade, *see* Slave trade. *See also* Slaves: of the West India Company

—employment with: as the basis for geographic mobility, 68–69, 72, 74–75, 82, 84, 95, 303; as the basis for class mobility, 98, 102, 120

—wages from: as the basis for credit, 31–35, 38–39, 69–70, 82–83; wives'

share of, 32n, 36–37, 73, 95; collection of, 44–46, 53, 57, 71, 93, 98–99; politics of, 85n

—workers of: indebtedness of, 31–36, 38–40, 65; empowerments by, 42, 44–46, 57; wives of, 42–44, 46, 57, 74–75; and transatlantic connections, 45–46, 51; foreign origins of, 71n; as settlers, 72. *See also* Soldiers; Soul selling

WIC. *See* West India Company (WIC)

Widows: travel by, 23, 74n, 75, 81–83; financial action of, 26, 28, 30, 47, 92–93, 117; debts to, 35, 58; overseas trade by, 54–56, 60, 65, 82–83, 95; legal capacity of, 60, 62n, 100n, 107–109; marriage of, 81–83, 112, 208, 209n, 222; family trading concerns and, 103–104, 106–110, 119; involvement of, in food trade, 153; among Africans, 208, 209n, 222; treatment of, by Munsees, 254, 263; sachemship of, 273

Wiechquaeskecks, 10, 14, 162–163, 258, 265–266

Witte Paert (ship), 205–206

Wouters, Marritgen, 26–28, 30, 41–42, 65, 66

Wyandanch, 270–273, 275, 278–279, 282–283

Zielverkopen. See Soul selling